approaching
the new
MILLENNIUM

approaching the new MILLENNIUM

an amillennial look at a.d. 2000

paul t. butler

COLLEGE PRESS PUBLISHING COMPANY • JOPLIN, MISSOURI

Library of Congress Cataloging-in-Publication Data

Butler, Paul T.
    Approaching the new millennium: an amillennial look at A.D. 2000 /
Paul T. Butler
        p.   cm.
    Rev. ed. of: Twenty six lessons on Revelation, 1982, and Daniel, 1970.
    Includes bibliographical references.
    ISBN 0-89900-812-7 (pbk.)
    1. End of the world.   2. Bible—Prophecies.   3. Eschatology.   4. Bible. N.T.
Revelation—Commentaries.   I. Butler, Paul T. Twenty six lessons on Revelation.
II. Butler, Paul T. Daniel.   III. Title
BT876.B77 1998
236'.9—dc21   98-35233
                                                                        CIP

DEDICATION

This book is dedicated to

John Stephen Butler

my precious grandson and "buddy"

TABLE OF CONTENTS

preface

This book is born of its times. It is not an ordinary book. If the Lord tarries, the end of history's second millennium and the beginning of the third, as some count millenniums, is fast approaching. We felt a need existed for a collation of some of the most often referenced passages of the Bible concerning eschatology. There will no doubt be a plethora of books dealing with biblical prophecy leading up to December 31, 1999. We can only hope this one will be of some help in understanding biblical eschatology, especially the often repeated phrase, "the consummation of the ages," i.e., the end of the world.

Biblical eschatology is not just about "end times." It is the study of the progress, goal and end of history from the perspective of divine revelation. Biblical eschatology often deals with various crucial "stopping places" in the history of the world as they relate to God's redemptive program. These "stopping places" are often indeterminately called "last days, latter days, time of the end, end of the ages," etc. God has revealed that history is lineal (not cyclical) and is oriented toward ending in eternity. But on the way to eternity God works in stages or phases. Occasionally he reveals that a particular phase will reach its termination and he announces it through his prophets in terminology that the cursory reader, disregarding context and stated fulfillments, will misunderstand to be referring to the end of the world. Biblical eschatology seeks to communicate eternal, invisible, and nonempirical concepts to human beings who presently live and think only in a transient, time-related perception. God experiences all time and eternity at once. Man experiences only time. And man's experience is only past and present — never future. This, too, may lead the occasional reader of the Bible to interpret every statement of "last days, time of the end," etc., to mean the end of **all** time.

The Bible is not an esoteric hodge-podge of mysticism and occultism like so many human religions and their "books." The origin of the Bible is divine, much of it history, revealed by the Holy Spirit of God. It was written in the human languages known by its authors — not in angelic or "unknown" languages. God's Spirit used human beings as instruments through which he verbalized his will to man. God communicated to man in human language guiding these human authors through his Holy Spirit to record both history and revelation without error. The Bible is to be understood by the usual rules for understanding any communication in human language.

To express any concept, human language is restricted to human experience. When God desires, at any point in the time line of history, to speak of eternal matters future to that point in time he must still use human language — words and symbols within human experience. This limitation tends to increase the complexities human beings face in discerning divinely revealed eschatology.

Our aim is to combine in one volume, a revised version of our former work entitled, *Twenty Six Lessons on Revelation, Parts I & II*, with the eschatological portion of our former work entitled, *Daniel*, along with additional exegesis of other major eschatological portions of the Old Testament Prophets and the New Testament. We will add to this certain appendices which have significant bearing on understanding biblical eschatology as compared to modern "prophetic" allegations about "the consummation of the ages."

We have arranged books and passages in chronological order believing this will facilitate an accurate and understandable interpretation of the passages. Eschatological literature is almost always apocalyptic in style. In Appendix A we have given a brief summary of the hermeneutical rules for interpreting prophetic literature. In Appendix B we have made a biblical word study of such words and phrases as "last days, end time, time of the end, latter days, end of the age(s)," et al.

Let the reader be aware from the start that we are not claiming to have dealt with all the prophecies in the Bible. Nor do we claim to have covered **all** the biblical texts of eschatological interest to everyone. However, we believe we have chosen a sufficient number of eschatologically significant texts to provide a "key" that will unlock the meaning of practically every prophecy in the Bible.

The questions remain: Will the world end at one millisecond after midnight on December 31, 1999? Will Jesus Christ come back to the world for his Second Advent precisely at A.D. 2000 and rule the world with a rod of iron from the physical city of Jerusalem for a thousand years? Are there "signs of the times" revealed in the Bible that when A.D. 2000 rolls around the true church of Christ will be "raptured" and unbelievers left behind to be given an opportunity to surrender to the rule of Christ on earth? Does God have something "more" for the Jewish race that they cannot appropriate now, before Christ's Second Coming? Will Christ rebuild the Jewish temple and reinstate the Jewish sacrifices — or will that be the work of **the** "Antichrist"? Are the answers to these questions found in the Bible? Where?

We believe the answer to every one of these questions is a resounding NO! And we propose to show it from some of the more significant eschatological passages in the Bible.

chapter 1

ESCHATOLOGY

"Well, what do you think, Preacher, is the world going to end at 00.01 in A.D. 2000?" "Say, Professor, what is your theory about the Rapture, the Tribulation, and the Millennium?" Perhaps you have sat in a Sunday School class when the lesson has been from Matthew, chapter 24, or First Thessalonians, chapter 4, or maybe even from the book of Revelation (for those hardy Christian souls bold enough to make a stab at studying Revelation). If you have, we're sure you've heard, "Well, I've read that there are things happening right now that are 'signs of the times,'" or, "I don't even study those places in the Bible that talk about the 'last days' because there are too many different opinions about such things."

If you are known to be a "conservative" or "evangelical" Christian and have never been asked what your eschatological inclinations are, you are one-in-a-million. That is because the "conservative" eschatological inclinations that get the most exposure today, with the help of an exulting media, are extreme, and not-so-extreme, Premillennialism and Dispensationalism. Every preacher, Sunday School teacher, and Bible college professor has been confronted, at one time or another, with the issues of **eschatology**. We hope this work, brief as it is, will be of some help in arriving at a biblically-oriented approach to eschatology.

The English word *eschatology* is a combination of two Greek words, *eschatos* meaning, "last, or end," and *logos*, meaning "study of, or science of." *Biblical eschatology*, for Bible-believers would be, one would think, a study of "last things from the *text of the Bible*. But that is not necessarily so! Russell Boatman's story of his boyhood introduction to *eschatology* in the 1930s illustrates this very well:

> As a teen age boy I was greatly impressed by an evangelist whose lectures on Revelation drew capacity crowds. He was reputed to know the Bible by memory.

Such Scriptures as he had occasion to refer to he certainly knew well enough to give credence to the report. Vividly do we recall how he used the apocalyptic Scriptures to show that all the wonders of the day, automobiles, airplanes, submarines, electricity, telephones, etc. were seen aforetime by the biblical prophets and described in their use, particularly in the warfare of the end-time predicted in Revelation.

Years passed and the teen age boy had become a preacher. My preaching did not pack the house, particularly on Sunday night. What could I do about it? I could preach a series of sermons on the book of Revelation. This intent was announced and to spark interest a preview was given of the wonders that would be disclosed.

The experience which ensued was traumatic. I couldn't find all those clear depictions of wonders and happenings! I frantically besought my father to send posthaste the four volume set, *Revelation Revealed*, authored by the aforementioned evangelist. The books arrived but still the goodies could not be found. The claims were there in a muted form, but the presence of the authority figure, his charismatic smile, the aura of being in the know, these were required to bring to light the things he had found 'uncovered' by the book of Revelation.[1]

Someone is going to say, "What, another book on last things?" Yes! We are impelled by the urging of the Scriptures to "test everything" and "teach sound doctrine." The past 60 years, which has included World War II, Nazism and Communism, the founding of the new Israeli state, the atomic age, the space age, and the high-tech communications explosion have fostered a deluge of erroneous eschatology. What will the turn of the third millennium, A.D. 2000, bring in eschatological meandering?

A Christian's eschatological perspective influences his entire view of life and the world. It impacts his interpretation of all the Bible; it prejudices his political ideology; it affects his evangelistic methods; it plays a leading role in Christian unity; and it is a determining factor in many ethical decisions a Christian must make.

There is a great deal of eschatology in the Bible. The Bible is God's propositional revelation of his divine program of redemption as it is being worked out in history. God's redemptive itinerary in the OT involved the interaction of his "chosen" people with the rise and fall of numerous heathen empires. Therefore, frequent *beginnings* and *endings* are predicted; some are documented as having been fulfilled within the time frame of the composition of the Scriptures. These eschatological crises are couched in prophetic symbolism which is often *highly apocalyptic* in style.[2]

Old Testament eschatology is focused *exclusively* on the beginning and ending of the Mosaic dispensation of God's redemptive agenda. In three and a half decades

OT – predicted end of mosaic dispensation only.

of daily studying and teaching the OT prophets, the Gospels, epistle to the Hebrews and Revelation, we have not found in the OT prophets one unequivocal, apostolical-ly-verified prediction of Christ's Second Coming, a literal millennial kingdom in Palestine, a rebuilding of the Jewish temple, a physical battle at Har-mageddon, a rapture of Christians, a seven-year-tribulation, or a special, extrabiblical invitation to the Jews to accept Christ. The Old Testament prophets were directed by the Holy Spirit to concentrate all their revelation on the *first advent of the Messiah, the spiritual nature of his kingdom, and Messiah's annulment, or fulfillment, of the Jewish system.* (cf. Luke 24:25-27, 44-49; Acts 3:17-25; 13:26-39; 15:14-18; 26:27; Heb. 1:1-4; 1 Pet. 1:10-12).

New Testament eschatology is threefold: (a) it plainly presages the once-for-all abrogation of Judaism, including the destruction of Jerusalem (e.g., John 4:21-24; Matt. 21:33-44 and parallels; Matt. 22:1-10: 23:29-39; 24:1-35 and parallels; 2 Cor. 3:7-11; Gal. 4:21-31; 6:14-16; Eph. 2:14-22; Col. 2:12-19; 1 Thess. 1:13-16; and the entire book of Hebrews). Jesus' "Olivet Discourse" depicting the signs and tribulations to come upon Jerusalem at the end of Judaism is so apocalyptic in expression, many have mistaken his predictions to be concerning his Second Coming[3] J. Marcellus Kik has succinctly evaluated this error: "They forget that the destruction of Jerusalem and the excision of the Jewish nation from the kingdom was one of the most important events that has ever occurred on earth, and had tremendous consequences for the future of earth;"[4] (b) NT eschatology also predicts the great tribulation upon the church of the first four centuries by the Roman Empire and the fall of Rome; (c) and it anticipates the second, *and final,* advent of Christ to this world for judgment and redemption, in both manifesto and inference (e.g. Matt. 24:36–25:46 and parallels; Acts 3:19-21; 17:29-31; Rom. 8:18-25; 1 Cor. 15:51-58; 1 Thess. 4:13–5:25; 2 Thess. 1:7-11; 2:1-12; Heb. 9:27-28; 2 Pet. 3:1-18; 1 John 3:1-3, etc.).

While the second advent of Christ is mentioned in nearly every book of the New Testament, it is not as pervasive as some eschatologists declare. The NT says much more about the past and completed work of Christ's atonement and its application to the tentative portion of life on this earth than it does about the end of the world and eternal life.

Almost constant warfare, natural disasters, grave moral dereliction and the explosion of technology in the last fifty years has, no doubt, provoked an abundance of eschatological intemperance and grievous error. As the turn of the third millennium, as some count millenniums, of the Christian dispensation becomes imminent, we can hardly anticipate an abatement of misinterpretations of eschatological Scripture and the lamentable consequences which inevitably ensue. Three *major* "millennial" inclinations, Postmillennialism, Amillennialism, and Premillennialism (divided into two distinct camps, Historical and Dispensational), are scattered across the spectrum of theological eschatology from liberal to conservative. Postmillennialism essentially holds that a "golden age" of spirituality will ensue and grow through religious (esp. Christian) influences upon society. Christ will return, after an indefinite time, to a thoroughly worldwide field of "wheat." Postmillennialists believe the church is the spiritual kingdom of God on earth. Postmillennialism, while clearly in disagreement with the Scriptures (e.g., Luke 12:49-53; 13:22-30; 18:8, etc.), is not widely embraced today. Amillennialism does not see the world Christianized before Christ's return (cf. Luke 18:8; 1 Thess. 5:1-3, et al.). It holds that the world will continue much as it is now, and has been since the days of Noah (cf. Matt. 24:36-44; Luke 17:25-37), with both good and evil existing in the same "field" (Matt. 13:24-30, 36-43). Amillennialsts believe that Christ will return *unexpectedly*, at a time *no one knows*, at which time *one*, general resurrection will take place. Those who are alive at his return will be united with the resurrected dead to be redeemed or condemned according to their response to the Gospel of Christ. They believe the kingdom of Christ is not political and economic, but spiritual, dwelling in the hearts of believers and outwardly manifested in the church. Historic Premillennialism was embraced by some early Christians, but is rare now. Dispensational Premillennialism, which permeates a large segment of conservative Protestantism and is highly profiled and "hyped" throughout the written and broadcast media, deserves a more lengthy analysis.

Despite a few minor differences within their camp, it is characteristic of all dispensational premillennial eschatologists to hold to the following generalized tenets:

1. The kingdom of God as prophesied in the OT is not now in the world, and it will not be instituted until Christ returns.
2. It is not the purpose of the present gospel age to establish the kingdom of God on earth, but to preach the gospel as a witness to the nations and so to warn them of and make them justly subject to judgment; also to gather out of all nations God's elect in anticipation of Christ's return to set up his kingdom for them on earth.
3. The world is growing worse and will continue to grow worse until Christ comes to establish his kingdom.
4. Immediately preceding the return of Christ there is to be a period of pervasive and intense apostasy and wickedness.
5. We are now in the latter stages of the "Church age" and the return of Christ is near, probably to occur within the lifetime of the present generation.
6. At Christ's coming the righteous dead of all ages are to be raised in the "first resurrection."

7. The resurrected dead together with the transfigured living saints who are then on the earth are to be "raptured" (i.e., caught up) to meet the Lord in the air.

8. The judgment of all the righteous then takes place, which judgment consists primarily in the assignment of rewards.

9. Before and during the "tribulation" period, the Jews are to be restored to the land of Palestine.

10. At the appearance of the Messiah the Jews will turn to him in a national conversion and repentance, thus "all Israel will be saved."

11. Christ at his coming destroys the Antichrist and all his forces in the battle of Armageddon.

12. After the battle of Armageddon Christ establishes a worldwide kingdom with Jerusalem as its capital. He and the resurrected and transfigured saints will rule for a thousand years in righteousness, peace and prosperity.

13. During this reign the city of Jerusalem and the temple are to be rebuilt and the feasts and fasts and the priesthood, the ritual and sacrificial system revived, but performed in a "Christian spirit" and by Christian worshipers.

14. The golden age (the thousand years) is also to be characterized by the removal of the curse from nature so that the desert shall blossom as the rose and the wild ferocious nature of beasts shall be changed.

15. During the millennium great numbers of the Gentiles will turn to God and be incorporated into the kingdom.

16. While many Gentiles remain unconverted and rebellious, they are not destroyed, but are held in check by the rod-of-iron rule of Christ.

17. During the millennium Satan is to be bound, cast into the abyss, and so shut away from the earth.

18. At the close of the millennium Satan is to be loosed for a short time.

19. The millennium is to be followed by a short but violent outbreak of wickedness and rebellion headed by Satan which all but overwhelms the saints and the holy city of Jerusalem.

20. The forces of wickedness are to be destroyed by fire which is cast down upon them from heaven.

21. The wicked dead of all ages are then to be raised in the "second resurrection," judged, and with Satan and the wicked angels cast into hell.

22. Heaven and hell are then introduced in their fullness, with the new heavens and the new earth as the future home of the redeemed, which will constitute the eternal state.[5]

Historical Premillennialism holds that the coming of Christ will be preceded by certain recognizable signs, such as the preaching of the gospel to all the nations, the apostasy, wars, famines, earthquakes, the appearance of the Antichrist, or Man of Sin, and the Great Tribulation. Some Dispensational Premillennialists, while acceding to most of the above tenets, do not hold to visible signs of Christ's return. However, they contend that the millennial kingdom will be predominantly Jewish, with Christian Gentiles in a subordinate position — in effect vassals of the Jewish kingdom in Palestine. Dispensationalists set forth seven dispensations — eight covenants (according to the *Scofield Bible*, p. 6):

1. The Edenic covenant — before the fall.
2. The Adamic covenant.
3. The Noahic covenant.
4. The Abrahamic covenant.
5. The Mosaic covenant.
6. The Davidic covenant.
7. The Palestinian covenant (Deut. 30).
8. The New covenant — instituted by Christ.

Dispensationalists also include the following eschatological theories in their system:

1. Two "Second Comings" — a coming of Christ *for* his people at the "rapture," and a coming *with* his people seven years later at the "revelation."
2. At least three, and perhaps four, resurrections — the righteous dead at the "rapture," the martyrs of the Great Tribulation, the wicked dead, the righteous who die during the millennium.
3. From four to seven judgments — the righteous immediately following the "rapture," the "sheep and goats" of the nations at the "revelation," the judgment of the wicked at the end of the millennium, the judgment of angels, and a judgment of the righteous who live during the millennium. Scofield adds a judgment of the believer's sins at the cross in the person of Christ, a judgment in the believer's conscience, and a judgment of Israel.
4. A second "rapture" will also be needed for the righteous who are alive at the end of the millennium.
5. And, according to some, there will be two eternally separate peoples of God, the church permanently in heaven, and Israel permanently on the earth. [6]

In chapter two we have cited a few examples of flawed biblical eschatology. Needless to say, there are hundreds more that could be made. Few people, however, have given much thought to the repercussions of aberrant hermeneutics applied to biblical "last things." Following are some of the effects of erroneous eschatology:

First, the 22 characteristics of Dispensational Premillennialism above violate the canons of biblical hermeneutics:

a. They reflect upon the integrity of Bible prophecy by implying that the Jewish rejection of Christ was a miscarriage in God's plan. The OT clearly foretold the rejection of Christ (cf. Isa. 53:1-12; Dan. 9:24-27; John 12:37-38; Psa. 118:22-23; Matt. 21:46, et al.).

b. They deny plain Bible teaching concerning the establishment of the kingdom of God upon earth in the first century (cf. Dan. 2:44; Isa. 2:2-4; Acts 2:16-17; Col. 1:13; Heb. 12:28; Rev. 1:4,6,9, et al.).

c. They suggest that the church was not a part of God's eternal purpose, but only an interim (parenthesis) emergency measure (cf. Eph. 3:10; Rev. 13:8; Acts 20:28, et al.).

d. They deny that Christ is *now* enthroned upon David's throne (cf. Zech. 6:12-13; Heb. 1:1-6; 8:1; Luke 1:32-33; Acts 2:30; 13:34; Rev. 3:21, et al.).

e. They deny we have been in the last days since the beginning of the first century, and that Christ's next coming will end this world (cf. Luke 17:26-30; Acts 2:16-17; 1 Cor. 10:11; 15:24; Heb. 1:1-4; 9:28, et al.).

f. They teach, contrary to the Bible, that Christ will come again to deal with sin through a Jewish system, and that violates the entire book of Hebrews (cf. Heb. 7:11-12, 26-28; 8:13; 9:12,28; 10:9-14; 13:10,14, et al.).

g. They affirm, contrary to Scripture, that there will be multiple *literal* resurrections from the dead, one thousand years apart. When John 5:28-29 is compared with Revelation 20:5-6, it is clear that there are *only* two resurrections. The "first" resurrection, which is one's new birth initiated by belief, repentance and immersion in water, redeems one from the "second death" (cf. Rom. 6:1-11; Eph. 2:1; Col. 2:12-13, et al.). The second and final resurrection is that of the body reunited with the spirit at the end of time.

h. They deny the *expressed* symbolic nature of the book of Revelation and much of the OT prophetic literature and history by literalizing their figures of speech. The Greek word *pneumatikos* in Revelation 11:8 is translated "spiritually" in the KJV and "allegorically" in the RSV. In Hebrews 9:9 the OT tabernacle is called, in Greek, *parabolē*, translated "figure" (KJV) and "symbolic" (RSV). Large portions of the Bible are "figurative, parabolic, and symbolic."

i. They deny that the redemptive work of the *first coming of Christ* is the only covenant by which both Jew and Gentile are saved and become one body (cf. Gal. 3:1ff; Eph. 2:11-22, et al.).

j. They deny that "Zion" of the OT prophets had its fulfillment in the New Testament church (cf. Gal. 4:21-31; Heb. 12:22-24).

Second, there is the aftermath of confusion and ridicule. The non-Christian world scorns and lampoons Christianity, the Bible and the church of Christ because *every* date for the Second Coming of Christ and the end of the world, so adamantly predicted in the past has been *wrong*! Unbelievers conclude, justifiably or not, that there is probably no truth or reality to the Bible, or if there is, no religious group has any truth since they all differ on such an important issue as the end of the world! It is a matter of record that a few unstable and scripturally untrained Christians have been prompted to become disillusioned and suspicious of the Bible and the church when faced with the contradictions of intemperate and erroneous eschatologists.

Third, the excising of a *potpourri* of OT passages from their historical and apocalyptic context, and a "pasting" of them into a New Testament text wherever it suits the presuppositions of one's eschatological system is evident to the careful Bible student who compares the dispensational viewpoint to what the Bible actually says.

Fourth, nearly every modern Israeli prime minister from Ben Gurion[7] to the present one, along with millions of Jews from rabbis to farmers to soldiers have emphatically declared that modern Israel has a "biblical mandate" to occupy the land of Palestine, even if it means evicting present day Palestinians from their homes and shops and farms. This Zionistic colonialism has been accepted, for purposes known and unknown, by political leaders across the western world, including numerous U.S. presidents and politicians as well as the United Nations. It is, of course, vigorously promoted and financed by Jewry throughout the world. It also has the fervent backing of most Christian dispensationalists. A Skevington Wood, well known preacher, broadcaster, author, and convention speaker in Scotland, is representative of "Israeli biblical mandate" policy: "The title-deeds to what we know as Palestine are clearly made over to Israel in irrefragable assurances."[8] Wood quotes Dr. Nahum Sokolow: "It is impossible to understand how it can be said that this covenant (see Genesis 13:14-15; Leviticus 26:32-45) will be remembered, if the Jewish people is to continue dispersed, and is to be forever excluded from the land here spoken of."[9]

In a more recent book, Theodore W. Pike said: ". . . the future of Israel, next to the Great Tribulation, is the most prophesied event in Scripture."[10]

The *New York Times* ran this piece: "He (God) made a covenant with Abraham, promising a large portion of the Middle East . . . for him and his descendants. The covenant is unconditional . . . and we, knowing Him who made the promise, totally support the people and land of Israel in their God-given, God-promised, God-ordained right to exist. Any person or group of nations opposed to this right isn't just fighting Israel, but God and time itself."[11]

Time magazine has printed numerous articles and editorials on the establishment of the Israeli state: "Thus Judaism . . . and Israel, have a commanding moral claim to Jerusalem. . . ."[12]

In a recent book by two men, one of whom has "written over twenty books," and his partner who "has over eight million Bible Study tapes in circulation around the world," we are told to "Look at what Jeremiah 16:14-15 prophesied and has literally come to fruition . . . 'I will bring them back into their land which I gave to their fathers.' Literally this came to be on **May 14, 1948; Israel was reformed as a nation**. This is not the only event that has been prophesied to happen in the twentieth century. . . . Both books, the books of Jeremiah and Ezekiel, provide the groundwork needed to realize that the Bible prophesies that Old Jerusalem would come to be under the Israeli flag again."[13]

Oswald T. Allis made an ethical evaluation of the Zionist/U.N. partitioning of Palestine. He asks rhetorically if the appeal to the promises God made to Abraham about the land of Canaan (Gen. 12:7; 13:14-15; 15:18; 17:8) proves the Jewish claim to sovereignty over the land of Palestine. His answer is, No! Allis contends that the promises in Genesis and other OT Scriptures were always conditioned upon the obedience of the Jews to God's law which includes, as the NT clearly demonstrates, the authority of Jesus Christ as the one and only Messiah of God. The majority of Jews have disobeyed God from the days of Moses to the rejection of the Messiah. They were warned by both Moses and the prophets that disobedience to God would forfeit their claim on possession of the land and they would be taken out of it (cf. Deut. 28:36,46,64,65,68; 30:2; Isa. 5:13; 7:23; 39:5-8; Jer. 6:8; 12:12; 16:13; 27:10; see especially, Ezek. 33:23-29; Hos. 9:3; Amos 4:1-3; 7:37; 9:9). Any restoration of the Jews to Palestine was conditioned upon repentance (Deut. 30:1-10). An Israeli nation that this very day has a law, enacted by its Knesset (Parliament), forbidding evangelism in the name of Jesus Christ should not expect to claim a "mandate from God" to forcibly dispossess people already living in Palestine, take it over, and forbid the Messiah's kingdom there! Any return to a Jewish system for spiritual reconciliation is *unacceptable* to God and would make it *impossible*, from divine perspective, for practitioners of that system to repent (Heb. 6:1-8; 10:26-39). The expatriation of the Jews and their dispersion was ordained of God upon their inflexible rejection of the Messiah (Deut. 18:18-19; 28:1-68; Matt. 21:43; 23:29-39; 24:1-34 and parallels; 1 Thess. 2:13-16). That Jesus and his apostles predicted the annulment of Judaism and nationalism hardly needs referencing.

What is more damning to this imperialistic arrogance of the Israeli state, however, is the fact that most Jews throughout the world, including most of those in Palestine today, *do not* accept the Old Testament *as the God-breathed, innerant, revealed, and authoritative* rule of faith and practice in either spiritual, cultural or civil matters. There is little spiritual difference between the Jews of America and the Jews of Palestine. A believing Jew is today as near heaven in the U.S., where 6 million of his fellow Israelites now live and apparently expect to live, as if he were in Jerusalem. An unbelieving Jew is just as far from heaven in Jerusalem as he would be in New York or London.

The most important thing about New Testament eschatology is its emphasis on the **certainty** of the obliteration of this world order and the return of Christ to judge the wicked and create a new heaven and a new earth in which righteousness will dwell. When that occurs, Christ will consummate the fellowship of redeemed mankind with God which he intended when he created us. There is only one credible affirmation that Jesus is coming again and that is the historical authentication he gave to his promise — his bodily resurrection from the dead (cf. Acts 17:29-31; 1 Cor. 15:20-28, et al.). Human predictions about "signs of the times" are subject to the enigma and vagary of speculation. Regulating eschatological study to this indisputable fact of history, and within the parameters of his *emphatic* assertion that the time of his return is unrevealed and unknowable, produces (a) faithfulness to Christ and purity of living (Matt. 24:37-51; 25:1-30; 2 Pet. 3:11-12; 1 John 3:2-3); (b) endurance for trials and tests (1 Thess. 4:17-18; 1 Pet. 4:13; 5:1-11); (c) aggressive evangelism (Acts 3:19-21; 4:19; 17:19-31; 24:25; 26:19-29; 2 Cor. 5:10-11; 1 Thess. 5:6-21; 2 Pet. 3:8-10); and (d) good works (Matt. 24:45-56; 25:31-46; Mark 13:34).

Anticipating the twenty-first century, social gurus are "hyping" as never before the refrain "relevancy." Every issue in the world is scrutinized for its "relevancy" for humanity. Two overriding issues are always at the forefront: the quest for personal identity (i.e., "self-awareness") and the quest for reality. Man has a gnawing in his soul to know what he is worth. Does he really matter in this seemingly limitless cosmos? Does he have a destiny beyond this life? Much of mankind is also skeptical of any theory of regeneration of society or the universe which is unsupported by hard facts. Is the Chrstian doctrine of a returning, redeeming Christ realistic in the twenty-first century? Is the Christian optimism that all will be well in the end justifiable? Isn't all that mere fantasy, a fairy tale like all the other myths of mankind?

That Christ *is* coming again in a *visible, personal* appearance to "dissolve with fire . . . the earth and the works that are upon it . . . and create a new heaven and a new earth in which righteousness dwells" (2 Pet. 3:8-13) is a message that is imperatively relevant in our depersonalized age! The Christ who came and is alive forevermore, and who is **coming again**, comes to us day by day, challenging us constantly for an entrance into our lives, seeking our fellowship (Matt. 18:20; 28:20; John 14:1–16:35; Rev. 3:20). God's purpose is to demonstrate now, in this transitory world, the beauty, power, holiness and permanence of the eternity to come. He who has called us out of this world is holy. He who comes for us is holy. In the meantime, he has given us his Holy Spirit to work out in our lives here something of the character of the eternity to come. Michael Green said it concisely: "I believe that in this biblical doctrine of the Christian hope (the Second Coming of Christ) we have an intelligible answer to the modern quest for purpose in the world."[14]

Notes

[1] Russell Boatman, *What the Bible Says about the End Time*, (Joplin, MO: College Press, 1980), pp. 4-5.

[2] See Appendix A for a study of apocalyptic style language in the Bible.

[3] See chapter 8 of this book.

[4] J. Marcellus Kik, *Matthew XXIV, An Exposition* (Philadelphia: Presbyterian and Reformed, 1948), p. 21.

[5] Loraine Boettner, *The Millennium* (Philadelphia: Presbyterian & Reformed, 1957), pp. 142-143

[6] Ibid., pp. 143-145.

[7] Ben Gurion declared during the hearing of the British Royal Commission on Palestine in 1937: "The Bible is our mandate. The mandate of the League (of Nations) is only a recognition of this right and does not establish new things."

[8] A Skevington Wood, *Signs of The Times* (Grand Rapids: Baker, 1971), p. 19.

[9] Ibid., pp. 19-20.

[10] Theodore Winston Pike, *Israel: Our Duty . . . Our Dilemma* (Oregon City, OR: Pike, 1984), p. 262.

[11] *New York Times*, advertisement over the name of the American Board of Mission to the Jews, supported by 48 named churches (1942).

[12] Spencer L. Davidson, "Building a New Jerusalem," *Time* (December 27, 1971).

[13] Woody Young and Chuck Missler, *Countdown To Eternity, Prologue to Destiny* (Fountain Valley, CA: Joy, 1992), p. 171.

[14] Michael Green, "Preaching the Advent, A Contemporary Approach," *Christianity Today* (January 1, 1965): 3-5.

chapter 2

THE IMPRUDENCE
OF SETTING DATES

Samples of date-setting concerning the Lord's return to earth gleaned from our personal files will suffice to establish the proposition. In spite of the specific warnings by Christ against setting dates about his second advent (Matt. 24:36–25:46), the practice of predicting it has been common and prolific ever since Christ's ascension into heaven. Even in the first century Paul and Peter had to correct misinformation that had been spread, saying "that the day of the Lord has already come" (2 Thess. 2:2; 2 Pet. 3:8-18).

There has been no dearth of "date-setters" in history since the first advent of Christ. In one of the last meetings Jesus had with his apostles on earth, they were anticipating the time of his establishment of the kingdom of Israel. He told them bluntly, "It is not for you to know times or seasons which the Father has fixed by his own authority" (Acts 1:6-7). We know the first century church was plagued with false teachers who predicted Jesus' second coming in their lifetime (1 Thess. 4:13–5:11; 2 Thess. 2:1-12), and with false teachers who said he was not returning at all (1 Cor. 15:1ff; 2 Pet. 3:1ff). Barnabas, A.D. 40-100, is said to have believed that as there were six days of creation so will God in six thousand years bring the present (Christian) dispensation of the world to an end. We are not informed by Barnabas as to the exact year when the 6000 years were to end.[1]

Indeed ". . . there have been many believers in *every* generation (from the Montanists of the second century through Joachin of Fiore (ca. 1125–1202) and Martin Luther to those Russian Mennonites who undertook a "Great Trek" to Siberia in 1880-84 and the nineteenth-century proponents of dispensationalism who have believed that *they* were living in the days immediately preceding the Second Coming of Christ. So far they have all been mistaken."[2]

Montanus, A.D. 135, a second century Christian, declared himself a prophet and announced the new Jerusalem would soon descend from heaven and take root in ancient Phrygia (Turkey). Christians throughout the Roman world were exhorted to move to the region to await the coming of the Messiah. Montanus was wrong but that did not deter others of that century (e.g., Cerinthus, A.D. 176) from also predicting the time of the Lord's return.[3]

A third century (A.D. 200-300) Roman Christian named Hippolytus relates that in A.D. 204, during severe persecution of Christians, a "bishop" became convinced the Lord would return immediately. He told his congregation to sell their farms, homes, and all property and accompany him into the wilderness to await the Lord's return. They did so, but when the Lord did not return, Hippolytus says the people were all reduced to poverty and begging.[4]

> In the third century, a prophet called Novatian gathered a huge following by crying, "Come, Lord Jesus!" Donatus, a fourth-century prophet . . . stressed that only 144,000 people would be chosen by God. Saint Martin of Tours, who died A.D. 397, wrote of the coming Antichrist whose reign would signify the last days. His prediction was, *Non est dubium, quin antichristus,* or, "There is no doubt that the Antichrist has already been born."[5]

The end of the first millennium was as mesmerizing upon the eschatologically obsessed as is the end of the second millennium. "As the last day of 999 approached, the old basilica of St. Peter's at Rome was thronged with a mass of weeping and trembling worshipers awaiting the end of the world believing that they were on the eve of the millennium. . . . This mistaken application of biblical prophecy happened again in 1000, 1200, and 1245. . . . In 1531 Melchior Hofmann announced that the second coming would take place in the year 1533. . . . Nicholas Cusa held that the world would not last past 1734."[6]

"Hans Nut, a German bookbinder, declared himself to be a prophet and in 1527 announced the end of time was to be in 1528 to be followed by a thousand years of free food, love, and free sex."[7]

Joachim (A.D. 1145) predicted that in 1260 the book of Revelation would be fulfilled in the destruction of the Roman papacy.[8]

The Anabaptists (originated ca. A.D. 1522 in Switzerland) denied the validity of infant baptism and practiced baptism of adults. Usually pacifist as to the use of force, their certainty of the imminent return of Jesus in 1528, led them to believe they should set up the Kingdom of God by force of arms at Esslingen. A dictatorship under Jan Matthys was established and a "purge of the unrighteous" in anticipation of Jesus' return ensued. A "communist" economic order was enforced at the point of the sword. What began as a belief in the certainty of the soon return of Christ ended in a reign of terror.[9]

There have been multitudinous prognosticators in centuries past who have calculated from the eschatological language of the Bible and proclaimed the year, month, and day when Jesus was to initiate his second advent. With rhetorical certainty, they wrote their tracts, drew their charts, and instructed their followers. *And every one of them was wrong!*

In light of the repeated statements (eight or nine) by Jesus that no one knows the day nor the hour, not the Son, nor the angels . . . that he would return when least expected . . . that it would be when times were normal, and with nearly 2000 years of conspicuous failures by date-setters, it would seem the eschatologically curious should have learned a modicum of restraint. Regrettably, they have not. Their unadvised and unashamed conjectures continue to blast through the airwaves and roll off the presses. The following sampling, in specific order, casts a shadow upon the integrity of those who persist in setting dates for Jesus' Second Coming.

A lengthy dissertation by a gentleman who refused to give his complete name declared: "The rapture will come between right now (August 1980), and no later than June 10, 1981."[10] And in a tract that would be ludicrous were it not so tragic a wresting of the Scriptures, it is stated: "The Vultures Are Already Circling in The Valley of Armageddon. God is preparing a feast of seven months for these vultures to feed upon. And a new breed of vultures has appeared in Israel . . . multiplying at three times the normal rate. . . . This is a sign of the end time . . . ." This same tract informs us that "Russia is stockpiling bows and arrows to fight against Israel in the battle of Gog and Magog."[11]

Some "end-times" seers insist, without any biblical sanction, that *God's invincibility* is inflexibly tied to *modern* Israel's invincibility. "Of the 46,000 plus Jews that returned to Palestine last year (1971), more than half of them were from Russia, A LAND THAT IS GOING TO INVADE PALESTINE in the not too distant future," but Russia "will not be able to successfully invade Israel. **ISRAEL IS INVINCIBLE UNLESS GOD IS VULNERABLE.**"[12]

While the following declaration sets no dates, it does illustrate the unabashed readiness of eschatology devotees to dictate the terms of Jesus' return to earth. It has been declared that:

> Christ will not return to the earth until the Jewish people ask Him to come back. This is the basis of the Second Coming of Christ. Satan . . . understands that Christ will not come back until the Jews ask Him to come back. If Satan can succeed in destroying all the Jews before they have a chance to ask Christ to come back, Christ will not come back and Satan will be safe. That is why Satan is in an

all-out campaign to destroy the Jews. The power of the Second Coming of Christ is very much in the hands of Israel.[13]

Circumscription was absent from this prediction: "Remember that year . . . 1982 . . . the church will have been taken before this happens. . . . that would place the Rapture in 1980-81."[14]

Radical eschatology always provides "meat" for the electronic press and the wire services. But it also gives the enemies of God's word occasion to bolster their claims that the Bible and Christianity are not to be trusted with the truth:

> Maupin is the spiritual leader of the Lighthouse Gospel Tract Foundation, a group of 40 to 50 people who believe (i.e., their own) Bible forecast that ascension (the rapture) will take place sometime Sunday (July 5, 1981) or before noon Monday (July 6, 1981). . . . according to the scenario, Satan will appear before December 1984 and will rule the world until May 14, 1988, when the Battle of Armageddon will be fought. . . . 'We're going,' Maupin said, 'I'm more sure of that than anything I know.'"[15]

None of the following "prophesied" events have come to pass except the establishment of the modern nation of Israel in 1948. "A.D. 1948–1952 — Israel's rebirth after the flesh S.A. 5952; A.D. 1967–1971 — Jerusalem restored S.A. 5971; A.D. 1974–1978 — Jewish Temple rebuilt? S.A. 5978; A.D. 1981–1985 — Beginning of the Tribulation S.A. 5985; A.D. 1985–1989 — Middle of the Tribulation S.A. 5989; A.D. 1988–1992 — End of the Tribulation S.A. 5992; A.D. 1995–1999 — Completion of Millennial Temple S.A. 5999; A.D. 1996–2000 — The Jubilee, a rest S.A. 6000; A.D. 1997–2001 — The Beginning of the Kingdom age S.A. 6001."[16]

Modern Israel's establishment was by decree of the United Nations and only achieved by terrorism and war. She has been sustained for nearly half a century largely through foreign aid from the United States and a few other nations, without which she would have long ago been conquered by her enemies.

The following teacher of prophecy needs to do further research: "*Christ Returns By 1988 — 101 Reasons Why*, Rev. Colin Deal. This book is beautifully researched, well documented, and is a must for a student of prophecy. For a contribution of $5.00."[17]

As tragic as the following wire story is, it is not an isolated case. Countless thousands of people continue to be exploited and violated by just such eschatology charlatans. The Associated Press reported:

> 2000 Koreans expecting Rapture . . . Seoul, South Korea — Kwon Tae-young,

seated cross-legged on the white linoleum floor, gestured excitedly as he explained; at midnight on Oct. 18 (1992), trumpets will blare and white-robed angels will carry him, his wife and three sons to heaven. . . . Hundreds or possibly thousands of Koreans who believe the beginning of the end of the world is at hand reportedly have sold property, abandoned their families, quit schools and jobs, deserted military posts, and even had abortions. . . . One group says the Rapture could occur as early as Oct. 10 (1992). At least three have already committed suicide. . . . Lee (the leader of this group of at least 20,000) was charged with swindling followers of up to $4 million. Prosecutors also said he had $380,000 worth of bonds with maturities as late as next May, indicating he did not believe his own preaching that the world was coming to an end.[18]

And speaking of quacks, this was another one for the press to sensationalize: "Rev. Rex Humbard installed an archive of videotapes in his 'Cathedral of Tomorrow' at Akron, Ohio." Rev. Humbard intends that all saved Christians who wish may videotape a message to be left behind for their unsaved relatives and friends when the "Rapture" comes. This service is offered to anyone for a donation of $100. "We have a responsibility to those who are left," he wrote. "The archives of faith will have the answer. At the archives, we will have a film that explains what has happened. The date of the rapture, or the second coming of Christ is uncertain," according to Mr. Humbard, but "all those who have been born again know we are on the verge of the Lord's return." The first testimony to be included in the archives, he said, will be that of country singer Johnny Cash. He said a major concern among many people would be when Humbard and all other saved Christians have been "raptured" away from earth, and the world is in the clutches of an evil Antichrist![19]

Even the secular prophets and prophetesses are "in on the act." "The Second Coming of Jesus for Christians and the First Coming of the Messiah to the Jews will be within the next 32 years," (i.e., A.D. 2000) predicted the famed seeress, Jean Dixon, from Washington, D.C., Monday night, October 7, 1968, to a standing-room-only crowd at State Fair Music Hall in Dallas, TX.[20]

Jean Dixon also claimed to have received a divine vision on February 5, 1962, about a coming world religious-political ruler who strikingly resembles the modern characterization of an Antichrist: "A child, born somewhere in the Middle East shortly before 7 A.M. (EST) on February 5, 1962, will revolutionize the world. Before the close of the century he will bring together all mankind in one all embracing faith. This will be the foundation of a new Christianity, with every sect and creed united through this man who will walk among the people to spread the wisdom of the Almighty Power." Mrs. Dixon claims that this man's influence will be felt in the early 1980s and that by 1999, the ecumenical religion will be achieved.[21]

And a Hollywood star has foreseen the end of the world, "I believe the world is coming to an end. I just feel that science, technology, and the mind have surpassed the soul — the heart. There is no balance in terms of feeling and love for fellow man," predicted Barbra Streisand.[22]

Jack Van Impe does not believe in setting dates for Christ's return, but he did speculate in his *Crusade NewsLetter* that 1975 might be the time of the Messiah's return and that 1976 might be the time of the Great Tribulation.[23]

John F. Walvoord said in an interview with *USA Today* that he believes the events described in Matthew 24:1-31 are being fulfilled and the time for the rapture is near.[24]

Hal Lindsey, author of *The Late Great Planet Earth*, and other pop-eschatology works, told his readers that "The decade of the 1980s could very well be the last decade of history as we know it." Lindsey believes "this generation" in Matthew 24:24 is the generation which saw the nation of modern Israel constituted in 1948. He contends that 40 years maximum constitutes a generation. That being the case, the "rapture" should have occurred in 1988, the Great Tribulation should have ended in 1995, and the millennial kingdom should have begun in 1996.[25]

Our *a cappella* brethren are not without their prognosticators. "While God's word tells us what will happen in the end time, God's word does not tell us when it will happen. With the amazing acceleration of human history in the last few years, we would expect to see the fulfillment of these prophecies in a very short space of time." We are not told what the "very short space of time" was to be, but this prediction was made nearly 30 years ago.[26]

Are people still "listening" to Harold Camping? When will Harold Camping predict again?

> *Broadcaster.* World will end in September. . . . When Harold Camping says the
> world is going to end in September, people listen. . . . Camping has convinced
> thousands that on one day this September (1994), the "saved" will be raised up
> and the "unsaved" living and dead condemned to everlasting damnation . . . .
> "The judgment throne is coming. In a few days it will be here," Camping said in
> a telephone interview from his office in Oakland, Calif. . . . According to
> Camping's dateline, the period of tribulation forecast in biblical books as leading
> up to the end began in May 1988, 13,000 years after the world was created in
> 11,013 B.C. It was in 1988 that Satan was turned loose on the Earth, and churches
> have been teaching what he calls "false gospels" that ignore the concepts of hell
> and damnation . . . . Working from the May 1988 date, he arrived at September
> 1994 as the date of the end of the world by taking literally a reference in the
> eighth chapter of the Book of Daniel to a vision of a sanctuary being rebuilt
> 2,300 days after it was desecrated.[27]

And the beat goes on!

Rapture Oct. 28 '92 — Jesus is Coming in The Air. . . . the seven days of God's creation in Genesis are symbolic of a 7,000-year probation for earth prior to eternity. . . . The Scriptures imply that the Lord will bring everything to an end in 6,000 years, and then will establish the 1,000-year Millenial [sic] Kingdom. . . . This, to allow for the 1000-year Millennium, Jesus will return about 6,000 years after the creation of Adam to fulfill the 7,000-year plan . . . 4000 years expired from Adam to Christ and 1,992 years since the birth of Christ. This gives us a total of 5,992 years that have alread passed since Adam. . . . Of course, the Rapture should occur around 7 years (1992) prior to the Kingdom's establishment. Thus, we know that the time of Rapture is imminent. [28]

A favorite way for eschatology aficionados to pass their time is to predict the identity and arrival of "The Beast." "If debit cards replace credit cards by 1982 as planned; and if both are replaced by body marking by 1984, 'the mark of the beast' decree could be enforced by computerization by late 1984 or early 1985." [29]

Date setters have many fish to fry and it is of no consequence to them where those "fish" are found in the Scriptures!

An update on the number of nations in the world when Jesus Christ returns; we again comment on the 21st chapter of John. We have noted in other publications, that in our opinion, this chapter in the Bible contains an important Kingdom Age teaching. In many Scriptures in the Bible, God catching the nations into His Kingdom for the Millennium is compared to a fisherman catching fish in their net and they brought in 153 large fish. In addition to the 153 fish in the net, there was a fish on the fire. We believe the fish on the fire represents Israel during the Great Tribulation (see Zech. 13:8-9). For several years, as far back as 1966, we have thought that there will be 153 nations involved in the Battle of Armageddon, and against Jerusalem. According to the 1980 edition of the *World Almanac*, as of July 1979 there were 151 members in the United Nations. Since that time, the following nations have been added: St. Vincent and Grenadines, St. Lucia and Zimbabwe, bringing the total number to 154. If we subtract one nation, Israel, the fish on the fire, we have 153 nations left — exactly the number of fish that were in the net. We are not overly dogmatic on this one point, but due to the fact that the signs of the time indicate that the return of Jesus is very near, the present UN membership provides further evidence. But the United Nations has rejected Jerusalem as belonging to Israel. [30]

Another miscalculation: The rapture was to occur September 15, 1975, on Rosh Hashana (OT Feast of Trumpets), according to Dr. Charles Taylor, Redondo Beach, CA. [31]

End-time predictions were rampant as the Nazis in Germany, under Adolph Hitler, began what was to become World War II. "The Great Tribulation, Revival of the Roman Empire, reign of the Antichrist, and the Battle of Armageddon must take place before the year 1933."[32]

The major "decisive conflict" between 1980 and 1992 was the Gulf War (1991) which Saddam Hussein boasted would be "the mother of all wars." It was hardly begun before it was over! It certainly was not "Armageddon." A gentleman in Indiana predicted, "In our view the 12 years between the Olympics (in 1980) and 1992 will produce the decisive conflict of our epoch" (meaning the battle of Armageddon).[33]

The following prediction, made numerous times, was *not* the eschatological position of the periodical in which it was noted — "Great banners at a widely attended men's clinic in the late 1950s proclaimed a college professor's prediction of Communist terror; 'Within four years we'll all be dead, or wish to God we were!'"[34]

And in the same periodical was this report:

> An equally firm and futile prediction came to our notice early in 1971 while we were enjoying one of Standard's Holy Land tours. Our Israeli guide was a delightful young Orthodox Jew who had made an extensive study of apocalyptic literature and had reached a firm conclusion about the coming of Messiah. This he shared with us via the tour bus speaker system as we climbed from Jericho to Jerusalem. The Mosque of Omar would be destroyed, he said, by an act of God — specifically an earthquake. That would clear the way for Israel to build her glorious temple on the sacred site to welcome her coming Messiah. Israel's enemies, led increasingly by Russia, would combine against her; and her friends — notably the United States — would withdraw their support. Armies would converge in the Plain of Megiddo for what would seem to be the inevitable destruction of Israel. Then Messiah would come to bring God's victory from disaster, and he would subsequently enter in triumph through the Beautiful Gate into the temple, not later than *May 20, 1974.*[35]

Jesus was supposedly coming in the lifetime of those alive in 1967. "This is the unquestionable SIGN (the Israeli six-day war in June 1967) to you and to me . . . that 'HE IS NEAR EVEN AT THE DOORS.' We do not know the day nor the hour, but we have to be blind to miss this historical fact that points to the **Generation That Will See the Lord Return** in His second advent. Amen!"[36]

The following prediction was reported in another major Christian periodical. "The outbreak of war in the Middle East temporarily stranded thousands of tourists in Israel and hundreds in Egypt . . . and prompted widespread speculative discussion on current events and Bible prophecy. . . . Pastor Chuck Smith of Calvary Chapel,

Costa Mesa, California, and eighty of his parishioners were in Israel the entire first week of the fighting. Many, convinced the return of Christ was near, wanted to stay and meet him there, said a church source."[37]

Wars in the Middle East are a never ending fuel for igniting the fires of end-time predictions. "In an interview, prophecy specialist Hal Lindsey . . . [stated] 'This [Israeli war] is a continuation of the priming of the fuse which will finally ignite the last war. . . . This is not the end, but the rapture is very close,' he concluded."[38]

Dr. Billy Graham surely knew, when he made the following statement, that self-appointed prophets had been predicting for centuries the Second Coming of Christ. "Evangelist Billy Graham predicted Monday night that the world is 'very, very close to war in the Middle East. . . . Graham said biblical signs for the second coming of Christ seem to be converging, 'perhaps for the first time in history.'"[39]

Joseph Smith, founder of Mormonism, made many false statements, not the least of which were his predictions concerning the Second Coming of Christ. "According to the Mormon prophet [Joseph Smith], Jesus Christ would return to earth before the close of 1891 . . . on February 14, 1835, 'President Smith then stated . . . the coming of the Lord was nigh — fifty-six years should wind up the scene.' . . . he told several church leaders that they would live until Christ returned. . . . His diary, dated April 6, 1843, reported, 'I prophecy (sic) in the name of the Lord God — & let it be written: that the Son of Man will not come in the heavens till I am 85 years old, 48 years hence, or about 1890.'"[40] It should also be noted that Joseph Smith never reached the age of 85 as he was murdered in 1844 before he was even 40 and only a year after making this prophecy!

Seventh Day Adventists have long been known for their eschatological predictions. "William Miller (Seventh Day Adventist) set the period from March 21, 1843, to March 21, 1844, as the year Christ would finally return. . . . 50,000 mostly in upstate New York and New England sold their property, refused to plow their fields, gave away their possessions, donned 'white ascension robes,' and climbed to the tops of trees and houses to await Jesus' reentry. Four times he set specific dates. Four times, he failed. The last effort declared by one of Miller's followers, Samuel S. Snow — October 22, 1844 — collapsed his prestige and believability."[41]

Let us not omit the Jehovah's Witnesses. Charles Taze Russell (Jehovah's Witness) predicted in his written work, *Studies in the Scriptures*, that Jesus "invisibly" returned to earth in 1874 . . . that the end of the world would come in 1914 and usher in the "full establishment of the kingdom of God on earth."[42]

Russell's followers have not learned caution for they continue to make predictions in their literature, e.g., "6000 Years of Human History Ending in 1975 . . . 1914 C.E. 'Last Days begin . . . 1975 C.E., end of 6,000 years."[43]

The *Moody Monthly* magazine published an article in which numerous predictions of Christ's second coming were recorded. The article quoted from a *Minneapolis Star* newspaper book review of Mr. Kenneth Aune's book, *God, History, and The End of the World*. For example, in January, 1963, a well-known Bible teacher in southern California entitled an article "Jesus Will Come in 1968. . . . It is my sincere conviction that the return of Jesus Christ to earth is immediately at hand."[44] Kenneth Aune claimed that in March, 1990, the battle of Jerusalem would ensue, Jesus Christ would return to earth and the battle of Armageddon would take place.[45]

Using the septa-millennial theory as a basis, Augustine (A.D. 354–430), predicted that the end of human history would be about A.D. 650.[46]

"The year 650 came and went with no notable events to fulfill the promise in Augustine's teaching. Attention was soon fastened on the year A.D. 1000. The belief was widespread that the second advent would occur on this date . . . also in the year 1044, and again in 1065, there was hope that the second advent would occur on Good Friday when Good Friday happened to coincide with the Day of Annunciation."[47]

"In 1911, the well-known prophetic speaker, I. M. Holdeman, pastor of First Baptist Church of New York, published a message, 'The Signs of the Times,' in which he declared that the increase in armaments, spiritual declension of the church, appearance of false teachers, Israel's return, earthquakes and famines all tell us that 'the hour is ripe for the moment when the Lord shall descend and gather His Church to Himself.'"[48]

The *Moody Monthly* continued its quotation of a *Minneapolis Star* newspaper reivew of Kenneth Aune's book, with these statements: "A popular author and conference speaker repeatedly declares that we are in 'this generation' of Matthew 24:34. He believes the 'paramount prophetic sign' is that Israel had to be a nation again in the land of its forefathers. This condition was fulfilled, he claims on May 14, 1948. After stating that a 'generation' is about forty years, he contends adamantly that we are in the last generation before Christ comes, though 'we may be twelve or thirteen years away.'"[49]

> Still a fourth spokesman, a seminary professor and author, while disclaiming date-setting, says, on the basis of Matthew 24:14, that Christ cannot come until the task of evangelizing the world has been completed. Thus, in essence, he is saying that Christ cannot come for His Church today.[50]

And there are some who believe Christ's Second Coming was completed in the destruction of Jerusalem in A.D. 70. They contend that the destruction of Jerusalem was a crucial point in God's scheme of redemption. They say it was the end of one world and the completion and beginning of another world that had been born on

Pentecost day. According to their eschatology the physical and spiritual results of the destruction of Jerusalem and significance of the fall of Judaism in A.D. 70 fulfills every need and purpose of the Second Coming of Christ. They say that the destruction of Judaism did not leave unfulfilled one single prophecy, promise, or blessing, the fulfillment of which is dependent upon the ending of this physical world.

So much for predicting the time of the Lord's return, the "rapture," the "tribulation," and the "millennium." We have not even mentioned David Koresh, Jim Jones, and a multitude of other "latter day prophets." Most of these intrepid interpreters of biblical eschatology would disavow any claim to be an official "prophet" but they are in effect, and *de facto,* making that very claim.

Moses instructed God's people, Israel, "And if you say in your heart, 'How may we know the word which the LORD has not spoken?' — when a prophet speaks in the name of the LORD, if the word does not come to pass or come true, that is a word which the LORD has not spoken; the prophet has spoken it presumptuously, you need not be afraid of him" (Deut. 18:21-22).

The true prophets of God in the divided kingdom of Israel had to deal constantly with the false prophets of false gods. Isaiah challenged them in his day, "Set forth your case, says the LORD; bring your proofs. . . . Let them bring them, and tell us what is to happen. . . . Tell us what is to come hereafter, that we may know that you are gods . . . ." (Isa. 41:21-23; cf. also Isa. 43:8-13). Jeremiah contended with false prophets, warning, "Thus says the LORD of hosts: Do not listen to the words of the prophets who prophesy to you, filling you with vain hopes; they speak visions of their own minds, not from the mouth of the LORD" (23:16). These false prophets said what the people wanted to hear, not what the Lord had revealed in his certified messengers. God warned, "Behold, I am against those who prophesy lying dreams, . . . and who tell them and lead my people astray by their lies and their *recklessness,* when I did not send them or charge them; so they do not profit this people at all" (Jer. 23:32, my italics). God charged Ezekiel to condemn false prophets, "Son of man, prophesy against the prophets . . . and say to those who prophesy out of their own minds: 'Hear the word of the LORD!' . . . Woe to the foolish prophets who follow their own spirit, and have seen nothing! . . . They have spoken falsehood and divined a lie; they say, 'Says the LORD,' when the LORD has not sent them, and yet they expect him to fulfill their word. . . . My hand will be against the prophets who see delusive visions and who give lying divinations; they shall not be in the council of my people, nor be enrolled in the register of the house of Israel, nor shall they enter the land of Israel . . . ." (Ezek. 13:1-9).

The apostle Peter characterizes false prophets who would come in the Christian dispensation as those whose greed would motivate them to exploit and entice with false words every unsteady soul they could find (2 Pet. 2:1-16). The apostle John gives us the New Testament criterion by which we may discern today what is the true word of God and what is false when he writes, "We (apostles) are of God. Whoever knows God listens to us (apostles) and he who is not of God does not listen to us. By *this* we may know the spirit of truth and the spirit of error (1 John 4:1-6, my italics). There is only one place from which to "listen to the apostles" and that is through the New Testament Scriptures. All other claims to be the word of God are false.

Notes

[1] Reinhold Seeberg, *Textbook of the History of Doctrines,* Vol. 1 (Grand Rapids: Baker, 1977).

[2] Gary DeMar, *Last Days Madness* (Nashville: Wolgemuth & Hyatt, 1991), p. 4.

[3] Albert Henry Newman, *A Manual of Church History* (American Baptist Pub. Society, 1953), p. 205.

[4] Ronald Heine, "Some Things Never Change," *Christian Standard* (April 7, 1996): 9.

[5] DeMar, *Last Days Madness,* pp. 11 and 142.

[6] Ibid. p. 13.

[7] Documented in Kenny Barfield, *The Prophet Motive* (Nashville: Gospel Advocate, 1995), p. 221.

[8] DeMar, *Last Days Madness,* p. 206.

[9] Ibid., pp. 107-109.

[10] "Ted," "Deadline 1981, Mockers Beware, Vol. 1," *The Gospel Truth* (St. Petersburg, FL): 12.

[11] Joel Darby, *Why All The Vultures?* an undated tract from Osterhus Pub. House, Minneapolis, which came into our possession in 1960.

[12] *Maranatha Trumpet,* Church bulletin of Central Christian Church, Colorado Springs, Dec. 11, 1972.

[13] Arnold G. Fruchtenbaum, "The Jews and The Tribulation," *The Chosen People,* Vol. LXXX, No. 9 (May 1975): 16-18.

[14] *WHITE PAPER, March 1977,* Total Evangelism, Inc., Altamonte Springs, FL, Raldo Cook, Director.

[15] Associated Press wire item, date line, Tucson, AZ, printed in the *Joplin Globe,* Joplin, MO, June 28, 1981.

[16] *The Gospel Truth,* Vol. 17, No. 11, October, 1977, The Southwest Radio Bible Church, Oklahoma City.

[17] *Current Events and Bible Prophecy Newsletter,* pub. Ministries Inc., Montgomery, AL Mar-Apr, 1981.

[18] Associated Press wire item, in the *Lexington Herald Leader,* Lexington, KY, Oct. 6, 1992.

[19] *Akron Beacon Journal,* Akron, OH, Sunday, May 11, 1975.

[20] *The Christian,* weekly bulletin of Heights Christian Church, Albuquerque, NM, Oct. 1968.

[21] DeMar, *Last Days Madness,* p. 142.

[22] Ibid., p. 10.

[23] Ibid., p. 71.

[24] Ibid., p. 72

[25] Ibid., pp. 72, 125, 128, 129.

[26] *The Exhorter,* Vol. X, No. 1, a publication of the Churches of Christ, Hammond, LA, January, 1969.

[27] Associated Press item, *Joplin Globe,* Joplin, MO., dated July 15, 1994.

[28] Tract from Mission For The Coming Days, Orange County Divison, Orange County, CA, undated.

[29] *666 Is Here,* Gospel Tract Society, Inc., Independence, MO, undated.

[30] *The Gospel Truth,* November 1980.

[31] Dr. Charles Taylor, *Get All Excited, Jesus Is Coming Soon, And Updated Addenda,* (Huntington Beach, CA: Today in Bible Prophecy, n.d.).

[32] Oswald J. Smith, *Is the Antichrist at Hand?* (Pastor of the Alliance Tabernacle, Toronto, Canada), pp. 16-19.

[33] *The Midnight Cry,* Vol. 39, No. 6 (Shoals, IN: MidNight Cry Publ. Co.): 10.

[34] Edwin Hayden, "Editorial,"*Christian Standard* (August 18, 1974): 3.

[35] Ibid., p. 3.

[36] William E. Parks, *Warning, Christ Will Come in Our Lifetime,* (Noel, MO, undated tract).

[37] Charles D. Kay, "The Middle East — Talk of the End," *Christianity Today* (October 26, 1973): 59.

[38] Ibid.

[39] "Graham Says Fighting Close in Middle East," *The Norman Oklahoma Transcript* (1976).

[40] Kenny Barfield, *The Prophet Motive,* p. 215.

[41] Ibid., p. 221.

[42] Ibid., p. 223.

[43] *Awake,* Watchtower publication, October 8, 1968.

[44] Earl D. Radmacher, "Signs of Confusion," *Moody Monthly,* May 1974, pp. 42-45.

[45] Ibid., pp. 42-45.

[46] Ibid., p. 43.

[47] Ibid.

[48] Ibid.

[49] Ibid., p. 42

[50] Ibid.

chapter 3

THE VALLEY OF
JEHOSHAPHAT

We begin here an adventurous stroll through the eschatological mind of God as he revealed it through pens and tablets of a few Old Testament and New Testament prophets. These men were privileged to prophesy "the grace that was to be yours . . . [of the] time . . . indicated by the Spirit of Christ within them . . . predicting the sufferings of Christ and the subsequent glory" (1 Pet. 1:10-12). You and I were being served by those men because they were announcing ". . . the good news . . . sent from heaven, things into which angels long to look." We will accumulate evidence for the inspiration of the Bible as we read of fulfilled predictions; we will be awed by God's power and faithfulness to bring his word to pass in spite of opposition by the most powerful forces man can muster against God; and we will be intrigued and impressed with the literary genius of these ancients who used figurative language with artistic skill and animated flair.

It is a fact of divine revelation that human history since the Fall in Eden is totally enveloped in spiritual warfare. That is the message of both the OT and the NT. God, and his Son, have victoriously concluded their major campaign. Satan and death have been defeated and their powers have been destroyed (John 12:31; 16:11; 1 Cor. 15:57; Col. 2:14-15; Heb. 2:14-18; 1 John 3:8). But there are skirmishes and battles yet to be fought by human beings, even by Christians (e.g. Rom. 7:13-25; Gal. 5:16-26; Phil. 1:27-30; 1 Tim. 1:18-20; 6:12; 2 Tim. 2:3-4; 4:6-8). And those who wrote our Bible "pictured" the struggle for human destiny in just those terms. Come with me now as we travel the "battlefields" of history from God's perspective.

The first OT prophet (in chronological order) whose writing provides the biblical student a *key passage* in understanding eschatology is *Joel*. Joel prophesied ca.

840-830 B.C., more than one hundred years prior to the captivity of Israel (the ten northern tribes) by the Assyrians in 722 B.C.

We learn from the historical parallels to Joel's account in 2 Chronicles 21:1ff and 2 Kings 8:25-29 and 11:1ff that the vicious Jehoram (Joram), king of Judah had slain his six brothers and married the wicked Athaliah. Athaliah was the daughter of the infamous royal couple Ahab and Jezebel who had ruled the northern kingdom Israel. Under the reign of Jehoram, and that of his father (Jehoshaphat) before him, Jerusalem was plundered by Arabians and Philistines. Jehoram died a horrible death and "departed with no one's regret" (2 Chr. 21:18-20).

After Jehoram's death, Ahaziah ruled Judah under the watchful eye of his mother, Athaliah. But Ahaziah was slain while visiting his uncle in Israel by Jehu at about the same time Jehu was killing Ahaziah's grandmother, Jezebel. The queen-mother Athaliah then took the throne of Judah for herself, murdering all her grandsons except one, Joash. She ruled Judah on her own 6 years, from 843 B.C. to 837 B.C. She, like her idolatrous Canaanite mother, was devoted to Baalism.

When Athaliah was carrying out her massacre of the royal princes, Joash was "stolen" away from the palace by his uncle and aunt, Jehoiada (the high priest) and his wife Jehoshabeath. They hid Joash and his nurse in a "bed-chamber" in the temple (the one built by Solomon). When Joash was 7 years old, Jehoiada instituted a sweeping religious reformation in Judah. The people joined him in tearing down the temple to Baal and all its altars and slaying the idolatrous priest to Baal, Mattan. Jehoiada then brought the boy-king Joash down from his hiding place to the royal palace, set him on the throne and had his wicked grandmother, Athaliah slain. And all the people of the land rejoiced! (2 Chr. 23:16-21). The high priest Jehoiada was *de facto* ruler of Judah (through the boy-king Joash) until he died at the ripe old age of 130 years. After he died Joash and the people of Judah fell back into idolatry and the social depravity ("drunkards" Joel 1:5) that invariably results from religious apostasy. They killed Jehoiada's son, Zechariah the priest, when he pronounced God's judgment upon them. The silence of Joel's prophetic discourse concerning a royal leader, and his call upon the "aged men" and the priesthood for leadership responsibilities during this time of crisis (Joel 1:2-3,9,13-24; 2:16-17) is strong confirmation for the dating of Joel's prophecy during this era.

In the midst of all this political anarchy and social degeneracy, God sent upon Judah a locust plague more terrible than any that had ever been seen before in Judah (1:1-3). Evidently, Judah was also being chastened by the Lord through devastating drought ("fire" Joel 1:19-20; 2:3). The land was so severely denuded of all vegetation the people of Judah had nothing to eat (1:16). They could not even present "cereal and drink offerings" to the Lord (1:9,13,16). The starving animals were "groaning" and "crying" to the Lord (1:18-20). This was indeed zero hour! So extreme was the situation it was called "the day of the Lord" (1:15; 2:11). The locusts were "the Lord's army" (2:11,25) executing his wrath upon Judah for all its sins.

Joel's summons was, "Blow the trumpet in Zion; sanctify a fast; call a solemn assembly; gather the people" (2:15). Every single citizen of Judah was summoned to cry unto the Lord, from the infant to the honeymooners to the elders of the land. They were to "return to the Lord with all their heart" (2:13-14). Joel used the Hebrew word *shûb* for "return" when he called for action from the people. But when he proposed that God might "repent" and lift his hand of judgment from them if they "turned" he used the Hebrew word *nacham*. The NASB has translated 2:13-14 most accurately of all the English versions and says that God would "relent" of the evil he intended to do upon Judah for its sins if Judah "repented." God does not "repent" of anything as if he had erred and needed to change his mind or his will (see Num. 23:19; Mal. 3:6; Jas. 1:17). God may very well change his action, in accordance with his immutable will, when man repents (changes his mind, confesses his sin, and changes his actions). This is Joel's proposition to the people of Judah.

Clearly, the people of Judah repented. The Lord "became jealous for his people," had pity upon them, removed "the northerner" (the locusts which came upon the land from the "fertile crescent" direction — north of Palestine), and restored the "years" the locusts and the drought had taken away (2:18-26). All of this was restored upon the condition that they would acknowledge Jehovah's sovereignty over their lives and land (2:27).

Now we have come to the major division of Joel's book of prophecy. We have at this point a classic example of the fourth axiom for interpreting prophetic literature (see pp. 275-276) called "**shortened perspective**." Joel makes a leap of nearly eight centuries from 2:27 to 2:28. Imagine Joel looking at a mountain range squarely in front of him. He sees one "mountain" which is very near to him — contemporaneous to him, in fact. That "peak" is God's blessing upon Judah as he restored their crops after the locusts. God is, in effect giving Judah back her life. Then, as Joel looks (actually, he is given this perspective by divine revelation) he sees another "peak," behind the first, which looks as if it was right up against the first "mountain" he has seen. He does not see the tremendous gap or "valley" between the two peaks. The "valley" is all the history of God's redemptive program between Joel's day and the coming of the Messiah at his first advent and the establishment of his "kingdom" (the church). The second peak Joel has seen is the completed redemptive work of God — the day of Pentecost, A.D. 30 — when the apostle Peter and the other apostles took the "keys of the kingdom" and opened its doors to people from sixteen different language groups. We have the inspired, inerrant apostolic word that this is the proper interpretation of Joel 2:28-29 (see Acts 2:14-41).

Our thesis is that the remainder of Joel's prophecy (2:30–3:21) is a "word picture" of the New Testament dispensation. The material blessings of God bestowed on Judah after her repentance and turning to the Lord became a **type** of the spiritual blessings God would bestow upon "all flesh" who repented beginning with the day of Pentecost, A.D. 30, and concluding with the end of time. The beginning point of Joel's messianic prophecy is stated in 2:28: "And it shall come to pass afterward . . . ," and the ending point is stated in 2:31: "before the great and terrible day of the LORD comes." All that comes *between* the beginning and the end is summarized by the statement, "And I will give portents in the heavens and on the earth, blood and fire and columns of smoke." Dr. Henry H. Halley's Handbook has sold over five million copies; his careful interpretation of Joel 2:28ff follows:

> In Acts 2:17-21 Peter quotes Joel 2:28-32 as a prediction of "the day" he was inaugurating. This means that God intended the passage to be a forecast of the Gospel era. It would be a day of judgment for the nations (3:1-12). To Joel himself that meant enemy nations of his own times, Sidonians, Philistines, Egyptians and Edomites (3:4,19). But more. The great battle in the valley of Jehoshaphat (valley of Kidron on the east side of Jerusalem, 3:9-12), is spoken of in connection with the "harvest" (13), the "valley of decision" (14), God "uttering his voice from Jerusalem" (16), the "heavens and earth being shaken" (16), and the "fountain flowing from the house of God" (18) — all of which is a continuation of the thought about the Holy Spirit era of 2:28-32. So, as a whole, the passage seems to be a picture of the Christian age, in which God's Word, embodied in the Gospel of Christ, and borne by the gracious influences of the Holy Spirit to all mankind, would be the sickle, in a grand harvest of souls.[1]

It is our view that the "gathering of all nations" into the "valley of Jehoshaphat" and arming themselves with every possible weapon available to them in order to do battle with Almighty God was fulfilled in the incarnation, crucifixion and resurrection of Jesus Christ because (a) it has to be a spiritual event, for a literal gathering of "all nations" into the valley of Jehoshaphat would be impossible; (b) the world of unbelief could never muster any greater powers to thwart God's redemption of creation than those which it brought to bear at the temptations of Christ (Matt. 4:1-11; Luke 4:1-13), Christ's own struggle with his "cup" (e.g., Luke 12:49-50; John 12:27-28; Matt. 26:36-46; Mark 14:32-42; Luke 22:39-46), and its murder of him at Calvary; (c) when Christ conquered sin in the flesh and fulfilled the law that condemned all mankind, God "disarmed the principalities and powers and made a public example of them, triumphing over them in him" (Col. 2:15; see also John 12:31;

16:11; Heb. 2:14-15; 1 John 3:8). **This** was the "valley of Jehoshaphat." **This** is where God won the greatest battle that shall ever be fought on the face of this earth. There will be no Armageddon or valley of Jehoshaphat or Gog and Magog greater than this! No literal battle of nations against nations with unprecedented masses of weapons could ever equal the intensity, the importance, or the consequence of **the battle at Calvary.** It was fought in history, at a place and time, seen by eyewitnesses and chronicled in divine writ for all succeeding generations to know and appropriate. At Calvary God fought man's battle for him and won man's victory for him.

One only has to read of the literal battle in the valley of Jehoshaphabt (2 Chr. 20:13-30) to see that Joel is using the physical to typify the spiritual. In the literal battle God told Jehoshaphat, "Fear not, and be not dismayed at this great multitude; for the battle is not yours but God's. . . . You will not need to fight in this battle; take your position, stand still, and see the victory of the LORD on your behalf . . . . Believe in the LORD your God, and you will be established; believe his prophets, and you will succeed." And the enemies of God's people "helped destroy one another." It is little wonder that Joel describes this event as, "confusion, confusion," or "raging, raging" as the Hebrew word, *hamonim*, should be translated (3:14). All this takes place, according to the Hebrew word *charūts*, in the "valley of sharp decisiveness or strict decision." Does this not read exactly like the magnificent messianic Psalm 2:1-11? Does this not read exactly like Paul's proclamation to the Corinthians (1 Cor. 1:18-31)? Rebellious mankind's *ultimate decision* in his *valley of confusion* was, and still is, his response to the redemptive work of Christ (e.g., John 3:16-21; 9:39). He faces no greater battle, no greater challenge, no greater decision than the gospel. What he decides about the gospel determines his eternal destiny! The very same Hebrew word, *hamonim*, ("confusion") is used in Ezekiel 39:16 to describe the figurative "site" where the ultimate enemies of God's people, "Gog" (led by "Magog") will be utterly defeated. The battle of "Gog and Magog" is the **same** battle as that in the "valley of Jehoshaphat!" It is the redemptive work of Christ and the institution of Christ's kingdom upon earth (the church), against which the "gates of Hades" are unable to prevail!

The Lord has "roared from Zion." Zion is unquestionably a **type** of the New Testament church. The author of Hebrews made that beyond dispute in his allegory of the two mountains in Hebrews 12:18-29. At Calvary, the Empty Tomb, Pentecost, and the fall of the Roman Empire, God potentially "shook down" every human, earthly kingdom (including the Mosaic system, Heb. 12:25-29) and inaugurated his "unshakable kingdom" the church of Christ. God continues to "roar" from Zion (the church) through the preaching of his Word. "And it shall come to pass that all who call upon the name of the LORD shall be delivered; for in Mount Zion and in

Jerusalem [the heavenly Jerusalem] there shall be those who escape . . . ." (Joel 2:32). And "Jerusalem shall be holy and strangers [those alienated from God] shall never again pass through it" (3:17). The church is the spotless bride of Christ (Eph. 5:27) and all those sincerely "purchased by the blood of his Son" (Acts 20:28) are no longer "strangers and sojounrers" (Eph. 2:19-22).

But what about the "portents in the heavens and on the earth, blood and fire and columns of smoke"? The Hebrew word *mophēth* is translated "portent" in the RSV and "wonder" in KJV and NASB. "The 36 appearances of this word are in all periods of biblical literature except wisdom literature. . . . this word signifies a divine act or a special display of divine power. . . . the word does not necessarily refer to a miraculous act, if 'miracle' means something outside the realm of ordinary providence . . . . the word can represent a 'sign' from God or a token of a future event . . . ."[2] The Septuagint translates the Hebrew word into the Greek word *teras* which means "something strange, causing the beholder to marvel . . . always rendered 'wonder.'"[3] So, Joel is not necessarily specifying "miracles" but "wonders." Some of these "wonders" might be "miraculous" and some might be cataclysmic or catastrophic developments which God providentially *permits* to occur through secondary causes, either through "nature" or human beings.

> There would be forerunners of judgment before the great and terrible day of the Lord would come . . . . Blood suggests bloodshed; fire upon the earth suggests the burning of cities, during which the pillars of smoke billow heavenward. . . . Jesus came not to judge the world but to save it (John 3:17-18); yet judgment became an inevitable result of His work (John 3:18-19). So, the outpouring of the Spirit and His work for the redemption and salvation of man would result in judgment on those who rejected His message. The rejection of the truth of the Spirit by the Jews, and their persecutions of Christians, became the forerunner of God's great judgment upon Jerusalem by the Romans, A.D. 70. The destruction of Jerusalem, which fulfilled the prophecy, in turn becomes a prophetic type of the ultimate end of the world and of the judgment of God on the world of the ungodly.
>
> And 'in those days, and in that time' identifies the judgment as being in the period of the outpouring of the Spirit, the dispensation following Pentecost. . . . Therefore this cannot refer to the return from Assyrian and Babylonian captivity, for this bringing back referred to by Joel is to be in the time of the Spirit (cf. 2:28-31). Also, Amos uses the expression 'I will bring back the captivity of my people Israel' (9:14) in a Messianic context (9:11-12; this is quoted by James and applied to the period under Christ (Acts 15:14-18), further strengthening the position that the judgments are after Pentecost. We must therefore look for the return of Judah and Jerusalem in a spiritual sense.[4]

Hailey proposes that the entire context from Joel 2:28–3:21 must be looked upon as a world view of things to come beginning with the outpouring of the Spirit and continuing until the Second Avent of Christ at which time the final judgment of God will occur and time will be no more.

The "portents" or "wonders" are hundreds of thousands of successive events in history, beginning with the Day of Pentecost, followed by the catastrophic destruction of Jerusalem in A.D. 70 and the numerous cataclysmic events that brought about the fall of the Roman Empire as predicted in the "seals, trumpets, and bowls" in the book of Revelation. They would also include continuous *judgments* or *blessings* (Acts 14:15-18) occuring in history since those days until today and which will continue until the end of time. These "portents" or "wonders" would be floods, hurricanes, droughts, famines, wars, or political freedoms, material affluence, victories over human tyrants, or other "natural" phenomena. All of these unquestionably constitute God's *modus operandi* in OT times to signal his omnipotence, his wrath upon sin, and his call to the world to repent (Amos 4:1ff). And they are clearly continued in NT times according to Romans 1:18-32 as ongoing revelations from God that can be plainly known and "clearly perceived in the things that have been made." Jesus confirmed this eschatological principle in Luke 13:1-9.

"Restoring the fortunes" of Judah and Jerusalem (Joel 3:1) in the RSV is a translation of the Hebrew phrase, *ashūb eth-shvūth*, and literally means, "return the unreturned (exiles)." It is a phrase used numerous times in messianic contexts (e.g., Jer. 30:3,18; 31:23; 32:44; Ezek. 39:25). Isaiah and Jeremiah specifically referred to the "return" of God's exiles in a *spiritual* sense and connected it to the Messiah's first advent, and Amos 9:11-15 is *certified* as a messianic prophecy by the apostles (Acts 15:16-17; see also Isa. 11:11; Jer. 50:4-5 compared with Rom. 11:5; 15:12).

Thus, Joel painted an exciting literary picture in apocalyptic "colors." It was to encourage a believing remnant in Judah at a very critical juncture of its history. The prophet predicted that "in the latter days" God would bring their enemies to defeat and confusion. He would give awesome signs that this world and man's attempts to save himself were condemned. These would continue until the "great and terrible day of the Lord." At the same time he would continue to provide deliverance, security, and righteousness to those who seek escape in "Zion" (the church of Christ).

Joel's "valley of Jehoshaphat" is **not** a prediction of some physical battle during some "tribulation" period, out of which the church of Christ has been "raptured." When Ezekiel was stationed down in Babylon by the Lord during the crisis of the exile, he "painted" the same picture of the same divine victory with word-colors very much like those of Joel: e.g., compare Ezek. 38:1-6 with Joel 3:11-12; compare Ezek. 38:8,16 with Joel 2:28; compare Ezek 38:21 with Joel 3:14; Ezek 38:23 with

Joel 3:11; Ezek. 39:10 with Joel 3:4-8 and 3:19; Ezek. 39:11-16 with Joel 3:14; Ezek 39:25 with Joel 3:1; Ezek. 39:28 with Joel 3:17; and Ezek. 39:29 with Joel 2:28. Word pictures — they are the same!

Jesus spoke of his redemptive work, as John wrote in the original Greek, *nun krisis estin tou kosmou toutou.* That would translate as *"Now is the crisis of the cosmos."* No greater crisis ever punctuated history than when he was choosing to drink the "cup" of God's judgment upon the sins of all mankind. This moment is the essence of all the apocalyptic battles and victories of the OT prophets. God knew that it would require the utmost skill and intensity for the OT prophets to persuade Israel of the spiritual nature of the First Advent of the Messiah. Thus, he led them by his Spirit to concentrate solely on that. It would be irrelevant for them to devote any of their predictions to the Messiah's Second Advent. This is readily seen in the almost total misunderstanding and rejection of Jesus' message concerning his First Advent by the Jews of his own time.

We turn, next, to "the mountains of Israel" and the "hordes" of "Gog and Magog." Hear the rattle of bows and arrows, spears, shields, and handpikes? It is God's victorious people piling a defeated enemy's weapons up to be burned.

Notes

[1]Henry H. Halley, *Halley's Bible Handbook, Large Edition,* 24th ed. (Grand Rapids: Zondervan, 1965), p. 357.

[2]Merrill F. Unger & William White, Jr., eds., *Nelson's Expository Dictionary of the Old Testament* (Nashville: Thomas Nelson, 1980), p. 478.

[3]W.E. Vine, *An Expository Dictionary of New Testament Words,* Vol. III (Old Tappan, NJ: Fleming H. Revell, 1957), p. 228.

[4]Homer Hailey, *A Commentary on The Minor Prophets* (Grand Rapids: Baker, 1971), pp. 54-57.

chapter 4

GOG AND MAGOG

Our next "battlefield" in the figurative (apocalyptic and symbolic) language of the OT prophets is the "battle of Gog and Magog." The description of this fierce "battle" by the prophet Ezekiel has piqued the curiosity of many, including some who have never even read it from the Bible. Numerous books have been written about it; it is alluded to occasionally in today's media; a few motion pictures have given it some mention. We want to examine it here through the lenses of literary hermeneutics hoping to arrive at the perspective God intended when he commissioned Ezekiel to picture it. The great "battle" involving "Gog and Magog" is outlined in Ezekiel chapters 38 and 39. We have already referred to it in our comments on "The Valley of Jehoshaphat" in Joel's prophecy.

Ezekiel's Israelite lineage was priestly (Ezek. 1:3). He lived in the southern kingdom of Judah during the crisis of the Babylonian assaults upon Jerusalem by Nebuchadnezzar (606, 596, 586 B.C.). Ezekiel was taken as a captive in the Babylonian deportation of 596 and was called to be a prophet of God some three or four years later. He was a contemporary of Jeremiah and Daniel. He lived down in Babylon by the "river" Chebar, which was really a man-made canal that connected the Tigris River with the Euphrates River, just above the city of Babylon. His ministry lasted at least 22 years, from 593 to 571 B.C. Jerusalem was destroyed by Nebuchadnezzar ten years after Ezekiel's arrival in Babylon, on the day Ezekiel's wife died (Ezek. 24:15-27). Jeremiah was stationed by God in the city of Jerusalem to preach to the people there of God's judgments upon them for their idolatry, but God allowed Ezekiel and Daniel to be taken down to Babylon as "prisoners of war" to minister to the exiles.

While there may be a few messianic prophecies in the first part of Ezekiel's book (e.g., 16:59-63), his messianic predictions essentially begin at chapter 34 and continue to the end of his book (48:35) with the pregnant phrase, "And the name of the city henceforth shall be, The Lord is there." It is our position that all of Ezekiel's prophecy from chapter 34:1 through chapter 48:35 is ultimately messianic written in graphic apocalyptic style. Here we give a basic outline of Ezekiel's messianic section:

    I. The Regeneration of God's Flock, ch. 34-37
        A. The Lord's Flock and the True Shepherd to Come, ch. 34
        B. The Lord's Deliverance, ch. 35-36
        C. The Lord's People Recreated, ch. 37
   II. The Release of God's Flock from Its Enemies, ch. 38-39
        A. God Challenges His Enemies, ch. 38
        B. God Conquers His Enemies, ch. 39
  III. The Rehabitation of The Flock by God, ch. 40-48
        A. Restoration of God's Dwelling Place, ch. 40-43
        B. Reorganization of God's Worship, ch. 44-46
        C. Re-peopling of God's Nation, ch. 47-48

This outline demonstrates that Ezekiel has simply conformed to the general pattern of all the literary prophets as they: (a) proclaimed an idolatrous and covenant-breaking people; (b) predicted a chastening punishment in order to preserve a remnant; (c) predicted a regenerated people of God; (d) predicted a great defeat of God's enemy; (e) predicted a rehabiting or reestablishment of God's covenant-keeping people into "a habitation of God in the Spirit" (Eph. 2:11-22).

Outlines of the OT prophets match the pattern of the book of Revelation as we shall see in a later chapter, i.e., Revelation (a) proclaimed sinning churches; (b) predicted a "great tribulation" to chasten the churches; (c) predicted a purified church; (d) predicted a great defeat of God's enemy; (e) predicted an establishment of God's faithful people into an "habitation" of God.

There can be no doubt (and there is hardly any disagreement among Bible expositors) that chapter 34 of Ezekiel finds its fulfillment in Jesus Christ, the Good Shepherd (e.g., John 10:11ff). The careful student of the OT prophets will also recognize the apparent parallel of Ezekiel 34:25-31 to Hosea 2:16-23, the latter confirmed as a messianic prophecy by Romans 9:25-26 and 1 Peter 1:10. "The entire passage relates to the new Israel of God — God's present-day chosen people (Gal. 6:16). The spiritual blessings which God in this Messianic age showers down upon His people are here portrayed in terms of agricultural prosperity."[1]

Ezekiel 35 predicts the total obliteration of the Edomites because they "cherished perpetual enmity" against God's people and coveted their land. While the prophet is predicting what will literally happen to Edom (as does Obadiah; Isaiah

34; Amos 1; Jeremiah 49), Edom is being used as a *metaphorical representation* of all those heathen who "touch the apple of God's eye" (Zech. 2:8) whether in the Old dispensation or the New. In the book of Revelation, Egypt and Babylon are used *metaphorically* to *represent* Rome. Rome "touched" Christ's church with severe persecution and seduction from A.D. 98–450, and Christ obliterated the Roman Empire (e.g., Rev. 19:11-21). God's judgment upon all heathen physical or ideological powers in conflict with his redemptive program and people occurred *de facto* at Calvary, the empty tomb, and Pentecost (cf. John 12:31; 16:11; 1 Cor. 1:18-31; Col. 2:15; Heb. 2:14-15). ". . . Edom is symbolic of every nation which had oppressed Israel. Only when all the enemies of the Lord are destroyed is the deliverance of God's people complete."[2]

We believe chapters 36-37 of Ezekiel are ultimately predicting, in hyperbolic language, God's "remnant" (the church) in the Messianic Age. So does Smith: "Properly understood, Ezekiel 36:22-38 points to the spiritual realities of this present Gospel age."[3] It is clear that the ultimate point of fulfillment of *all* this *crisis* language is the Messianic Age. Phrases in both chapters demand a Messianic Age fulfillment, e.g., ". . . you shall be clean from all your uncleannesses. . . . A new heart I will give you . . . . And I will put my spirit within you . . . . [you] shall be my people and I will be [your] God. . . . My servant David shall be king over them; and they shall all have one shepherd. . . . David my servant shall be their prince forever. I will make a covenant of peace with them; it shall be an everlasting covenant with them . . . and . . . set my sanctuary in the midst of them for evermore . . . ." If the NT (esp. Romans, Galatians, and Hebrews) is to be accepted as God's final revelation to man, these are circumstances that could *not possibly* be fulfilled in a physical Israel with a physical temple and a physical David. These are probably the very prophecies that Jesus expected Nicodemus to know so as to understand when he spoke to that "teacher of Israel" about the *new birth* (John 3:10).

This brings us to Ezekiel, chapters 38-39! First, if our thesis is correct that Ezekiel 40-48 is a glorified prevision of the NT kingdom of God and the church of Christ (e.g., Eph. 2:11-22), and Ezekiel, chapters 34-37 find their ultimate fulfillment in regeneration through the Messiah, then chapters 38-39 are *surrounded* by messianic predictions. This is a distinct *contextual* signal that chapters 38-39 are also messianic in fulfillment.

Second, notice some significant elements of the entire bizarre "scene" being verbally painted here:

1. *Magog* is mentioned only once elsewhere in the OT (Gen. 10:2) among the sons of Japheth. Meshech and Tubal are also mentioned in Genesis 10 as sons of Japheth (Gentiles). Josephus (*Ant.* I.vi.1) identifies the people of Magog as the

ancient Scythians. *Gog* is to be identified as a potentate of this people-group called *Magog*.

2. The RSV translates the word *rosh* in 38:2, "the **chief** prince of Meshech." The Hebrew word *rosh* in this verse means **chief** and *not* "Russia." As DeMar has stated: "If *rosh* is a prophetic name for Russia because it sounds like Russia, then why don't the other nations sound like their modern counterparts?"[4] There is no evidence that *Rosh* was ever a nation of antiquity, or a nation at any other time.

3. Please notice the location of these enemies of God at a *very remote* distance away from Palestine, from "the uttermost parts": (a) Meshech and Tubal (known as *Moschi* and *Tabal* in Assyrian cuneiform) were peoples of Asia Minor (modern Turkey) living near the headwaters of the Tigris River to the far reaches west of Palestine; (b) Persia (Indo-Europeans) from the far reaches east of Palestine; (c) Cush or Ethiopia (descendants of Ham, Gen. 10:6) from the far reaches south of Palestine; (d) Put or Libya (descendants of Ham, Gen. 10:6) far across the great Mediterranean Sea from Palestine; (e) Gomer (descendants of Japheth, Gen. 10:3) perhaps from north of the Caucasus mountains far to the northeast of Palestine; (f) Beth-Togarmah (descendants of Japheth, Gen. 10:3) from Armenia in the southern Caucasus, still to the far north of Palestine; (g) "the coastlands" (39:6), includes the Mediterranean, Adriatic, Aegean, Black, Red and Caspian Seas, and the Persian Gulf. Thus, these "enemies" symbolize *all* Gentile heathendom from the "ends of the earth" as it were.

4. The foregoing "nations" were so far apart they were unlikely to form any literal coalition against Judah — further indication they were symbolic.

5. Please notice the battle was not to occur immediately but in *"the latter years"* (38:8,16), a phrase that is clearly messianic (see Appendix B, "Word Studies").

6. Gog and Magog and allies are identified with the enemies of God "of whom the former prophets spoke" (38:17). Compare Isaiah 66:7-9 where God will bring forth a new "Zion" in "one moment" (the church of Christ at Pentecost) and at the same time show his glory to Tarshish, *Put*, Lud, *Tubal*, and *Javan* (66:18-21), and God's people will "look on the dead bodies of the men that have rebelled against" him (66:24). Thus, Gog and Magog are symbolic enemies. Joel's "all nations" in the "valley of Jehoshaphat" is another symbolic parallel to symbolize "Gog and Magog."

7. The result of the cataclysmic struggle symbolized in Gog and Magog will be to manifest God's holiness and to make God known in the eyes of many *nations* (Hebrew, *goyim*, "Gentiles") 38:23. This was the predicted purpose of the coming Messiah (Isa. 52:13-15; 56:6ff; 60:3,10; 61:9) as well as the predicted pur-

pose of other *apocalyptic, symbolic* battles in the OT prophets (Isa. 34:1–35:10; Joel 2:28–3:21; Zech. 12:1–14:21).

8. The huge *hordes* of people (called, "bands" in KJV and *agapim* in Hebrew, which means, "men in armor") in this combined force of Gentile nations is pictured as spoiling and plundering a land that could **not** literally furnish room for them to stand in, let alone provide sustenance for them to prosecute a literal war.

9. God causes them to defeat themselves (38:21). Remember the enemies of Jehoshaphat destroyed themselves! (2 Chr. 21). After God's defeat of Magog the wood of their weapons will furnish fuel in Judah for seven years! If this great battle is to be a literal battle between Russia and Israel, or China and Israel, or any other modern nation and Israel, it must be fought by literal horsemen, on literal horses, with literal bows and arrows, shields and swords!

10. The dead carcasses of "Gog and Magog" were to take seven months to bury. There would be at least 1,000,000 literal citizens of Judah in Ezekiel's day. If each Judean buried two corpses per day (in an age of hand tools), that would factor a total of 360,000,000 putrefying corpses lying around waiting to be buried — slowly. Human life could not endure the diseases which would result from such carnage. This is clearly apocalyptic, symbolic and hyperbolic language depicting Satan's defeat at the cross and the empty tomb of Jesus Christ (see Col. 2:14-15).

11. If the biblical prophets are predicting some literal, physical battle between Jews and Russia or China, or some other nation, as the ultimate battle on earth, then they contradict one another for: (a) Ezekiel 38-39 says the battle is upon the mountains of Israel; (b) Isaiah 34 says it is upon the mountains of Edom; (c) Joel 2-3 says it is in the valley of Jehoshaphat; (d) Zechariah 14 says it is in the immediate environs of Jerusalem; (e) Revelation 20 says it is "around the camp of the saints." So, where is it?! And why is it made by literalists to be the same as "Armageddon" (Rev. 16:16) when there is no mention of Gog and Magog in the first 19 chapters of Revelation? The word "Armageddon" in Revelation 16:16 is a transliteration of the Hebrew word *Har-Meggidon. Har* is the Hebrew word for a single "mountain" — not plural "mountains"; (a) the great battle in Ezekiel 38-39 does not take place upon a single mountain; (b) the term *Battle of Armageddon* never appears in the Bible — the actual term for the battle used in Revelation 16:16 is "the great day of God the Almighty;" (c) the name *Armageddon* does not appear in ancient geographical or historical writings, nor on modern maps; (d) there is a "plain of Megiddo" in Zechariah 12:11 but that is in reference to an event in the days of Josiah (see 2 Chr. 35:20-25) ca. 608 B.C.

12. Pointing, as all the above do, to the struggle of the Messiah and his church at his first advent into the world during the "latter days," if it is to be a literal battle, it would be a grossly carnal struggle involving the church in attaining its victory through force. That would contradict the plain teaching of the NT that the church is to conduct its "warfare" strictly on the **spiritual** plane (e.g., 2 Cor. 6:7; 10:3-5; Eph. 6:12-20).

The "Valley of Abarim" (39:11) is in the Mountains of Moab, just east of the north end of the Dead Sea near Heshbon ("Heshbon" means, "reckoning"). The Hebrew words for "Valley of Abarim" mean "valley of those who are passing-by," or, "valley of travelers." It was a mountain pass for travelers. But according to Ezekiel's apocalyptic symbolism there were to be "dead bodies" piled high enough to block travelers from passage in the valley. It is prophetic hyperbole to emphasize the *total* victory of God over his enemies.

Ezekiel 39:16 gives the locale of the battle's burial ground as "The Valley of Hamon-Gog" and "a city Hamonah is there also." The Hebrew word *Hamonah* is the very same word used in Joel 3:14 characterizing the "valley" of Jehoshaphat as the valley of "confusion" or "multitudes in chaos." Neither Joel nor Ezekiel are referring to a geographical location. Both are using the word to symbolize the "crisis of the cosmos" which occurred when God confounded, confused, disarmed, and defeated all the powers that could possibly be arrayed against him. This was at the cross, the empty tomb, the founding of and the victory of his church over the fourth great beast of Daniel, ch. 7, i.e., the Roman Empire (Col. 2:15; Heb. 2:14; 1 John 3:8; Rev. 1:1–20:7). The incarnation, Gethsemane, Calvary, the resurrection, the infant church struggling against the Jewish onslaught (1 Thess. 2:14-16) and against the "great tribulation" of the Roman Empire for 350 years was the *greatest conflict* against God's redemptive program ever fought. Those events also included the greatest *victory* ever accomplished on the face of this earth. Christians are to conquer "by the blood of the Lamb and by the word of their testimony" (Rev. 12:11).

Note the following citations of parallel similarities between Joel's "valley of Jehoshaphat" and Ezekiel's "Gog and Magog":

1. Ezekiel 38:1-6 — the gathering of the "hordes" from the "uttermost" parts of civilization; Joel 3:2,11,12 — the "gathering of all the nations round about."
2. Ezekiel 38:8,16 — "in the latter years, or latter days"; Joel 2:28 — "in the latter days" (Acts 2:14-21).
3. Ezekiel 38:21 — every man's sword of God's enemies will be against his brother (i.e., they will self-destruct); Joel 3:14 — Joel took his symbolic battle from the real battle in the valley of Jehoshaphat (2 Chr. 20:23) in which God's ene-

mies destroyed one another. Compare Rev. 17:15-18 where God puts it into the heart of Rome to destroy herself!

4. Ezekiel 39:7,28 — God shows his greatness and holiness and makes his name known in the midst of his people; Joel 3:17 — the valley of Jehoshaphat is so "you shall know that I am the LORD your God, who dwell in Zion . . . ."
5. Ezekiel 39:9-10 — massive amounts of weapons; Joel 3:9-10 — even the implements of peace made into weapons for war.
6. Ezekiel 39:10 — God will "despoil those who despoiled" his people; Joel 3:4-8, 19-21 — God will despoil those who despoiled his people and avenge the blood of his people.
7. Ezekiel 39:11-16 — the great defeat of the heathen nations will take place in "Hamonah" ("confusion"); Joel 3:14 — the great defeat of the nations will take place in "Hamonah" ("confusion").
8. Ezekiel 39:25 — God will "restore the fortunes of Jacob"; Joel 3:1 — God will "restore the fortunes of Judah and Jerusalem."

Briefly, for the sake of continuity, a few observations concerning Ezekiel's *symbolic* "temple" (40-48):

1. Ezekiel's measuring tool is a (Heb. *qaneh*) "reed," and a "reed" is six (Heb. *amōth*) "cubits" long (Ezek. 40:5. Traditionally, a "cubit" was approximately 18 inches. Ezekiel here describes a "long cubit" which was approximately 20½ inches, making the "reed" ten feet three inches.
2. The original Hebrew text in Ezekiel 42:15-20 should be translated "500 reeds by the measuring reed" as it is in the NASB and KJV — not "500 cubits by the measuring reed" as it is in the LXX and RSV.
3. Properly translated the temple area would therefore measure 5,125 feet square or just under one mile square.
4. A temple area 5,125 ft. square could be superimposed over two cities of Jerusalem the size of Hezekiah's Jerusalem (the one Ezekiel would have known). Hezekiah's Jerusalem was approximately 4000 ft long and about 2000 ft. wife (see *Oxford Bible Atlas*, p. 81).
5. No such temple was ever built by the Jews. The returning exiles certainly must have known that Ezekiel's "temple" was never intended to be literally built for the one they built ("The Second Temple") was nowhere near that size or complexity.

Consider now Ezekiel's partitioning of the land of Palestine (47:13–48:29) in those "latter days" **after** the battle with "Gog and Magog."

1. The Hebrew word *terumah* as specified in 45:1-5 and 48:8-22 (esp. 48:12) is translated "portion." It means literally, "a high or elevated portion."

2. The *terumah* (which was to contain the new city and the new temple) was to be built squarely in the geographical center of the land of Palestine, with seven tribes to the north of it and five tribes to the south of it. Each tribe was to receive an *equal* portion of the land. This clearly conflicts with the Mosaic legislation as to the distribution of the land. Furthermore, the distribution of the land to the tribes of Israel according to Ezekiel would necessitate the occupation of a large portion of Egyptian territory from the Nile River to the south end of the Dead Sea, and a large portion of the land to the north of Palestine belonging to ancient and modern Lebanon. Locating Jerusalem in the geographical center of Palestine certainly does violence to OT legislation and does not fit any dispensational schematic we have ever read. But accepted as *symbolic* it clearly fits Jesus' statement to the woman at the well (John 4:19-24) which dismisses literal Jerusalem as necessary to the worship of God in the Messianic Age.

3. The *terumah* was to be 25,000 "somethings" long (the Hebrew text does not supply a word for a measuring tool — the KJV and ASV supply the word *reeds* while the RSV supplies the word *cubits*). Fairbairn says it is most logical to supply "reed," the same word as the Hebrew text used for measuring the temple area itself. The *terumah* was to be 20,000 *reeds* wide. Altogether, the *terumah* was to be approximately 48½ *miles* long and 38.8 *miles* wide or 1882 square miles in area.

4. Literally fulfilled, this "raised portion" of Palestine (upon which the "new city and new temple" were to be built) would have jutted out into the Mediterranean Sea up to five miles. That would require accomplishing what would be an impossible construction project even with today's modern technology.

5. The *terumah* was to be divided into three parallel tracts. The "city" was to be located in the southern tract; the "temple" located in the "middle of the city." There were to be two equal areas on either side of the *terumah* for the "Prince."

6. According to Ezekiel it will not be the people who erect the temple — God will set his sanctuary in the midst of them (37:26-27). When it was shown to Ezekiel it was already there in Palestine (40:1ff). Jesus Christ built his own church (Matt. 16:18; Eph. 2:19-22) and there the Godhead dwells forever.

7. The people of Ezekiel's temple are represented as serving Jehovah in accordance with ordinances that would violate the Law of Moses! "Some of the sacrifices spoken of here (45:18-25) and in the next chapters were unknown in Solomon's Temple. . . .The prince was to *prepare*, i.e., provide, a bullock as a sin-offering for himself and for the people. No such sacrifice was connected with Passover in the Mosaic dispensation. . . . The offerings prescribed for the Sabbath and new moon of the new Temple age (46:1-7) do not correspond with

those prescribed in the Law of Moses (cf. Num. 28:9, 11-15)."[5]

8. Flowing from under the threshold of the temple of Ezekiel was a never-failing, never-fading, *miraculously increasing* river of fertility (47:1-12). This is a clear symbolic picture that in the Messianic Age, the "temple" of God (the church) would be the source of life and fruitfulness. The same symbolic "living waters" flowing from Zion are used by Zechariah to pictorialize the Messianic Age (Zech. 14:8). This "river of life" is that which flows from Jesus to his church (his disciples) and from his church to the world (John 7:37-39).

9. God was going to dwell in this temple, in the midst of his people, *forever*! (43:7 and 48:35). See also Joel 3:17; Jer. 12:6; 33:16; Isa. 12:6; 24:23; Jer. 3:15-17; Zech. 2:10 — all messianic. This can only be a prediction of the New Testament church of Christ.

To understand the prophetic idiom one must not "miss the forest from looking at too many individual trees." Especially must the apocalyptic language of the prophets be visualized as verbal pictures portraying the climactic point of human history, as Jesus called it, "the crisis of the cosmos" (John 9:38-39; 12:31; 16:11), when the world of sin would be both judged and redeemed in the **finished work of the Messiah** (e.g., John 19:30; Heb. 9:23-28; 10:11-18).

Through the prophets God was preparing the Jewish people for the **end** of their religious system, the Mosaic Law (e.g., Jer. 3:15-18; 31:31-34; Heb. 1:1-4; 8:13; 12:25-29) which would also end, from God's perspective, most of their civil, social, cultural identity. At the same time God was saying through the prophets that all the utopian schemes of the heathen empires to unite the world of mankind in a mono-lithic, humanistic, idolatrous system would also be exposed, judged, and **conquered** by the messianic kingdom's spiritual warfare, i.e., worldwide militant evangelism (Acts 15:12-18; Rom. 1:1-7; 16:25-27; 1 Cor. 1:18-31; 2 Cor. 10:3-6; Col. 2:15; Rev. 11:15).

The message of the coming King and his Kingdom to be set up on earth (the church) to supplant the 1400-year-old Israelite system, and its conquest of the "wealth of the nations" was **cataclysmic**! The "wealth of the nations" is, of course, their people. In the coming kingdom of the Messiah there would be no racial, cultur-al, fleshly incongruities. The Messiah's coming was to be **the turning point of all history**! It would in effect be **the end of the world** for that Old Testament era where the Law of God had been restricted to a "chosen" people which had rejected that Law and had out-heathened the heathen. It would also be the **end of a kind of world** for the rest of mankind which was essentially left to wallow in the depravity of its self-chosen idolatry (Rom. 1:1-32). The "glad tidings" would come and those who were walking in darkness would see a great light; a child would be born, God

Incarnate, and of the increase of his government and of peace there would be no end (Isa. 9:1-7).

How is God to communicate these mind-boggling concepts? In newspaper prose? How is he to get the attention of a world steeped in humanistic egocentricity? With a "ho-hum" sermon? Hardly! So God put electrifying, vivid, bizarre, hyperbolic, symbolic words into the mouths of the prophets.

1. God will enter into **battle** (spiritual, mental battle) with the **old** world. He will utterly confound all its presuppositions of humanistic self-sufficiency. He will expose to that **old** world the futility in the "big lie" of its self-appointed "god" (Satan).

2. God will set up his Kingdom on earth and rule in the hearts of men through the spiritually regenerating news of a redemption by vicarious atonement. It will be a "resurrection from death" of his "chosen" people.

3. His Kingdom will be secure, prosperous, and worldwide. And God himself will dwell in its midst in the Spirit, empowering, protecting, and blessing its citizens, never to leave them again.

One must approach the literary prophets from this comprehensive perspective and take into account their need for a provocative vernacular to communicate to an "impudent . . . stubborn . . . unwilling to listen . . . of a hard forehead . . . nation of rebels" (Ezek. 2:1–3:11). Without such an approach, one gets caught up and confused attempting to find literal fulfillments of the minute details when the prophets intended the details to be only a vernacular background to the "cosmic drama" to be acted out "in the latter days."

And the apocalyptic idiom should not be thought unique to the OT prophets! It is found in the literature of every civilization, past and present. One of the great hymns sung by Christians for a century and half now is clearly portraying its author's apocalyptic viewpoint of the tragic American "War Between the States." It begins, "Mine eyes have seen the glory of the coming of the Lord, He is trampling out the vintage where the grapes of wrath are stored. . . ." Modern movie makers produce films actually named, "Apocalypse Now!"

With this point clarified we proceed to a survey of the "battlefield" of redemption as it is portrayed by the latter half of the book of Daniel.

Notes

[1]James E. Smith, *Ezekiel* (Joplin, MO: College Press, 1979), p. 378.
[2]Ibid., p. 380.
[3]Ibid., p. 391.
[4]DeMar, *Last Days Madness*, p. 202.
[5]Smith, *Ezekiel*, pp. 468-470.

chapter 5

THE FOUR BEASTS AND THE SEVENTY SEVENS

For all those who are intrigued with biblical eschatology, the book of Daniel seems to be the "mother lode." And this is as it should be! Numerous reasons might be cited:

a. Daniel predicts in minute detail a span of history that encompasses at least a *millennium* (one thousand years) from 606 B.C. to approximately A.D. 457 — from the Babylonian empire through the fall of the Roman Empire.

b. Daniel's language is highly symbolic and intensely apocalyptic. There are sufficient fulfillments, coupled with occasional inspired interpretations from Daniel, in which we are furnished explicit "keys" to interpret other apocalyptic language in both the OT and the NT.

c. Daniel 7:12 fits right into Revelation 13:1-4 like an extension cord "plugs into" an electrical outlet on the wall of a building. By this we mean to say that the book of Revelation is a *continuation* and *amplification* of Daniel's "*fourth beast*" (the ancient Roman Empire).

d. Daniel 9:24-27 "plugs right into" the Gospel accounts of the first advent of the Messiah, his redemptive work, and the institution of the church at Pentecost, the fall of Jerusalem in A.D. 70, and the "decreed end poured out on the desolator," i.e., the fall of the ancient Roman Empire.

We are not going to review the first six chapters of Daniel in this study, except to note later the parallel between the four successive empires in chapters 2 and 7. Those interested in the first six chapters are referred to our commentary.[1] Daniel has written most of the eschatology of his book in chapters 7 through 12, and that is where we concentrate our analysis.

Every child who has been to Sunday School knows the story of Daniel, the young lad exiled from his homeland by the Babylonians, there to become a fearless and faithful witness to his God. He became a highly placed executive in the Babylonian and Persian governments because of his integrity and courage. Daniel was a prophet of God and an advisor to emperors. The fact that Daniel was an historical personage is confirmed by one of his contemporaries, Ezekiel (Ezek. 14:14,20; 28:3), and by the Lord Jesus Christ himself (Matt. 24:15). The canonicity of the book of Daniel is well established by (a) its inclusion in the Septuagint (250–150 B.C.); (b) being referred to in 1 & 2 Maccabees (125–70 B.C.); (c) the witness to it in the NT (A.D. 60–100); (d) its inclusion in the Jewish *Baba Bathra,* a Talmudic tractate (A.D. 200–500), which is a "canonical" listing of the OT books by order and author which was first in oral tradition and later committed to writing; (e) its listing in the canon of 2 Esdras (A.D. 81–96); (f) and its being considered canonical by Josephus (ca. A.D. 100). It is not within our purpose here to deal with the details of authorship, date, and textual difficulties.

Daniel 7:1-28

Daniel had a dream during the first year of Belshazzar's reign over Babylon (ca. 553 B.C.).[2] In his dream the "four winds of heaven" stirred up the sea until out of the sea burst four terrifying beasts, each succeeding the other and each different from the other. The first was "like a lion and had eagles' wings." Its wings were plucked off so that it could not fly, but then it was lifted up from the ground and stood on its hind legs like a man, and a man's mind was given to it. The second beast was like a bear with its feet on one side lifted up as if it were going to stride ahead. It held three ribs in its mouth between its teeth. Daniel heard a voice say, "Arise, devour much flesh." The third beast was like a leopard, but it had four wings on its back like those of birds and it had four heads. Extensive power was given to it over all mankind. Finally, a fourth beast came up out of the sea but it was so fearful and dreadful Daniel could find no metaphors by which to describe it. The fourth beast was exceedingly strong. It devoured some of its victims by tearing them apart with its huge iron teeth; others it crushed beneath its powerful feet. It was far more brutal and vicious than any of the other beasts, and it had ten horns. In his dream, Daniel suddenly saw a small horn appear among the ten and three of the first ten were pulled out by the roots to give the little horn room; this little horn had a man's eyes and a boastful, bragging mouth.

It is not unusual for God to "stir up" the nations and their rulers and through his permissive will allow them to carry out his redemptive purposes (e.g., Isa. 10:5-16; 13:17; 45:1-7; Jer. 27:5-7; 2 Chr. 36:22-23; Ezek. 1:1-4; Hos. 9:6; 11:5; Obad. 1; Hab. 1:5-11). The "stirring up" of the great sea is clearly a biblical metaphor for the disturbed and "confused" state of the Gentile world powers in their hostility toward God and his chosen instruments of redemption (faithful Israel in the OT and a faithful church in the NT) (e.g., Isa. 8:7ff; Jer. 46:7-9; 47:2; Isa. 17:2ff; Rev. 13:1-5; 17:1-15). This symbolism is a parallel to the texts from Joel and Ezekiel and the valleys of Jehoshaphat and Hamonah — "confusion, confusion."

And these four "beasts" are unquestionably parallel to the four parts of the "great image" in Daniel 2:31-45. On that occasion it was Nebuchadnezzar who had the dream and Daniel, by divine guidance, interpreted those four parts of the image to be symbols of four successive world-encompassing empires beginning with the Babylonian empire (Dan. 2:36-45). Daniel is told in his revelatory dream the meaning of the "four beasts" (Dan. 7:17-27). The "four great beasts" were revealed as "four kings who shall arise out of the earth," and the description of the fourth beast in 7:19-22 is an "exceedingly terrible" one with iron teeth and claws of bronze, devouring and smashing everything under its feet until it is finally destroyed by the "kingdom of God." This is precisely the same description of the "fourth" part of the great image of Nebuchadnezzar's dream (2:40-45). The first three parts of Nebuchadnezzar's image and the first three beasts of Daniel's dream also bear striking resemblances in their descriptions. Beastliness is a fitting symbol for human governments — especially tyrannical ones. All human governments are *predatory* by nature. They survive only as they prey upon their citizens for the citizen's time, money (taxes), and at times, physical life. Interestingly enough, most human governments today have adopted certain "beasts" as national symbols (e.g., the Russian bear, the American eagle, and the British lion, etc.).

Since the winged lion (Dan. 7:4) is parallel to the head of gold (Nebuchadnezzar) as Daniel specified, it represented *ancient* Babylon — not a future, modern, "resurrected" Babylon located in Europe. Archaeological discoveries of *bas reliefs* in the ruins of ancient Babylon confirm the fact that the Babylonian empire had adopted a winged lion as its national symbol! The plucking of the wings from the lion, its being *made* to stand on two feet like a human, and its being *given* the mind of a man is a prediction of the de-beasting and humanizing of Babylon. It undoubtedly refers to the humiliation of Nebuchadnezzar when his proud lust for power and conquest were taken away from him by successive providential acts of God (Dan. 2:46-49; 3:28-30; 4:1-37). Nebuchadnezzar came to confess that the God of Daniel "does according to his will . . . and none can stay his hand or say to him, 'What doest thou?'" Nebuchadnezzar had a "conversion experience!"

The second beast is parallel to the second part of the "image" and follows immediately after Babylon. The bear "raised up on one side; . . . three ribs in its mouth" symbolizes the Persian empire inaugurated by Cyrus the Great from a coalition of

Medes and Persians. He conquered Babylon and voraciously "gobbled" up the Middle East, Asia Minor, and Egypt, and tried to step across the Aegean Sea to devour Europe (cf. Isa. 44:28; 45:1ff; and Isa. 13:17; 51:11; Dan. 5:24-31). The Persian wars with Greece began about 490 B.C. when the Persians invaded Greece. The Persians were eventually defeated in battles at Marathon, Salamis, Plataea, and Mycale.

The "leopard, with four wings . . . and . . . four heads" was ancient Greece. It was under the leadership of Philip II of Macedonia, and his eighteen-year-old son later to be called "Alexander the Great," that the Greek city-states were eventually conquered and became part of the Macedonian empire. Then the Macedonian "leopard" (Alexander) in 334 B.C., leading an army of some 35,000 men and a retinue of philosophers, historians, poets, agronomists, etc., began to extend the "dominion given to it" (by God). The next eleven years were spent in a whirlwind of warfare, hardships, and revelry. Entering Babylon in the spring of 323 B.C., on his way back to Greece, worn out by wounds, hardships and over-drinking, Alexander fell ill of a fever. Within two days Alexander died. He was not yet 33 years old. His empire stretched half way around the world — from Europe to Asia — from Macedonia to the Himalayas in India and China. The leopard, ferocious agile, swift and cunning is a very appropriate symbol of Alexander and his empire. The four wings on its back symbolize the rapidity with which Alexander conquered "the world." The four heads on the leopard symbolize the four-way division of this empire at Alexander's death. Ptolemy, one of his generals, received Egypt; Antigonus received rule of Asia; Cassander received rule of Macedonia; and Lysimachus received rule of Thrace. Antigonus was later killed in a battle, his Asiatic empire came to an end, and Seleucus, another Greek general, received rule of Palestine and Syria. These four kingdoms continued as prominent factors in world politics until the next empire (Rome) appeared on the scene and amalgamated the parts into a whole!

The fourth beast, with ten horns is *ancient* Rome. It is the Rome of the Caesars, not a modern "resurrected" Rome (neither the Roman Catholic Church, the Communist bloc, the European Common Market, nor the United Nations). Remember, these "kingdoms" *immediately* succeed one another (Dan. 2:36-43). Remember, it is in the days of the "fourth" kingdom (Dan. 2:45) that God sets up his kingdom on earth. God's kingdom on earth is the church of Christ which was established on the Day of Pentecost A.D. 30 (Acts 2).

There is no beast in all the fauna sufficiently fierce and terrible to symbolize so awesome and savage an empire as the fourth one seen by Daniel. Everything points to the Roman Empire as being the world power typified by this beast. Using its great "iron teeth" it broke things in pieces and devoured them, and what it could not devour it stamped with its "feet," grinding it into dust. Rome was voracious, cruel and destructive — even vindictive — as a world power. She could never get enough of conquest. She continually "went out conquering and to conquer" (Rev. 6:2). And wherever she went, war, famine, pestilence, death in the arenas, and martyrdom of Christians and others followed. Rome had no interest in raising the conquered nations to any high level of development for their sake. All her designs were exploitation and imperialism for Rome's sake. If they could not "devour" a victim by plunder and taxation, they would "stamp'" it under foot, sack and burn, and leave it in desolation and ruin.

The "ten horns" (7:20) symbolize the first ten recognized emperors of Rome: Augustus (i.e., Octavian), Tiberius, Caligula, Claudius, Nero, Galba, Otho, Vitellius, Vespasian, and Titus. Julius Caesar was in the process of making himself emperor when he was assassinated (44 B.C.), but he was never recognized as sole ruler of Rome (he was one of the ruling Triumvirate). It was Octavian (Augustus) who destroyed the Triumvirate and centralized the emperorship in himself. These "ten horns" are specified by Daniel as "ten kings," *not* ten kingdoms. Daniel uses the Hebrew word *malkin* which is always translated "kings" — he does not use the Hebrew word *mamlakōth* which is always translated "kingdoms." Of course, each *administration* of the Roman Empire varied somewhat as the different emperors came to the throne. But Daniel's "ten kings" will be "plugged into" by John in the Revelation with the *eleventh* emperor to follow these ten. And Daniel's attention immediately focuses on a "*little horn*" originating from this fourth beast (fourth empire). This is *not* the same "little horn" of chapter eight. The "little horn" here is "Domitian, the eleventh emperor of Rome, a son of Vespasian," who, according to Suetonius[3] spent a "poverty-stricken and rather degraded youth," before being declared emperor at the death of his brother Titus Vespasian. Suetonius says that a Roman official had a letter in Domitian's handwriting offering to engage in a homosexual affair with him. It was also said that Domitian and his eventual successor, Nerva, engaged in homosexual affairs.[4] William L. Langer, in his *Encyclopedia of World History*, describes Domitian, "Naturally of a suspicious, perhaps cruel temperament . . . Domitian . . . came to the throne determined to rule without respect for others, especially the Senate."[5] Domitian was left in Rome by his father and brother who were campaigning in Judea, where he narrowly escaped death at the hands of Vitellius' followers. By disposition he was aloof, humorless, avaricious, and cruel. Suetonius charges him with constant plotting against his brother, Titus, and with degrading his memory after death.

The "three horns plucked up by the roots" would be the three "barracks emperors," Galba, Otho, and Vitellius, not really in the royal Julian line of succession to the throne, but declared emperor by their troops. In *one year* A.D. 68-69, these three

ruled and were successively slain or committed suicide to keep from being assassi-
nated. Domitian came to his absolute rule in A.D. 81 after the rule of his father
Vespasian, A.D. 69-79, and the rule of his brother Titus, A.D. 79-81. It is possible
that the "three horns plucked up" could be later conspirators to Domitian's throne;
Senecio, Rusticus and Priscus, all slain by order of Domitian. The "*little horn*"
(Domitian) had eyes like the eyes of a man, and a mouth speaking great things.
Daniel is to understand from this symbolism that the fourth "beast" is human
regardless of how many great claims he may make for himself. This is explained
later (7:24-25) as the "little horn" making claims to deity. Precisely the same warning is given by John in the Revelation that the "beast" of Revelation is not superhuman, but human, when John assigns him the number "666" (see comments in this
work on Rev. 13:4,18). While some of Domitian's predecessors were deified after
their deaths by the populace, they did not issue any decrees that they *must be worshiped.* However, Domitian made it a law that he must be addressed as "Lord and
God."[6] Will Durant says of Domitian, ". . . he filled the Capitol with statues of himself, announced the divinity of his father, brother, wife, and sisters as well as his
own, organized a new order of priests, the *Flaviales,* to tend the worship of these
new deities, and required officials to speak of him, in their documents as *Dominus
et Deus Noster* — 'Our Lord and God.' He sat on a throne, and encouraged visitors
to embrace his knees."[7] This is not said of any other emperor!

In Daniel's dream, "thrones were placed." There are more thrones than one
involved in what follows. They could be the "24 thrones" of Revelation 4:4.
Daniel's vision is presently focused on one throne. Who sat upon the other thrones
is not germane to the vision here.

The "Ancient of Days" signifies One who has lived ever since anyone can
remember, and longer than anyone can remember. In other words, it symbolizes an
eternal and divine personage. We get much the same picture of the throne in heaven
here as we get in Revelation 4:1–5:15. The "Ancient of Days" is the Eternal One,
God, the Father, who sits on the throne in Revelation 4:1-11. The "one like a son of
man," who came to the Ancient of Days and was given dominion (Dan. 7:13-14), is
the "Lamb" (Rev. 5:1-14), the Lion of the tribe of Judah, who conquered and was
worthy to take the scroll of history and open it. The Eternal One's throne is fire, and
fire issues forth from it representing judicial power, splendor and majesty (e.g., Psa.
50:3; 97:3; Exod. 3:2; Deut. 4:24; 1 Tim. 6:16; Heb. 12:29; Rev. 4:4-5). Fire may
also symbolize a purifying, purging, sanctifying agent issuing forth from the throne
of God. "Wheels" symbolize the omnipresent God "riding" through his creation,
dispensing judgment through secondary agents (e.g., Ezek. 1:15-21; 10:1-22; Zech.
6:1-8), bringing "rest" to the earth in order that his work of redemption may be car-

ried on according to his providential emanation into history. God has at his command "myriads and myriads" (LXX) of heavenly creatures to do his bidding in the judgment upon the fourth beast and the little horn.

The "books" are symbolic of the fact that God records the actions of his creatures (e.g., Isa. 65:6; Jer. 17:1; Mal. 3:16; Luke 10:20). In the Revelation, John makes a point to show that those who worshiped the "beast" and had its mark upon them were judged by what was written "in the books." Those who had passed from death to life through the "first resurrection" (belief and baptism), over whom the second death had no power, had their names written in the "book of life." Nothing escapes the eyes of God.

Daniel sees the "beast" slain by the One before whose judgment court it had been arraigned. This would be the "fourth" beast which had incorporated elements of the three beasts that had preceded it. When the "fourth" beast was slain, the "dominion" of the other beasts was taken away, "but their lives were prolonged for a season and a time." Daniel's vision correlates precisely with John's vision of the end of the "beast" in Revelation 19:2-21 where it is "thrown alive into the lake of fire . . . ." The rest of the beasts, the first three (the lion, bear and leopard) had their "dominion" taken away. Universal imperialism would never again envelope civilization just as Daniel interpreted Nebuchadnezzar's dream (2:44-45). When the "fourth" was destroyed, they were all destroyed. The "lives" of Babylon, Persia, and Greece *had been prolonged for a season and a time* in the Roman Empire. The phrase literally says "a prolonging of life was given." The LXX translates the Hebrew word *yᵉhaybath* (from *yahab*) into the Greek word in aorist tense, *edothē.* Both of the words, Hebrew and Greek, literally mean, "given, arranged with." Aorist tense in Greek is essentially the "past" tense of the language. Thus, the first three great universal empires ("beasts") had their "lives" *given,* or *arranged with,* the life of the fourth ("beast") empire, Rome. When Rome fell, they, and what they represented — universal imperialism — fell. This idea of the three empires being absorbed by, and preserved in, the fourth, and finally having their universal dominion destroyed by the universal kingdom of God parallels, exactly, the idea in Daniel's interpretation of the "great image" (2:44-45). And the same concept correlates, again, with John's "beast" (Rome) where it is depicted as a *composite* of the "leopard, bear, and lion" (Rev. 13:1-2).

There appears in Daniel's dream "one like a son of man" to whom is given "dominion and glory and kingdom." His kingdom shall be universal, i.e., from "all peoples, nations, and languages" (cf. Rev. 7:9-17 — those who had "come out of the great tribulation"). This person of Daniel's dream is Jesus Christ (Rev. 1:13). He comes "with the clouds of heaven." That is an OT apocalyptic symbol depicting judgment from God coming into history, upon the earth (e.g., Isa. 19:1; Jer. 4:13; Lam. 2:1; Ezek. 1:4; Joel 2:2; Zeph. 1:15). Jesus used the same symbolism to warn his enemies that he was coming back with divine power, "on the clouds of heaven," to destroy Jerusalem (Matt. 24:30; 26:64; Mark 13:26; 14:62).

The kingdom that God would establish during the "days of those kings" (those of the fourth empire, 2:44-45) would be an *everlasting, universal* kingdom and it would belong to the "son of man." The saints of the Most High were to be "given into the hand of the beast for "a time, two times, and half a time." Daniel's dream predicted the kingdom of the "son of man" would be victorious over the *fourth* "beast" (Rome) and bring about its downfall. The Roman Empire *began* its plunge into ruin in the reign of Domitian (A.D. 81-96) and *ended* about A.D. 450. If we allow a "time" to roughly prefigure a century, then we have predicted here the 350 years from about A.D. 100 to A.D. 450. John sees the same time period as "the great tribulation" upon the churches of Christ in Asia Minor (cf. Rev. 11:2-3 and 12:14, 1260 days are 42 months and 42 months are approximately 3.5 years, and "years" symbolize centuries). From the end of the first century A.D. to A.D. 450, the history of the ancient Roman Empire is a story of financial disaster, civil war, decimation by famine and plagues, a sapping of its strength and morale by the constant attack of its enemies, and a terrible moral and social depravity and disintegration.

The apostle John clearly identifies Domitian in his "riddle" of Revelation 17:8-11. Counting from Tiberius (omitting the "barracks emperors") who was emperor when Jesus was crucified and the church was established, to Domitian, there are seven emperors. Five had fallen, one was and the other had not yet come. There was a myth popular in the Roman world of John's day that Nero had not died in battle but was still alive and would return to Rome and resume his reign.[8] Some scholars believe the apostle John satirically adapted this myth to symbolize that Nero (the "king that was and is not and was an eighth which belongs to the seven) was "reincarnated" in Domitian, "the eighth." Many other clues within the book of Revelation itself indicate it was written in the time of Domitian and was predicting the future death of ancient Rome beginning with that time.

Since it would have been irrelevant to Daniel's purpose to write in great detail about the fall of the *fourth* "beast," it is left to John the apostle in his Revelation to "plug in" 700 years later, exactly where Daniel left off his divinely-revealed "dream" of this future time. Daniel will give one more predictive "hint" about the "fourth beast" (Dan. 9:27) as he is filling in the details concerning the second and third "beasts" and their impact upon God's messianic people before the coming of the Messiah.

Finally, Daniel is given a capsulized interpretation of the dream (7:15-27). Four powerful, beastly empires will arise in history. But their beastliness either separately or combined in one final culminating and all-encompassing "beast" will not stop God's redemptive work. That work will reach its apex after God has "nurtured" his church in the "wilderness" of the "great tribulation" of the fourth beast (Dan. 7:25; Rev. 12:13-17). God established his eternal kingdom *before* the fall of the fourth empire. But its universal spread into the far-flung corners of the earth had to await the taking out of the way of the most threatening of all beasts — the fourth one.

The most crucial time for the infant "kingdom of God" (the church) was during the reign of Domitian and especially in Asia Minor where Paul had accomplished his greatest missionary success and where most of the Christians were near the end of the first century. That is why John's Revelation is addressed to the churches of Asia Minor. That is when it appeared as if the fourth "beast" of Daniel (the same as the "beast" in Revelation) was invincible (Rev. 13:4) and could not be withstood even by God! But Daniel (and other prophets, see Rev. 10:7)) had been shown that *any concentration of human power, regardless of how mighty*, would **never** thwart the purpose of God to redeem his creation. And Daniel was shown specifically the eventual rise of the mightiest of all the beastly monoliths of human power — Rome — arrogantly and presumptuously boasting that it would "wear out the saints of the Most High, and . . . think to change the times and the law . . . ." But Daniel is also shown that God's saints will have their victory over the worst enemy of God's redemptive plan in the person of the Anointed One (cf. Dan. 9:24-27). The Messiah would establish God's eternal kingdom on earth *in the days of the fourth world empire*. That is Daniel's goal; beyond that he does not go. It is significant that the Son of God, God in the flesh, was put to death during the Roman Empire, by order of a Roman procurator. That was the ultimate blow that could be exercised by rebellious mankind to stop the establishment of the kingdom of God on earth. But God was not stopped! He used, in fact, the death of his Son to accomplish man's redemption. Then he raised his Son from the tomb, and turned over to him the "scroll" (Rev. 5:7-8) which contained the awful destiny of a Roman Empire presuming to usurp the sovereignty of its Creator.

John wrote Revelation to tell the saints of Asia Minor (and all saints down through the centuries who would subsequently read its words) that the "beast" was "human" and not divine and would be destroyed while the church would be victorious (Rev. 13:18). But before the beast was to meet his doom, he would: (a) deceive all the world except believers; (b) cause the world to worship him; (c) withhold food from those who would not; (d) and persecute and kill many believers (Rev. 13:1-18). John is quick to inform believers that in the war of the beast upon the church, those who die will "rest from their labors" (Rev. 14:12-13). Both Daniel and John predict that the war of the beast upon the saints will continue until the judgment upon the beast (Dan. 7:26; Rev. 16:1-20; 17:1-15; 18:1-24; 19:1-21).

Domitian was human but he was beastly in his character. By getting himself elected consul and censor for life, he openly subordinated the republican aspect of the Senate and lesser magistrates to a monarchial totalitarianism. Thus he "changed" the law of Rome. He instituted a reign of terror that kept Rome in a state of constant fear. He assumed the right of voting first in the "Senate" (Senate in name only) so that anyone who voted differently would be a marked man. He issued his letters and imperial edicts with the salutation: "Our Lord God instructs you to . . . ." He demanded that anyone addressing him say, *Dominus et Deus*, "Lord and God." He renamed September and October (the months of his accession of the emperorship and his birthday) calling them "Germanicus" and "Domitianus." Thus, he sought to "change the times." Finally, he paid no attention to the policies of the Senate at all but insisted on the finality of his own decisions. He demanded to be hailed as the Roman god Jupiter's son and heir, the earthly viceregent and representative of the "king of the universe!" Suetonius says of Domitian that "he was extremely lustful," consorted with prostitutes and homosexuals, seduced his young niece who became pregnant by him, and forced her to have an abortion which brought about her death.[9]

Domitian was just one of the emperors who transformed Rome into the "fourth" and mightiest "beast" of all. Rome's beastliness toward the church continued, intermittently, until A.D. 476 when the Western Empire fell. It was not until then (ca. A.D. 500) that Christianity became, through missionary endeavor, a worldwide "kingdom." At that point in history "the kingdom and the dominion and the greatness of the kingdoms under the whole heaven" were given to the people of the saints of the Most High (Dan. 7:27). Rome was at the zenith of its power from Julius Caesar (46 B.C.) until about A.D. 180 That was when the "seventh angel" blew his trumpet" (Rev. 11:15-19) and the "seven bowls full of the wrath of God" *began* to be poured out upon the "beast" (Rev. 15:1–18:24) and the "great city" and all her subordinate "cities" eventually fell. Her fall was first, from the human perspective, because of natural disasters which brought about economic ruin. Second, Rome's moral depravity resulted in social and civil anarchy. Finally, these internal collapses made the empire vulnerable to invasion by the "Barbarians" (Goths, Visigoths, Ostrogoths, Huns, Scythians, et al.).

Chapter seven of Daniel has *nothing* to say about the "end of the world" and the Second Coming of Christ. Clearly, Daniel is talking about the fourth ancient empire that would have to be taken out of the way by Almighty God in order that God's *eternal* kingdom might be *universally* established on earth. In fact, there is not even one word in the original text of Daniel that might be translated "time of the end, end time," or "the last day" in chapter seven.

The two visions (Daniel's and John's) reveal exactly the same message. Man, in his attempt to usurp God's sovereign rule over this creation, would attempt to do so by monolithic mechanisms of humanistic governments. But God planned to intervene in history and establish, once for all, his kingdom on earth. The Old Testament prophets were not given revelations concerning the Second Coming of the Messiah. This would have been irrelevant to the purpose for which God called them. They had to concentrate all their skills coupled with the guidance of the Holy Spirit (1 Pet. 1:10-12), on convincing the Jews that the kingdom of God, established by the coming Messiah, would be a spiritual kingdom, victorious over any and all attempts of humanistic socialization to create its own *utopia* on earth. The prophets had difficulty persuading their contemporaries that the Messiah would come and set up his kingdom in the earth as a spiritual kingdom, in the midst of carnal power, at his *first* coming. The history between Messiah's first coming and his second coming was not given to them. What would be germane and edifying to Daniel's contemporaries would be to know that worldly dominion, regardless of how powerful it might grow, would ultimately be overthrown by the kingdom of God. This he revealed!

However, since the pattern of carnal opposition to the kingdom of God adopted by the Romans has been followed by practically all the succeeding world powers, Daniel's revelation and John's revelation are sufficient to demonstrate that God is able to make his kingdom survive their utmost beastliness. And this, even to the extreme of attempting to eliminate God's anointed. All worldly powers oppose God's kingdom because the spirit of the devil is incarnated in them (Dan. 10: Rev. 13). But with the destruction of the "fourth beast" God "bound" the devil for "a thousand years." "Thousand years" simply means a long time from man's viewpoint. The devil's power to bring about another universal pagan rule over civilization has been restricted by the release of the gospel into the whole world. This was made possible when Rome fell ca. A.D. 500.

Daniel 7 is prophecy fulfilled, and therefore trustworthy as a divine revelation and perspective for history. By it man may know how history must run its course. The kingdom of God, the church, will stand forever while all other institutions, societies, cultures and governments will ultimately fall into the lake of fire and brimstone. God permits his saints to be tested and tried by those forces which oppose his kingdom in the world. He does this to purify their lives and strengthen their faith. The church is "nurtured" in the "wilderness" of carnal opposition (Rev. 12:13-17). As the Christian takes God's perspective of history from God's revelation, he sees the transitory nature of the world and the way of destruction chosen by those who worship the beast. This is the essence of biblical eschatology. "For the testimony of Jesus is the spirit of prophecy" (Rev. 19:10).

Daniel 8:1-27

The eighth chapter of Daniel is self-explanatory. Readers need only to compare Daniel's vision recorded in it to the outcome of the historic struggle between ancient Persia and Greece and Daniel's *interpretation* will guide them to the message God conveys in it.

Elam was a country situated on the east side of the Tigris River in a mountainous region opposite Babylonia. Its population was made up of a variety of tribes. Their language, different from the Sumerian, Semitic and Indo-European tongues, was written in *cuneiform* (written in wedge-shaped characters) script. It has not yet been totally deciphered. Elam was one of the earliest civilizations. In Sumerian inscriptions it was called *Numman*, meaning "high mountain people." This same term became *Elamtu* in Akkadian texts. In classical literature Elam was known as *Suisana*, which is the Greek name for *Susa*, the capital city of Elam. The city *Susa* was located on what today is the Iraqi, Iranian border. The river *Ulai* runs through the province of Elam, flowing on through the city of Susa, and eventually into the Tigris-Euphrates rivers. Daniel takes great care to mention these places because *Shushan* (or, *Susa*) was later to become the summer capital of the Persian empire. When this vision appeared to Daniel nothing concerning the future importance of this territory was known. But since the fortunes of Persia were to be significantly involved in the messianic destiny of God's people, the future center of Persian life and political activity would be important. The contemporary Jewish readership of Daniel's prophecy would know little about *Shushan* when Daniel first "published" his book, but Daniel's citation here would certainly authenticate the canonicity of his book when his predictions came to pass. Archaeological effort in the last part of the 1880s uncovered in Shushan the great palace of King Xerxes (486-465 B.C.) in which Queen Esther lived. Many Jews lived here in the captivities and became prominent in the affairs of the city as the books of Esther and Nehemiah document.

Daniel saw in this vision, a "ram" with "two horns" standing on the bank of the Ulai River. This two-horned ram symbolized the Medo-Persian Empire (see Dan. 8:20). The two horns are the component parts of the empire — Media and Persia. More than a hundred years before Daniel, Isaiah predicted the Medes would be "stirred up" against Babylon (Isa. 13:17; 21:2; see also Jer. 51:11). The taller horn came up last which coincides with the history of this empire. Persia eventually became supreme and assimilated the Medes. The ram represented in the Israelite mentality that which was more "sanctified' than a "he-goat" (Ezek. 34:17). Persia's conquest of the civilized world is symbolized by the butting of the ram "westward, northward, and southward." Persia did not "charge" toward the east because *she* was the easternmost part of her empire. The three-way charge of the ram agrees with the three ribs in the mouth of the bear in Daniel 7. That "no beasts could stand before him" refers to the imagery of chapter 7 also, and the command there, "Arise and devour much flesh," shows the lack of resistance to the Persian conquest of the world (cf. Isa. 44:28–45:17).

Cyrus the Great, the initial Persian conqueror, was equally as great as Alexander the Great. Cyrus ruled from the Aegean Sea in the west to the Jaxartes River and the Himalayas on the east. A later Persian emperor, Darius, increased the size of the Persian Empire from the Balkans and Egypt on the west and well into India on the east. This empire lasted for two centuries and gave the world a relative peace and many innovative social improvements. They introduced an international language, Aramaic, a "pony-express" rapid communications system throughout the empire, good roads, and an international currency for commercial exchange. The Persian respect for truth, honor, and the rule of common law (cf. Esther) was the secret of their imperial success. The "Law of the Medes and Persians" was sacrosanct. Even the emperors could not change it once it had been legislated. That created great stability within the structure of civil government. Persia also allowed their "provinces" much latitude in self-governance (cf. Ezra and Nehemiah), even permitting them to institute their own religious practices. Alexander the Great would later find the Persian forms of government so practical he would adopt them *in toto* and simply graft into them his Hellenistic culture.

The "he-goat" symbolizes the empire of Greece (Dan. 8:21). It represents sure-footedness and quickness just like the leopard of chapter 7. Alexander the Great's conquests are described in 1 Maccabees 1:3: "He went through to the ends of the earth and took spoils of a multitude of nations; and the earth was quiet before him." The rapidity of his conquests is pictured by the he-goat going across the face of the whole earth "without touching the ground." The he-goat had a "conspicuous horn" between his eyes. This represents Alexander the Great, born ca. 356 B.C., who invaded the Persian Empire and fought his first major battle at the Granicus River. The "great anger" points to the cry for vengeance from the Greek people after years of assaults across the Aegean Sea by the Persians in 490-480 B.C.[10] By 331 B.C. the known "world" lay at his feet. Alexander swept across Asia Minor (present day Turkey), on through Persia (modern Iraq and Iran) and into India. At the Beas River, his troops threatened to mutiny if he did not turn back and allow them to return to their homes on the Greek mainland. When he had give in to his army's demand, one of his philosophic retinue, Anaxarchus, needled him, reminding him that there were a great many other worlds besides the Eastern, Alexander replied, "Do you not think it worthy of lamentation that when there is such a vast multitude of worlds, we have not yet conquered *one*?"[11]

Idealized by his men, hailed as divine in lands he won, Alexander was adopted into the legends of three continents. Central Asia worshiped him as *Iskander*, founder of cities and one of the Asian cities, Bucephala, named itself in honor of his horse. Chiefs in Turkistan claim descent from him; Afghan mothers frighten naughty children with tales of *Iskander*. Persians called him "son of Darius;" Egyptians, "son of the last Pharaoh." Ethiopia made him a saint, and Islam enrolled him as a prophet. Medieval Europe depicted him as a knight of chivalry. Romans, first to call Alexander, "the Great," held themselves to be heirs to his empire and ambitions. Caesar Augustus (Octavian) wore Alexander's image on a signet ring and emulated his deeds. Even Buddha owes his image to Alexander's march into the Orient. Inspired by statues Greeks brought to Bandhara, sculptors created Buddha in the image of Alexander, but added to his forehead the Oriental third eye, which allegedly emits spiritual light. He won an empire covering more than one and a half million square miles. He had mapped unknown territory, built cities, opened trade routes, and stimulated the exchange of philosophies. From the Mediterranean to the land of India, Greek became the *lingua franca* of court and commerce. He died, some historians say in a drunken stupor, in 323 B.C. at the young age of 33 years.

His vast realm survived for only a few years because the *Diadochi* — his successors — had his only son (by his Persian wife Roxane) assassinated and fought each other for power. It is said that on his deathbed, Alexander called his army generals to his bedside and divided his empire between four of them. The "four notable horns" of 8:8 which came up, "toward the four winds of heaven," in the place of the "great" horn are parallel to the four heads of the leopard of chapter 7 and represent the four-way division of Alexander's empire. He divided it between Ptolemy (Egypt), Antigonus (Asia), Cassander (Macedonia), and Lysimachus (Thrace). Antigonus was later killed in a battle. His Asiatic empire came to an end, and Seleucus (Ptolemy's leading sub-general) was given Palestine and Syria over which to rule.

The "little horn" that came up out of the four and "grew exceedingly great toward the south, toward the east, and toward the glorious land" is Antiochus IV. His immediate predecessors, the Seleucids, were a dynasty of Greeks who ruled Syria or what we call today, "The Fertile Crescent." It included modern Syria, Palestine, and Iraq. The Seleucid dynasty was a result of 150 years of war between them and the Ptolemies in Egypt outlined by Daniel in the revelation he received from the angel in chapters 10 and 11 of his book, i.e., the "kings of the north and the kings of the south." In this dream all the Seleucid rulers prior to Antiochus IV are passed over so as to get to the heart of the Jewish messianic destiny as it would be played out beginning with their restoration from exile. This was a matter of cosmic significance involving the length of time the Jews would have to endure the Seleucid holocaust before God's "Anointed" (Messiah) should come to "save them from their enemies" (8:18-26).

It is important to note that the "little horn" here in chapter 8 grows out of *one of the four* which in turn had displaced *the great horn* which was "broken" and which is **explicitly** interpreted by the angel (8:21-26) as Greece, the **third** "beast." This "little horn" grows out of the third "beast." The "little horn" of chapter 8 is **different** than the "other horn" in chapter 7. The "other" horn of chapter 7 came out of the **fourth** "beast." The "other horn" of chapter 7 is Domitian, the Roman tyrant; the "little horn" of chapter 8 is Antiochus IV, the Syrian "madman."

This little horn grew great even to the "host of heaven and some of the host of the stars it cast down to the ground and trampled upon them." Daniel uses apocalyptic and symbolic language here to designate God's covenant people with, "the host of heaven" (see Exod. 7:4; 12:41; Jer. 33:22; Dan. 11:30-35; 12:3,7). Anyone who causes contemptuous injury to God's covenant people in any age is contemptuous toward heaven and the throne of God (Zech 2:8). Antiochus IV (the "little horn" of chapter 8), called himself "Epiphanes" ("Illustrious One"). The Jews called him "Epimanes" ("The Mad One"). He actually considered himself a god and commanded that a likeness of himself be placed in the temple of the Jews and worshiped. He forbade the Jews to offer their regular sacrifices and placed in the office of Jewish High Priest the person (whether Levite or not) who offered him the biggest bribe or who could produce the most political favors (cf. 1 Macc. 1:4-47). He desecrated the Jewish temple by offering a sow upon its altar and by substituting an altar to Jupiter for the altar of burnt offering. This was the crowning "abomination" that made the temple desolate for the Jews (8:11-12; 11:31). Great numbers of the Jews consorted with Antiochus and welcomed his Hellenization of their culture (8:12; 11:30-35).

There are two principal interpretations of the "two thousand and three hundred evenings and mornings" (8:14) until the sanctuary (temple) shall be restored to its rightful state:

(a) It means 1150 days; i.e., the prophecy is related to the daily morning and evening sacrifices, and 2300 such sacrifices would therefore be offered on 1150 days; this view equates the "little horn" of 8:9 with the "little horn" of 7:8,24,25, contending 1150 days is nearly *equivalent* to 3½ years, i.e., "time, two times, and half a time." But it should be obvious that 1150 days do not equal 3½ years for even if a year is considered to be 360 days long, we would have 1260 days; it **is** obvious that the "little horn" of 7:8,24,25 and the "little horn" of 8:9 are **different**.

(b) It means 2300 full days and is probably a derivative of Genesis 1:5,8,13,19, 23,31 where "evening and morning" are reckoned as a full day; in the OT an expression such as 40 days and 40 nights does not mean 20 days, nor does 3 days and 3 nights mean either 6 days or 1½ days — it means 3 days. Keil says: "A Hebrew reader could not possibly understand the period of time 2300 evening-mornings as 2300 half days or 1150 whole days, because evening and morning at the creation constituted not the half but the whole day."[12] Clearly, the 2300 are full days. The number 10 and any multiple of it (e.g., 1000 years; 1000 hills; 1000 times) is a "round number" and should not be taken literally. The number 2300 should be considered as measuring *nearly* a time span of 2300 days. The period is clearly referring to the period of Antiochus Epiphanes' abominable treatment of the Jews. This began in the year 171 B.C., one year before his return from a second expedition to Egypt. This is the year he began desecrating the Jewish temple. The termination would then be the death of Antiochus in 164 B.C. The 2300 days covers a period of six years and about four months. Keil believes that the number (being a little short of 2520 days or seven years) possesses a symbolic meaning, namely, not quite the full duration of a period of divine judgment.[13] That it is expressed in "days" would serve to remind the Israelites reading it hundreds of years after it was predicted who actually experienced the pogrom of Antiochus, that the Lord would not let the tribulation extend a day beyond what they could bear. The 2300 days would culminate in the restoration of the sanctuary to "its rightful state" (cleansed and rededicated), see 1 Maccabees 4:36-59.

As the angel began explaining the symbolic message, Daniel was told it was going to be made known to him *what time* the vision was for, and told *what experience* would be "at the latter end of the indignation; for it pertains to the appointed time of the end" (8:17,19). Now we have come to an *eschatological* statement in Daniel's book! Here the Hebrew text uses two of the words of eschatology listed in our Word Study (Appendix B). In 8:17 Daniel used the Hebrew words '*ēth qēts*. The Septuagint translated these words into the Greek words, *kairou*, and *peras*, and *horasis*, which literally mean, "time of . . . end . . . vision." In 8:19 Daniel used the Hebrew words, *acharith*, *mo'ēd*, and *qēts* translated by the Septuagint into the Greek words, *eschatōn*, and *kairou*, and *peras,* and *horasis*, literally, "last . . . of time . . . end . . . vision." The whole idea is, "Behold, I make known to you the things that shall come at the last of the wrath ("indignation"), for unto a time appointed is the vision."

The Hebrew word translated "indignation," *za'am*, is sometimes translated, "enraged." In the Septuagint (or, LXX) it is the Greek word, *orgēs*, from which we get the English words, "orgy, orgiastic, orgasm." The term "indignation" or "wrath" refers **specifically to the captivities of the covenant people of the OT** by Assyria and Babylon. For confirmation of this we need only to look at the biblical use of the

Hebrew *za'am* in Isa. 10:5,25; 26:20, et al. Daniel is predicting that when the abominations of Antiochus IV occur, it will signal that the indignation of God against the covenant people for their idolatry during the divided kingdom period is coming to a fierce finality. The "appointed time of the end" is the *appointed time signalling the end of the OT dispensation.* It would be a sign that the messianic dispensation (the first advent of Christ and the establishment of the church) was about to begin. When Antiochus IV died (ca. 164 B.C.) the Maccabean brothers were able to liberate the Jews and give them about 100 years of self-rule until about 63 B.C. when Pompey, one of the Roman Triumvirate, occupied Palestine as a part of the Roman Empire. "In the fullness of time" God sent forth his Son, the Messiah, to establish his kingdom, the church. The Jews, for the most part, rejected the Messiah and crucified him, but God raised him from the dead, enthroned him upon David's throne, established his church (Acts 2), and in A.D. 70 permitted the Jews and the Roman army to destroy the Jewish temple. A million Jews were slain and a half-million were sold into slavery all over the Roman world. The OT dispensation was nailed to the cross at the death of Jesus (Col. 2:8-15). Even the OT predicted that it would be supplanted with the new and ultimate word of God (Jer. 3:15-18; 31:31-34; Heb. 8:13).

God warned the Jews in the earlier prophets that because of their idolatry he was going to bring his "indignation" upon them in the form of exile and oppression. This would be to chasten them and prepare them for the glorious blessings to come to all who believed and accepted the promised Messiah and his kingdom. God revealed through Daniel that this *indignation* was going to end one day and when it ended, it would be a sign that the Messiah was (in his first advent) to appear. But since the events were for a long time after Daniel's *last* prophecies were to be fulfilled (some 300 years) he was to preserve ("shut up") the words of his prophecies. This does not mean it was to be kept "secret" or not be understood. It simply means that it was to be *permanently* preserved for posterity's sake (cf. Rev. 22:10). History records that Antiochus IV took up residence in Tabae, Persia, where he became mad and died in 164 B.C. Thus, Daniel's prophecy in 8:25-26 was fulfilled.

The phrases "time of the end" (Dan. 8:17), "the latter end of the indignation" (Dan. 8:19), and "the appointed time of the end" (Dan. 8:29) **do not apply** to any alleged tribulation, rapture, earthly millennial rule of Christ, or Antichrist, in the year A.D. 2000. They were predictions of an holocaust upon the Jewish people perpetrated by a cunning king of "bold countenance" arising out of Alexander the Great's four-way division of the empire of Greece. There are **only** four **scriptural** notations concerning Antichrist." They are:

1. 1 John 2:28 which may be literally translated, "Little children, a last hour has come, and as you heard that Antichrist is coming, even now many Antichrists

have arisen and are continuing to arise, so we know that this is a last hour." Note: (a) there is no definite article before "last," so John is not writing about *the* last hour; (b) there is no definite article before Antichrist, so John is not writing about *the* Antichrist; (c) John says, in fact, **many** Antichrists (plural in the Greek text) had *already* arisen and were continuing to do so (the Greek verb for "arisen" is perfect tense).

2. 1 John 2:22 translated literally would read, "Who is the liar except the one denying that Jesus is the Christ? This is the Antichrist, the one denying the Father and the Son." Note: (a) this passage does have the definite article before Antichrist; (b) but an Antichrist is *anyone* who denies that Jesus is God's "Anointed," and, *anyone* denying the divine relationship of Jesus to God the Father.

3. 1 John 4:3 literally translated would read ". . . and every spirit which does not confess Jesus is not from God — and this *is* the Antichrist which you have heard is coming and is already in the world." Note: (a) *every* spirit which does not confess that Jesus is of God is the Antichrist (that would mean there are "many" Antichrists); (b) there were Antichrists in the world **already** when John was writing his epistle (ca. A.D. 95-100).

4. 2 John 7 literally translated would read, "Because many deceivers have gone forth into the world, those not confessing that Jesus, God's Anointed, has come in the flesh are the deceivers and the Antichrists." Note: (a) the Greek verb for "went forth" is in the aorist — past — tense, i.e., the deceivers and Antichrists had *already* gone forth into the world; (b) while John uses the definite article before "Antichrist" he still says there were **many Antichrists** who had already gone forth; (c) and *anyone*, at that time, denying that God's "Anointed" had come in the flesh, in the person of Jesus of Nazareth, was an Antichrist.

Clearly, the "king of bold countenance" in Daniel 8:18-26 and the "contemptible one" of Daniel 11:21-45 are the same person. But this person in Daniel cannot be "the" Antichrist. And, further, while "the man of lawlessness, the son of perdition," in 2 Thessalonians 2:3-12 is definitely an enemy of Christ, if proper hermeneutical science is to be observed, he should **not** be called "the Antichrist."

The "latter end of the indignation" or the "appointed time of the end" which was revealed to Daniel is **the consummation of the ages**, the *first* coming of the Messiah (cf. 1 Cor. 10:11). The holocaust of Antiochus IV was to be a chastening discipline of the Lord, "to make them (the idolatrous Jews) white until the time of the end," preparing Israel to welcome the Messiah (Dan. 11:35; 12:1-3, 10-13). Tragically, most of them, when the Messiah came, "received him not" (John 1:11; Acts 13:44-47; 28:25-29). Next we will learn about Daniel's prediction of the exact time the Messiah was to appear, how most of his "people" would reject him, and the consequences of that rejection.

Daniel 9:1-27

"Darius the son of Ahasuerus" of Daniel 9:1 is the same person as "Darius the Mede" of Daniel 5:31–6:28. Darius, the son of Ahasuerus (see our discussion of his identity in *Daniel, 3rd edition*).[14] The "first year of his reign" was probably near 536 B.C., the year in which the first increment of Jewish exiles were allowed to return to Palestine by the edict of Cyrus (see 2 Chr. 36:22-23; Ezra 1:1-4). Apparently Daniel had received word from the first of the Jews to return to Jerusalem that they had encountered "trouble" as they sought to inhabit their land (see 9:25).

That is exactly what had happened. When the Jews first returned to Jerusalem to rebuild, they found nothing but trouble. The territory of Judea had been inhabited by squatters on the farms and in the villages vacated when the people of Judah had been exiled to Babylon. These "squatters" were people from all over the area of ancient Mesopotamia and Asia Minor. They had been forced to immigrate there by the Assyrians when they exiled the nation of Israel (the ten northern tribes) in 721 B.C. These squatters came to be known as "Samaritans." They did not want to move out of Judea so they accused the returning Judeans of trying to revolt against Persia. Furthermore, so many Jews considered building homes for themselves to be the first priority in their lives, their rebuilding of the temple had ceased — it still lay in ruins sixteen years after their return from exile. This very real trouble the Judeans faced is documented in Nehemiah, Haggai, and Zechariah. This disturbed Daniel! He thought he had read in the scroll of Jeremiah that God's "indignation" was to last only 70 years — so he checked Jeremiah (25:9-11) again. Sure enough, it said, "And this whole land shall become a ruin and a waste, and these nations shall serve the king of Babylon seventy years." Daniel prayed! He confessed Israel's sin; confessed the justice of the Lord in their punishment; and besought the Lord for a cessation of the "troubles" facing his brethren back home in Jerusalem.

Daniel's understanding was faulty, but his motive was singularly pure. His prayer was not for any selfish reasons, but that God should vindicate his own Majesty and Holiness by providentially intervening on behalf of the beleaguered Jews back home. The Lord did answer Daniel's prayer. He sent the angel Gabriel to tell him that the covenant people must yet face 490 years of "indignation" or "trouble" before God provides *ultimate* forgiveness in the Messiah. That answer came to Daniel in the revelations which begin at 9:20 and end at 12:13!

It would be difficult to exaggerate the prominence the text Daniel 9:24-27 finds in works on eschatology — especially in the system of dispensationalists. It is often appealed to as definite proof that the entire "church age" is supposed to occur *between* the events listed in 9:26 and those listed in 9:27. Verse 27 concerns the seventieth week which is supposed to be, according to some, the "seven years of tribulation" following the "rapture" of the church and preceding the literal "millennium" on earth.

The Hebrew text of 9:24 begins with the words, *shavu'im shiv'e'im*, which would be translated, literally, "sevens–seventy." The correct interpretation, however, in light of other passages (e.g., Ezek. 4:6) which show the Hebrew's use of figurative language, the "day–year" symbolism should be *"Seven times seventy years,"* i.e. 7×70 years = 490 years (the LXX translates the Hebrew into the Greek words, *hebdomekonta hebdomades* from which we get the English word *heptad* — "a series of seven"). Furthermore, all 490 years *are a unit*! The Hebrew verb, *chatak* ("cut off, determine, decree"), is singular and the nouns (i.e., the "sevens seventy") are plural. This means the entire 490 *is* one unit. This will be an important distinction in a later discussion concerning the seventieth seven. These 490 years are a divine revelation that a definite period of time has been *decreed* (Hebrew, *nechtak*) for the accomplishment of the six redemptive events enumerated in 9:24. When these six objectives are finished, the "indignation" of God upon Israel (and all mankind, for that matter) will come to the "appointed time of the end" (Dan. 8:17,19,26; 10:14; 11:35; **11:36**; 12:4,7,13). Jeremiah clearly shows that the "end of the indignation" of God will come in the Messianic Age (Jer. 32:36-41) tying it to the "everlasting covenant." See the "indignation" in other messianic contexts in Zechariah 1:12-17 and Isaiah 10:24–11:16. When the 490 years and redemption through the Messiah are accomplished, God will have "restored the fortunes of Judah and Israel" (i.e., "brought them back"). This "bringing back" will involve Gentiles being brought into the **new Israel, the church of Christ** (e.g., Isa. 2:1-4; 19:16-25; 56:68; 60:3; 66:18-23; Rom. 9:24-29; Gal. 6:15-16). The six redemptive objectives are:

1. *The transgression would be finished*: that is, the cup of iniquity of the Jewish people, indeed of the whole world, would be filled to the brim. At the instigation of the Jews, the world would reject and crucify its Messiah. The full height and depth of their iniquity was yet to be shown but would be within the 490 years allotted to the Jewish people. In putting the Messiah to death they reached the culmination of all their wickedness. No greater sin was possible (Matt. 23:32; Acts 2:22-23; 3:13-14; 1 Thess. 2:16; Heb. 6:6; 10:29).
2. *Sin would be put to an end*: that is, God would conquer sin in the incarnate work of Christ (Rom. 8:1-4). In the death of the Messiah, God would triumph over man's rebellion and Satan's power (Col. 2:13-15; Heb. 2:14-18) and do so "publicly" (i.e, in history). All sin, even that done from Eden to the end of time was done away in the death of Christ (Rom. 3:21-26; Heb. 9:15-28).

3. *Iniquity would be atoned for*: that is, the vicarious, substitutionary death of Jesus Christ would atone for human iniquity. The wrath of God upon sin would be satisfied and man would be reconciled. God would be both just and the justifier of those who believe (Rom. 3:21-26). And this was borne witness to in the law and the prophets! (See also 2 Cor. 5:14-21; Eph. 2:11-22).

4. *Everlasting righteousness would be brought in*: that is, God would bring in everlasting righteousness through the willing sacrifice of Christ (Heb. 10:5-18) and impute it to those who are constrained by the love of Christ (2 Cor. 5:14-21) to enter into covenant with him. By this redemption of grace God also provided the impetus for men to practice righteousness (Rom. 1:16; 1 Tim. 6:18; 2 Tim. 1:7).

5. *Prophecy would be sealed*: that is, God put his "seal" on (validated) all the prophecy of the Bible through the redemptive work of the Messiah (e.g., Luke 24:25-27, 44-49; John 6:26-27; 2 Cor. 1:20-21; Heb. 1:1; 6:13-20; Rev. 19:10). "All the promises of God find their **Amen** in him." See also Acts 3:24; 1 Pet. 1:10-11.

6. *A Holy of Holies would be anointed:* The word "anointed" is from the Hebrew root word *mashach* from which comes the English word, "Messiah." Since there are no definite articles before the Hebrew words, *qodesh qadashim*, or, "holy [of] holies," it is difficult to determine whether the author means Christ (Messiah) will be "anointed" (e.g., Matt. 3:16; 16:16; 17:1-8; 22:41-46; 26:64; 28:18-20; Luke 7:38; 24:44-49; John 12:3; 20:28; Acts 2:24-36; 4:12, 26; 10:38; 13:26-40; Rom. 1:1-5; Heb. 1:9; 5:5-6) or the church will be established (e.g., Eph. 2:1-22; Col. 1:15-20). We opt for the first interpretation because the only "anointing" said to be upon the church is in 1 John 2:27, and upon the apostles (2 Cor. 1:21), but there are many predictions of Jesus being "anointed" as the Christ.

Oswald T. Allis indicates that there are points of agreement and points of difference between those who interpret the prophecy of the 70 weeks traditionally and those who interpret it dispensationally. Points of **agreement** are: (1) the 70 weeks represent weeks-of-years, to a total of 490 years; (2) only one period of weeks is described, as is proved by the fact that the subdivisions (7 + 62 + 1) when added together give a total of 70; (3) the "anointed one" of verses 25-26 are the same person, the Messiah; (4) the first 69 weeks or 483 years had their ending point in the period of the first advent; their fulfillment is long past. The points of **difference** revolve around two significant questions: (1) have the great events described in verse 24 been fulfilled, or is their accomplishment still future? (2) is the 70th week past or is it still to come?[15]

Dispensationalists insist that all the events of verse 24 are still in the future. They say, for example, "to make an end of sins" means to eliminate moral evil completely from this world. Dispensationalists *must* insist that verse 24 refers to the future for if the fulfillment of the prophecy is still incomplete, and if the predictions relating to the 69 weeks are long past, the 70th week must be still future. That view, in turn, *must* insist on an interval between the end of the 69th week and the beginning of the 70th week which has continued now for some 2000 years! The entire "church age" is thus to be considered a 2000-year "parenthesis."

The great events of verse 24 are unequivocally declared in the New Testament to have been fulfilled with the *first* coming of Christ. We cannot exegetically abide the idea that these events are in the future. The epistle to the Hebrews in the NT represents all these objectives as having been fulfilled at the first advent. Jesus Christ was the perfect sacrifice, the one and only sacrifice, made **for all time.** His sacrifice is able to perfect for **all time** those who are being sanctified by it (Heb. 9:11-12, 25-28; 10:12-14). A return to a Jewish state, a Jewish temple and sacrifices would be apostasy. Notice in Hebrews 9:25-28 Christ will appear a *second* time **not to deal with sin**! And why would there be a need to make further atonement, validate prophecy, produce everlasting righteousness, or confirm he is God's Anointed after his first advent? The "traditional" and in our opinion, the scriptural view, is that all these goals (vs. 24) were reached and completed in the birth, life, death and resurrection of Christ and the establishment of the church. These objectives completed **are** the **consummation of the ages**, (1 Cor. 10:11, et al.). They certainly are not yet to be, at the end of the world. All that remains for God to implement is eternity with the second advent of Jesus.

Since all six objectives of verse 24 were finished with the first advent of the Messiah, that settles the *terminating point* of the prophecy and the 70 weeks as well. The termination of the 490 years coincides then, *not* with the times of Antiochus IV, nor with the Second Coming of Christ, but with Christ's *first advent*! When Jesus ascended into heaven and the Holy Spirit descended to inaugurate the kingdom through the apostolic preaching, there remained *not one* of the six items of Daniel 9:24 that was not fully accomplished.

Now, in verse 25, we are told exactly how many years would intervene between the return of the Jews to restore the Jewish commonwealth and the coming of an "Anointed One." Daniel uses the Hebrew words *mashiach* and *nagid*, "Messiah" and "Leader" so there can be no mistake as to whom he points in his prophecy. That expiration of time would total 69 weeks-of-years or 483 years. This prophecy was fulfilled in a marvelously accurate way.

There are only four decrees that might be taken as answering to "the commandment that went forth to . . . restore and build" Jerusalem:

a. The decree of Cyrus in 538 B.C. (2 Chr. 36:22-23; Ezra 1:2-4) — This decree authorized the building of the temple but did **not** include the authorization to restore the Jewish commonwealth. Mauro makes his case for *this* edict, citing Isaiah's prophecy (Isa. 44:24-28). Mauro also claims that to take any other decree than that of Cyrus indicates "that expositors have turned aside from the Scriptures, and have accepted, for the 500 years immediately preceding the coming of Christ, a defective chronology based upon heathen traditions," name-ly, those of the *Canon of Ptolemy*."[16] If, however, the "coming of an anointed one" (Jesus' ministry beginning in A.D. 26 is the ending date, the year 458-457 B.C. must be the beginning date. Furthermore, it appears that Cyrus issued a *generic* statement that Jerusalem and the temple *shall* be built. He does not include the *mandate* so emphatically given Ezra by Artaxerxes (Ezra 7:11-26) to *restore* the Jewish *laws, magistrates, and judges* which makes Judea a com-monwealth, not merely a province of Persia.

b. The decree of Darius, 518 B.C. — a decree continuing the building authorized by Cyrus which seems to have been hindered; it was a repetition of the first decree and did not authorize the reestablishment of the Jewish commonwealth (Ezra 4:4-5).

c. The decree of Artaxerxes, 458-457 B.C. — The seventh year of Artaxerxes' reign was 458-457 B.C. An exact copy of this decree is found in Ezra 7:11-26. It is written in Aramaic, which was spoken in Persia at that time. The rest of the book of Ezra is written in Hebrew. There is something very significant in the preservation of the *original language* of this decree and considering how much depended on it one must regard it as providential. By this decree permission was granted to Ezra to go up to Jerusalem, taking as many as he desired that were willing to go. It also granted him *unlimited* finances. It *empowered* him to ordain laws, set magistrates and judges who had authority to execute punish-ments, confiscations and banishments, and even the death penalty was included. In other words, by this decree Ezra was authorized to *restore the common-wealth*, and means were placed at his disposal to enable him to do so. We opt for this decree. It appears that the decree of Artaxerxes was the one regarded by Ezra (Ezra 6:14) as the "final word."

d. The fourth decree was given to Nehemiah ca. 444 B.C. The purpose of Nehemiah's going to Jerusalem was to assist in accomplishing the work under-taken by Ezra which was being retarded. He accomplished his mission in 52 days after his arrival at Jerusalem. It is doubtful that this was the "command-ment" which went forth to "restore and rebuild Jerusalem."

Smith makes a persuasive argument in *The MajorProphets* proposing "the com-mandment that went forth" was made by God through Ezra. "The reference is probably not to the decree of some Persian king, but to the command of God himself. . . . the word to restore Jerusalem would have been issued by God through Ezra in the year 457 B.C. . . . The year 457 B.C., then, is the *terminus a quo* for the seventy heptad prophecy."[17] He has a much more detailed discussion of this prophecy in *What the Bible Says about the Promised Messiah* but admits, "Though Scripture nowhere so states explicitly, it is surely reasonable to believe that Ezra must have issued the first command to rebuild Jerusalem."[18] One of Smith's objections to the 'traditional view" (i.e., the decree by Artaxerxes in Ezra 7) is that "the destruction of Jerusalem foretold in verses 26-27 must be removed from seventy sevens . . ." but he adds, "While the implication may be present that the seventy heptads terminate in the destruction of Jerusalem, the passage does not directly affirm such to be the case. The word *determined* in verses 26-27 may suggest that what would happen during the seventy heptads would seal the fate of Jerusalem, and of the Roman armies which would attack Jerusalem. Taken this way, the passage would not be saying that the desolations would take place during the seventy heptads, but only that they would be determined during that period."[19]

Taking the view that the last seven was one "week-of-years," i.e., seven literal years, and that the Messiah was "cut off" in the middle of that "week," and the "cutting off" was A.D. 30, making the destruction of Jerusalem the final event of the 490 years would necessitate the destruction of Jerusalem in A.D. 33-34 or 3½ years after the "cutting off" of the Anointed One. *But, Jerusalem was destroyed in A.D. 70, 37 years after the Messiah was "cut off."*

While we prefer the traditional view that the beginning marker was Artaxerxes "commandment" because permission was granted for pervasive independence for the Jewish commonwealth, the *crucial* matter is the *date* when the "word went forth."

Reckoning from 457 B.C., the first seven heptads (i.e., $7 \times 7 = 49$ weeks-of-years) would make the end of this first period 408 B.C. That date accords accurately with historic facts. Thus the work was completed in 49 years. This was accomplished in 'troubled times" (9:25 in Hebrew it is *vubetzoq haityim*, "oppressive, afflicting times") as the biblical record bears out in Nehemiah, Ezra, Haggai, Zechariah.

Reckoning from 408 B.C. through the next period of time, 62 heptads (62×7 weeks-of-years), or 434 years added to the 49, we come down to the year A.D. 26 as the ending date of the second period. That brings the timeline to the Messiah ("Anointed Leader"). Jesus was "anointed" by the Father at his baptism when the Holy Spirit descended upon him in the form of a dove and God said, "This is my beloved Son in whom I am well pleased." He was approximately 30 years of age. Here the second period of the "70 weeks-of-years" ended and 483 years would elapse beginning from 457 B.C.

The third period of the "70 weeks-of-years" consists of but one seven (or seven years). This is the ardently debated *70th week*. The text states that the *cutting off* of the "Anointed Leader" would cause "sacrifice and oblation to cease." The two events are coincidental; therefore his cutting off is determined to be "in the midst of the week" (i.e., in the midst of the last seven years). This *settles once for all* that the *70th week* is **not** waiting for Christ's second advent!

Dispensationalists are fond of using the illustration of a clock to promote their view of the 70th week. The ticking clock, they say, represents *Jewish* time. The church age *parenthesis* (now 2000 years long) is "time-out" because, they allege, God only counts time in dealing with Israel when the Israelite people are living in their land. Some add the further specification that time is counted only when "the people of Israel are governed by God." Neither of these requirements, according to dispensationalists, are met by the interval which they call the "church age." Consequently, they affirm the "clock ceased to tick" at the time of the triumphal entry of Christ into Jerusalem 30 A.D. They believe God's "clock" will not "tick" again until that moment, still future, when God resumes his direct dealings with Israel during the *millennium*. This will be when the Jews are once more in their own land. According to dispensationalists, the millennium will follow the *rapture* and be marked by the appearance of a resurrected Roman prince ("the" Antichrist). So, they conclude, those of us who live now in the so-called "church age" exist, as far as God's time clock" is concerned, in a sort of suspended animation, while God's "clock" has ceased to tick and God's time is at a standstill.[20]

None of this is found in the canonical Scriptures! It is all *apocryphal!* And a large portion of it has been copied from Jewish and so-called Christian apocrypha (A.D. 200-400). If the 69 weeks-of-years are exactly 483 consecutive years, exact to the very day, as dispensationalists admit, it is incredible to think that one week-of-years (i.e., seven years) has now taken 2000 years (and the "clock" is still not "ticking") to transpire! It seems inconceivable that an interval which is already more than 1900 years past, nearly four times as long as the period covered by the prophecy, is to be introduced into this whole prophecy and be allowed to interrupt its fulfillment. Some dispensationalists have contended that God's "clock" began "ticking" in 1948 when the modern nation of Israel was founded. One popular writer in this vein warned that since Israel was back in her land in 1948, and a "generation" is approximately 40 years, the world would experience the "tribulation and rapture" shortly after his book was published in 1988. DeMar states in *Last Days Madness*, "There is no *biblical* warrant for stopping Daniel's prophecy of the seventy weeks after the sixty-ninth week. *The idea of separation and an interminable gap is one of the most unnatural and non-literal interpretations of Scripture found in any eschatological system.* This interpretation is taught by those who insist on a literal hermeneutic."[21]

It seems much more plausible that since the 62 weeks are regarded as following directly on the first seven, that the last seven (the *70th week*) is to immediately follow the 62 "weeks." There are two very serious objections to the "Jewish time clock theory:" (1) Israel was still in the land for nearly 40 years after the death of Christ. In other words, Israel was still in the land for nearly 40 years (to A.D. 70) *after* the clock stopped "ticking;" and, (2) if the clock could only "tick" when Israel was "governed by God" can we say this condition was really fulfilled at any time during the period of the 69 weeks? The "times of the Gentiles" (dispensationalists mix Luke 21:24 in with Daniel's 70 weeks) are regarded by dispensationalists as beginning with Nebuchadnezzar's destruction of Jerusalem which began in 606 B.C. The exiles returned in 536 B.C. but except for a few years under Zerubbabel and a few years under the Hasmoneans, the Jews were successively ruled by foreign empires even though they remained in Palestine. Most of this entire period, then, was distinctly *not* a period when Israel was "governed by God." If the clock represents "Jewish" time, with Israel in the land and "governed by God," how then could it "tick" at all during the entire period from 606 B.C. to A.D. 30?

What most dispensationalists really have with such a theory is a *parenthesis* (i.e., the "times of the Gentiles" beginning with Nebuchadnezzar) within which they have placed *another parenthesis* (i.e., the so-called "church age"). By dispensational principles the one parenthesis is no more entitled to be called Jewish time than is the other. If the "clock" could "tick" during *part* of the "times of the Gentiles," obviously, it could "tick" during the *whole* of it! If the clock stops ticking at A.D. 30, instead of A.D. 70, it does so quite arbitrarily. For Israel continued to be in their land and under foreign rulers during those 40 years from A.D. 30 to 70, quite as much as from 457 B.C. to A.D. 30.

To sum up so far, the 70th week follows *immediately* upon the 69th week; there is *no parenthesis*! In the midst of the 70th week the Anointed One is *cut off.* That much we know. His "cutting off" and his "causing sacrifice and oblation to cease" are one and the same thing. When Jesus was nailed to the cross and died, the law of Moses in its entirety was fulfilled, completed, and the "bond which stood against us with its legal demands" was "set aside" and "nailed to the cross" with Christ (Col. 2:14-15; Eph. 2:15). The emphatic doctrine of the whole book of Hebrews is that Christ, by his death, abolished the sacrifices of the Old Covenant (e.g., Heb. 7:11; 8:13; 9:25-28; 10:8-9).

Christ was actually "cut off" in the "midst" of the *70th week.* He was crucified three and one-half years after the beginning of his public ministry, in the spring of A.D. 30, thus fulfilling this part of the prophecy to the letter!

Only the last half of the *70th week* (3½ years) is left to be accounted for. The gospel *privileges* were, with only a few exceptions like the centurion Cornelius, *limited* to the Jews for approximately 3½ years after the death of Christ. After that, ca. A.D. 34, Paul took the gospel to the Gentiles. This may be determined from the record of events taking place *after* (Acts 8:1–13:52; esp. Acts 13:46-48) Christ's death and resurrection. This three and one-half years fulfilled the last half of the *70th week* and the prophecy that the Jews would be allotted 490 years is *finished*! All that remained for the Jews was about 35 years of God's grace before his "*wrath unto the end*" came upon them (1 Thess. 2:14-16; see also Matt. 23:34-39; 24:1-35).

The text predicts "the people of the *prince* who is to come shall destroy the city." We take this to mean that the *people* of the *prince* of verse 25 (the Messiah) shall destroy their own city. Some commentators think "the prince who is to come" is the Roman general, i.e., Titus Vespasian, who with his Roman armies accomplished the final destruction of Jerusalem. Thus, this predicted desolation of Jerusalem forces the termination of the *70th week* to be in A.D. 70. While we believe verses 26 and 27 predict this *final* "desolation" of Jerusalem in A.D. 70, we do not believe it necessary to find the termination of the 70th week in this destruction. The destruction was a *consequence* of the Jews "cutting off" their Anointed One, but the accomplishment of the destruction itself was extended by God to a time beyond the strict limits of the 70th week. Allis writes:

> None of the predictions of desolation and vengeance contained in these verses (9:26-27) can be regarded as so definitely included in the program outlined in vs. 24 that we can assert with confidence that they must be regarded as fulfilled within the compass of the 70 weeks. They are consequences of the cutting off; they may be regarded as involved in it, but their accomplishment may extend . . . beyond the strict limit of 70 weeks, since the destruction of Jerusalem was much more than three and a half years after the crucifixion.[22]

It is, after all, Jesus who "comes" with power on the clouds of heaven (see Matt. 26:64), and God the Father (Matt. 22:7), to "destroy those murderers and burn their city." See also our comments in this work on Matthew 24:29-35; Mark 13:24-31; Luke 21:25-33).

Daniel lends to the difficulty of interpreting the passage when he uses the Hebrew words *sar* and *nagid* for "prince" interchangeably throughout his book whether they be heathen or Jewish. Josephus interprets the destruction of Jerusalem (mainly by the Jews themselves) as a fulfillment of this prophecy of Daniel! He wrote, "In the very same manner Daniel also wrote concerning the Roman government, and that our country should be made desolate by them."[23] But Josephus also records that much of the destruction of the city was done by the Jews themselves as they fought one another.[24] The Romans besieged the city, intermittently, for three years beginning in A.D. 66 before they assaulted and overwhelmed it. Inside the city violent wars ensued between various Jewish factions killing one another and burning food supplies and razing buildings. One faction of Jews set fire to the temple. Then, in A.D. 70, "upon the wing of abominations [came] one who [made] desolate, until the decreed end [was] poured out . . . ." *That* was Titus Vespasian.

There can be no doubt that God intended to bring the Jewish dispensation to an end. The Old Testament predicts its own end in a number of places.[25] The apostle Paul indicated God's *finale* was *already* come upon the Jews when he wrote 1 Thessalonians, for in chapter two, verse 16 of that book Paul uses the Greek word *telos* explaining that God's wrath had come upon them fully, completely, at last. Paul is undoubtedly referring to the destruction of Jerusalem 20 years hence from the time he wrote 1 Thessalonians. So, Daniel anticipates the coming end of Judaism by saying, "Its end shall come with a flood, and to the end there shall be war . . . ."

An important part of Daniel's prediction is that *during the 70th week* the Messiah will make a firm covenant with many. Jesus spoke of his "blood of the covenant" which was to be "poured out for *many*" (Matt. 26:28). The Hebrew word translated *firm* (RSV) and *confirm* (KJV) is *gabar* which is often translated "mighty, powerful, strong, prevailing." It is the same word used by Isaiah (Isa. 9:6) to name the coming Messiah, "Mighty (Warrior) God." The English version translates verse 27, "And he shall make a strong covenant with many *for* one week . . . ." There is no preposition in the Hebrew text; "for" is a supplied word. Certainly Jesus Christ did not confirm his New Covenant *for* only one week. It would be more correct to supply the word *during* for it was *during* the 70th week (in the "midst" of it) that Christ confirmed his New Covenant. When the Anointed One of God was "cut off" and raised from the dead he mightily confirmed the covenant made with Abraham (Rom. 15:8) by which all the nations of the earth would be blessed.

Daniel has given in this passage (9:24-27) an encapsulation of the time and manner by which God is going to fulfill his cosmic redemptive plan typified, symbolized and predicted in the patriarchs, the law of Moses, and the prophets. *This is one of the most amazing and significant prophecies in all the Bible.* It was given to the Jews centuries before its fulfillment so they might "be wise" and be ready to endure the 490 years of "trouble" (detailed in Dan. 11:1–12:13) until their Messiah came. It was also given so that Jews who were "wise" would understand the Old dispensation was earthly and perishing (Col. 2:20-23). In the six objectives of 9:24, Daniel emphasized the *spiritual* essence of the New covenant to be *empowered* by the Anointed Prince to come.

Dispensational View of Daniel 9:24-27
"The Seventy Weeks of Years"

1. 483 yrs. (from 457 B.C. to A.D. 26)
2. Then God quits counting on the 490 years (or 70 7s)
3. The last week (or 70th 7) is yet future

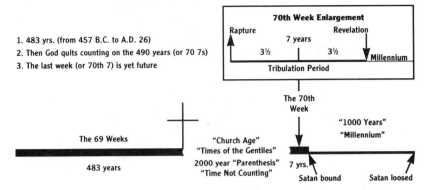

70th Week Enlargement

Rapture — 7 years — Revelation

3½ — 3½ — Millennium

Tribulation Period

The 70th Week

The 69 Weeks

"Church Age"
"Times of the Gentiles"

"1000 Years"
"Millennium"

483 years

2000 year "Parenthesis"
"Time Not Counting"

7 yrs.

Satan bound — Satan loosed

Author's View of Daniel 9:24-27

"Seventy weeks of years are decreed concerning your people and your holy city . . ."

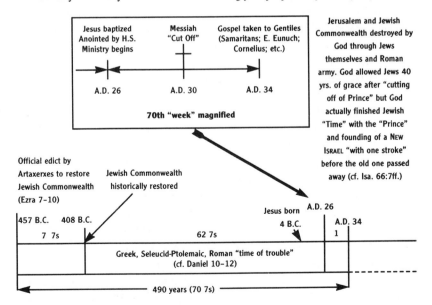

Jesus baptized
Anointed by H.S.
Ministry begins

Messiah
"Cut Off"

Gospel taken to Gentiles
(Samaritans; E. Eunuch;
Cornelius; etc.)

A.D. 26 — A.D. 30 — A.D. 34

70th "week" magnified

Jerusalem and Jewish Commonwealth destroyed by God through Jews themselves and Roman army. God allowed Jews 40 yrs. of grace after "cutting off of Prince" but God actually finished Jewish "Time" with the "Prince" and founding of a NEW ISRAEL "with one stroke" before the old one passed away (cf. Isa. 66:7ff.)

Official edict by Artaxerxes to restore Jewish Commonwealth (Ezra 7–10)

Jewish Commonwealth historically restored

Jesus born
4 B.C.

A.D. 26

A.D. 34

457 B.C.   408 B.C.

1

7 7s

62 7s

Greek, Seleucid-Ptolemaic, Roman "time of trouble"
(cf. Daniel 10–12)

490 years (70 7s)

"And for half of the week he shall cause sacrifice and offering to cease . . . ." (RSV) is not a good translation of this phrase. The Hebrew text has the word *vachªtsi* which means literally, "and in the middle or half." A more correct translation is "and in the midst of the week he shall cause the sacrifice and the oblation to cease" (KJV). It could very well be translated, "at the middle." That would fit the context and what the rest of the Bible says about the Messiah's atonement. The substitutionary atonement of the Suffering Servant of God was to be an "everlasting" covenant and it would become efficacious when the Messiah was "cut off." The NASB translates it correctly, ". . . but in the middle of the week he will put a stop to sacrifice and grain offering . . . ." The LXX translates the phrase, *kai en tō hēmisei tēs hebdomados*, or, "in the midst of the week . . . ."

From predicting the new covenant which the "Prince" (Messiah) will make to take away sacrifice and offering, Daniel turns once again to predict more about the destruction of Jerusalem. In the final phrase of chapter nine, Daniel predicts, "upon the wing of abominations [plural] shall come one who makes desolate." Unquestionably that was the Roman legions under Titus Vespasian in A.D. 70. Their very presence around and in the city, with their idolatrous standards deifying Caesar, would make them "abominable." Josephus describes how, once they penetrated the walls and entered the city, they desecrated the temple. They made obscene remarks about it and did obscene actions in it and began systematically to burn all that was left that would burn and to tear it down stone by stone. Jesus foretold the Roman invasion of the temple would be "the abomination" which Daniel predicted (Matt. 24:25; Luke 21:20-24). Daniel also predicted God had "decreed an end" to be "poured out on the desolator." The "desolator" is Rome, and Daniel had already predicted the demise of Rome, the "fourth" beast (7:26).

Daniel brings his predictions concerning the "four great beasts" (7:11–9:27) to a significant conclusion with the prophecy of the 70 weeks-of-years. He will proceed in the next section (10:1–12:13) to amplify the 490 years of "trouble" the Jewish people must endure until the "indignation is accomplished" (11:36) and "the time of the end" (12:9), i.e., the arrival of the Messiah and his blessings in the "latter days" (Joel 2:28ff; Hos. 3:5; Isa. 2:2; Micah 5:2-3, et al.).

Contextually there is not the slightest hint that the 70 weeks-of-years has anything to say about a 2000 year long "church age" *parenthesis* (or longer) beginning with the "cutting off" of the Messiah. Nor does Daniel 9:24-27 indicate the *70th week* will be "seven years of tribulation" preceded by a "rapture" of the church and ending with the institution of a millennial reign of Jesus Christ upon the earth. In this section Daniel has predicted the **first coming** of the Messiah which is called in the New Testament the "close of the age" (Matt. 24:3) or "the end of the ages"

(1 Cor. 10:11). Indeed, as Daniel has predicted, **the consummation of the ages** came when the Anointed One of God was cut off and empowered his everlasting covenant. Most of the Jews of the first century would not believe that, so God literally left their house "forsaken and desolate" (Matt. 23:38) to confirm in history the predictions of Daniel and his fellow prophets.

The tragic intransigence of many Jews to acknowledge the fulfillment of Daniel 9:24-27 in the person of Jesus Christ is illustrated in a portion of the Talmud prohibiting the teaching of the book of Daniel:

> In Ketubot we read that "the prophets shall not make known the end" and Rabbi Jonathan says in Sanhedrin "Blasted be the bones of those who calculate the end." Rabbi Jonathan ben Uzziah is even rebuked by a voice from Heaven (a Bat Kol) because he "reveals my secrets" and *he is prevented from teaching on the book of Daniel because "The date of the Messiah is in it."* [emphasis ours]. It could . . . mean that study of this passage by later readers might suggest that the Messiah had already come. [26]

Notes

[1] Paul T. Butler, *Daniel*, 3rd Edition (Joplin, MO: College Press, 1982).

[2] For the date of Belshazzar's reign see, Charles F. Pfieffer, *Exile and Return* (Grand Rapids: Baker, 1962), pp. 84-88.

[3] Gaius Suetonius Tranquillus, *The Twelve Caesars*, trans. Robert Graves (New York: Penguin Books, 1957), p. 295.

[4] Ibid., p. 295.

[5] William L. Langer, *An Encyclopedia of World History* (Cambridge, MA: Houghton-Mifflin, 1952), p. 109.

[6] Suetonius, *The Twelve Caesars*, p. 304.

[7] Will Durant, *The Story of Civilization, III, Caesar and Christ* (New York: Simon & Schuster, 1944), pp. 291-292.

[8] Suetonius, *The Twelve Caesars*, pp. 240-241.

[9] Ibid., pp. 295-309.

[10] For a more detailed account of this history see Butler, *Daniel,* pp. 290-316.

[11] Tom Burnam, *The Dictionary of Misinformation* (New York: Thomas Y. Crowell, 1975), p. 4.

[12] Keil and Delitzsch, *Daniel,* Commentaries on The Old Testament (Grand Rapids: Eerdmans, 1971), p. 304.

[13] Ibid., pp. 306-308.

[14] Butler, *Daniel,* pp. 205-206.

[15] Oswald T. Allis, *Prophecy and The Church* (Philadelphia: The Presbyterian and Reformed, 1945), pp. 112-113.

[16] Philip Mauro, *The Wonders of Bible Chronology* (Swengel, PA: Bible Truth Depot, 1961, pp. 86-99.

[17]James E. Smith, *The Major Prophets* (Joplin, MO: College Press, 1992), pp. 606-607.

[18]James E. Smith, *What the Bible Says about the Promised Messiah* (Joplin, MO: College Press, 1984), p. 396.

[19]Ibid., p. 390.

[20]Allis, *Prophecy,* pp. 111-128, notes pp. 306-311 and pp. 192-217, Notes pp. 317-321.

[21]DeMar, *Last Days Madness,* p. 58.

[22]Allis, *Prophecy,* pp. 114-115.

[23]Flavius Josephus, *Antiquities of the Jews,* X. XI. 7, trans. William Whiston (Philadelphia: The John C. Whiston Co., 1737).

[24]Josephus, *Wars of The Jews,* VI. II. 9, 10; VI. III. 1-5.

[25]See our comments on Isaiah 66:1-24 in Paul T. Butler, *Isaiah,* Vol. III (Joplin, MO: College Press, 1990); see also Jeremiah 3:16; Daniel 12:7.

[26]Rev. M.G. Bowler, M.A., B.D., *The Hebrew Christian,* Vol. LIII, No. 2, The Quarterly Organ of The International Hebrew Christian Alliance, Summer 1980, 45.

chapter 6

THE KINGS OF THE
NORTH AND SOUTH

Daniel 10:1-21

The last three chapters of the book of Daniel form a *unit* which Daniel literally calls a "word" that was revealed to him. The LXX translates the Hebrew word *galah* ("uncover, reveal") into the Greek word, *apokalypto*, from the same word that forms the title of the NT book *Revelation*. Chapter 10 is introductory, chapter 11 is the main body, and chapter 12 is the conclusion of the "revelation." This is the *last* revelation of all the astounding things to come upon the OT covenant people prior to the **consummation of the ages** which would usher in the Messianic Age. Daniel's *last* revelation is going to fill in numerous *details* of the "time of trouble" which the Jewish people would have to endure before the "Anointed Prince" arrived on the scene.

A very powerful "messenger" from God (an angel) gave Daniel this revelation. This angel had been sent to Daniel after he had finished struggling with "the prince of the kingdom of Persia" which had been trying to withstand God's messenger. Evidently the messenger of God had been engaged in spiritual combat against an evil spirit for the mind and will of the ruling dynasty of Persia. Zechariah 1:1–6:15 describes the cosmic warfare that went on as God was protecting the covenant remnant of the Jews. Zechariah saw in a vision "horsemen" sent to patrol the earth; "smiths" to cast down the "horns" (i.e., powers) of the nations; God "shaking" his hand over the nations so that they would give material aid for the Jews to restore and rebuild Jerusalem; God sanctifying a Jewish high priest for restored worship; wickedness purged from the land; and a résumé of it all in chapter six. All these visions were fulfilled initially in the restoration of the Jewish commonwealth beginning in 457 B.C. but were ultimately fulfilled in the Messiah (cf. Zech. 6:12-15).

The high priest and his fellows were to be for a sign that God would fulfill their true significance in the Branch (3:8). Isaiah had introduced Him as "a shoot out of the stock of Jesse" (11:1), as "the root of Jesse" unto whom the nations would seek (v. 10). Jeremiah had further identified Him as "a Branch of righteousness" who would "grow up unto David" and who would "execute justice and righteousness in the land" (33:15). [1]

All of Zechariah's visions are *apocalyptic* symbols (revelations) of the providential work of God as he continued in history to produce the Messianic covenant he had made with Abraham. Zechariah's visions correlate precisely with Daniel's *last* revelation. God's messenger and message prevailed, for Cyrus and Darius (Dan. 10:13,20; 1:1) and their successors freed the Jewish exiles and gave them finances to return and rebuild their commonwealth (see Ezra, Nehemiah, Haggai, and Zechariah).

God's messenger was sent to Daniel to give him specific instructions from "the book of truth" (10:21). This gave Daniel some understanding of what would happen to the Jewish people "in the latter days" (10:14). And, as Daniel introduces the revelation, he says it was "true, and it was a great conflict" (10:1). Daniel was told that God's celestial powers would continue to "fight against" opposition to the restoration of the Messianic program through both *Persian* and *Greek* regimes (10:20). As we have seen in this study, the term "latter days" in OT prophecy always refers to the Messianic Age — the **first** advent of the Messiah — *not* the second advent. Daniel was reminded over and over in this *last* revelation that it was for "the time of the end," "till the indignation was accomplished," "for the time appointed," and "for the end of the days" (11:35,36; 12:4,7,9,13).

Daniel 11:1-45

The angel from God begins to give Daniel the main body of the *last* revelation. Three more kings were to arise *after* Cyrus: (1) Cambyses (Cyrus' son) who would die of a wound accidentally self-inflicted when mounting his horse; (2) Gaumata (called Pseudo-Smerdis) who claimed to be the brother of Cambyses — he was taken prisoner and executed; and (3) Darius Hystaspis whose claim to the throne was considered by many of his contemporaries a usurpation. The Behistun inscription was deciphered in 1835 by Sir Henry Rawlinson, about 200 miles northeast of Babylon. It was an inscription engraved ca. 516 B.C., by order of Darius Hystaspis in the Persian, Elamite and Babylonian languages. The account shows the pains which Darius Hystaspis took to prove that he was the heir of the dynasty of Achemenes. It also records Darius' conquests of Asia Minor, large portions of India, and Egypt. But he was defeated when he tried to conquer Greece. Darius Hystaspis was a great administrator of the Persian empire which reached its peak of power and influence during his reign. For more detail concerning these rulers see our commentary on *Daniel*, pp. 406-410.

Daniel is told that "a fourth" king would arise in Persia, "far richer than all of them" and he would attempt what Darius was unable to do — conquer Greece. This was Xerxes (in Ezra and Esther he is named Ahasuerus). He was murdered by an assassin, Artabanus, who reigned seven months and was, in turn assassinated by Artaxerxes, the third son and legitimate heir of Xerxes. From the time of Artaxerxes the strength of the Persian empire began to wane, and was finally overwhelmed by Alexander the Great (see notes on chapters 7 and 8).

The "mighty king" (11:3) who was to rule "with great dominion" was Alexander the Great. He would no sooner "arise" than his kingdom would "be broken and divided toward the four winds of heaven." His kingdom would not pass to "his posterity" nor would it ever be united again "according to the dominion with which he ruled" (11:4). When Alexander died in 323 B.C., he left no heir. A son was posthumously born to Roxane, Alexander's Bactrian wife, but the *Diadochoi* ("successors") of Alexander seized power before he could reach maturity. One of the *Diadochoi*, Cassander, murdered Roxane and her son. Alexander had many able generals, but there was not one that arose with enough power to assume rule of the empire. By 315 B.C., after seven years of struggle, four outstanding leaders appeared: Antigonus, Cassander, Ptolemy Lagi, and Lysimachus. We have detailed their hegemonies in comments on chapter 8. In 301 B.C. after much fighting between these four "kings," Antigonus died on the battlefield and his suzerainty (Syria and Palestine) was given to *Seleucus*, one of the generals in Ptolemy's army.

It is nothing short of supernatural and miraculous to observe how the *actual history* of this period and these people, in this part of the world, confirm in minute detail the prophecies here made by Daniel some 300 years before it transpired! Its actual fulfillment to the letter is the one factor motivating the destructive critics of the Bible to place the book of Daniel as late as the 2nd century B.C. For if the book of Daniel was written near 600-500 B.C., his prediction of these details of history, which could only have happened to the Ptolemies and Seleucids, is proof positive of supernatural revelation!

Daniel 11:5-6: This prophecy concerns Ptolemy I (the "king of the south" or Egypt) and Seleucus Nicator, Ptolemy's general (the "king of the north"), who was given rule over Syria-Palestine. As a matter of actual historical fact, the dominion of the Seleucids did greatly exceed that of the Ptolemies. It reached from Asia Minor in the west to the Indus River in India on the east. Ptolemy I was succeeded by his son Ptolemy II (Philadelphus) in 283 B.C. Two years later, 281 B.C., Seleucus Nicator was murdered and succeeded by his son, Antiochus I. In 275 B.C., Ptolemy II invaded Syria and was repulsed by the Seleucid forces. Ptolemy's naval power, however, enabled him to prolong the war. Hostilities ceased in 272-271 B.C. without a decisive victory for either side. When Antiochus II (261-246) succeeded his father to the Syrian throne, war broke out again. Again the results were indecisive, and peace was concluded in 252 B.C. At this time Berenice, the daughter of Ptolemy II (the "king of the south"), was married to Antiochus II (the "king of the north"), for political purposes. But Antiochus was already married to Laodice, who had given him two sons, Seleucus II (also known as Callinicus), and Antiochus III. Berenice was brought to Antiochus in great pomp. Two years later Ptolemy II died, and Antiochus divorced Berenice, taking back Laodice. Laodice, fearing lest her husband might again turn to Berenice, had him poisoned and encouraged her son Seleucus II to murder both Berenice and her infant, thus obtaining the throne for himself. Daniel knows the intrigues of political marriages between two powerful enemies of God's covenant people centuries in advance of their occurrence!

Daniel 11:7-9: "[A] branch from her roots . . . ." concerns Berenice's Ptolemaic family "roots." In 246 B.C. Antiochus II was murdered and his son Seleucus II succeeded him. In 245 B.C., Ptolemy II died and was succeeded by Ptolemy III (Euergetes). Ptolemy III was the brother of Berenice. Thus is fulfilled the prophecy that "a branch from her roots" (i.e., from her ancestry) will stand in the place of Ptolemy II (Philadelphus). Daniel knew some 300 years before the event, that even in the midst of wars and political intrigue, it would *not* be a usurper who would take the throne of Egypt but "a branch from" Berenice's "roots" — another Ptolemy. When war broke out again between the Seleucids and the Ptolemies, it was learned that Berenice, with her infant son, had been murdered. The murder of the daughter and grandson of Ptolemy II was an outrage to the honor of the Ptolemies and resulted in the "Laodicean War." After a series of brilliant victories in which Syria was completely subjugated, Ptolemy III was called back to Egypt to care for a local problem. "The king of the north," Seleucus II, marched against Ptolemy III (11:9) again ca. 240 B.C. but was soundly defeated. Peace was concluded and no further attacks were made on Syria during Ptolemy III's reign. He died in 221 B.C. and was succeeded by Ptolemy IV (Philopater), one of the worst of the house of Ptolemy. Seleucus II was succeeded, in 226, by Seleucus III, who died by poison, and he in turn was succeeded by his younger brother who is known as Antiochus III, or, Antiochus "the Great."

Daniel 11:10-20: "His sons . . . ." are the sons of Seleucus II, Seleucus III and Antiochus III, who became the "king of the north" when he was only 18 years of age. Daniel predicted that one of the two sons would campaign against the "king of the south." History actually records that Antiochus III attempted an invasion of Palestine (held by Ptolemy IV) in the summer of 221 B.C. He did not get very far until he was forced to withdraw by the Egyptian forces in Syria. Antiochus III invaded Palestine again in 219 B.C., and Ptolemy's general deserted and joined Antiochus's ranks, delivering to his new sovereign the cities of Acre and Tyre. There were more skirmishes until Antiochus had conquered (217 B.C.) all of Palestine and had reached the Egyptian frontier town of Raphia. An Egyptian army under the personal command of Ptolemy IV met the Syrians south of Raphia. Here the armies of Antiochus met a disastrous defeat (11:11). Ptolemy IV was too much of a braggart and a rake (11:12) to utilize his victory to the fullest and died in 203 B.C. from a life of luxury and dissolution.

Meanwhile, Antiochus III was busy making plans to annex Palestine. He gathered a vast army and better equipment than before and launched an attack (11:13). The son of Ptolemy IV, only a child of four, was Egypt's titular ruler, and Egypt was rent with turmoil and rebellion . The phrase, "he shall come on at the end of the times, *even of years* . . . ." (ASV) does not refer to any alleged "Antichrist" coming at the end of the world but simply describes the years intervening between Antiochus's defeat by Ptolemy IV and Antiochus's victory at Panion (also known as Caesarea Philippi). Antiochus III made a league with the Macedonians, had the help of the malcontents in Egypt, and had the support of certain violent and factious Jews whose aid to their enemy eventually brought trouble upon their country (11:14). He besieged the Egyptian forces at Sidon and in the spring of 198 B.C., the Egyptians were compelled to surrender, leaving the whole of Syria (including Palestine — "the glorious land") in the hands of Antiochus III (11:15-16). Antiochus III came to Jerusalem where, according to Josephus,[2] the inhabitants gave him a cordial welcome. Antiochus had complete control of the land of Palestine and its people. Antiochus III "set his face" to throw all the power and cunning he possessed against Egypt to conquer her. God knows the schemes of men before they are carried out. God knew Antiochus III would plot to give his daughter in marriage to Ptolemy V (204-181 B.C.), the "king of the south," to corrupt him. Secular history states that in 198 B.C. Antiochus III betrothed his daughter Cleopatra to Ptolemy V, who was then only seven years of age. The marriage was not consummated until five years later. Antiochus hoped by this stratagem to gain an advantage over the king of Egypt. He trusted his daughter to be her father's ally. But, as history records, Cleopatra constantly sided with her husband, Ptolemy V, against her father; fulfilling the words, "she shall not stand, neither be for him" (11:17).

When Hannibal was defeated by the Romans at Zama (202 B.C.) he fled eastward and took refuge in the court of Antiochus III. Hannibal encouraged Antiochus to invade Greece (11:18). Rome thereupon declared war on Antiochus, moved into Greece, defeated Antiochus in Macedonia and forced him to retreat back across the Aegean Sea to Asia Minor. Rome moved into Asia Minor, where the brilliant Roman general, Cornelius Scipio, defeated Antiochus (190 B.C.) at Magnesia (between Sardis and Smyrna) (11:19). Antiochus paid an enormous indemnity to Rome, surrendered his war elephants and his navy, and his younger son, Antiochus IV was taken to Rome as hostage in partial payment of the indemnity. Antiochus marched against the Armenians (187 B.C.) and attempted to plunder their temple where both he and his soldiers were slain by the Elamites.

Next to rule Syria (the "king of the north") was Seleucus IV (187-175), son of Antiochus III and brother of Antiochus IV (who was away at Rome as a hostage). Rome dominated the defeated Syrians and demanded an enormous tribute of a thousand talents annually. Syria, in turn, exacted heavy taxes from its tributary nations (including the Jews in Palestine). A special tax collector by the name of Heliodorus (cf. 2 Macc. 7) was sent by Seleucus IV (11:20) to appropriate the rich treasure of the temple at Jerusalem. Archaeology has confirmed the position of Heliodorus as prime minister at this juncture in Syria's history. After a short time on the throne of Syria, Seleucus IV was suddenly and mysteriously removed, possibly through poisoning administered, according to Appian, by Heliodorus. Daniel had predicted "a time of trouble" (Dan. 9:25) to come upon the Jews after the Persians would allow them to restore Jerusalem. But thus far in Daniel's prophecy, the troublous times are mild compared with what was to come under the "Contemptible One," Antiochus IV, who is next on the scene.

Daniel 11:21-28: The first twenty verses of Daniel 11 merely set the stage for the escapades of the "Contemptible One." Antiochus IV (175-164 B.C.) spent 12 years as a hostage in the city of Rome. There he learned to live and rule as the Romans did. He called himself, "Epiphanes" ("the Illustrious One"). The Jews called him, "Epimanes," ("the Mad One"). The term "Contemptible One" probably has reference to his nonroyal lineage and illegal usurpation of the Syrian throne. There were three possible aspirants to the throne of Syria: Demetrius I, son of Seleucus IV and nephew of Antiochus Epiphanes (Demetrius I had been taken to Rome as a hostage and remained there, so he was not likely to take the throne of Syria); the younger brother of Demetrius I, a very young child also named Antiochus; and Antiochus (Epiphanes) IV. When Seleucus IV died, his brother, Antiochus IV, was at Athens, Greece. Immediately, Antiochus IV returned to Syria and posed as the "guardian" of the "heir apparent," the boy-prince Antiochus. When the boy-prince was murdered by a man named Andronicus, Antiochus IV promptly put Andronicus to death. Through intrigue and flattery, (11:21) Antiochus IV won the king of Pergamum to his assumption to the throne, and the Syrians gave in peaceably.

Antiochus IV attempted three invasions of Egyptian territories; the first ca. 174 B.C. (11:22); the second, 170 B.C. (11:23); and the third, 168 B.C. (11:25). Antiochus subjugated the Jews, of course, in his obsession to conquer all that territory, including Egypt. In these troublous times the Syrian army made Palestine little more than a "no-man's-land." Many Jews decided that survival was more important than Jewish culture and religious orthodoxy. Some Jews welcomed the conquest of their land and adopted the Syrian-Greek lifestyle. A gymnasium was built in Jerusalem and young Jewish men exercised there in the nude. Greek names were adopted in place of the Jewish names for both people and cities. A man named Jason bribed Antiochus IV to depose the Jewish High Priest, Onias II, and Jason secured the position for himself. Jason (who had changed his name from Joshua to Jason) encouraged the Hellenizing of Palestine.

Antiochus, campaigning against Egypt, by intrigue, deceit, and flattery won a significant victory at Pelusium and subsequently captured Memphis and all of northern and central Egypt. He deceived two royal Egyptian princes (his nephews) and played one against the other, and was thus able to do what his royal Syrian predecessors were unable to do (11:24) — control a part of Egypt.

Antiochus IV left Egypt to quell a revolt in another part of his vast kingdom. While he was gone, the Ptolemy princes began to regain control of northern and central Egypt. So Antiochus (the "king of the north") raised a great army and went against the Ptolemies (the "kings of the south") a second time (11:25). In this expedition Antiochus came as close as he ever came to subduing the empire of the Ptolemies. The Ptolemies, fighting among themselves to gain the rule of Egypt (11:26), were soundly defeated by Antiochus IV. Antiochus and Ptolemy (Philometor) called a truce and met at the conference table. But they were lying to one another (11:27) and there was really no "truce" intended by either one. The phrase "for the end is yet to be at the time appointed" is very significant here (11:27). The pretended truce "was of no avail" because "in the appointed time" of God it was not "yet" time for the end of the wars between Syria and Egypt (which were bringing such "troublous times" upon the covenant people). Daniel had already predicted the Jews would have "troublous times" until the end of the "sixty-nine sevens" (cf. Dan. 9:24-27). The trouble for the Jews would come to an end in the "seventieth-seven" when the "Anointed Prince" would be "cut off." Peace for the troubled saints of God was to be found in the Messiah. Physical circumstances were to have no bearing upon the end of "troublous times" except to mark the point in history where the

Messiah would be ushered into the world. And that would be the end of the Syrian and Egyptian struggles and the beginning of the Roman era (the fourth kingdom of Dan. 2:44; 7:7-27).

After apparent success (history later proved to be temporary) and laden with the spoils of conquest, Antiochus returned to his own land (11:28). A part of his land was now "the glorious land" (the Jews' homeland), and Antiochus IV had to pass through Palestine to get to Syria proper. In the phrase ". . . his heart shall be set against the holy covenant. And he shall work his will . . . ." is the prediction of a burning hatred in Antiochus against the Jews. First Maccabees 1:20-28 records his plundering of the Holy Land. This prophecy by Daniel was intended to let the Jews understand that the evil machinations of Antiochus IV were only temporary and in the appointed time of God they would come to an end.

Daniel 11:29-39: This section details the *finale* in the life of Antiochus IV. Some exegetes believe that at verse 36 Daniel is predicting "The Antichrist" to come, supposedly, at the end of the Christian age and the alleged "beginning of the seven years of tribulation" after the church has been "raptured." We shall discuss this view later.

"At the time appointed" (11:29) is simply a reference to God's providential schedule for "the kings of the north and the kings of the south" — especially for Antiochus IV. The third expedition of Antiochus IV against Egypt ("the kings of the south") took place in the spring of 168 B.C. This expedition would be quite unlike the former ones. "Ships of Kittim" (11:30) is metaphorical for any military forces that might come toward Syria from the *west*. It is undoubtedly a prediction that was fulfilled when the Roman legate confronted Antiochus IV. What happened to Antiochus IV on this third expedition to conquer Egypt is a famous historical episode that has often been retold. C. Popillius Laenas headed the Roman embassy at the time when it encountered Antiochus besieging Alexandria. The Roman legate apprised him of the demand of the Roman emperor and senate that he leave Egypt immediately and return to his own land. Antiochus hesitated, so the Roman official drew a circle in the sand around Antiochus and told him curtly that his decision must be reached before he stepped out of the circle. Should he decide to stay in Egypt, he was told, he would meet the Roman army in battle. Having lived in Rome as a young man for years, Antiochus knew well the strength and grandiose ambitions of Rome. Although humiliated and irate he decided "the better part of valor is discretion" and gave his word he would withdraw from Egypt immediately.

The rage he was unable to vent on Egypt is now turned against the people of Palestine (11:30). If Egypt was to remain a rival power outside his domain he found it more necessary than ever to retain his hold on Palestine. He dispatched Apollonius, his general, to occupy the city of Jerusalem. In a Sabbath attack, when he knew the orthodox Jews would not fight, he slaughtered large numbers of the Jews. The city walls were destroyed and a new fortress, the Akra, was built on the site of the citadel. Syrian forces were assisted by Menelaus and his apostate Jewish followers. Antiochus's forces "gave heed" to these Jewish apostates who had "forsaken the holy covenant." The Akra was garrisoned by a large force of Syrian soldiers to keep the Jews in submission for the paganizing policies of Antiochus. One of the darkest periods of Jewish history began (11:31). A systematic persecution was instituted to Hellenize the Jewish people by force. An edict demanded the fusion of all the nationalities of the Seleucid empire into one people. Greek deities were to be worshiped by all. An elderly Athenian philosopher was sent to Jerusalem to supervise the enforcement of the policy. He identified the God of Israel with Jupiter and ordered a bearded image of the pagan deity set up on the Jewish temple altar, which incidentally looked very much like Antiochus IV, himself. The Jews spoke of this as *"the abomination of desolation."* Syrian soldiers and harlots performed licentious heathen rites in the very temple courts. Swine were offered on the temple altar.[3] Drunken orgies associated with the worship of Bacchus (god of wine and revelry) were made compulsory. Conversely, the orthodox Jews were forbidden to practice circumcision, Sabbath observance, and observance of all the feasts of the Jewish year — upon penalty of death. Copies of the Hebrew Scriptures were ordered destroyed. This is documented in First Maccabees and the works of Josephus.

During this holocaust of persecution, Antiochus was able to "seduce" (Heb. *chanaph*, translated "corrupt" and "pollute" in KJV, used only in Num. 35:33; Psa. 106:38; Jer. 3:1,2) some Jews, both the cowardly and the ambitious, to "violate" or abandon their Hebrew covenant law and adopt idolatrous, pagan ways (11:32). But "the people who [knew] their God [would] stand firm and *take action*." In opposition to this paganization of their culture there arose a resistance movement among the Jews so zealous it became fanatical. The *maskilim* (11:33,35; 12:3,10 meaning "wise ones") swore to follow the ways of their forefathers, even welcoming death to do so. This caused consternation in the Syrian palace and Antiochus IV sought means by which to solve the "Jewish problem." An aged scribe named Eleazar was flogged to death because he refused to eat swine's flesh. A mother and her seven sons were successively butchered, in the presence of the Syrian governor for refusing to pay homage to an image. Two mothers who had circumcised their newborn sons were driven through the city and cast headlong from the top of Jerusalem's city wall. Such loyalty to God's law in the face of suffering served to fan the spark of righteous zeal in the hearts of the pious Jews and this would later ignite and burn into a flame in the Maccabean freedom-fighters.

Daniel's *maskilim* ("wise ones") were called the *Hasideans* (meaning, "righteous ones") in the era of the Jewish exile, probably during the very times being here predicted by Daniel (see 1 Macc. 1:63; 2:42; 7:13; 2 Macc. 6:18; 14:6; Judith 12:2; Josephus, *Ant.* XIV. iv. 3). The *Hasideans* were later called *Pharisees* (meaning "separated ones") in the New Testament era. These "wise ones" would teach others the faithful way of God, and many of them suffered much for their faith (see Heb. 11:32-40). The "little help" they would receive probably refers to Judas Maccabeus whose efforts were valiant enough, but he was never able to put an end to all the distresses of the people (cf. 1 Macc. 3:1ff; 4:14ff). Many Jews who did not really believe in the Maccabean struggle played the hypocrite and joined it for fear of being classified as apostates. The suffering this righteous remnant endured for its faith had a purging, purifying effect. It separated the hypocrites from the true righteous ones. And this purging process continued "until the time of the end" for it was yet for the "time appointed." God appointed the exact time when the *troublous times* (Dan. 9:25) would end. Their end came with the end of the Syrian domination and the occupation of Palestine by the "fourth kingdom" (Dan 2:44) at which time the 490 years would bring the "shattering of the power of the holy people" (Dan. 12:7) and the "Anointed Prince" would come and the "kingdom of God" would be instituted.

The predictions of Daniel 11:21-45 parallel and amplify the predictions of Daniel 8:18-27. That Daniel predicts this holocaust *twice* indicates it is indeed the point in God's redemptive program for the fulfilling of the "time appointed," the "time of the end," and the time "till the indignation is accomplished." Chapters 10 and 11 are clearly amplifications of chapters 8 and 9.

The "king" who shall "do according to his will" (11:36) is none other than Antiochus IV (the "king of the north") who is attacked by the "king of the south" (11:40). Numerous speculations have been offered to identify the "king" of 11:36 as one different than Antiochus IV, e.g., (a) Constantine the Great; (b) Omar ibn El-Khat-tab; (c) the Roman Empire; (d) a supposed Christian apostate also identified as the "little horn" of Daniel 7:8,20, who establishes his palace in Jerusalem, from which time runs the alleged "great tribulation," the last 3½ years of Daniel's 70th week (*Scofield Reference Bible*); (e) the alleged singular "Antichrist," an apostate Jew who will assume kingly honors, and be recognized by the Jewish apostates as the Messiah-King, and by the Christian apostates as the Antichrist who in the middle of the 70th week will come and take his seat in the Jerusalem temple and claim divine worship (Gaebelein); (f) the pope of the Roman Catholic religion; (h) Herod the Great, etc., etc. It is contrary to sound principles of *contextual* exegesis to suppose that, in a continuous description, with no indication whatever of a change of subject, part of this text (11:21-45) should refer to one person, and part to another, and that "the king" of verse 36 should be a different "king" from the one whose actions are described in verses 21-35. There would be no purpose served for Daniel to predict for those Jewish exiles the machinations of some Antichrist whose deeds some 2500 years later would have no relationship whatsoever to their present predicament or their future hope for a Messianic deliverance. The "king" of verse 36 cannot be the "little horn" of Daniel 7:8,20, which grew out of the fourth world empire (Rome) because this king very evidently grew out of the "he-goat" (Greece). Lange writes, "The king can be no other than the one hitherto represented, the anti-theistic persecutor of Israel, the king of the north, Antiochus Epiphanes. It is there-fore not Constantine the Great . . . or the Roman state as a whole, . . . or the New-Test. Antichrist — all of which interpretations contradict the context and arbitrarily interpose an hiatus of centuries between ver 35 and the closing verse of the chapter."[4] To apply this to Herod the Great would require an hiatus of nearly a cen-tury and a half between verses 35 and 36.

Antiochus IV conceived of himself as the only "god" and caused to be ascribed to himself the following: "King Antiochus, God, Manifest, Victory-bearer." He magnified himself above every "god" on earth, plundering temples at Jerusalem, Elymais and other places. He commanded that all national religious systems under his power should be united in one which he himself had decreed. He blasphemed the name of Jehovah in word and action.

Another scriptural parallel which ties "the king" of verse 36 to Antiochus IV is the phrase "the indignation" (11:36). Daniel 8:19 clearly indicates that "the indigna-tion" belongs *contextually* to the time of the successors of the *he-goat* (Greece). The power of Antiochus to "do according to his will" continued until the God-deter-mined end of the period of "indignation" which is the beginning of the end of the "troublous times" which will culminate with the "cutting off" of the "Anointed Prince" in Daniel 9:24-27. Antiochus IV, who had lived some years at Rome, learned to despise the Syrian gods, and prefer Jupiter, Lympius and Xenias of the Romans and Greeks. But secretly he had contempt for *all* religion except a "reli-gion" of military power. He inflicted gross indignity on the worship of the great goddess Nanea (Artemis) by attempting to plunder her temple in Elam or Persia (Elymais — 1 Macc. 6:1-4; 2 Macc. 9:2 — there is no contradiction in these two accounts, one is simply more specific than the other). Antiochus imbibed of the worship of war and conquest that so intoxicated the Romans (Rev. 6:2), and he courted and rewarded those Jewish apostates who would join him in his idolatrous devotion to power through violence (11:37-39).

"At the time of the end" (11:40) introduces, we believe, a *summarization* of the warlike career of Antiochus IV (Epiphanes) especially as it was directed against

Egypt and the Jews in the land of Judah. This section cannot be a prediction of Herod the Great as "the king of the south" for that would necessitate a "king of the north" (the Romans) rushing upon Herod like a whirlwind and this never occurred. This section recapitulates the life and death struggles between Syria and Egypt with the land of Judah in the middle. It reiterates that Antiochus was plundering peoples to the south of Syria but was eventually forced to a humiliating retreat taking his furious spite out upon the "glorious land" (the Jews) (2 Macc. 9:1-4). "But the all-seeing Lord, the God of Israel, struck him with an incurable and invisible blow." The death of Antiochus IV (164 B.C.) is described in vivid detail in Second Maccabees, concluding, "So the murderer and blasphemer, having endured the more intense suffering, such as he had inflicted on others came to the end of his life by a most pitiable fate, among the mountains in a strange land" (see 2 Macc. 9:5-29; 1 Macc. 6:8-17; see also Josephus, *Antiquities*, XII.9.1,2,3).

The heroic, bloody, Hasmonean (also called Maccabean) war for Jewish independence from Syria was begun in 167 B.C. by an aged priest named Mattathias. He had five sons: Judas, Jonathan, Simon, John and Eleazar. Mattathias died in 166 B.C. Leadership of the struggle passed to his eldest son Judas (1 Macc. 2:1ff) who was nicknamed "Maccabeus" which means "Hammer." Judas Maccabeus won battle after battle against incredible numbers of Syrian armies. He reconquered Jerusalem and purified and rededicated the temple of Jehovah on December 25, 165 B.C. The Feast of Dedication (Hanukkah) (cf. John 10:22) has been observed by Jews to this very day (also called "The Feast of Lights").[5] Antiochus IV died in 164 B.C. A wounded elephant fell on Eleazar during battle and killed him. Judas Maccabeus, with most of his army having deserted him, died bravely in battle (161 B.C.) near el-Bireh (Berea — not the Berea mentioned in Acts), opposite Ramalah, 10 miles north of Jerusalem (1 Macc. 9:1-18). Judas united the priestly and civil authority in himself, and established the Hasmonean dynasty which a few years later began to rule an independent Judean nation for the following 100 years. Judas was succeeded in the leadership of the Jews by his brother Jonathan. On Jonathan's death his brother, Simon, was installed as leader and high priest, and Judea was granted independence by Demetrius II (144 B.C.). At Simon's death in 135 B.C., John Hyrcanus, his son, became ruler, and corruption, intrigue, murder, chaos and abuse of the Jewish populace ensued and lasted until the Romans, under Pompey, invaded Palestine in 63 B.C. Palestine was then occupied by the Romans, the fourth world empire of Daniel 2:40-45; 7:7-27. Pompey appointed Antipater, an Idumean (Edomite) ruler of Judea. He was succeeded by his son Herod the Great who was made titular "king of the Jews" by Rome (37-4 B.C.). During this Roman era the "Anointed One" of God (the Messiah) was born (Dan. 9:25; Micah 5:2) and the "kingdom of God" was instituted.

Thus Daniel has, in fine detail, painted a panorama of history from the exile of the Jews and their release from Persia, through 490 years of troublous times, to the death of Antiochus IV, and the "end of the indignation" (the coming of the Messianic kingdom), and to the downfall of the "fourth kingdom." That is approximately one thousand years of history predicted and long since come to pass. If that will not substantiate the authenticity, credibility and claims to divine inspiration and inerrancy for the Bible, nothing will! God's message in this is that he will not desert his people and his holy covenant in any of the storms and changing events of the history or raging beastliness by heathen empires, but he will send deliverance in the precise moment he, himself, has determined. History is linear, and it is being guided inexorably, inevitably, toward the redemptive goal of Almighty God.

Daniel 12:1-13

What follows in chapter 12 is connected to the whole vision which began in chapter 10. This is hardly disputable since Daniel connects it by saying, "At *that* time . . . ." Chapter 12 is clearly connected to what has been predicted in chapters 9, 10, and 11 by words and phrases such as, "a time of trouble," "those who are wise," "the man clothed in linen," "when the shattering of the power of the holy people comes to an end," and "[m]any shall purify themselves, and make themselves white, and be refined." Disregard the imposed chapter and verse divisions, and read chapters 10 through 12 as one unit and observe the continuity of subject matter. Chapter 12 is the *epilogue* to all that Daniel has predicted concerning the time allotted by God to the Jewish nation for divine redemptive purposes.

The holocaust of human suffering under Antiochus IV and its termination is still the primary revelation being made to Daniel. For in the termination of this convulsion of "abomination" shall be the sign that the age of the Messiah and the eternal kingdom of God is beginning to rise on the horizon. That there shall be "a time of trouble, such as never has been . . . ." may, or may not be, hyperbole for communicative purposes. Surely, the troubles that came upon the Jewish people under the persecution of Antiochus IV surpassed any the Jewish nation had experienced until that time (war, degradation, humiliation, deprivation, apostasy, torture, death, desecration of their holy place — see 1 & 2 Macc., Josephus, Heb. 11:35-38). The Lord Jesus spoke of the Roman tribulation of A.D. 66-70 in the same terms (Matt 24:21) and that was no exaggeration.

The time of the end of God's "indignation" and their troubles with the "little horn" which arose from the "four horns" (Dan. 8:9, etc.) will be the *signal* that the time for establishing the predicted eternal kingdom of God has come. At *that* time all those who were true Israelites (the faithful remnant) would have been enrolled in "the book" of God and those who had remained faithful unto death would find deliverance. This *epilogue* may have both an initial, intermediate fulfillment and an ultimate fulfillment. Many OT prophecies do (e.g., Hos. 11:1; Isa. 7:14ff). While it may find its initial fulfillment in certain pious Jews delivered from physical death at the hands of the Syrians by the Maccabean revolt, it does not necessarily find its ultimate fulfillment in that.

Initially Daniel is predicting in 12:1-3 the events that would occur in the time of Antiochus. Many would be aroused to defend their faith as if called from the dust of the earth. They would be summoned by the Maccabean brothers from "wandering over deserts and mountains, and in dens and caves of the earth" (Heb. 11:38) and raised to honor and freedom from the yoke of heathen oppression. On the other hand, many of that era arose and attached themselves to Antiochus and the shame of idolatry and wickedness. The "wise" would continue walking in their "resurrection" to faithfulness to God and provide the remnant through which the Messiah would be born into the world and by whom he would institute his kingdom. Those who capitulated to heathenism in the days of Antiochus would provide the "seed" to bring forth a materialistic, hedonistic, self-righteous majority of Jews who would shamefully bring the judgment of God upon themselves for rejecting and crucifying the "Anointed One" of God!

The initial fulfillment of this prophecy was undoubtedly intended, also, to typify and teach the literal and final resurrection from the dead at which time those who are "wise" and have believed and accepted the Messiah will arise to everlasting life and those who are not, to everlasting shame. Bringing the *final* resurrection and damnation into view, even though typically and secondarily, would focus the thoughts of Jews who had faith in God's word far beyond the "troubles" and triumphs of the days of the Maccabees to the time when the rewards and retribution of eternity should occur. There are a few places in the OT prophets where a "resurrection" is spoken of in figurative terms, and with a possible *double* reference point (Isa. 25:6-12; 66:7-24; Ezek. 37:1-28; Hos. 6:2)

The angel revealing this to Daniel has passed in rapid succession from the "time of trouble" in the days of Antiochus IV (12:1), to the end of that trouble and "deliverance" to be accomplished in the first advent of the Messiah in 9:24-27, and thence to the final resurrection of the dead (12:2). In so doing, the angel has "shortened the perspective" of the redemptive time schedule through predictive prophecy (see an explanation of "shortened perspective" in Appendix A, p. 273). Widely separated events, often times separated by many centuries, are spoken of in unseparated succession in prophetic literature. Two successive verses in the same chapter may be divided by 700 unspoken centuries (e.g., Joel 2:27 and 2:28). The reason for unspoken centuries between the days of the prophets and the fulfillment of their predictions is the spiritual immaturity of their audiences. And this is no surprise, for Jesus and his apostles found spiritual immaturity a hindrance to apprehension of the OT prophets as well as the profound teachings of God in the New Testament! The aim of the angelic revelation is the birth of hope in the hearts of the Jews when they would be undergoing the "troublous times" of the 490 years after the return from their exile. There was no need to reveal or explain any of the history that should transpire between Christ and the end of time. Their *ultimate* deliverance, as well as ours, finds its accomplishment in the work of the "Anointed One" at his "cutting off" and the making of a "strong covenant" in the "midst of the 70th week." *That* is the work which is the **consummation of the ages** (1 Cor. 10:11). The death of Christ (authenticated by his resurrection) was efficacious for all people who will enter into covenant by faith and obedience to him (Rom. 3:21-26; Heb. 9:15). The "wise" (*maskkil*) will understand (Psa. 111:10; Hos. 14:4-9) what the angel has revealed to Daniel, will remain faithful unto death in the midst of "trouble," and will be "delivered" at the final judgment.

The angel has revealed all that God wishes to be disclosed (12:4). Daniel is commanded to discontinue writing and ensure that what has been thus written is *confirmed* or *authenticated* as a revelation from God. In spite of the fact that nothing more is to be revealed, when these prophecies began to be fulfilled, much more would be understood (i.e., "knowledge would be increased") about the place and purpose of the Jews in the redemptive history of God upon the earth. Lange comments: ". . . many shall search it through, and the understanding shall become great."[6] Barnes comments: ". . . by diffusing information, and by careful inquiry, those of coming ages would obtain much clearer views on these points; or, in other words, that time and the intercourse of individuals and nations, would clear up the obscurities of prophecy."[7] When Christians "run to and fro" as missionaries in all the earth, preaching the gospel of Christ, the fulfillment of these predictions would be understood. It is altogether possible that a part of what moved the "magi from the East" to find and pay homage to the "king of the Jews" (Matt. 2:1-2) was their knowledge of Daniel's prophecies.

Daniel is visited by *two* angels so that every word of God is established at the testimony of two or more witnesses. But Daniel, like all the other prophets, (1 Pet. 1:10-12) desired to know how long it would be till the end of these "wonders" (i.e., the "troublous times"). Daniel was told (9:24-27) it would be 490 years, but he had heard many other things since he was told that, and his mind is brimming over with a multitude of names, times and events. He is asking for clarification and elucidation which, of course, had to wait until the fulfillment of all those "wonders."

The angel swears by the name of the Almighty God to emphasize the "kingdom-shaking, power-breaking" (Heb. 12:25-29) *significance* of the announcement about to come. What must necessarily guide in the determination of the "time, two times, and half a time" (i.e., 3½ seasons) is Daniel's question: "How long shall it be till the end of these wonders?" The Hebrew word *haphelaoth* translated "wonders" is found in the OT only here in Daniel 12:6 and may mean "wonderful" in the sense of "hard, difficult." The Hebrew word *lemoed* translated "time, times" is more specifically, "seasons." The question of Daniel concerns the extraordinarily difficult wonders predicted in the times of the "kings of the north and the kings of the south" (i.e., the Ptolemies and the Seleucids, and more specifically, the "Contemptible One" Antiochus IV). The angel is **not** revealing to Daniel some alleged "Antichrist" of the 21st century, removed from Daniel's contemporaries *two and one-half millennia* (some 2600 years) and removed from the Jews of Jesus' day over *two millennia* (some 2000 years).

It is necessary to note here that the *2300 days* (Dan. 8:14) is *longer* than the *3½ years* (or "time, two times, and half a time") here. The *2300 days* begins when Antiochus first began persecuting the Jews in 171 B.C. The *3½ years* begins when Antiochus desecrated the temple in Jerusalem in late May or early June of the year 168 B.C. Both periods end when Judas Maccabeus rededicated the cleansed and purified temple on December 25, 165 B.C. There is no chronological problem between the two predictions of the end of Antiochus's holocaust. The "time, two times, and half a time" is an indefinite prediction of the end of the reign of Antiochus IV. The angel adds that when the "shattering of the power of the holy people comes to an end, all these things would be accomplished" (12:7b). History confirms it! When the oppressed, persecuted Jews were finally rallied under the Maccabeans, the purifying of the temple took place and the subsequent death of Antiochus IV was announced. An even more exact time to denote the beginning and ending of this extraordinary trouble is declared in the next section (12:11-12).

Daniel heard the revelation but he did not understand. The angel informs him that this revelation is "shut up and sealed *until the time of the end.*" "The sufferings of Christ and the subsequent glory" was not understood by those who predicted it (1 Pet. 1:10-12) for it could only be comprehended after it was fulfilled. And even when the time arrived that the prophecies had come to pass, it took a considerable amount of evidence and teaching to be understood by those who were eyewitnesses to its fulfillment (Luke 24:25, 38-43, 44-52; John 20:24-29; Acts 1:3). It is reiterated to Daniel that the "wise" (*maskkil*), god-fearing Jews will, by faith, endure and profit spiritually by the terrible experiences to come upon them during the days of the "Contemptible One." They will trust the promises of Messianic deliverance which God announced through the prophets and perpetuate holiness and faith in their progeny. And some 17 generations (600 years) later there would be Jews, like Simeon and Anna (Luke 2:25-38), eagerly anticipating and ready to receive the Messiah and his redemption. But there would still be some Jews who would do as wickedly as those apostates from the days of the prophets through Antiochus Epiphanes down to the Sadducees, Herodians and Pharisees. These wicked would not understand (Acts 3:17; 13:27) because they did not *want* to understand (Acts 13:45-47; 28:25-28), just as they did not want to understand in the days of the prophets (Isa. 6:9-10; 30:9-12; Jer. 6:16-17; Ezek. 2:3-7; 3:4-11).

The angel reveals that the time-span during which the terrible "wonders" will ensue will be a total of 1335 days. The terrible "wonders" will begin when "the continual burnt offering is taken away, and the abomination that makes desolate is set up." The "abomination" will last for 1290 days. Another 45 days will be added to the 1290 to make 1335 days, and the terrible "wonders" will be over. At the end of May or the beginning of June, 168 B.C., Antiochus IV forced the cessation of Jewish temple services and commanded his general Appolonius to erect an altar to Jupiter in the temple. From this time until Judas Macccabeus removed this "abomination" and purified the temple on December 25, 165 B.C., is 1290 days. The phrase "time, times and half a time" (12:7) is a "round number" which is half of *seven*, the sacred number. The phrase "a thousand two hundred and ninety days" is more specific. They are both essentially the same amount of time: 3½ years is *approximately* 43 months and 1290 days is exactly 43 months. The work of Judas Maccabeus is the ending point for the 1290 days.

Now add to the 1290 days 45 more days and the angel's "blessed" 1335 days are completed. The total of 1335 days constitutes the time-span between the "abomination that makes desolate" until the time of Antiochus's *death!* Lange writes: "The meaning of this [verse] can only be as follows: After 1290 days have expired, the tribulation shall end; it shall not be *completely* ended, however, until forty-five additional days . . . have elapsed, hence, until a total of 1335 days has been reached."[8] The Jewish temple was rededicated December 25, 165 B.C. In early spring 164 B.C. Antiochus undertook the plundering of the temple to Artemis in Elymais. He was defeated and humiliated. This exacerbated the mental and physical sickness already debilitating him. The account of Antiochus's death is recorded in 1 Macc. 6:1ff and Josephus, *Antiquities*, XII.9.1. Counting forward from December 25, 165 B.C. another 45 days brings the time-span to 1335 days and the death of Antiochus IV in early spring, 164 B.C. History has not anywhere recorded the *precise* day of Antiochus's death, so we cannot confirm the angel's revelation with calendar exactness. But the death of Antiochus is certain as to the order of events, and as to the season of the year, as well as the year itself. Of the general accuracy there can be no doubt. It would be chronicled as follows:

Abomination of desolation set up	First of June, 168 B.C.
Purification of temple by Judas	December 25th, 165 B.C.
Time elapsed:	Three and one-half years plus one month, or 1260 days plus 30 = 1290 days.
Death of Antiochus IV	Early spring, 164 B.C., 1335 days after abomination of desolation set up, or 45 days after the 1290 days.

This interpretation of the meaning of the time periods is, we believe, historically and contextually sound. Daniel's primary mission in recording this angelic revelation was to comfort and strengthen *his contemporaries* and *succeeding generations of Jews* as they endured the terrible "wonders" of the 490 years of troublous times. During some of those 490 years it might have appeared to some of God's saints as if the covenant people were about to be exterminated. It might have appeared to those of Antiochus's day that God's redemptive covenant with Abraham might fail. God's people would need to know that the terrible days would *end* and they would need to know, as specifically as possible, *when the troubles would end.*

The information in Daniel chapter 12 has nothing to do with predicting a "rapture of the church," or a "tribulation" upon the whole world, where a singularly powerful and wicked "Antichrist" will institute a "one-world-government" and seduce the majority of mankind to join his wickedness, or a literal "millennial reign" of Christ, who has come to the earth a *second time*, enthroned in a literal Jerusalem, in a world that is for the most part unconverted where a Jewish temple will be rebuilt and sacrifices and offerings will be once again made by Jews, and where Christ and "Antichrist" will meet in one huge, carnal battle at Armageddon at the end of 1000 years, so that a second, third, or fourth resurrection may take place. A reinstitution of a Jewish temple, theology, and religion would be a direct contradiction of the predictions of Christ (Matt. 23:37-38; 24:1-3; Luke 21:5-6) and the doctrine of the book of Hebrews (e.g., Heb. 6:1-8; 7:18-28; 8:13; 9:25-28; 10:1-18; 12:18-29; 13:14, etc.)

What consolation would a post-Christian, dispensational interpretation be for those faithful Jewish exiles who had returned and found themselves in the throes of "troublous times" (490 years of trouble) as they tried to rebuild their temple and nation? What consolation and guidance would it be, especially, to those who had to endure the terrors of Antiochus IV, to have a prediction of the eventual overthrow of some unknown "Antichrist" in some unknown age more than two millennia removed from their struggles? Daniel assures the future readers of his prophecy here that if they "wait" in faith for God to bring about its fulfillment they will be "blessed." Those "wise" ones in the days of the "Contemptible One" will see definite proof that divine providence is at work according to the promises of the covenant-keeping Jehovah-God.

Further, to rob the OT of its prophecies and their fulfillment in past history by forcing them to refer to the end of the world (as dispensationalists do with practically all the apocalyptic prophecies in the OT) is to destroy the most incontrovertible evidence of the veracity of the Bible which is so desperately needed by today's saints of God and an unbelieving world.

Notes

[1] Hailey, *Minor Prophets*, p. 352.

[2] Josephus, *Antiquities*, XII:III:3.

[3] Ibid., XIII.8.2

[4] John Peter Lange, *Daniel*, Commentary on the Holy Scriptures, Vol. 13 (Grand Rapids: Zondervan, 1876), p. 251.

[5] Josephus, *Antiquities*, XII.7.6-7.

[6] Lange, *Daniel*, p. 263.

[7] Albert Barnes, *Notes on the Old Testament, Daniel*, Heritage Edition (reprint of 1873 edition) (Grand Rapids: Baker, n.d.), p. 262.

[8] Lange, *Daniel*, p. 268.

Dispensational View of "The Chronology of the End"
according to Daniel 12:4-13

1. There will be 1260 days plus 30 from the middle of the Tribulation (see Dan. 9:27) to an "undefined" termination (or 3½ yrs. + 30 days).
2. The purpose of the "plus 30 days" beynd the return of Christ is an extra month for the judgment of Gentiles and Jews to determine who will be worthy to enter the Kingdom.

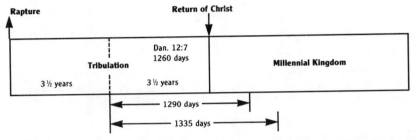

1. An additional 45 days added to the 1290 (making a total of 1335) will be "necessary for setting up the governmental machinery for carrying on the rule of Christ . . . the true border of Israel will have to be established and appointments made of those aiding in the government (Donald K. Campbell, *Daniel: Decoder of Dreams* [Wheaton, IL: Victor Books, 1977]).

Author's View of Daniel 12:4-13

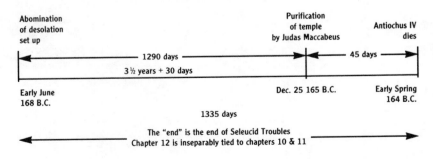

chapter 7

ZECHARIAH AND DAVID'S RIGHTEOUS BRANCH

"Behold, the man whose name is the Branch . . . he shall build the temple of the Lord . . . . and shall sit and rule upon his throne."
Zechariah 1:1–8:23

Few of those today who read the Bible comprehend that Zechariah's book, for the most part, is an *apocalyptic* work predicting the same times as Joel, Daniel, and Ezekiel — i.e., the first advent of the Messiah, the Messianic Age. Many of today's Bible believers have been exposed to so much dispensational distortion of the OT prophecies they are unable to read it within the proper hermeneutical rules for symbolic, crisis, revelatory literature. A few simple references to parallel symbolisms and figures in other apocalyptic OT books would be of great value in interpreting Zechariah. But the most valuable assistance the Bible reader gets to interpret Zechariah's symbolisms are the unquestionable NT fulfillments. We endeavor in this brief work to employ both hermeneutical aids to show that Zechariah is one of the most prolific and pointed prophets of the Messianic Age in the OT.

Zechariah was a prophet of priestly lineage. His grandfather, Iddo, (see Neh. 12:1,16) was one of the first to return from the exile in Babylon. Zechariah was probably born in Babylon and returned to Judea with the increment of 50,000 led by Shesh-bazzar (see Ezra 1:8) in 536 B.C. Zerubbabel was Shesh-bazzar's successor to leadership. Zechariah wrote his book of prophecy ca. 520-518 B.C. When the Jewish exiles first returned to Judea in 536 B.C. they began immediately to rebuild Jerusalem's walls and the temple on the foundation of the one that had been razed by Nebuchadnezzar some 50 years earlier.

When the exiles returned to Judea they found "squatters" from among the neighboring Arab peoples, especially from the Samaritans, occupying their cities, villages and farms. The land itself and the buildings had been desolated by the Chaldeans. The "squatters" were openly hostile to the returning exiles. The Samaritans had offered to help the Jews rebuild Jerusalem and the temple, but their offer was refused (Ezra 4:1-5). The Samaritans attempted to intimidate the Jews by planning war upon them (Neh. 4:7-23) but the Jews armed themselves and began their work of rebuilding "with one hand laboring on the work and with the other hand holding a weapon." The Jews did get an altar built and sacrifices and offerings were made upon it under the direction of Joshua (or Jeshua) the high priest. Joshua was the grandson of Seraiah who had been the last high priest serving when the temple was destroyed.[1]

But soon after beginning the temple construction, the Jews ceased working on it to build their own homes and plant their fields (see Haggai 1:1-15). Discouragement and self-centeredness gripped them (Neh. 5:1ff). The Samaritans and other "squatters" apparently convinced the satrap of Palestine and Syria (Tattenai) that the Jews were planning to rebel against Persian rule (Ezra 5:1–6:22). That accusation was soon squelched when Darius found the decree of Cyrus and ordered Tattenai to assist the Jews in their work. But political unrest and their own materialistic avarice kept the Jews in a state of turmoil and depression. Thus it was that God called Zechariah and Haggai, contemporaries, to call the people back to *spiritual priorities* (rebuilding of God's temple) and to prepare them in holiness of character that they might proceed with their national messianic destiny. Zechariah and Haggai were sent to predict the *certain fulfillment* of God's Messianic program. This demoralized, disorganized, fleshly-minded, leftover (*remnant*) of Jews needed to be refocused on the ultimate purpose of their recent chastisement (exile) and present restoration to the Land of Promise. They needed to be reminded of the hope of their forebears and the Messianic Age which had been so gloriously predicted by the former prophets. These Jews were still only a part of the Persian Empire, but they did have those promises of Isaiah, Jeremiah, Daniel, Ezekiel, et al., of a day when God's Anointed, "a shoot from Jesse" would come from their people to rule all nations with pervasive righteousness and justice. These Jews had recently left a seventy-year expatriation in the midst of a rich and secure pagan Babylon. God did not send them there to be slaves (Jer. 29:4-7). Most of them lived a moderately prosperous economic life. Some of their contemporaries became very powerful and affluent (e.g., Daniel, Esther, Mordecai). Now, back in Palestine, they were reverting to a lifestyle they had been used to in Babylon. Some of them saw nothing wrong even now in "intermarrying with those who practiced abominations" (Ezra chs. 9 & 10). If Zechariah is to excite and motivate these spiritual dullards to give priority to their messianic goal, *he must use graphic, vivid, provocative language.*

Zechariah's prophecy is probably the *most messianic* book of the literary prophets. Zechariah verbally paints an arresting picture of the advent and work of the Messiah, and the establishment of his kingdom for the mind's eye of his audience. He does this through the dramatic visions given him by the Lord, often through the mediation of angels.

There appears to be a division of Zechariah's prophetic work between chapters eight and nine. The first eight chapters deal with contemporary problems of rebuilding Jerusalem and the temple, into which Zechariah interposes a few Messianic prophecies. But from chapters nine through fourteen, this book is distinctly an eschatological treatise in highly figurative and symbolic vista, predicting the *first advent of the Messiah and his earthly work.* His prophecy is saturated with *apocalyptic, symbolic* idiom and it is emphatically *eschatological* in orientation. The contemporary issues Zechariah preaches and predicts in the first eight chapters; in the last six chapters he preaches and predicts their *eschatological consummation* in the redemptive work of the Messiah at his *first coming.* In our opinion, Zechariah says nothing in his book concerning the Second Coming of Christ.

"As the Lord of Hosts Purposed . . . ."

After encouraging and exhorting his people that the words and commandments of the Lord do *faithfully and inexorably* come to pass, and urging them on that basis to repent (1:1-6), Zechariah reveals a series of eight *visions* (1:7–6:8). These visions are apocalyptic (revelations about impending crises) and are couched in graphic symbolism. In these visions it is revealed to the prophet that the everlastingly faithful Jehovah *has the immediate future* of the Jewish people completely under his control.

Vision #1, Zech. 1:7-17: Zechariah sees "four horsemen" of apocalyptic nature. These four are on missions exactly opposite to the "four horsemen of the Apocalypse" in the book of Revelation. In the Revelation the four horsemen bring turmoil upon the earth and not "rest." In Zechariah, the Lord has sent his heavenly horsemen throughout the earth to ensure that the world of heathenism remains "at rest" to such an extent that the Jews may be assured their temple and Jerusalem *shall* be rebuilt so that God may fulfill his covenant promises there through the Messiah.

Vision #2, Zech. 1:18-21: The *goyim* (Gentile nations symbolized by "horns" which mean "powers") which scattered Israel in the captivities will be scattered.

Vision #3, Zech. 2:1-12: God is intensely concerned about Jerusalem for it is the "apple" (actually, *pupil* or "eyeball") of his eye (2:8). Anyone who touches Jerusalem anthropomorphically touches God at his most sensitive spot. Jerusalem here is a metaphor for the covenant people of God, for God is not primarily concerned with land and buildings. This Jerusalem cannot be measured. It is a type of the future church of God in the New Testament, a universal city (Heb. 12:22) composed of Christians from every tribe, tongue, people, and nation on earth. Zechariah exhorts his people to flee from the "nations" and their heathen ways and rejoice in *spiritual Zion.*

Vision #4, Zech. 3:1-10: The people of God are assured they will have access to him, which was theoretically and theologically taken from them when Jerusalem and the temple were destroyed and they were cast into the heathen nations (cf. Ezek. 8 through 11). Joshua is cleansed, symbolizing a restoration of the Jewish priesthood and typifying the coming, ultimate, High Priest, Jesus Christ. Joshua and the forgiven people together represent the "Branch" to come through whom absolute and perfect access will be provided (Heb. 5:1-10; 7:1-28).

Vision #5, Zech. 4:1-14: Zerubbabel is further encouraged that *no obstacle,* no world power, will stand in the way of God's accomplishing his goal of redemption for the world. God predicts he will work, "not by might, nor by power, but by his Spirit" (see Isa. 44:28; 45:1ff.; 2 Chr. 36:22-23; Ezra 1:1-4). Some of Zechariah's contemporaries had compared the "new" temple with the old (Solomon's) and "despised" the new (Ezra 3:12). Little did they know! God was going to do something in the Messianic age through Christ's *perfect, ultimate redemption,* and the establishment of his church, that would make these "despisers" rejoice! The "seven eyes" (or "lampstand with seven lamps") symbolize the *complete, perfect* Spirit of God watching over his work of restoring these people in their Messianic work. The two olive trees represent the two "anointed" offices through which God dispensed his grace to the people — the high priest and the king (Exod. 30:30; Lev. 8:30; 21:10; 1 Sam. 10:1; 2 Kgs. 9:1-6). Immediately they represent Joshua and Zerubbabel, respectively. Ultimately they are combined in the Messiah as Zechariah clearly states in 6:12-14.

Vision #6, Zech. 5:1-4: The flying scroll symbolizes God's "book of deeds" and written upon it are the misdeeds of the restored Judeans. Upon the scroll is written the "curse of God." The people returned from captivity had grown careless and needed purging, so God would send "curses" appropriate for the crimes committed. "Curses" would remind these Jews of God's covenant with them through Moses (see Deut. 27:1–29:29).

Vision #7, Zech. 5:5-11: The ephah (a basket with a lead lid) and the woman called "Wickedness" — this vision symbolizes that their wickedness must be completely removed. Holiness and sanctification must precede the coming of the "King." So "wickedness" is consigned to the land of Shinar. Shinar symbolizes all that is rebellious and wicked in human, secular kingdoms. Shinar is where Nimrod led the infamous "united nations" (Gen. 10:10-11) in its attempt to build a tower to heaven — apparently to assault God's throne and usurp his rule over the world. God would have none of it! Now, Zechariah tells the covenant people they must purge themselves of such rebellion and wickedness.

Vision #8, Zech 6:1-8: The series of visions ends as it began. Zechariah sees four warriors in chariots which were dispatched by Jehovah to various parts of the earth. They would "patrol" the earth to the "four winds of heaven." There would be judgments upon the enemies surrounding Judah (cf. Jer. 49:36; 51:1; Dan. 7:2; Psa. 104:4). The purpose for this is that sufficient international tranquility may ensue for the Jews to complete their restoration and ultimately bring the Messiah into the world.

In chapters seven and eight Zechariah tells of an historic event during the restoration work. Some people of Bethel came to Jerusalem to inquire about the practice of fasting. They had made ritualistic fasts for 70 years during the exile. Now that they had returned to the Promised Land and the temple was being rebuilt, they seemed to think fasting (repentance, "afflicting the soul") would no longer be appropriate. Zechariah, speaking the word of the Lord, answered sharply that all their fasting in Babylon had been "for themselves." They had been no better than their forefathers. They had been hypocrites. A solemn warning is followed by a promise of the Lord's blessing if they will do true "fasting" (compare Isa. 58:1-14). Zechariah directs their attention from outward observance to the real substance and ultimate goal of fasting. The prophet closes this "lesson" with a startling Messianic prophecy (8:20-23). Their *true fasting* would result in a pilgrimage of the *goyim* (Gentiles) to *spiritual Zion* (the NT church) in order that they might share in Israel's fellowship with God.

"Lo, Your King Comes to You"
Zechariah 9:1–14:21

The last half of Zechariah's book is Messianic in its overall orientation. Beginning in 9:16 through the end of the book, the Hebrew phrase, *ba yom*, i.e., **"on that day"** is repeated *eighteen* times and the conjunction **"then"** is used *seven* times! Clearly, the antecedent for "on that day" and "then" throughout to the end of the book is 9:9 ("Lo, your king comes to you") which is unquestionably referring to the *first advent* of the Messiah (see Matt. 21:1-5; John 12:12-15). This Messianic *orientation* holds true even when Zechariah refers in chapter 9 to nations and places and times that appear to be contemporary with Zechariah (e.g., Damascus, Tyre, Gaza, Ekron, et al.). The prophet is implementing the prophetic vehicle we have called "Historical Contemporaneity" or "Time's Coloring"; i.e., he is using names and situations contemporaneous with his immediate audience as symbols to predict future events that will transpire with the *first advent of the Messiah*. The phrase, "on that day" connects all the words of the prophet to the *first coming of Christ*. The following overview-outline will help understand the goal of this section:

The King Will Come and Be Victorious over the People's Enemies (9:1-17)

I. God's Enemies (whomever they be) Will Be Defeated, 9:1-8
II. The Enigmatic King Will Come Humbly but Victoriously, 9:9-10
III. **Then**, God's Covenant People Will Win, 9:11-15
IV. **On That Day**, *God* Will Save and Shepherd His People, 9:16-17

God Will Gather His People from All the World (10:1-12)

I. His People Will Be Scattered by False Shepherds, but Out of the Scattered Shall Come "The Cornerstone," 10:1-5
II. **Then**, He Will Gather with Compassion, 10:6-7
III. He Will Gather from All the World by a Signal, More Than Was Ever in Palestine, 10:8-10
IV. It Will Be Greater Than the Redemption from Egypt, 10:11-12

The Old Order (Judaism) Will Be Done Away (11:1-17)

I. The Jewish "Flock" Will Be Destroyed — Its Corrupt Shepherds Will Wail, 11:1-3
II. **On That Day**, the True Shepherd (Messiah) Will Be the Shepherd of a Flock "Doomed to Slaughter," and He Will Be Rejected and Esteemed Worth Only the Price of a Wounded Slave, 11:4-14
III. **Then**, the Old "Flock" Will Be Given into the Hands of Worthless Shepherds (in the hands of such the Jews have been ever since Messiah's coming), 11:15-17

The New House of David (The Church of Christ) Shall Have the Nature of God (12:1-9)

I. **On That Day**, It Will Have the Strength of God against All the Nations of the Earth That Come against It, 12:1-5
II. **On That Day**, It Will Devour All around It and Endure Forever, 12:6
III. On That Day, Everyone in It Will Be Equal and Have Divine Glory, 12:7-9

There Shall Be a Fountain Opened (12:10–13:9)

I. **On That Day**, the New House of David Will Be Purified, 12:10–13:1
II. **On That Day**, the New House of David Will Be Purged of Idolatry and False Prophets, 13:2-9a

III. The New House of David Will Become God's Peculiar Possession, 13:9b

And the Lord Will Become King over All the Earth (14:1-21)

 I. **On That Day**, "Zion" (The Church of Christ) Will Be Tested, but Sustained by the Lord, 14:1-8

 II. **On That Day**, The Name of the Lord Will Be "Sovereign" and "Security," 14:9-11

 III. **On That Day**, a Curse Will Be upon Those Who War Against "Zion," 14:12-15

 IV. **Then**, a Remnant of the Nations (Gentiles) Will Turn and Worship Jehovah at "Ingathering" (i.e., "the Feast of Booths," or "Tabernacles"), 14:16-19

 V. **On That Day**, Everything Belonging to Him Will Be Holy unto Jehovah, 14:20-21

Other passages in the literary prophets and their New Testament fulfillment show that Zechariah has adopted the usual symbolism of the apocalyptic and eschatological idiom of messianic *first-advent* prophecy. We have listed some of them in Appendix A on principles of interpreting the prophets.

In chapter nine (9:1-8) Zechariah lists enemies of the covenant people of God contemporary with his immediate audience (the Jews returned from the exile). But the ultimate goal of his prophecy is the *spiritual victory* of the Messiah (Zech. 9:9-10) at the cross and resurrection (1 Cor. 1:18-31; Heb. 2:10-18) where he conquers the "mind that is set on the flesh" of believers, Jew and Gentile alike (see Rom. 8:1-8; 2 Cor. 10:3-5; Eph. 6:10-20; Col. 2:13-15). The Hebrew word in 9:10, translated *command* is from the root word *dabar* and is better translated *word, sue,* or *speak.* The usual Hebrew word for *command* is *tsavah* and for *commandment* it is *mitsvah.* The humble and lowly "king" will *sue for* peace. He will not *force* or *order* anyone to be at peace. The controlling peace of Christ comes through *persuasion* and *conviction* (2 Cor. 5:14f). The *supreme* warfare of Christ is *spiritual — mental,* not carnal (2 Cor. 10:3-5). Zechariah's symbolism is routinely used in practically all the prophetic books to point to the Messianic Age, and used profusely by the *apocalyptic-style* books of Daniel, Ezekiel, and Revelation. Compare Hosea 2:16-23 with Rom. 9:22-29 and 1 Pet. 2:9-10. Compare Amos 9:11-15 with Acts 15:16-17. Compare Joel 2:28–3:21 with Acts 2:17-21. Initially the prophetic judgments in Zechariah chapter 9 may have transpired upon those enemies of the covenant people trying to thwart the restoration of Jerusalem and the temple in 536 B.C., but the prophecy has only one **ultimate** goal and that is the *first coming of Christ.*

In chapter ten Zechariah predicts (10:1-2) that God will gather his scattered people who are "like sheep without *a shepherd*" (singular). This is a familiar messianic symbolism in Isaiah's messianic prophecy (Isa. 40:1-11); in Ezekiel's messianic prophecy (Ezek. 34:1-31); in Jesus' words (Matt. 9:35-38); John 10:1-18). And who but the Messiah is "the cornerstone" (Zech. 10:4). It is all symbolism. Chapter ten clearly is not some carnal battle yet to be fought between literal modern-day Israel and an enemy "riding on horses" (Zech. 10:5). Isaiah's prediction that "in that day" there would be a "highway from Egypt to Assyria" and that "Israel would be the third with Egypt and Assyria" (Isa. 19:16-25) is messianic and similar to Zechariah 10:9-12.

> The question arises as to whether these promises . . . have a more far-reaching implication . . . . to limit the prophecies to that particular period is to do violence to the general nature of prophecy. Often the prophet is laying down general principles of God's divine government and leadership . . . . for the ultimate and complete fulfillment of the prophecy one must look to the Messianic age when Judah and Ephraim were joined together in a spiritual union, fighting a spiritual warfare.[2]

In chapter eleven, Zechariah is told by the Lord, first, to portray and symbolize the "shepherd of the flock doomed to slaughter" (11:4,7), **then**, second, he is to portray a "worthless shepherd. . . . who does not care for the perishing . . . ." (11:15,16). There is nothing strange about a prophet "acting" out one of his messages. Isaiah did it (Isa. 8:1-4; 20:1-6). Jeremiah did it (Jer. 13:1-7; 18:1-11; 19:1-13). Ezekiel did it (Ezek. 4:1-17; 5:1-12). Hosea was told to take "a wife of harlotry and have children of harlotry" and his whole marriage experience was a dramatization of God's future dealing with the covenant people. What Zechariah depicts in his first "role" is the Messiah sent to be the "Good Shepherd" (Ezek. 34:20-24; John 10:1-18) but rejected and esteemed worthless (the price of a slave). The "thirty pieces of silver" are applied to the Messiah (Matt. 27:3-10). Isaiah predicted the Suffering Servant (the Messiah) would be rejected as one whom God had "smitten" (Isa. 53:1-12). But the "flock's" rejection of the "Shepherd" would result in the "death and destruction" of the flock (cannibalizing one another). *Zechariah is predicting the end of Judaism* — end of the old covenant. Again, this is not an unusual prediction. Isaiah predicted the "old nation" would be destroyed and a "new nation" would be created "in one day" (Isa. 66:7-9,24). That took place on the Day of Pentecost, Acts 2, when the church of Christ, the new kingdom of God, was created. Jeremiah predicted the old covenant (symbolized by the "ark of the covenant") would "not come to mind, or be remembered, or missed; . . . [or] made again" (Jer. 3:15-17) and that God would make a "new covenant, not like the old" (Jer. 31:31-34). Daniel predicted that when the Anointed Prince came (Dan. 9:25-27) he would be "cut off" and "the people of the prince" would destroy the city. Josephus records that a major portion of the destruction of Jerusalem in A.D. 66-70 was by the Jews themselves. Jesus predicted the destruction of Judaism and Jerusalem as a consequence of the Jews not knowing "the day of their visitation" (Luke 19:41-44) and of not receiving him (Matt. 23:37-39; see also Matt. 24:1-35 and parallels in Mark 13 and Luke 21). When the "flock" rejected their Messiah-Shepherd, the Shepherd broke both his staffs ("Grace" and "Union"). God annulled everything he had covenanted with the Jews, gracious preservation and internal cohesion. John the Baptist said so (Matt. 3:1-12; Luke 3:1-17). Jesus said so (Matt. 21:33-46; Mark 12:1-12; Luke 20:9-19; Matt. 22:1-14; 23:35-39; 24:1-35; Mark 13:1-31; Luke 21:5-33). Stephen said so (Acts 6:14–7:53). Paul said so (1 Thess. 2:13-16; Heb. 6:1-8; 8:13; 12:25-29; 13:10).

The second symbolic shepherd Zechariah portrayed was the "worthless shepherd." This was a shepherd who cared not for the sheep. This is the same shepherd Ezekiel condemned for devouring the flock of God (Ezek. 34:1-10) and the one Jesus identified as the "hireling" (John 10:1,12,13). These are false, hypocritical religious and political Jewish leaders who, for their own benefit, exploited and savaged the flock of God. There were many false prophets and ungodly kings in the days of the Old Testament prophets. And there were many *after* the *first advent* of the Messiah as the book of Acts, the Epistles, and subsequent world history testifies! The Israel that rejected God's Anointed in A.D. 26 and the Israel that has rejected him today has been given over to foolish and worthless shepherds. From the time of Christ until this very day a succession of false messiahs and false prophets and manipulative ideological leaders has led the Jewish people to disbelieve the only Messiah (Jesus) they shall ever have. God does not have any promises left for Jews, or anyone else in the world for that matter, except through Jesus Christ. It is imperative that those who have become convinced of this proclaim it constantly, consistently, and lovingly.

Chapter twelve follows through on the eschatological theme being revealed. Having rejected the king who had come to them humble and lowly, God's Anointed, the unbelieving world (including both Jew and Gentile) thought to rid itself of God's sovereignty, conquer "Jerusalem," and enthrone itself over creation. But **on that very day**, God gave divine strength to the *spiritual* "house of Judah." Again, this is apocalyptic and highly symbolic. God gave the house of David (the church of Christ) victory and compassion. He did so **when** they looked "on him whom they have pierced." We have *apostolic confirmation* that this applies to the Messiah, Jesus Christ (John 19:37). It should be apparent from 9:9-10; 10:4; 11:12; and 12:10 that all Zechariah has thus far predicted is to be applied to *the first advent of Christ*.

Chapter thirteen is indisputably connected to all that has preceded it from 9:9-10 with the phrase, **"on that day** there shall be a fountain opened . . . to cleanse them from sin and uncleanness." Who but Jesus Christ could qualify to be this "fountain?" Furthermore, the statement, "Strike the shepherd, that the sheep may be scattered . . . ." (13:7), is *applied* by none other than Jesus, himself, to the Messiah at his *first advent* (Mark 14:27). And in 13:9 Zechariah appears to be quoting a part of Hosea's messianic (*first advent*) prophecy (Hos. 2:16-23). In the closing verses of chapter thirteen the prophet predicts that judgment and refining will follow the smiting of the shepherd. Two-thirds, symbolic of the major portion of those who smote the shepherd, will be "cut off." This became a fact when Jesus was crucified and the gospel was offered to the Jews, the majority of whom rejected it (compare Matt. 10:14-15; 21:33-43; 22:1-10; 23:29-39; 27:25 with Acts 13:46,51; 18:6; 28:25-28; Rom. 10:21; 11:7,20; 1 Thess. 2:14-16). The one-third symbolic minority will be put to the fire of testing and will, as a result, call on God's name and he will call them his people. This minority is "the remnant" (Rom. 11:5) who became Christians and the majority is those who "were hardened" (Rom. 11:7) and remain hardened to this day.

In chapter fourteen, Zechariah continues predicting the results of the great redemptive climax **on that day** when the Messiah comes to accomplish a victory in humility and lowliness (cf. Phil. 2:5-11; Heb. 2:5-14; 5:7-9) by becoming a shepherd who is rejected by a people who are under the influence of "worthless" shepherds. The Messiah by being "pierced" becomes a source of strength, compassion, intercession, cleansing and purging to a minority which repents and accepts him.

God gives half of this minority, symbolized by "Jerusalem," who had stricken the Good Shepherd but had repented (cf. Acts 2:38-41,47; 4:4; 5:14; 6:7, et al.), to the nations "to be plundered . . . and . . . ravished" (14:1-2). This is the early church. The persecution of the church of Christ from A.D. 34 to A.D. 450 is documented and predicted in the Acts, the Epistles, and Revelation. The New Testament symbolizes the church of Christ as "Jerusalem" and "Israel" (see Rom. 2:28-29; 9:6-13; 11:26; Gal. 4:21-31; 6:15-16; Heb. 12:18-29).

> . . . which Jerusalem is the prophet speaking of? Some have concluded that he speaks of physical Jerusalem and its destruction by the Romans, A.D. 70. But this interpretation is made untenable by the assurance "and the residue of the people shall *not* be cut off from the city." Of Jerusalem's destruction by the Romans Josephus says, "Now as soon as the army had no more people to slay or to plunder, because there remained none to be the objects of their fury . . . Caesar gave orders that they should now demolish the entire city and temple" (*Wars*, Book VII., 1:1). . . . The more probable explanation is that the Lord is here pointing to the spiritual Jerusalem as the capital of His spiritual kingdom (cf. Heb. 12:22; Gal. 4:26) and the assault upon it by the world. Daniel described such an attack on the saints by the "little horn" of the fourth world power, in which the saints

were given into his hand (7:21). In his vision on Patmos John saw this fulfilled in the persecution of the saints by imperial Rome (Rev. 13:7). This does not exhaust Zechariah's prophecy, for his description is that of the conflict which would come time after time. "The residue," which is used of Jehovah's remnant (Mic. 5:3; Zeph. 2:9), would never be cut off from spiritual Jerusalem.[3]

The apostle Peter warned the church that she would be "tested by fire" (1 Pet. 1:6-7; 4:12-19; 5:1-11). Revelation 12:13-14 plainly states that the persecution of the church was God's *modus operandi* for "nourishing" (testing) her. So, Zechariah, like the NT "prophets" to follow him, informed the church that the Lord (Jesus) would be *there,* "with all authority in heaven and on earth," to guard them as he promised (Matt. 2:18-20), symbolized as the Lord standing on the Mount of Olives, for that is where he made the promise! The Lord Jesus will display his sovereignty (Zech. 14:9-11) **"on that day."** He will "disarm" those "nations" that go against his church, and "make a public example of them, triumphing over them in him" (Col. 2:15).

> Jehovah stood by His saints as they were scattered from Jerusalem (Acts 8); He brought Jerusalem to an end by the Romans (Matt. 24:30-32); He cast the beast, the Roman Empire, and the false prophet, paganism, into the lake of fire (Rev. 19:11-21). These incidents are only a few that illustrate the Lord's fulfilling of the prophecy.[4]

The curse and defeat of her enemies and the future glory of "Zion" (the church, Heb. 12:22) is portrayed by Zechariah (14:12-15) much as Isaiah did in his prophecy (chapters 60-66) and we have the word of Jesus that Isaiah was speaking of the *Messiah's first advent* (compare Isa. 61:1-2f with Luke 4:16-28). Zechariah continues (14:16-19), **"on that day"** a surviving remnant of all the nations (in Hebrew, *goyim,* specifically, Gentiles) will turn to the *King* and *worship him as the Lord of hosts!* The "King" of 14:16 is the same "King" as the one in 9:9 — *the Messiah at his first advent.* The worship of the converted *goyim* (Gentiles) is symbolized as "keeping the feast of booths." In Hebrew the word for "booths" is *sukkoth.* The feast is also known as the "Feast of Tabernacles" and "Ingathering" and held by the Jews five days after *Yom Kippur* or the Day of Atonement. The major Jewish feasts, and in fact the entire Israelite system and history, were all symbolic-prophetic of the Christian age. See 1 Cor. 10:11 where Paul indicates they were all *typikos,* or "typical" of the "end of the ages," and see Hebrews 9:9 where the writer uses the Greek word *parabolē,* or "parable" to indicate the tabernacle itself was "symbolic of the Christian dispensation. The apostle Paul used Passover to symbolize the entire Christian life (1 Cor. 5:6-8). Jesus was undoubtedly thinking of the symbolic meaning of *sukkoth* when, attending that feast, he spoke of "rivers of living waters" (compare Zech. 14:8 with John 7:37-39) in connection with a question about going to the Gentiles! Ezekiel makes the land of Canaan, the temple and its services symbolic of the Messianic age (Ezek. 40-48). The "ingathering" of the Gentiles by the Messiah's *first advent* is a major subject in the prophecies of Isaiah. We are on solid biblical ground when we interpret Zechariah 14 as parabolic of the New Testament Church!

Finally, Zechariah (14:20-21) predicts that when the "King" comes to bring victory and security to God's people, everything will be sanctified and holy to the Lord. **"On that day,"** everything and everyone in the "King's" kingdom shall have been cleansed. There will be no separate "priesthood" but every worshiper of the "King" will be his own priest. The Hebrew word translated "trader" is *kena'aniy*, and means "Canaanite" or "Trafficker." There will be no "unclean" (heathen) in the kingdom of this "King." This parallels the scenes of the Messianic Age as described by Isaiah (60–66); as described by Ezekiel (40–48); as described by Joel (2:28–3:21); as described by Micah (5:1-15); as described by Zephaniah (3:8-20); as described by Daniel (7:1-27); as described by Jesus in his parables; as described by the epistles of the NT; and as described by the book of Revelation.

None of these amazing and inspiring prophecies of Zechariah are predicting a literal, carnal war between a millennial army led by a literal Christ ruling in a literal Jerusalem against a literal Russia, China, other nation, or coalition of nations, which might literally invade modern Israel. These prophecies **began** their fulfillment at the *end (consummation) of the ages* (1 Cor. 10:11), the *first advent of the Messiah*, and the establishment of the church on the Day of Pentecost (Acts 2). Their application continues for the church as it wins its *spiritual warfare*, and they will find their ultimate realization in heaven.

Notes

[1]Charles F. Pfeiffer, *Exile and Return*, (Grand Rapids: Baker, 1962), p. 105.
[2]Hailey, *Minor Prophets*, p. 377.
[3]Ibid., p. 395.
[4]Ibid., p. 396.

chapter 8

THE OLIVET
DISCOURSE

"Tell us when will this be? And what will be the sign of your coming and the close of the age?"

What is often called "The Olivet Discourse" is the **polestar** of most people's concept of biblical eschatology. Jesus gave this important prophetic revelation during the last week of his life upon earth. Many people do not know it is recorded in all three synoptic Gospels, Matthew chapters 24 and 25, Mark chapter 13, and Luke chapter 21. While it is a significant part of biblical eschatology, it should not be as all-absorbing as some have made it. The Olivet Discourse deals fundamentally with two issues: (1) the end of Judaism with the destruction of Jerusalem and the Jewish temple; (2) the Second Coming of Christ at the end of time. Coincidentally, it also deals with the biblical doctrine of **"the consummation of the ages."**

Because Matthew contains the extended version of the discourse, we will use his account as the primary source. We will interject the salient portions of the other two, Mark and Luke, wherever appropriate to clarify a statement by Matthew or supplement with variations or omissions made by him. In short, we will make a harmony of all three accounts.

A Chronology of Introductory Discourses
(in the order in which they were proclaimed)

The complexity of this text demands that the student avail himself first of a biblical harmony of the Gospel accounts. Second, the eschatological focus of the Olivet Discourse can only be appreciated when the reader of it has become aware of the impact of the five statements by which Jesus prefaced it. These are, in chronological order, (1) Luke 19:41-44; (2) Matthew 21:21-46 and parallels in Mark 12:1-12; Luke 20:9-19; (3) Matthew 22:1-10; (4) Matthew 23:1-39 (especially, vv. 34-39); (5) and John 12:27-33. The disciples (apostles) were privy to all these startling statements. In the midst of gleeful patriotic cheering they saw him sobbing almost convulsively and saying the enemies of the Jews would cast up a siege-bank around Jerusalem, dash their little ones within her to the ground, and leave not one stone upon another (Luke 19:41-44). Then Jesus predicted that the kingdom of God would be taken from the Jewish rulers and given to another nation (Matt. 21:43); that the "angry king" would send his troops and destroy them and burn their city (Matt. 22:7). Next, he called the Pharisees "sons of hell" and announced that upon their generation of Jews would come all the righteous blood shed from Abel soon after the Garden of Eden up to that very era, and, that the "house" of Judaism was adjudged *desolate and forsaken* (compare Jer. 19:8; Lam. 1:4; Ezek. 8–11 regarding the desolation of Judaism in the Babylonian exile).

After Jesus' condemnation of the ruling oligarchy of Pharisees, he paused to teach a lesson about faith using the widow who cast all her living into the temple treasury (Mark 12:41-44; Luke 21:1-4), one "point of light" in the midst of darkness and impending doom upon the Jewish nation.

Just then some Greeks, not permitted into the temple court where Jesus was, asked to see him. That triggered a soul-wrenching reminder to Jesus of his imminent trek to a place of crucifixion where he would be made to be sin on our behalf that we might become the righteousness of God in him (2 Cor. 5:21). He preached a short sermon on death and life (John 12:20-50) in which he agonized over the "trouble" in his soul and the struggle in choosing the cross (John 12:27). The profound words that become a prelude to his great Olivet Discourse, however, are these: "Now is the judgment of this world . . . ." (John 12:31). If the key words of the Greek text of John 12:31 had been *transliterated* it would have had more impact, for if transliterated it would read, *"Now is the crisis of the cosmos!"*

That alone was enough to precipitate the questions of the apostles about the destruction of Jerusalem and the "consummation of the age." Combined, all these statements shocked and confused the apostles. It seemed to them that Jesus was predicting, that in *their generation*, the city of Jerusalem and the temple would be desolated and forsaken by a calamity upon the Jewish system which sounded like the world was coming to an end. As Jesus left the temple at the end of that exhausting day of challenging confrontations and threats upon his life, his disciples came "to point out to him the buildings of the temple" how wonderfully they were adorned with "noble stones and offerings." His apostles appear to be ambivalent; filled with incredulity as well as excitement as they poured over these amazing statements of

Jesus. Some of the great stones of Herod's temple measured, according to Josephus, approximately $38 \times 12 \times 18$ feet. Eight large-sized American automobiles could be stacked within those dimensions! The "noble offerings" were the gold-plated columns and the huge grapevine decorating the door of the temple, forged of gold, donated by Herod the Great in his 46-year job of remodeling the temple. When Jesus predicted twice (Luke 19:44 and Matt. 24:2 and parallels) "not one stone would be left upon another" the apostles felt compelled to ask him "privately," two questions: "Tell us, when will this be?" "And what will be the sign of your coming and of the close of the age?" Mark says they asked, "When will this be? And what will be the sign when these things are all to be accomplished?" Luke reports it: ". . . when will this be? And what will be the sign when this is about to take place?" The phrase reported by Matthew, ". . . and of the close of the age" is, in the Greek text, *kai synteleias tou aionos.* The word *synteleias* is translated *close* by the English translators but more correctly means **consummation** (i.e., bring to perfection, fulfillment, completion, see our discussion of *synteleias* in Appendix B).

These Jewish apostles could hardly help from being influenced by their boyhood years with the eschatology taught in the synagogues by the rabbis of their day. Jewish scribes and rabbis had divided their eschatology into three eras (more or less): (a) *Olam hazzeh,* the order then existing; (b) *Athid labah,* the age to come after that existing order; and (c) *Olam habba,* the world to come. In some rabbinic traditions, the age to come and the world to come blended into one. The *existing order* was to be succeeded by the "days of the Messiah," which would stretch into the *coming age* and end with *the world to come.* According to the rabbis, the birth of the Messiah would be unknown by the *am-haretz,* i.e., the "common people of the land." He would appear, carry on his work, then disappear — probably for 45 days — reappear and destroy the hostile powers of the world (notably, then, Rome). Israelites would be brought back to Palestine from all over the world through miraculous deliverance and, according to the Midrash, all circumcised Israelites would then be released from Gehenna, and the dead Jews raised by the Messiah (according to some rabbis). This resurrection would take place in Palestine so that those who had been buried elsewhere would have to roll underground — in great pain — until they reached the holy land of Palestine.[1]

In the coming age, *athid labah,* the rabbis wrote that all resistance to God would be concentrated in the great war of Gog and Magog (Ezek. 38–39) and there would be an intensified focus of wickedness upon Israel in her land. Israel's implacable enemies would three times assault the Holy City to destroy it, but each time be repelled. The city would suffer some destruction but not completely so. When Israel's enemy was destroyed completely, by the Messiah, the Holy City would be gloriously rebuilt and inhabited. The new city would be lifted to a height of some nine miles — some said it would even reach as high as the throne of God — and extend from Joppa to the gates of Damascus. The new temple the Messiah was to erect, would contain every glorious item which had been absent in Herod's temple: the golden candelabra, the ark of the covenant (in direct contradiction of Jer. 3:15-16), the heaven-lit fire on the altar, the Shekinah glory, and the cherubim. Some rabbis insisted that the whole of the ancient ceremonies of Moses' Law plus rabbinic traditions would be practiced. More liberal ones believed that only the Day of Atonement and the Feast of Purim, and the Feast of Tabernacles would be observed and only the thank-offerings (not the bloody animal offerings) made. Some insisted that the many stipulations concerning lawful and unlawful foods would be abolished.

The end of the age of *athid labah* would blend right into *olam habba* or "the world to come." *Olam habba* was to be a glorious period of holiness, forgiveness and peace. In this vast new land and new Holy City (not heaven, but literal Palestine), angels would cut gems 45 ft. long and 45 ft. broad and place them in the city's gates. The walls of the city would be of silver, gold and precious gems, and precious jewels would be scattered all over the land which every Israelite was at liberty to take. Jerusalem would be as large as all Palestine and Palestine as large as the world. Every event and miracle in the history of Israel would be repeated, only on a much more magnificent scale. Wheat would grow as high as the mountains and the wind would miraculously convert the grain into flour and blow it into the valleys of the land. Every woman was to bear a child daily, so that ultimately every Israelite family would number as many as all Israel at the time of the Exodus. All sickness and disease would pass away; Israelites would not die; some Gentiles would live hundreds of years. The Messiah was to rule the entire world from Jerusalem, for Jerusalem was to become the capital of the world and take the place of the fourth world empire, Rome (as the rabbis interpreted Daniel 2:44-45).

A war, a revival of the earlier Gog and Magog conflict during *athid labah*, would close the Messianic Era. The nations, which had to this point given tribute to the Messiah, would rebel against him, and he would destroy them by the breath of his mouth, so that Israel alone would be left on the face of the earth. That period of Gentile rebellion was to last seven years. Then the final Judgment would commence. There seems to be no resurrection for Gentiles at all, except to immediately die again at Judgment. Gehenna, where all Jews except the perfectly righteous ones went, served as a Jewish purgatory, from which they were *all* ultimately delivered by Abraham to go to Paradise. No such deliverance was ever considered for the heathen, or apostate Jews — they were to be fuel for the fires of hell. The final Judgment would be held in the Valley of Jehoshaphat by God, presiding over the

Heavenly Sanhedrin, composed of the elders of Israel. After the final Judgment there would be a renewal of heaven on earth and the full implementation of *olam habba*, the world to come.[2]

Now when Jesus spoke of the judgment of the Jewish hierarchy, the desolation of Jerusalem, and the *crisis of the cosmos*, the apostles concluded that such catastrophic events would be signaling the end of the existing order, *olam hazzeh*, and ushering in of *athid labah*, the coming age, and perhaps, *olam habba*, the world to come (i.e., **"the consummation of the age"** as Matthew recorded their last question). The questions of the apostles indicate how influential the rabbinic interpretations had been on them and how confused they were trying to reconcile them with these statements of Jesus about cataclysmic events (i.e., *Jerusalem torn completely down, the kingdom of God taken from the Jews and given to another nation, their city burned and citizens killed, the Pharisees in hell, Jerusalem desolate and forsaken,* **and,** *the crisis of the cosmos*).

Remember the apostles' three questions: (1) *When* will this destruction be? (Matt. 24:3a; Mark 13:4a; Luke 21:7a); (2) *What* will be the *sign* that *You* are coming to do this? (Matt. 24:3b; Mark 13:4b; Luke 21:7b); (3) and Matthew alone records the third part to their questioning, *What* will be the *sign* of *the consummation of the age*? (Matt. 24:3c). It is doubtful at this stage in their conscious understanding of all Jesus had been teaching the apostles that they were asking about his *Second* Coming. They were still confused about his *First* Coming! They were still wrestling with his Messiahship, his hints about being God Incarnate and his return as the Holy Spirit (cf. John 14:8, 18-22; 16:16-28, 29-33). The entire discourse in John, chapters 14–16, is an explanation of his *return as the Holy Spirit* (see specifically, John 14:17) and **not** a prediction of his *visible* Second Coming. So, the questions of the apostles at the Olivet Discourse, are precipitated by their dreams of an earthly kingdom of Israel and the rabbinic traditions they had learned coupled with the *apocalyptic language* of Jesus (i.e., kingdom taken from the Jews, city burned, citizens killed, crisis of the cosmos, desolate and forsaken, et al.).

Recognizing the dangers inherent in their confusion, Jesus sets out immediately to reveal a number of future events. He will clearly specify that what is soon to come from him (the cataclysmic abrogation of Judaism) when he is ascended to heaven and given all power and authority is **NOT the end of the world and his Second Coming**. He will explain that what **IS** going to transpire **IS** the consummation, or "close," of the age (cf. Acts 2:14-21; 1 Cor. 10:11; et al.). He will conclude his answer to their questions by telling them that there will be **NO** signs of the end of the world and his Second Coming — it will be unexpected, unanticipated, and without prior signs.

The devastation of Jerusalem and the Jewish nation was a generation away — forty years from the time Jesus gave this dissertation. Events leading up to the firestorm to come would be so severe the apostles and other believers might be led astray from the faith. They might also flee the country too early thinking the early catastrophes were the end. On the other hand, there is the danger they might see the city encompassed by the Roman legions and rush into the city for safety when, actually, they would need to flee to the hills east of the Jordan. Thus, for their immediate future it is imperative that they, and other Christians, have some very practical instructions about the apocalyptic end of the Jewish dispensation, for it was going to be a holocaust of suffering and destruction. The apostles have not yet understood that Jesus must "go away." When he returned to his heavenly throne they would long to have him back (Luke 17:22), but he had a work for them to do immediately after his ascension, right there in Jerusalem and Judea (Matt. 28:18-20; Luke 24:44-49; Acts 3:26; 13:46). They must live in daily expectation of the end of the world and his Second Coming, but they would first be vulnerable to false expectations of an earthly Messianic Age as portrayed by rabbinical tradition (Matt. 20:20-28; Mark 10:35-44; Luke 22:24-30; Acts 1:6). Actually, the circumstances preceding the destruction of Jerusalem were to be *similar* to rabbinic messianic eschatology. So Jesus spoke these warnings:

1. Preliminary Signs of the Destruction of Jerusalem
Matt. 24:4-14; Mark 13:5-13; Luke 21:5-19

A. *Pseudo Christs*

Jesus warned the apostles that their generation would experience the rise and fall of many who would come in his name, saying they were the Messiah. But the first century Christians were not to be led astray by these claims. In spite of all the excitement and troubles attending these pretenders, Jesus was **not** then returning, **nor** was "the time at hand" for the destruction of Jerusalem. According to Jesus, pseudo-Christs proclaiming the new age would *precede the destruction of Jerusalem*. Josephus mentions numerous impostors who deluded multitudes of first century Jews into following them, claiming they would prove they were Christ by exhibiting wonders and signs by the power of God.[3] Two such pseudo-Christs are mentioned in the book of Acts, Theudas and Judas the Galilean (Acts 5:35-37). These ersatz-Messiahs came to a climactic fervor 62 years *after* the destruction of Jerusalem in a rebellion against Rome under the false Messiah, Bar Kokhba, A.D. 132-135. Jesus says *nothing* here about "The Antichrist" or "antichrists." According to apostolic revelation, "antichrists" are those who "will **not** acknowledge the coming of Jesus Christ in the flesh" (2 John 7). Pseudo-Christs did just the opposite.

B. *International Wars*

Rome was having increasing difficulty with civil wars between Roman emperors and army generals. There was also an ever-recurring necessity for Rome to defend her empire against foreign invaders. Jesus predicted also an increase of rebellious attitude by the Jews against Rome when he said ". . . you will hear of wars and rumors of wars." Herod Agrippa, given his uncle Philip's territory by Caligula, set out to avenge his uncle Philip against Herod Antipas who had stolen Philip's wife, Herodias. Agrippa spread the *rumor* to Rome that Antipas would make war and that he had in his arsenal at Tiberias enough armor to equip 70,000 men. Riots broke out in Alexandria, Egypt among the Jews of that city in A.D. 37-38. A riot broke out in Jamnia in western Judea in A.D. 39 when Jews tore down an altar some Gentiles had erected to the Roman emperor. The Roman emperor Caligula sent two Roman legions, 12,000 men, to Jerusalem to set up his statue in the Jewish temple. Jews vowed to resist to the last Jewish death. Some Jewish Christians in Palestine thought this impending bloodbath was a fulfillment of Jesus' prophecy here. Claudius was forced to put down another riot in Alexandria with bloodshed in A.D. 53. There were the rebellions of the pseudo-Christs already mentioned. In the days of the procurator Cumanus (A.D. 48), a Roman soldier from the garrison in the Tower of Antonia, on the north environs of the Jewish temple, exposed his genitals to the Passover crowds which precipitated a skirmish where hundreds of Jews were killed by Roman soldiers. Frontier disputes between Jews and Samaritans caused bloodshed.[4] Luke reports that Jesus said his followers would hear of *wars and tumults* (instability, political chaos). Whole nations and small social groups would hate and kill one another. The news of such bloodshed would be reported widely. Jesus warned his disciples they must not be "alarmed" (Matt. 24:6) or "terrified" (Luke 21:9). Jesus' statement, "The end is not yet" refers to the "end" of Jerusalem and the temple which he has already predicted (Matt. 23:37-39; 24:2; Mark 13:2; Luke 21:6). He has work for the Christians, especially the apostles, to do in Jerusalem and Judea which will take years to accomplish. They must not flee when social chaos, injustice, and their persecution takes place. When the final catastrophe becomes imminently discernable, Jesus will want all who are able to escape (cf. Matt. 24:15-22; Mark 13:14-20; Luke 21:20-24).

C. *Famines, Earthquakes, Pestilence, Terrors, and Great Signs in Heaven*

They are not to be alarmed when great disturbances in nature "in various places" are reported. One famine (Acts 11:29ff) occurred about A.D. 45-46 and was very severe in Palestine. Josephus and Tacitus (Roman historian) record numerous natural disasters that "shook" the Roman world of the first century.[5] These historians speak in awesome words of famines, pestilences, plagues, droughts, floods, hurricanes, fires, storms. Josephus writes, in *Wars*, IV.4.5: "These things were a manifest indication that some destruction was coming upon men, when the system of the world was put into this disorder; and any one would guess that these wonders foreshadowed some great calamities were coming."[6] As Harold Fowler points out, "The basic message of these verses is, whatever you do, DO NOT CONSIDER THESE DISASTERS AS SIGNS OF ANYTHING! They are not indications of the end, but *of the beginning!*"[7] Some of the "signs" mentioned by Josephus and Tacitus may have been mere products of rumor. But the very fact that they were recorded indicates they were having impact upon the emotions of the people at that time. This is the point of Jesus' warning here in counseling his disciples. Should they see or hear of unusually frightening natural phenomena, Jerusalem's destruction is **still not imminent**.

D. *Persecution from Countrymen and Families*

Persecutions and severe afflictions would come upon his followers, Jesus warned. But even this was no signal of any *imminent* eschatological end. Such times, distressing as they would be, were only preliminary to the carnage to come. Until Jesus was tried and murdered, there were no severe persecutions against his followers. An instance or two of hostility toward followers of Jesus occur in the Gospel records, and at least one instance of a believer in Christ being betrayed to the authorities by parents is recorded (John 9:1ff). The authorities had determined to kill Jesus, but his followers were still free of such malice. But immediately after his death, the tribulation would fall upon his followers. All of this persecution is documented in Acts of the Apostles and the Epistles, all of which were written (except John's epistles and the Revelation) before A.D. 66. Even this should not cause them to flee from Jerusalem and neglect to fulfill their mission to preach the gospel there first. Being brought to trial in Jewish synagogues and prisons, and before Jewish rulers, would be an opportune "time for them to bear testimony" (Luke 21:13). Jesus predicted that before the destruction of Jerusalem many of his followers would "fall away and betray one another, . . . false prophets would arise and lead many astray," and the love of many would "grow cold" (Matt. 24:9-12). It hardly needs to be said that the book of Hebrews, especially, shows the "love of many grown cold" toward Christianity. The author of the Hebrew epistle warns Christians they must not let persecution intimidate them into forsaking their worship assemblies "as they see *the day* approaching (see Heb. 10:19-39). The only *day* any Hebrew-Christian could **see approaching** would be the destruction of Jerusalem as Jesus prophesied it in the Olivet Discourse and gave the signs of its commencement.

E. *The Gospel Will Be Preached throughout the Whole World*

"The very existence of our New Testament Epistles, addressed to widely separated congregations, attest the presence of important Christian centers around the Mediterranean world."[8] The gospel was preached to Jews from all over the known world of the first century on Pentecost (Acts 2:5). Paul said the gospel had gone into all the world and had been proclaimed to every creature under heaven (Rom. 10:18; Col. 1:6,23). Paul does not say it is "going to be preached," but, "it has been preached to every creature under heaven." Paul also said the faith that the Roman Christians had was "proclaimed in all the world" and was "made known to all the nations" (Rom. 1:8; 16:26). The "world" of Jesus and Paul was not the "world" of the twentieth century! The "whole world" for people of the first century included little more than all the "civilized" and subjugated world of the Roman Empire. Josephus, quoting Roman historians and Herod the Great, declared that *all the inhabitable world* was subject to Rome.[9] It is not only improper exegesis, it is close to blasphemy, to say, as some "prophecy evangelists" are saying today, that Christ cannot come until the gospel is preached unto the whole world. The world will end and Christ will return for his final judgment upon this wicked cosmos *any time he wishes to do so* whether everyone in the world has heard the gospel or not.

Jesus stated that **when** the gospel had been preached to *that* world, "**then the end would come.**" The end of what? **When and what the end was that was to come** is *specified* in the next section of Jesus' discourse.

2. Precise Signs of the Destruction of Jerusalem
Matt. 24:15-34; Mark 13:14-30; Luke 21:20-31

A. *The Abomination That Makes Desolate*

Jesus began to predict signs that would be observable to *the generation then living* and plainly indicates that a *terrible holocaust* was imminent upon Jerusalem and its inhabitants. He would give a solemn warning to the women of Jerusalem, on his way to the cross, that they should not weep for him but for themselves and their children. He told them the days were coming when they would desire the hills to fall upon them and cover them (Luke 23:26-31). The first of the *imminent* signs of the end of Jerusalem was to be what Matthew and Mark call *the desolating sacrilege spoken by the prophet Daniel.* Daniel predicted the desecration of the Jewish temple and the city of Jerusalem by the fourth world empire, Rome, when the Messiah would be "cut off."[10]

After a series of Jewish uprisings and riots, the city of Jerusalem was first besieged in November, A.D. 66, by Cestius Gallus, the Roman legate of Syria. He had marched to Judea in November with the Twelfth Legion and surrounded the city on orders from the emperor, Nero. Gallus occupied the northern edge of the city, called Bezetha, but concluded his forces were too small to take the whole city, so he withdrew. The Jews, assuming divine providence had intervened to spare the city, took no advantage of the opportunity to flee. Many Jews living in the immediate environs outside the city fled *into* the city for what they thought would be protection.[11] Meanwhile, on the way back to Syria, Gallus and his forces were ambushed by Jewish insurgents at Beth-horon and the Romans suffered great losses. When Cestus Gallus began his retreat to Syria, Christians, remembering Jesus' prophecy, fled to Pella, east of the Jordan. Eusebius writes, ". . . the people of the church in Jerusalem, being commanded to leave and dwell in a city of Perea, called Pella, in accordance with a certain oracle which was uttered before the war to the approved men there by way of revelation . . . ."[12]

Nero sent Vespasian with 60,000 men to Judea in the spring of A.D. 67. Vespasian subdued all of Judea and was about to besiege Jerusalem when he was called back to Rome as a result of Nero's suicide. Vespasian left his troops encamped at Jerusalem, traveled back to Rome, became emperor and sent his son, Titus, to Judea to put down the Jewish revolt. On July 24, A.D. 70, Titus recaptured the Tower of Antonia at the northern edge of the temple courts. August 5, he caused the daily sacrifices of the Jewish priests to cease. August 27, the temple gates were burned, and on August 29, A.D. 70, the anniversary of the Babylonian destruction of Solomon's temple in 587 B.C., the sanctuary itself was torched. While the sanctuary was burning, Roman soldiers brought their legionary standards into the temple area and offered sacrifices to the Roman emperor there. By September 26, A.D. 70, the whole city was in Titus's hands. All during the siege and assault on the city by the Romans, the Jews within the city had been reduced to such desperation they committed atrocities upon one another almost too horrible and gruesome to recount. At one point several women killed their children, roasted their flesh, and ate it.[13]

Luke *explicitly* defines what the *desolating sacrilege* is by saying, ". . . when you see Jerusalem surrounded by armies, then know that its desolation has come near" (Luke 21:20-21). The time to flee the city and Judea would be easily recognizable for Jesus' followers. When they saw the Roman army building siege walls they could understand that Jerusalem's desolation was forthcoming.

B. *Great Tribulation and Distress*

Luke reports Jesus saying, "for these are days of vengeance to fulfill all that is written" (Luke 21:22). Over 1400 years earlier than this Moses predicted that such tribulation would befall the Jews if they rejected *The* Prophet (the Messiah) and

Daniel predicted destruction and desolation would come upon the Jews because they would "cut off" their "Anointed One" (Deut. 18:15-18; 28:15-68; Dan. 9:26-27). Jesus proclaimed the Jews would "Fill up . . . the measure of [their] fathers. . . . that upon [them would] come all the righteous blood shed on earth" because they were going to kill the Son of God (Matt. 23:31-36). And Luke reports that Jesus denominated a *specific generation of Jews* upon whom this great tribulation was to come. It would be "wrath upon **this** people" (Luke 21:23).

Harmonizing the reports of Matthew and Mark, they describe it as a "great tribulation, such as has not been from the beginning of the creation which God created until now, and never will be" (Matt. 24:21; Mark 13:19). This is one of the points of the Olivet Discourse which causes major confusion. Many readers insist that such language cannot be referring to the destruction of Jerusalem by the Romans, even though that event was certainly terrible in its time. Of course, there have been many tribulations since the destruction of Jerusalem *statistically* much worse than that one. The universal deluge during Noah's day (see Gen. 6–9) was prior to the destruction of Jerusalem. Nineteen hundred years after Jerusalem's tribulation two world wars caused more death and destruction. The Nazis of Germany killed some six million Jews[14] during World War II. Statistically, that is more than the estimated million and one half slain and captured in A.D. 70.

But the term, *such as*, in the description of Jesus, really does not refer to the *statistical* magnitude of the tribulation. It refers, rather, to the *kind of tribulation.* Jesus is anticipating the uniqueness of the cause and effect of the suffering. It is hardly possible for any tribulation to exceed in magnitude that of the Noachian flood. The explanation has to be sought in the issues of quality and uniqueness.

a. This tribulation involved the final destruction of what once had been God's holy nation. This had never happened before. God rescued a remnant from exile and restored their nationality and their religious system. But this judgment would not be rescinded — God would not restore them as he had before. This *kind* of tribulation never happened again. The church of Christ is *now* God's holy nation and religious system (1 Pet. 2:9; Matt. 16:18; Dan. 2:44).

b. The circumstances of the Jews trapped in Jerusalem was unique in all of history. God had withdrawn his presence. They were abandoned to their own evil. The residents had cried at Jesus' trial, "His blood be upon us and upon our children" and thus it was. The residents turned on one another in hatred and panic, and inflicted on themselves atrocities more horrible than even the Romans could invent.

c. It was a tribulation suffered only by those Jews who had rejected Christ. Those who believed Jesus' prophecy were saved from the disaster of A.D. 66-70.

d. Consider: The Bible was written for all time, for the atomic age as well as the age of bows and arrows. For Jesus to try to compare the tribulation of Roman warfare with Hiroshima's atomic-bomb destruction would mean nothing to the apostles. So, Jesus is simply saying, "In the frame of reference of what you apostles know and can visualize, Jerusalem's suffering is going to be the greatest." This is no contradiction of Jesus' omniscience. He is, in fact, condescending to the human limitations of the apostles. He did this at other times. He told them a few hours later, "I have many things to say to you which you are not presently able to bear" (John 16:12ff).

e. The holocaust of A.D. 66-70 was unique in the way the Jews tortured, murdered, and despised their fellow Jews. Josephus contends that *the Jewish sedition destroyed the city, and the Romans destroyed the sedition.*[15] Jerusalem was really self-destroyed. Titus, the Roman general, made every effort to spare the people, the city and the temple; but the Jews were implacable in their intention to never surrender to the Romans again. Titus eventually could wait no longer and went into Jerusalem, killing those still alive and destroying that which had not yet been destroyed.

f. It may be that this "great tribulation" which began with the destruction of Jerusalem in A.D. 66 has continued with more or less intensity up to the present time! The Jews since A.D. 70, have, in many lands and many centuries, suffered "great tribulation and distress" (1 Thess. 2:13-16).

g. Even Josephus saw the holocaust of A.D. 66-70 as singular in the history of the world when he wrote, "Accordingly it appears to men, that the misfortunes of all men, *from the beginning of the world*, if they be compared to these of the Jews, are not so considerable as they were. Neither did any other city ever suffer such miseries, nor did any age ever breed a generation more fruitful in wickedness than this was, *from the beginning of the world.* . . . The multitude (1,100,000 slain and 97,000 taken captive) of those that perished exceeded all the destructions that either men or God ever brought upon the world."[16]

In his *Wars*, Josephus fills two "Books" (60 pages in William Whiston's translation) detailing the "great extremity to which the Jews were reduced" in the Roman siege:

a. They fought one another with such abandoned hatred they slew thousands of innocent Jews in their cross fire — even priests and worshipers in the temple courts were killed in the act of making offerings.

b. They burned their own storehouses filled with food, polluted water reservoirs to keep others from them, and caused the starvation of thousands of their countrymen.

c. Those seeking to escape the city, if caught by fellow Jews, had their throats cut on the spot.

d. It was impossible to bury all the dead bodies so they let the cadavers rot, tramped over them, or threw them over the walls.

e. Those who attempted to escape and save coined money by swallowing it were captured by either fellow Jews or Romans, thrown to the ground, and disemboweled alive and their gold taken from their intestines while they writhed in death throes.

f. Jews plundered the city's stores, homes and government buildings, torturing and killing anyone found inside in search of food or other valuables.

g. Children yanked the very morsels of food out of the mouths of their parents, and parents did the same to children.

h. Many Jews sold everything they possessed, homes, children, spouses, clothing, for *one* measure of wheat or barley.

i. Jews tortured other Jews by driving wooden spikes up their "private parts" and this, for no reason at all except to express anger.

j. Romans crucified escaping Jews at the rate of 500 per day — they ran out of wood with which to make crosses.

k. Tens of thousands died of pandemic disease and pestilence.

l. Leaping from the tops of the walls of the city, many Jews either crushed their bodies or died instantly. If they survived and escaped, they ate anything they could find and so much, so rapidly, they died.

m. Dead bodies were stacked as high as houses and blood ran down street gutters ankle deep.

n. Some ate from public sewers, they ate cattle and pigeon dung, wood, leather, shields, hay, clothing, and things even scavenger animals would not eat.

o. After one mother roasted her child and ate its flesh, Josephus says the "whole city was full of this horrid action immediately."

p. When great crowds took refuge in the temple at the word of a "prophet" 10,000 were burned alive when Titus burned the temple.

q. The Romans, upon capturing the entire city, slew every living person they found — "they obstructed the very streets with their dead bodies, and made the whole city run down with blood, to such a degree that the fires in many houses were quenched with these men's blood."

r. Josephus calculated 1,100,000 perished and 97,000 were taken captive. Some estimates go as high as 2,000,000 casualties.

s. He concludes, ". . . thus the city was thoroughly laid even with the ground . . . ." Only three towers and a little part of one wall were left by Titus to "memorialize" his victory over the Jews.[17]

Jesus continued, Luke reports by stating that "Jerusalem will be trodden down by the Gentiles, until the times of the Gentiles are fulfilled." The "times of the Gentiles" are surely in the hands of God and not of men, i.e., the "desolation" of Jerusalem would continue as long as God sees fit. The passage in Romans should provide a clue: ". . . a hardening has come upon *part* of Israel, *until the full number of the Gentiles* come in, *and so all Israel will be saved*" (Rom. 11:25-26). The crucial issue focuses on *all Israel*. It is plain from the New Testament that "Israel" is the church of Jesus Christ. Paul says, ". . . not all are children of Abraham because they are his descendants . . . . it is not the children of the flesh who are the children of God, but the children of the promise are reckoned as descendants" (Rom. 9:7-8). Paul also writes, "And if you are Christ's, then *you are Abraham's offspring*, heirs according to promise" (Gal. 3:29).

Thus, the "until" in the Olivet Discourse points to a time when God will have "grafted" all who through obedience of faith in Jesus Christ have become heirs of Abraham into *spiritual Israel*. *Spiritual Israel* is the church of Christ — Jew and Gentile. When God is through bringing all those who are being saved by faith in Christ into *spiritual Israel*, then the "times of the Gentiles will have been fulfilled" and **that will be the end of time**! The Jews had their time. They were allotted 490 years from the return after their exile, to bring the Messiah into the world (457 B.C.–A.D. 34), to accept him, and fulfill their messianic mission as a nation of believers. For the most part, they rejected the Messiah and crucified him. They adamantly rejected his kingdom from the day of Pentecost onward. So the kingdom was taken from the Jews and given to the Gentiles. God gave his kingdom to a mixture of all races and tribes and languages which would produce the fruits of repentance. This would include, of course, all Jews who would become Christians. In this kingdom neither circumcision nor uncircumcision counts. *It is the new creation that counts!* Those who walk by this rule *are the Israel of God* (Gal. 6:15-16; 2 Cor. 5:16-17). God has not absolutely rejected the Jews, neither have all the Jews rejected Christ. A "hardening" has taken place only in part (Rom. 11:25). And if any one of them does not persist in unbelief, he will be grafted in (Rom. 11:23). The only way anyone becomes a citizen of the *new* "Israel of God" from the death of Christ until the end of time is through the *New* Covenant accomplished by Jesus and inscriptured in the *New* Testament (John 5:23; 14:6; Heb. 10:10, 12-14). When the Jews were given their allotted time and when the apostles had completed the first part of Jesus' Great Commission to take the gospel to Jerusalem, Judea and Samaria, and the Jews had, for the most part, rejected it, the kingdom was delivered to the Gentiles (Acts 13:46). The time allotted for the Gentiles to carry out the work of the kingdom continues from A.D. 34 until the end of time — until Christ delivers up the kingdom to God after destroying every authority and power.

Until the end of time Jerusalem will be "trodden down by the Gentiles." Geographical Jerusalem and national Israel can only be characterized as "Gentile" so long as the present world exists. So long as a Jew will not come to God by faith in Jesus Christ, he is a heathen, an unbeliever, one who crucifies Christ afresh, and for him there is no possibility that God will accept his attempts at repentance (see Heb. 6:1-8; 10:1-31). There is no grace of God for anyone outside of Christ, certainly not in Judaism, for Christ's work fulfilled the law of Moses, at *the end of the ages*, **once for all time** (Heb. 9:12, 26-28; 10:12,14; Gal. 5:4). There are passages in the Scriptures which indicate that Jews in Jerusalem or anywhere else, today, outside of Christ, are as "Gentile" as any unbeliever practicing any form of idolatry, **because God's covenant is in Christ** (Zech 13:2-6; Heb. 3:12-19; 6:1-8; 10:26-31; 12:22-29; 13:9-14; Rev. 2:9; 3:9).

All the "Israel" there is from now to eternity is the church of Christ. If Paul is predicting in Romans 11:26 that by some coincidence *all Jews alive* at Christ's Second Coming will have become Christians and thus "all" Israel (alive at that time) will be saved, then he must also be predicting in Romans 11:32 that by some coincidence all Gentiles will have become Christians at the time of the Second Coming and we can anticipate that they shall all be saved. The word *all* in Romans chapters 9–11 is evidently being used *qualitatively* rather than *quantitatively*. In other words, *all* who are *really* "Israel" by being in Christ, will have been saved by the time the "full number of the Gentiles has come in."

When Christ comes again, are we to expect everyone alive at that time to be saved? Hardly! (see Matt. 7:13-14; 25:45-46; Luke 13:24; 18:8). Paul recognized that only *some* (Greek, *tinas ex auton*, literally, "some out of them") of his fellow Jews would be saved if God could make them jealous through sending the gospel to the Gentiles (Rom. 11:14). Paul says the "others," referring to Jews, "if they do not *persist* in their unbelief, will be grafted in, for God has the power to graft them in *again*" (Rom. 11:23).

Yes, God has the power to graft Jews back into the kingdom; Christians must pray and work and give, in order that it may be a reality — but only *in Christ!* Are we to expect that not *one Jew* will be persisting in unbelief at the moment of Christ's return? If there is *one* still in unbelief at that time, then the phrase "all Israel shall be saved" must be *qualified!* Paul has qualified *all* in this Romans context and also in Romans 2:28-29; 4:9-15; 9:6-8; Galatians 6:15-16; and in the entire book of Hebrews! The New Testament doctrine of the Second Coming clearly teaches that the majority of people all over the world and in every race — and Jews are everywhere — will be *unprepared for Christ's coming!*

C. *False Messiahs and False Prophets Showing False Signs and Wonders*

At this point in the discourse Jesus points to another *sign indicating the imminent destruction of Jerusalem*. This sign would be when pseudo-Messiahs and false prophets would take advantage of the catastrophic circumstances of the siege and try to build large groups of followers. They would pretend to work wonders and show omens. They would try to convince many to follow them into alleged places of safety. But Jesus exhorts his disciples to "take heed; I have told you all things beforehand" (Mark 13:23).

Josephus refers to numerous "pseudo-Messiahs" who had deceived themselves and large numbers of other people with false hopes which inevitably ended in disastrous calamities. In one instance he reports:

> A *false prophet* was the occasion of these people's destruction, who had made a public proclamation in the city that very day, that God commanded them to get up upon the temple, and there they should receive *miraculous signs* of their deliverance. Now there was then *a great number of false prophets* suborned by the tyrants to impose upon the people, who denounced this to them, that *they should wait for deliverance from God* . . . . Thus were the miserable people persuaded by these deceivers, and such as believed God himself; while they did not attend, nor give credit, to the signs that were so evident, and did so plainly foretell their future desolation; but, like men infatuated, without either eyes to see or minds to consider, did not regard the denunciations that God made to them.[18]

Despite Jewish guards within the city, and Roman troops without, many Jews succeeded in escaping Jerusalem by one means or another.[19] Even after Titus had allowed 40,000 Jews to leave the city alive[20] the majority of Jews, still believing in the promises of the "pseudo-Messiahs" chose to remain inside the city. At the siege of Jerusalem, a few Jews of the countryside, led by Eleazar, a commander of the *Sicarii* (Jewish "freedom fighters") fortified themselves in *Masada*, a stronghold about 35 miles south of Jerusalem near the western shore of the Dead Sea, built by Jonathan the Maccabean and improved by Herod the Great. Reduced to starvation by a Roman army siege of the fortress, these loyalists all committed suicide rather than surrender.[21]

Jesus concludes this warning saying, "For as the lightning comes from the east and shines as far as the west, so will be the coming of the Son of man" (Matt. 24:27). In effect, Jesus is warning his disciples not to follow pseudo-Messiahs because their signs will be *obscure, deceitful, and false*. On the other hand, when the Son of man comes in *his judgment upon Jerusalem, his* signs will be *unmistakable*. The signs which Jesus gave would be as clearly visible as when lightning fills the skies. The signs Jesus gave would be as visible and easily interpreted as when one sees *vultures* circling in the skies — these signs will indicate Jerusalem is *dead!*

The *real* Messiah did "come" with *his army,* not to deliver but to destroy Jerusalem in A.D. 66-70. The reader is referred to Matthew 22:7 where Jesus plainly allegorizes the destruction of the Jewish nation at the hands of the "King's troops."[22] This reference to the destruction of Jerusalem as a symbolic "coming" of the Son of man is Jesus' method of giving an interpretative key for the proper understanding of the highly apocalyptic and symbolic statement that is to follow.

D. *The Heavenly Powers Brought Down*

Matthew reports Jesus saying that cataclysmic events would occur there, "Immediately after the tribulation of *those days.*" Mark reports the predicted events thus: "But *in those days, after that tribulation.*" Luke simply quotes Jesus saying, "And there will be signs in sun and moon and stars," etc. (Matt. 24:28-31; Mark 13:24-27; Luke 21:25-28).

Contextual continuity and biblical parallels give conclusive endorsement to the interpretation of this text as a **continuation** of the prophecy of the destruction of Jerusalem and Judaism: (a) *"Immediately"* does not sensibly make room for a time gap that would postpone the fulfillment of this text for over 2000 years from its utterance until sometime future to the present; (b) *"When these things begin to take place"* (Luke 21:28) surely is not referring to the Second Coming for there will be **no signs** pointing to its nearness; (c) and the chronological statement by both Matthew and Luke, that . . . *"this generation will not pass away till all these things take place"* (Matt. 24:34; Luke 21:32) undoubtedly includes the sun and moon being "darkened," stars "falling from heaven," "perplexity and distress of nations," and "the powers of the heavens being shaken."

This section is difficult for the occidental mind-set, but not for the oriental. The careful Bible student will find much help in understanding this by giving attention to context, comparable passages from the OT and biblical word usage. This section is plainly couched in *apocalyptic* style language. It is word-for-word like that of the OT prophets and the book of Revelation when predicting the "coming" of God in judgment upon both the Israelite nation and the pagan nations (e.g., Isa. 13:1-22; 14:12-31; Hab. 3:1-15, et al.). Apocalyptic language is distinguished by its figurativeness, symbolism and high drama. It is used at *crisis* points in the history of God's unfolding plan of redemption. The apocalyptic language of Jesus here should be interpreted in light of the following considerations:

(1) Sun, moon, and stars darkened or falling is often stated symbolically in the OT to picture any inexpressible calamity such as an overturning of empires, kingdoms, cities, emperors, kings, or religious potentates thought otherwise to be invin-

cible. It is clear that Isaiah, Jeremiah, Ezekiel, Joel, Amos, Micah, Habakkuk, and others refer to the fall of empires and emperors, kingdoms and kings in such terms (e.g., Gen. 37:9; Isa. 13:10; 14:12ff; 24:23; 34:1-4; Jer. 4:23-28; 15:9; Ezek. 32:7ff; Joel 2:10; 2:30–3:21; Amos 4:9; Mic. 3:6; Hab. 3:11).

(2) Luke reports Jesus saying, ". . . distress of nations in perplexity at the roaring of the sea and the waves . . . ." This is picturing the distress of the wicked as these calamities of the destruction of Jerusalem roll over them like waves of the sea. Isaiah and Jeremiah both used this terminology to describe "floods" of judgments coming upon the wicked, even at the hands of human "messengers" of God (Isa. 23:9-12; 57:20-21; Jer. 6:23ff).

(3) "The powers of the heavens being shaken . . . ." is a figurative prophecy of the "shaking down" of the system of Judaism and the obsolete priesthood (cf. Heb. 8:13; 12:25-29; 13:13-14 with Isa. 14:12ff; 24:21-23; Hag. 2:6-9). Daniel spoke of Antiochus IV as growing "great, even to the *host of heaven*; and some of the *host* of the *stars* cast . . . down to the ground, and trampled upon . . . ." (Dan. 8:10,23ff; 11:36ff). "Host of heaven" and "host of the stars" are "the mighty men and people of the saints" (the Jewish hierarchy) many of whom Antiochus IV murdered or deposed in his persecution of the Jews (see 1 & 2 Maccabees). Modern news media personnel used this very phrase to describe the fall of Russian communism!

(4) Matthew writes, "then will appear the sign of the Son of man in heaven . . . coming on the clouds . . . with power and great glory." Both Mark and Luke put it, "And *then they* will see the Son of man coming in a cloud(s) with great power and glory." Jesus plainly told his apostles some of them would not taste death before they saw the kingdom of God come *with power* and they *saw the Son of man coming in his kingdom* (Mark 9:1; Matt. 16:28).

God deemed it necessary to *punctuate* his sovereign will about the abrogation of Judaism and the implementation of Christianity with physically catastrophic measures! Because of the implacable intransigence of the Jewish leadership against God's Anointed, God is "tested" as the Jews "tested" him in the days of Moses (see 1 Cor. 10:1-22; Heb. 3:1-19; 4:1-13). And we must remember that what God was going to do would annul a religious, cultural, and political system which was his "chosen" system for 1400-years-worth of the "scheme of redemption." Fowler cites Milton Terry:

> We might fill volumes with extracts showing how exegetes and writers on New Testament doctrine assume as a principle not to be questioned that such highly wrought language as Matthew 24:29-31 . . . taken almost verbatim from Old Testament prophecies of judgment on nations and kingdoms which long ago perished, must be literally understood. Too little study of Old Testament ideas of

judgment, and apocalyptic language and style, would seem to be the main reason for this one-sided (literalist) exegesis. It will require more than assertion to convince thoughtful men that the figurative language of Isaiah and Daniel, admitted on all hands to be such in those ancient prophets, is to be literally interpreted when used by Jesus or Paul.[23]

The English word *earth*, in the phrase, "then all the tribes of the earth will mourn," is misleading since the Greek word *ge* also means a land, region or country.[24] The mourning will be by the nation of Israel, not by the whole world of that time as Zechariah predicts (Zech. 12:10-14; John 19:37). The whole Roman world would have its time of "wailing" at the "coming" of Jesus in judgment upon the "beast" (i.e, the Roman Empire, see Rev. 1:7; 6:12-17; 16:17-21; 18:9-19). But the Gentile world of Rome hardly noticed when Jesus was crucified.

When the Son of man comes "on the clouds of heaven with power and great glory," *they will see it*. First, the nearest antecedent of *they* is those who are going to mourn (the tribes of Israel who have pierced him) *at his first coming* as Zechariah and John confirm. Second, there is not the slightest indication in this sentence that Jesus is "coming" *toward the earth in a total, final judgment*. Jesus has adapted an OT prophecy and its language to portray his "coming" in judgment upon Judaism. Daniel saw the "son of man" come to "the Ancient of Days" to assume his everlasting "dominion and glory and kingdom" and Daniel's vision concerns the fall of the fourth world empire, Rome (Dan. 7:11-27). Upon Jesus' resurrection and imminent ascension he told his apostles that "all authority in heaven and on earth *had been* given to him" (Matt. 28:18-20). Jesus' pronouncement of the fall of Judaism coincides with his promise to his apostles that *they would not die before they saw the Son of man coming in his kingdom with power* (Matt. 16:28; Mark. 9:1). Furthermore, Jews had been scattered all over the world ever since their Babylonian exile. These would certainly mourn and faint with fear when they learned of Jerusalem's obliteration by the Romans, fearing the same treatment might come to them.

Sending out his "angels" with a loud trumpet call to gather *his* (i.e., those belonging to the Son of man) elect from the "four winds, from one end of heaven to another" is further apocalyptic language. The first thing we notice is that these "angels" are *not* sent from *celestial* realms! Second, it is not unusual for the Greek word *angelos* to refer to earthbound, human *messengers*. John the Baptist is called *angelos*; some of John's disciples are called *angelos*; the two spies sent into Jericho by Joshua are called *angelos*; some of Jesus' emissaries are called *angelos*; most students of the Revelation conclude that the "angels" to the seven churches of Asia Minor were human messengers, perhaps evangelists at specified churches (cf. Matt. 11:10; Mark 1:2; Luke 7:24,27; 9:52; Jas. 2:25; Rev. 1:20). These *angeloi* are probably the "prophets, wisemen, and scribes" Jesus sends the Jewish nation in Matthew 23:24. And the "loud trumpet call" is prophetic idiom used to "announce" *solemn* warnings of impending judgment and redemption (see Isa. 18:3; 17:13; 58:1; Jer. 4:5; 6:1; 51:27; Ezek. 33:3,6; Hos. 5:8; 8:1; Joel 2:1,15; Amos 3:6; Zech. 1:16; 9:14; Rev. 1:10; 4:1; 8:13; 9:14; 18:22). Fowler points out,

> Among its other uses, the trumpet, as a symbol, would bring to the Jewish Jubilee a trumpet song of the emancipation of Hebrew slaves and of the restoration of alienated property to its true owners. . . . In this same vein, Jesus established the keynote of His own ministry, citing Isa. 61f (Luke 4:18f). . . . Then he claimed, "Today this scripture is fulfilled in your hearing." So doing, He initiated the great spiritual era of freedom, rest and restoration. . . . Then, as He sent forth His heralds to proclaim this same dispensation of God's grace now available to all in the Gospel, these messengers (*angeloi*) but echoed the Jubilee trumpet's function to "proclaim liberty throughout the land to all its inhabitants.[25]

Luke notes that Jesus concluded this highly figurative section by saying, "Now when these things *begin* to take place, look up and raise *your* heads, because *your* redemption is drawing near (Luke 21:28). This statement is clearly *parallel* to Jesus' statement in the next section (i.e., the lesson of the fig tree) where he also says, "So also, when you see all these things taking place, you know that he is near, at the very gates (Matt. 24:33; Mark 13:29; Luke 21:31). Now the nearest antecedent of "you" in this text is "his elect." *The elect will believe the signs of Jerusalem's destruction which he has been giving.* They will understand that the great "mountain" (the perpetuated religious system and the persecuting powers of Judaism) that stood in the way of the expansion of the kingdom of God has been "moved." It is interesting that Jesus used this figurative prediction in connection with his withering of the fig tree during his last week of ministry! He uses the "fig tree" picture again, in the next section, for the sake of *that generation* (Matt. 21:18-22; Mark 11:12-14; Matt. 24:32-34; Mark 13:22-30; Luke 21:29-32). It was indeed the Judaizers who presented the greatest "mountain" to the church of Christ between its establishment on Pentecost and the destruction of Jerusalem in A.D. 70. The Acts and Epistles (especially Romans, Galatians, and Hebrews) emphatically attested to it!

E. *The Lesson of the Fig Tree*

"And he told them a parable, 'Look at the fig tree, *and all the trees*'" is Luke's report. Matthew and Mark report Jesus saying, "From the fig tree learn its lesson." This is an illustration anyone may understand. "Jesus was using an illustration his disciples, as outdoors men, could readily understand. A budding tree, whatever its specie, is a sign that 'spring has sprung' and 'summer is nigh.' Thus He was telling his disciples that when they should see the things He had enumerated, they should know the fall of Jerusalem was at hand."[26] Some dispensationalists would make the fig tree, in its "bursting forth with leaves," symbolically represent a revived nation of Israel. But Luke's report emphatically shows that Jesus was *not* using any particular tree for his purpose. Besides, it is the grapevine that most symbolically represents Israel in the Scriptures (e.g., Ps. 80:15; Isa. 5:1-7; 27:2; Jer. 12:10; Ezek. 15:1-8; Hos. 10:1; Matt. 20:1-16; 21:33-46; John 15:1-11).

The RSV translates Matthew 24:33 and Mark 13:28 thus: "So also, when you see all these things [taking place (Mark)] you know that *he* is near, at the very gates." The Greek text has no personal pronoun of any kind (i.e., *ho*) for the English *he* in the text; it has *only* the Greek verb *estin*, translated *is* in English. The sentence, as Luke reports it reads, "So also, when you see these things taking place, you know that the kingdom of God is near" (Luke 21:31). Jesus is **not** the subject. "**It**" (i.e., the kingdom of God) is the subject. Only the KJV and NIV translate it correctly. The "signs" Jesus had given up to this point were all to be as easily recognizable as the arrival of spring is unquestionably recognizable by the budding and leafing of trees. And what was to be so easily ascertained was *not Jesus' second advent*, but the messianic "kingdom of God" in its ascendancy over Judaism, for Judaism was about to be taken out of the way. When the preceding signs were seen, Jesus' followers would know that the Son of man had assumed absolute, divine sovereignty in heaven and that he was coming on the clouds in power, with his "army," "to destroy those murderers and burn their city" (Matt. 22:7). They would know that the kingdom of God had come in its power and destroyed the usurpation of the wicked husbandmen who tried to take the kingdom ("vineyard") for themselves (Matt. 21:43).

The Hebrew epistle was written to encourage Hebrew Christians not to go back to Judaism, but to hold fast to Christianity, "and all the more as [they were *seeing*] (the Greek verb for *seeing* is present active indicative — not future — meaning something they were presently and continually seeing) the Day drawing near (Heb. 10:25). The only "day" the Hebrew Christians of the first century (A.D. 65-66) could see approaching was the desolation and destruction of Jerusalem! They certainly could not see the *second advent of Jesus Christ* "approaching." Physical "redemption" for Hebrew Christians of the first century would be effectuated at the fall of Jerusalem and Judaism. The Greek word used by Luke (21:28) is *apolytrosis* and is the same word used of the "deliverance" from torture refused by those faithful saints of God mentioned in Hebrews 11:36. The first century Christian's "redemption" would be the breaking of the stranglehold of Judaism from the throat of the infant church of Christ, allowing it to survive the Judaizers.

Matthew and Mark record Jesus' final statement about the destruction of Jerusalem and Judaism thus, "Truly, I say to you, *this* generation will not pass away till ("before," Mark) all these things take place" (Matt. 24:34; Mark 13:30). Luke records it thus, "Truly, I say to you, *this* generation will not pass away till all has taken place" (Luke 21:32).

The critical issue is the meaning of the word, "generation" (in Greek, *genea*). Before treating that issue, let it be understood that *all those things Jesus predicted* **did** *take place!* (a) Jerusalem *was* surrounded by armies, and Christians *did* flee; (b) Jerusalem and the temple *were destroyed*; (c) Judaism *was* never a threat to the kingdom of God thereafter; (d) there *were* pseudo-Messiahs who led many Jews astray in the siege of Jerusalem; (e) the Jews *did fall by the sword* and *were* led captive among all the nations; (f) Jerusalem *was* trodden down by the Gentiles *and continues* to be so today; (g) the gospel *was* preached to the *whole* world of the first century by A.D. 66-70; (h) God's "elect" *were* gathered from the "four corners of the earth" (John saw them in A.D. 95, in the Revelation from every tribe, tongue, nation and people); (i) the theological "world" of Judaism *was shaken* down (Heb. 8:13; 12:25-29); (j) comparatively, the destruction of Jerusalem *was* uniquely a "great tribulation" upon Israel unparalleled before and afterward.

J. Marcellus Kik has categorized the statement of Jesus, "Truly, I say to you, this generation will not pass away till all these things take place," as *the pivotal time text.*[27] The problem is the meaning of the Greek word *genea*, "generation." Some dispensationalists wish to make the word *always* mean "race." While it *may* mean "race," it does not **always** do so in the Bible. The careful student will first compare other usages of the word "generation" in the NT (e.g., Matt. 1:17; 11:16; 12:41; 16:28; 23:35-36; Mark 9:1; Luke 1:48,50; 9:27; 16:8; 17:25; Acts 13:36; 14:16; 15:21; Eph. 3:5,21; Col. 1:26; Heb. 3:10; Psa. 95:7ff). Exegesis carefully done always abides by the simplest explanation of a text (within its context) unless there are other reasons not to do so. The simplest explanation of "generation" in *this* context is that it means a life-span of some 35-40 years. The word "generation" is clearly modified by all the tribulations that were to come upon Jerusalem when the "armies" encompassed the city in A.D. 66-70. Dispensationalists have assigned the events listed of *"this generation"* to be fulfilled in *numerous succeeding generations!*

The next thing the careful Bible student will notice is Jesus' significant and *continued* use of the word "these" (contemporary things) all the way through this discourse until coming to Matthew 24:35. From that point on he always uses the adjective, *that*, to refer to his Second Coming. Jesus predicted that the final crisis of Jerusalem would take place during the lifetime of men, women and children who were presently inhabiting the city (Luke 19:41-44; 23:27-31). Up to this point in the discourse, Jesus says everything that is to happen is to happen in those "days" (plural). Everything **after** this point (after Matt. 24:34; Mark 13:30; Luke 21:32) is in that "day" (singular)! The phrase, "that day" (singular) is *almost* singularly used in the NT to speak of the end of the world and judgment (see Appendix A). The conjunction "But" (Matt. 24:36; Mark 13:32; Luke 21:34) is a definite word separating that which has been predicted earlier and able to be known, from that which follows the conjunction, and which **cannot** be known.

The evaluation of the word "generation" in this context by J.W. McGarvey, cited by Fowler, is significant: ". . . it contained in itself a challenge to that generation of Jews to watch the course of events in their own national history, and to say whether its predictions proved true or false. No generation has lived that was so competent to expose a failure had it occurred, or that would have done so more eagerly. But the events, as they transpired, turned the prophecy into history, and demonstrated the foreknowledge of Jesus."[28]

3. "Heaven and earth will pass away, but my words will not pass away."

This is the *transitional* statement of the Olivet Discourse. What Jesus had just said must have registered on the minds of the apostles. The terrible destruction predicted of Jerusalem and Judaism would result in a shock to their Jewish mentality! He sounded like the world was going to come to an end. So, Jesus said, "Indeed, the world *is* going to come to an end, however, the destruction of Jerusalem *is not the end of the world.*" Jesus emphasizes that his words concerning the ravaging of Jerusalem will not fail to come to pass. They *will* be fulfilled! Every prediction he made came to pass regardless of how incredible it may have seemed to the Jewish mentality.

Then, as Matthew and Mark report, Jesus said, "But of that day and hour (i.e., the passing away of heaven and earth) no one knows, not even the angels of heaven, nor the Son, but the Father only" (Matt. 24:36; Mark. 13:32). From this point onward, to the end of Matthew, chapter 25, Jesus gives one illustration after another reinforcing his warning that *no one would be able to know* when he would return and heaven and earth would pass away. Luke merely summarizes all these illustrations with one statement (Luke 21:34-36).

Now if the knowledge of the end of the world was withheld from angels and the incarnate Son by God the Father (Matt. 24:36; Mark 13:32), how do present-day eschatology "experts" presume to be able to figure it out from Scriptures which even Jesus and the Jews had in their day? Was Jesus, with all his wisdom, unable to interpret Daniel, chapters 7 through 12, while modern-day dispensationalists are? To say that Jesus simply did not know *the year or day of the month and the exact minute*, but that he *did* tell us certain signs to look for and know that it is *near*, makes this whole context ridiculous!

If Jesus knew the time of the end of the world but declared he would not or could not tell it, the temptation to read into his every statement some subtle prediction as to the exact time would be almost overwhelming. Not only does Jesus *not* predict the time of the end, he *could not* during his incarnation because God did not reveal it to him while he was on earth. There is no excuse for anyone trying to predict the time of the Second Coming when we understand that even Jesus himself did not know. The most important thing about eschatology is the emphasis on the *certainty* of the end of this world and of judgment (Acts 17:30-31). There are some "times and seasons" which God has reserved only to himself to know (Acts 1:7).

Where and *when* the rotten universe needs dealing with, there the Lord will come and deal with it (Luke 17:37). *Where* it needs dealing with is, of course, all over! *When* it needs dealing with, only he knows. The NT never speaks of Jesus' Second Coming in terms of *time* or *specific place* but in terms of God's preordained will that this sin-flawed creation *shall* be redeemed (cf. Rom. 8:18-25; 1 Cor. 15:12-58; 2 Cor. 5:1-21; Phil. 3:20-21; 1 Thess. 4:13–5:11; 2 Thess. 1:5-12, et al.). Nowhere in the Bible are we told *when* it will be redeemed. We are told to *watch and wait every day*. In the meantime, we are warned, men will try to exploit the word of God and the faith of believers for their own egotistical ends by telling everyone they know when the time of his Second Coming will be. For emphasis we insert here a brief résumé of the remainder of Jesus' discourse on the end of the world as recorded by Matthew, Mark, and Luke.

It is as if Jesus said, "Let me illustrate." The remainder of this entire discourse, from Matthew 24:37 through Matthew 25:46 (including Mark 13:34-37) is a combination of TEN DIFFERENT prosaic statements and parabolic stories to accentuate Jesus' categorical declaration that the time of his Second Coming will be *totally unknown and unexpected*:

a. Matthew 24:36 — ". . . of that day and hour, no one knows . . . ."
b. Matthew 24:37-39 — ". . . as the days of Noah . . . . they did not know . . . ."
c. Matthew 24:42 — ". . . watch . . . for you do not know . . . ."
d. Mark 13:35 — ". . . watch . . . for you do not know . . . ."
e. Matthew 24:44 — ". . . at an hour you do not expect. . . ."
f. Matthew 24:51 — ". . . when he does not expect him . . . an hour he does not know . . . ."
g. Matthew 25:13 — ". . . you know neither the day nor the hour. . . ."
h. Matthew 25:19 — ". . . after a long time . . . ."
i. Matthew 25:31 — "When the Son of man comes . . . ."

j. Luke 21:34 — ". . . and that day come upon you suddenly like a snare . . . ."

Luke notes that Jesus pictured the day the world ends like a "trap springing shut" — unexpectedly! (Luke 21:34). So Jesus warned those who believe in him to keep themselves from excessive attention to this world as if it is all the world there is ever going to be. The parables of Jesus in Matthew and Mark clearly indicate the following *conditions* when the end comes **suddenly and unexpectedly**:

a. Matthew 24:37-41 — "As the days of Noah" illustrates the end will come at a time of normalcy. People will be going about their lives normally; they will "not know" when the Lord is coming as those did not know when the flood was coming "until" it came.

b. Mark 13:34-37 — The parable of the householder illustrates God expects each human being to be doing his work, but many will not be, as if they were asleep.

c. Matthew 24:43-44 — The parable of the thief at night illustrates God is not going to signal the world ahead of time as to the time of Jesus' coming (see also 1 Thess. 5:2; 2 Pet. 3:10).

d. Matthew 24:45-51 — The parable of the wise versus the wicked servants illustrates that some will be ready for the Master's return because they were *always* ready, while others will believe he is delayed and continue to exploit their fellow servants.

e. Matthew 25:1-13 — The parable of the ten virgins illustrates that some are *always* prepared for the Bridegroom's coming, while others give no concern to prepare to meet him.

f. Matthew 25:14-30 — The parable of the talents illustrates the need for faithful use of the blessings God has given in proper *preparedness* for the end of the world.

g. Matthew 25:31-46 — The parable of the separation of the sheep and the goats illustrates that the way to *prepare* for his coming and the judgment is to be found in practicing love for the needy in the affairs of everyday living.

Every statement concerning Jesus' Second Coming or the end of the world in the Epistles confirms Jesus' teaching that *no one will know the time and it will be when no expects it*. Paul writes, ". . . the day of the Lord will come like a thief in the night" and believers should "not let that day surprise them like a thief" (1 Thess. 5:2,4). Peter writes, "But the day of the Lord will come like a thief" (2 Pet. 3:10).

Those who believe Jesus is coming back should expect him momentarily, every moment of every day. With the great apostle John of old, they should say, *"Maranatha* — "Our Lord, come!" Etched upon my mind are the words of a banner one of my beloved teachers and, later, esteemed colleagues, placed in his Bible college classroom. It was in large letters that all his students might see and heed, "PERHAPS TODAY!"

Notes

1. "Olam," *Encyclopedia Judaica*, Vol. 12 (Jerusalem, Israel: Keter Pub. House. Ltd, 1971), pp. 1355-1357.

2. "Afterlife," "Eschatology," "Messiah," and "Resurrection," *Encyclopedia Judaica*, Vols. 2, 6, 11, and 14, respectively.

3. Josephus, *Ant.* XX.5.1.; *Wars* II.13.4-5; *Ant.* XX.8.10; *Wars* II.13.5.

4. Josephus, *Ant.* XVIII.5.1-3; XVIII.8.1-9; XX.5.3; *Wars* II.10.1-5; II.12.1; II.14.2.; II.16; II.17.2.4; II.18.1.3; IV.3.2.; IV.9.1-2,9-10. See also, F. F. Bruce, *Israel and The Nations* (Grand Rapids, Eerdmans, 1969), pp. 197-225.

5. Josephus, *Ant.* III.15.3; IV.5.2; XVI.9.8; XX.2.5; *Wars* VI.5.3; Tacitus, *Annals*, XII.43; XV.22,47; XVI.13, Norma Miller, trans. (Bristol, UK: n.p., 1987); Tacitus, *Histories*, I.2, P.V. Jones, ed. (Cambridge, UK: Cambridge University Press, 1995).

6. Josephus, *Wars*, IV.4.5.

7. Harold Fowler, *The Gospel of Matthew*, Vol. IV (Joplin, MO: College Press, 1985), p. 418.

8. Ibid., p. 433.

9. Josephus, *Antiquities*, XIX.2.4; 3.1.

10. See our comments in this work on Daniel 9:24-27.

11. Josephus, *Wars*, II.19.2.

12. Eusebius, *History*, 111.5.3.

13. Josephus, *Wars*, VI.3.4.

14. This figure includes both descendants of Abraham and descendants of the Khazars of the Caucasus area. See Appendixes C and D for more information.

15. Josephus, *Wars*, IV.5.3-5; IV.6.2; V.6.1.

16. Ibid., V.10.5.

17. Ibid., Books V & VI.

18. Ibid., VI.5.2.

19. Ibid., IV.6.3; 7.1; V.10.1; 13.7; VI.2.3.

20. Ibid., VI.8.2.

21. Ibid., VII.8 & 9.

22. See such figurative language in Joel 2:11,25 where God speaks of the destructive locusts as "my army;" and Isa. 10:5-10; 44:28; 45:1; Jer. 27:5-7 where God speaks of using human beings as secondary agents of his chastening judgments.

23. Milton Terry, *Hermeneutics*, cited in Fowler, *Matthew*, Vol. IV, p. 466.

24. Fowler, *Matthew*, Vol. IV, p. 484.

25. Milton Terry, *Hermeneutics*, p. 466, cited in Fowler, *Matthew*, Vol. IV, pp. 496-497.

26. Boatman, *What the Bible Says about the End Time*, p. 259.

27. Kik, *Matthew XXIV*.

28. J.W. McGarvey & Philip Pendleton, *The Fourfold Gospel* (Cincinnati: Standard, n.d.), p. 351, cited in Fowler, *Matthew*, Vol IV, p. 509.

chapter 9

THE REVELATION
OF JESUS CHRIST
PART I

"Here is a call for the endurance and faith of the saints."
The Revelation of Jesus Christ

Introduction

Before we begin our exegesis of the text of the book of Revelation, a few preliminary issues need clarification. We intend to present only the author's interpretation of the Revelation. We have neither the space nor the inclination to discuss in any detail the multitudinous viewpoints about the meaning of this book.

First, the book of Revelation is ONE revelation. It is not entitled, "Revelations" as it is erroneously called. The Greek title is APOKALYPSIS, (in English it is APOCALYPSE) and it is *singular*! It needs to be studied with this in the forefront of the consciousness. It is one large *drama* with many *scenes or acts*, but it is ONE drama, not many. Too many people have never "seen the forest" of Revelation because they have been too busy "looking only at the trees." It is important that the "plot" of the drama be seen before the "review" begins.

The plot is: The "kingdom of God" was then enduring, as John received the Revelation, and in the very near future was going to suffer, a "great tribulation" (Rev. 1:9). This "great tribulation" was to be brought against the "saints" by the ferocious "dragon" (the devil) who tried to thwart God's redemption for man by devouring the "male-child." But the dragon was foiled in that attempt, so he proceeded to give his power (which consists only in deception) and authority to the "beast" representing political and military power, the "false prophet" representing false religious power, and the "harlot" representing the power of carnality. The "kingdom of God" (the churches of Asia Minor in the initial focus) needed, first, to

repent of its failures in order to survive this great, three-pronged, assault by its enemy (see Rev. 2:1–3:22). Second, the church needed a divine perspective of what was coming. She needed to know that the throne of God and the Lamb was aware of her predicament and that heaven was in control of all that exists (see Rev. 4:1–5:14). Third, the church needed to have revealed to her the intensity, the scope, and the methodology these enemies would use against her (see Rev. 6:1–20:10). Finally, she needed to know that ultimate, blessed, eternal victory belonged to her, not to the "beast" (see Rev. 20:11–22:21). That, essentially, is the dramatic overview of the book of Revelation as it unfolds in vivid apocalyptic style and symbolic language throughout its 383 verses in the English version.

Christians should not undertake to decipher the book of Revelation until they have learned the "decoding" books. Those are the Old Testament books written in apocalyptic symbolism, especially Daniel, Ezekiel, and Zechariah. Of the 348 OT quotations or references in Revelation, 235 of them (68 percent) are from the OT Prophets. Since the Revelation "plugs" into Daniel right where Daniel is in the process of predicting the fourth great world empire (Rome),[1] it is imperative that anyone who wishes to understand where John "is coming from" (to use a modern colloquialism) in Revelation, he must familiarize himself with Daniel's predictions and their fulfillments.

Remember, the Bible affirms that man is free to think and act. And the Bible obliges man to think precisely. Any interpretation of the Revelation (including the "thousand years") which does not leave man a free agent, thinking according to accepted rules of interpretation, is false! There can be no "age" this side of the final judgment when man will be free from temptation and sin in an absolute sense. And, as the "thousand years" are said in Revelation to precede the final judgment, the "millennium" can be no exception to this rule. Any theory that places a meaning on figurative language that is contrary to the plain, literal statements of Jesus and his apostles, must be false. There is very little information in Revelation that may not be learned from the rest of the Bible. In the more prosaic books doctrines and events are presented to the mind, but in Revelation they are presented in dramatic form to the imaginative and excitable capacities of the human psyche. The message is the same — Christ and the church are to be victorious over the worst the world can do against them; the style of communicating that message is more vivid and esoteric in Revelation than the Gospels and Epistles.

It is our firm conviction that through serious and honest use of the accepted canons of hermeneutics, *all* readers of the Bible should see *all* the Bible **alike!** And that includes the book of Revelation (see Deut. 29:29; John 20:30-31). God deplores the fact that his creatures are ignorant of his word (see Luke 24:25; Rom. 1:18-32;

11:25; 1 Cor. 3:1-2; 10:6ff; 12:1; 2 Cor. 1:8; 2:11; 1 Thess. 4:13; 2 Pet. 3:5,8). Please see our notes on interpreting Biblical prophecy in Appendix A. What we have said there applies *in toto* to the book of Revelation. The Revelation is prophetic, but it is also exhortative, revelational and edificatory. Actually, Revelation is *epistolary* in both statement and style! It was specifically to be written "in a book and sent to the seven churches" of Asia Minor. Revelation is *eschatological* in that it is a *continuation* of the history of God's covenant people from the Old Testament, through the Gospels, Acts, and Epistles of the New Testament, into the second, third and fourth centuries to *the end of the Roman Empire*. The Revelation portrays the struggle of the church against this great "beast" (Rome) and predicts the victory of the church. It predicts the *end* of the last great obstacle to the spread of the Gospel to the four corners of the earth. Revelation presents a divine perspective to human history. That is what makes it *eschatological*. But Christ meant *all* Christians to understand the message of Revelation — to "keep it" and to *continue* to read and keep it! (Rev. 1:3; 2:7,11,17,29; 3:6,13,22; 22:16,17,18,19).

There are about five different interpretations of the book of Revelation:

(a) *Preterist* (from Latin meaning "past") — Revelation is viewed as a history of the Jewish nation and pagan Rome.

(b) *Futurist* — Revelation centers around the time of Christ's Second Coming and the end of the world; everything from chapter 4 through 22 is still future, and the book of Revelation is a volume of unfulfilled prophecy (e.g., the Scofield Bible) and is understood in mostly literal terms.

(c) *Historical* — The book of Revelation outlines history so that most of it has been fulfilled during the Christian age with only a small portion yet to be fulfilled (e.g., B.W. Johnson's "Notes" on the NT).

(d) *Philosophy of History* — Revelation is divorced from an historical background and is viewed as an expression of the principles of divine government whose operation may be observed in every age — mostly a theologically liberal viewpoint.

(e) *Historical Background* — The book is written primarily for the encouragement of the seven churches of Asia Minor and other Christians of those centuries of Roman imperial antagonism against Christianity. H. B. Swete concluded that since the book starts with well defined historical situations to which reference is made again at the end, as well as in the intermediate visions, the entirety of the work could not **reasonably** be dissociated from its historical setting.

Without apology we follow the *Historical Background* approach because we are convinced it most clearly conforms to the fundamental canons of biblical hermeneutics and, certainly, to the rest of the Scriptures. The purpose of the book was to strengthen the courage and faith of the Christians in Asia Minor and the rest of the

Roman imperial world by visualizing the downfall of the Roman Empire and the final victory of the kingdom of God and the victorious Christ.

Evidence that the author of the book of Revelation is John the apostle is beyond reasonable doubt: (a) it takes an apostolic, authoritative posture toward the churches; (b) it has the spiritual insight and background of an apostle and eyewitness of the incarnate Christ; (c) early church historians attribute the book to John the apostle (i.e., Justin Martyr, Irenaeus, et al.); (d) the internal evidence of Johannine idioms.

The date of its writing is approximately A.D. 95: (a) the rule of the Roman emperor Domitian (A.D. 81-96) is most characteristic of the circumstances outlined in the book (Will Durant says of Domitian, "he began like Gabriel and ended like Lucifer"[2]); (b) Irenaeus, Victorinus, Eusebius, and Jerome all agree on this date; (c) the condition of the churches of Asia Minor is definitely *later* than Nero and best fits a time span of 35-40 years after their establishment by the apostle Paul (The First Epistle of Clement of Rome to the Corinthians was contemporaneous with Revelation and reflects the external social conditions of the Domitianic era.); (d) the severity of the persecution predicted better conforms to the era of Domitian; (e) and history records that the major struggle of the church against the imperial power of Rome took place early in Asia Minor for that is where most of the Christians were congregated until after the fall of the Roman Empire. Merrill C. Tenney says: "The later date (Domitian) has the advantage of being confirmed by definite historical evidence."[3]

Revelation was written in a cultural milieu in which Christians had become *personae non gratae*. Although most Christians were in Asia Minor, Christianity had spread throughout the Roman Empire. It was exclusive and quite unlike the polytheism of the pagan people of that day. There were numerous misconceptions among the heathen philosophers and writers of that era — one was that Christians practiced cannibalism because it was rumored they "ate the body and blood of Christ." While some Roman soldiers became Christians, most Christians were pacifists toward Rome's insatiable lust to invade and conquer other nations. Most Christians were poor and came from the lower social classes — many were slaves. Romans tended to think of Christianity as a "sect" of Judaism and thus considered it to be an aberrant rather than normal lifestyle. The austere morality of Christians toward the excesses of the heathen conflicted with Roman social norms and was a "thorn in the flesh" against the materialism of the day. But the most significant aspect of Christianity that caused Roman antagonism was the refusal of Christians to burn incense and worship the Roman emperor. For their adamant opposition to idolatry Christians were considered to be threats to Rome's political, economic and social existence. Christians were categorized as seditionists!

At the end of the first century, the Roman Empire had reached the apex of its impact upon civilization for good. Actually, its demise had begun when it became an empire rather than a republic. The excesses and extravagances of Rome's political and financial elite is almost beyond imagination. The ruling classes indulged in every imaginable vice — blood-letting and violence in the gladiatorial games, gluttony, drunkenness, fornication, adultery, divorce, abortion, homosexuality, bestiality, incest, abortion, murder, and extortion.[4]

Religion (except for Judaism and Christianity) was totally idolatrous. The empire tolerated all religions which tolerated her paganism and idolatry. It was Domitian who "filled the Capitol with statues of himself, announced the divinity of his father, brother, wife, and sisters *as well as his own.* He instituted a new order of priests, the Flaviales, to tend the worship of these new deities. He made the first official decree throughout the empire that he was to be worshiped and addressed as *Dominus et Deus Noster* — "Our Lord and God." As he sat on his throne he insisted that his visitors embrace his knees. In A.D. 93 he executed some Christians for refusing to offer sacrifice before his image; according to tradition these included his nephew Flavius Clemens.[5]

Under the Flavian emperors, Vespasian (69-79) and his sons, Titus (79-81) and Domitian (81-96), there was a veneer of prosperity and growth. Imperial conquest and expansion became the obsession of the Flavians. Domination of the whole civilized world seemed inevitable; all nations and all languages seemed destined for their control. The emperor was the living "god" of the world and the benefactor of all people. He was expected to feed the world, to protect it against barbarians, to administer its justice, control its weather and its history, entertain it, and educate it. According to the emperor's whims people lived or died, ate or starved to death. His abilities and deeds seemed superhuman and divine to the common man. Pagan people, so long skeptical of the mythological gods of Olympus, felt that in the emperor of Rome they at last had a real person whose position and powers made him worthy of worship (Rev. 13:4).[6]

There were several early periods of localized persecutions upon Christians. Some of them took place during the reigns of Caligula, Claudius, Nero, and Vespasian. But Domitian is the emperor who has gone down in history as the one who bathed the empire in the blood of the Christians because they refused to worship him as god.[7] He was assassinated in A.D. 96 in a plot in which his own wife was a participant.

The purpose of Revelation is inseparable from the background of all this as it affected the Christians and the churches, especially in Asia Minor, in the latter centuries of the Roman Empire. It is to show that the alleged "invincible" power of the Roman emperor (the "beast") was doomed to be overthrown, and that in the end the kingdom of God would triumph for its King, Jesus Christ, reigns supreme. But, as John points out at the very first of his Revelation, the church must *repent* if it wants this victory and triumph. Revelation presents a clear and vivid call for Christians to maintain loyalty to the faith at all costs, even martyrdom. The saints must not allow the dragon to deceive them through the powers of the beast. This message is peculiarly relevant today. It is the call to choose the eternal rather than the temporal; to resist temptation; to refuse to compromise with pagan secularism; to place the claim of conscience above all demands against it; to cherish the confidence of ultimate victory for the kingdom of God, not only in the reign of Domitian, but in every other chaotic period of world history, including the twentieth and twenty-first centuries — if our Lord tarries.

The following commentary on the Revelation will focus on eschatological issues and will not emphasize exegetical concerns or contemporary applications. We have already produced a commentary on the book dealing with those aspects.[8]

Revelation 1:1-20
"I am the Alpha and the Omega . . . the first and the last . . ."

The events revealed by Jesus Christ were imminent on John's horizon of history. The Greek word *tachei* translated *soon*, means "shortly, quickly, imminently."[9] What Jesus revealed to John was *not* to wait for two thousand years before coming to pass! So, Jesus reiterates! The *time* for this to come to pass was *near* or *ready* (*engus*) in relation to John's time, not ours.[10]

This revelation came from the now glorified Lord who had previously been the humble and humiliated Messiah on earth. He was *the* faithful witness, *the* firstborn *from the dead*. They did not annihilate him when they crucified him. He is alive forever more. Now he is ruler of history and *ruler of kings on earth*. If there are any eschatological issues or points of time to be decided, he will decide them and reveal them.

He is about to "come on the clouds." This does **not** refer to his Second Coming. "Coming with the clouds" is an apocalyptic, symbolic phrase used frequently in the Bible to portray God's "coming" in judgment, sometimes by direct providential intervention and sometimes by using secondary agencies to carry out his judgments. (See Exod. 16:10; 19:9; 34:5; Lev. 16:2; 2 Sam. 22:8-16; Psa. 18:6-15; 97:1-5; 104:3-4; Isa. 19:1; Jer. 4:13; Ezek. 1:4; 10:4; 30:18; 32:7; 38:9,16; Dan. 7:13; Amos 4:12; Micah 1:3-7; Nahum 1:3; Joel 2:2; Zeph. 1:15; Matt. 24:30; 26:64; Mark 13:26; 14:62; Luke 21:27; Rev. 14:14,16.) That "every eye will see him" does not demand an assumption that John is referring to Christ's Second Coming. Jesus used the same figurative idiom when predicting that those Jews who were condemning him to be crucified would *see him coming* in powerful judgment upon them and

Climactic Parallelism Chart
Revelation 6–22
by Paul T. Butler

4

Chapters 19–20:6: Bride of Christ rejoices at victory of Bridegroom over Harlot (Rome). Bride antici- pates consummation of marriage; marriage not yet to be consummated so invitation still extended until Bride comes down from heaven after "1000 years." When harlot falls, Satan bound; destruc- tion of last universal humanism severely limited Satan's power, while saints given more expansion to reign, be priests and bring others to life by first resurrection (new birth). Second (eternal) death cannot harm these.

Chapters 15–18: Heaven readies to pour out judgment on Rome; time for intercession for Rome no more. Seven bowls of judgment essentially parallel 7 seals and 7 trumpets. While Rome destroyed itself, God was using such destruction, accompanied with his providential judgments, to warn and destroy at the same time. The "harlot" is destroyed because she prostituted humanity and made the whole world join in her "fornication" (idolatry). The world does not offer to help the harlot — only bemoan her fall.

3

Chapter 14: Saints (churches of Asia Minor) given vision of ultimate destiny of redeemed and unredeemed as encouragement in endurance. Redeemed are those who follow the Lamb wherever he goes; they are blessed forever. Unredeemed those who worship beast; tormented forever. History moves inevitably toward judgment, but reaping need not await end of time — God about ready to reap Rome.

Chapter 12–13: Rome's attempt to thwart God's redemption by trying to kill Son of God and devour Bride of Christ ("woman"). Devil enlists aid of Rome ("beast"). Beast gives power to another beast (differ- ent phase of Rome's satanic role). John exposes the "beast" as merely human and warns against worshiping it for its destiny and that of all who worship it is to be destroyed forever. Whole world (including church) tempted to worship beast who appears invincible.

2

Chapters 10–11: God warned his enemies; they do not repent; God delays their judgment no longer; thunder sounds — it is coming; sour to the world, sweet for the saints. God's house (church & Word), but God receives them. Great shaking of Roman Empire as portent; heavenly band rejoice because victory is apparent. God is always faithful. Enemies think they have slain God's witnesses (church).

Chapters 8–9: Tribulations on world by desire to conquer must be warned against. God sounds 7 "trumpet" warnings in form of natural disaster, internal chaos, international assault. Rome is given up to destruction (cf. Rom. 1:18ff.), but Rome does not repent. Judgment must come. It is por- tended in ch. 10–11.

1

Chapter 7: During the great tribulation of Rome's imperialism, God's saints are safe. God has all his numbered; he will not lose one; they are his new "Israel." No human knows how many belong to God; all washed in Lamb's blood, though martyred, are safe.

Chapter 6: Rome's insatiable desire to conquer produces war, famine, pestilence, death. Christians will suffer during this tribulation and cry out for vindication. God will bring such destruction on Rome it can only be described in apocalyptic, cataclysmic terms. Even the enemies of God will acknowledge it as the Lamb's wrath.

5

The 1000 years

From Rome's fall until the end of time and the Second Coming of the Lord in judgment on the whole world

(shortened perspective in style of O.T. prophets)

6

Revelation 20:7–22:5

Satan sets himself to conquer the church but God destroys.

God then brings whole creation to judgment.

Bride's marriage is consum- mated.

Second death for unredeemed; life everlasting for redeemed.

All of John's vision after the Throne Room is one vision, seen from different perspectives, running parallel to one another. The one vision is Rome's attempt to usurp the Lamb's sovereignty over the world by destroying his redemptive kingdom in the world (the church). As Rome attempts this, the Lamb is seen using the chaos caused, and adding his own providential control of events, to warn Rome to repent, chasten and save his church, and finally bring Rome's downfall. ALL THESE PREDIC- TIONS RUN PARALLEL TO ONE ANOTHER UNTIL THEY REACH A CLIMAX AT THE DESTRUCTION OF ROME. This severely restricts the powers of Satan (binds him), a victorious era of the church ensues (symbolized by "1000 years"). The fall of Rome and destruction of the "beast" typifies and presages the consum- mation of all history (time unknown), described by the Lamb in Rev. 20:7–22:5.

their nation in A.D. 66-70.[11] The Roman Empire (i.e., those who pierced him and all the tribes of the earth) will *see* him come in judgment, just as the Jews did.

The Jesus who is "coming" in judgment upon the "beast"[12] is none other than The Beginning and the End, the Eternal One, and the Almighty One. This is the Jesus Rome, and the Jews, cursed, abused, crucified and whom they thought they had exterminated. This One is the Lord of history, Lord of all that exists, and the One who has the "keys of Death and Hades." He is Lord of life beyond time and space and earth.

The person writing this Revelation was widely known to the Christians of Asia Minor. He was *one sharing* (Greek, *synkoinonos*) or *participating* with the Christians of Asia Minor in the *tribulation*, the *kingdom* and the patient *endurance*. This is unequivocal proof that the "kingdom" and the church of Christ were, and are, one and the same! John was *participating* with the seven churches of Asia Minor in "the kingdom." The "kingdom" of Christ is not in the future; it is here and has been ever since the day of Pentecost in Acts, chapter 2! John's exhortations to faith and endurance would have much more impact on the persecuted Christians of Asia Minor because they came from one suffering tribulations as a Roman prisoner in the copper mines of the island of Patmos.

The Revelation is specifically begun in historical circumstances. It is written in a book and sent to seven named churches. It is *epistolary* as well as *prophetic*. Revelation ends in historical circumstances with instructions, promises, warnings, and a perpetual invitation (see Rev. 22:6-21). It is hermeneutically proper, then, to conclude that what is dramatically symbolized in between is referring to historical circumstances relatively contemporary with, and imminently future to, John and the seven churches!

The Greek article is absent in the phrase "one like a son of man," so John is saying that which he saw was *like* a human being, i.e., it was not like an animal or some material object. "Son of man" is an eschatological, symbolic title for the Messiah.[13] It was Jesus' favorite title for himself while he was on earth. Thus, John is also signifying that the One he sees is the formerly incarnated Lord God, now exalted as Sovereign Lord God. He stands "in the midst of the seven churches" and they are to know that he is aware of their condition and circumstances. He has eyes that penetrate like a flame of fire beyond the facade of the churches' outward appearances. He "holds" the messengers of the churches in his right hand. They belong to him. They are to deliver the message to the churches which he wants them to hear — not what they want to hear. His symbolic regalia portrays his omnipotence, omniscience, intercessory priesthood, and his purpose to speak words of judgment (the sword coming out of his mouth) upon both the churches and the "beast." (Compare

Rev. 2:16; 19:11-16; Jer. 5:14; Hos. 6:5; Eph. 6:17; Heb. 4:12; 2 Cor. 10:3-5; 6:7; 1 Tim. 1:18.)

The Greek phrase *mellei genesthai meta tauta* is translated, "what is to take place hereafter." More precisely it means, "what is about to, or is on the point of happening."[14] What John sees, in the entire Revelation, and is to write, is not relegated to the far distant future, for it "is on the point of happening."

Revelation 2:1–3:21
"He who has an ear, let him hear what the Spirit says to the churches."

Our comments on the letters to all seven churches will be subsumed as one section. To do so aids in understanding the overview of the Revelation. Jesus has revealed *himself*, in all his glorious omnipotence and omniscience. He is the "ruler of kings on earth" and no longer the incarnate "smitten, afflicted Lamb led meekly and mute to the slaughter." He is also Lord of the church, and the churches of Asia Minor needed to be reminded of that! We will comment on the seven churches only as their situations relate to the eschatology of the Revelation.

The churches of Asia Minor (modern Turkey) were going to face great pressure (the Greek word *thlipsei*, translated "tribulation," means *pressure, constraint*). That pressure was already starting. It would manifest itself in three areas: political persecution, false religion, and sensual materialism (i.e., the "beast, false prophet, and harlot"). When all this *tribulation* came, the Christians (churches) of Asia Minor would be asking "Where are God and Jesus now?" The answer began in chapter one, "I am here, in your midst, and I will be forevermore. I am sovereign and am prepared to sustain you so that you may *get through the great tribulation*." The rest of the Revelation verifies that Christ knows in great detail what the churches will endure and that he has the power to sustain them.

But the imperative question is: "Where is the Lord's *church* in Asia Minor? Is it prepared to stand the onslaught of the beastly Roman Empire?" God's program for the sanctification and edification of the church has always been for it to see the sovereignty and love of God, see man's failures and the need of God's grace, then relate that to the heathen, antagonistic world around the church. This is God's program throughout the Bible — for both the Old Testament church and the New Testament church. Revelation is no different; it portrays the same program. These churches of Asia Minor are going to be thrust into the "wilderness" (an hostile environment) where they are to be "nourished" for an indefinite time (Rev. 12:6,14; Deut. 8:2,3,16).

Most of the seven churches of Asia Minor appeared outwardly to be worthy of praise. Judged by themselves and worldly standards most were very successful. Two of them (Smyrna and Philadelphia) apparently judged themselves *unsuccessful.* Judged by the Lamb there were a few worthy things to be commended. With all their outward successes one would think nothing negative should be sounded toward these churches at all. But the letters from the Lamb are to the contrary! This should prove once for all that the world's evaluation of the church's success, and even the church's evaluation of itself, is much different than that of the Lord!

The apostle Paul wrote his letter to the Ephesians from his imprisonment in Rome under Nero about A.D. 60-61 and closed it with these words: "Grace be with all who love our Lord Jesus Christ *with love undying*" (emphasis ours). Now, 35 years later, the church at Ephesus had "abandoned" the love it had at its beginning. They must restore it. Love is more than emotion or sentimentality. It is *commitment* of mind and will and life in the service of others. Toil may be done without love for God or man. Praying, giving alms, and fasting may be done for self-glorification (Matt. 6:1-18). Only love that is "genuine," "sincere" (Rom 12:9; 1 Pet. 1:22), and "fervent" will sustain the church facing the three-pronged assault of the devil in the persons of the beast, false prophet, and harlot. *Agape* love, God's love, is a choice to care in spite of feelings and emotions. Jesus asked Peter, "Do you love me?" Peter replied, "Yes, Lord, you know I love you." Jesus demanded, *"Feed my sheep!"* Loving the Lord is *"keeping his commandments"* (John 14:21,23; 15:10,14; 1 John 2:24; 3:23,24; 5:3). Christian love is a *reaction*. It is a reciprocation for the love of God given (2 Cor. 5:14; 1 John 4:10,19).

The church at Smyrna was surrounded by an affluent elite who loved Roman ways and idolatry. Polycarp, an elder in the church there, was martyred some 50 years after John wrote Revelation. A community of Jews were there "slandering" the Christians — probably rumoring that they were a rabble of "outcasts" and slaves. The Christians in Smyrna evaluated themselves as "poverty" stricken. They must repent of that attitude and see themselves as Christ sees them. Jesus evaluated the church as "rich." A recognition of the *true* riches is necessary to prepare for the assault of the "beast and the harlot." The cares of this world and delight in riches induce a vulnerability that allows for "choking-out" of mature spirituality (Matt. 12:23; Luke 8:14; 1 Tim. 6:6-10). The *true* riches of a church lie in the character of its people (like Polycarp), not its property. Jesus is about to put this church into the crucible of the great tribulation of Rome to purify it and make it truly rich. If the church at Smyrna does not recognize this, she will not endure.

Idolatry was endemic in the city of Pergamum, and the resultant carnality was rampant. The carnal philosophy of the Balaamites and Nicolaitans had infected the church there. Jesus warns that if they are to resist the "beast," their carnality must go. Repentance was imperative. Fleshly-mindedness wars against spiritual-mindedness

(Rom. 8:6-8; Gal. 5:16-17; Jas. 4:1-4). Carnality unchecked leads human beings to live like animals (Rom 1:18-32; 2 Pet. 2:12,22). Carnality is the "mark of the beast." The church at Pergamum, if it was to survive the seduction of "beastly" Rome, had to repent of its own beastliness.

Thyatira was corrupted with the false teaching of Jezebel! Militant false teaching by this "woman" was destroying the church. Love, faith, service, patient endurance and growth in good works are to be pursued, *but not at the cost of doctrinal orthodoxy!* The pragmatism that tolerates false doctrine in order to produce outward "growth" is an abomination to Christ. False teaching cannot be tolerated by the Lord of the church. He *forbids* it in his church! "More" and "bigger" are not always better. If this church was to resist being led astray into the false religion of the "second beast which was the false prophet" and its consequences, it was imperative that they purge themselves of "Jezebel" and her pseudo prophesying. Tolerating false doctrine is as much a "mark of the beast" as carnality.

One of the earliest elders of the church at Sardis was Melito, the first known commentator on the book of Revelation. The church here had a reputation of "being alive." But Christ saw through the veneer of "liveliness" and pronounced her "dead." Jesus could find none of the works of the saints at Sardis perfect (finished). Evidently this church had, by its busyness and its bustling activities, fooled itself and the secular community into thinking it was a "live-wire" congregation. It enthusiastically engaged in many religious-appearing activities, but it never *finished* anything. It had the if-I'm-excited-and-doing-something-I'm-holy syndrome. It was all on the surface. What would a "finish the job" attitude have to do with preparing to endure the beastliness of Rome? Christ warns the church that it must be more dogged than delirious — more consistent than "charged-up." Jesus always cautioned would-be disciples to *count the cost of finishing before starting* (Luke 14:25-35). Paul, about to be martyred, wrote to Timothy about those who deserted him at his first defense (2 Tim. 4:14-16). Superficiality in relationship to Christ will not sustain the soul in the face of the beastliness of a sinful world.

The saints at Philadelphia evidently complained of their powerlessness. The city of Philadelphia in Asia Minor sat on a huge seismological fault and was repeatedly devastated by earthquakes. A "synagogue of Satan" was there as in Smyrna. Once Christ came to fulfill the redemptive program of God, impenitent, unresponsive Judaism would be viewed by God as aligned on the side of Satan. Those not with Christ are *against him* (Matt. 12:30). For Jewish Christians to revert to Judaism was classified in the book of Hebrews as apostasy, crucifying the Son of God afresh and holding him up to contempt, profaning the blood of the covenant, and outraging the Spirit of grace (Heb. 6:6-8; 10:29). Thus, in my opinion, *any* Jewish synagogue after the once-for-all redemptive work of Christ, *is a synagogue of Satan!* The book of Acts and the Epistles of the NT show clearly that the Jews were violently against the church of Christ, undermining and debilitating the church's power during the first century. Remember John the Baptist said of the recalcitrant Jews they were, a "brood of vipers" (Luke 3:7ff). Jesus said they were "sons of the devil" (John 8:44) and "children of hell" (Matt. 23:15). Paul called the Judaizers, "dogs" and "evil workers" (Phil. 3:3) and associated them with "Satan" (2 Cor. 11:13-15). But Christ insists to the church at Philadelphia it must prepare for the onslaught of Rome by ceasing to view itself as powerless. In the face of the huge "beastliness" of secular Rome, the saints had to see themselves as imbued with the power of Christ who overcame the world. Yes! Even in the soon-coming "great tribulation" Philadelphia Christians would have an "open door" set before them. Christ had promised and was able to make a fearless church victorious over her enemies. If Christ opens, no one will be able to shut!

Egotism and complacency go hand-in-hand. That was the condition of the church at Laodicea. The Christians there believed themselves to have everything they needed because they had a congregation of "prosperous" members. They had become tepid, indifferent, putrid in their Christian witness. Christ saw them as wretched, pitiable, poor, blind, and naked. Christ wanted the church at Laodicea to be "hot" *for* him and "cold" toward paganism. What he demanded was total *loyalty* or none at all. But the Laodiceans tried to be "in the middle." He knew that only a firm, stable, unwavering, Christian lifestyle would endure the temptations which came from the world of Rome.

Fundamentally, then, the threat to the churches of Asia Minor was from **within**, not from without! The churches did not know that — but Christ did. And, loving these churches, he reproved, threatened, and chastened them through these letters and the great tribulation that was soon to come. Christ "knocked" on their doors, but he did not force himself into their fellowship. If they were to survive and receive the divine reward, they would have to repent!

There are significant lessons for today's church to be learned from the admonitions of Christ to its brethren 2000 years ago in Asia Minor: (a) Christ exposes the church to herself as realistically as possible in his word; (b) the church usually sees her great threat as from without, but Jesus reveals it as *from within*; (c) the church must evaluate itself and everything else in its experience according to Christ's revelation, not its own standards or those of the world; (d) Christ stands at the door of his church and "knocks," sometimes with words, sometimes with "tribulation"; (e) survival of Christ's church does not depend on worldly power, worldly sophistication, or worldly financial status — its survival depends on its response to Christ's call for *repentance*.

Thus the vision of the churches portrays the glorified Christ in the midst of the churches, aware of their conditions and circumstances, revealing, protecting, and calling them to *repentance*. He alone has the "keys" to death and Hades (the life beyond death). The next scene of this great drama connects the former vision to the visions (scenes) that are to come later.

Revelation 4:1–5:14
"... and lo, a throne stood in heaven ..."

Throne-visions are called "theophanies." God appeared numerous times in the OT. He appeared to Abraham, Isaac and Jacob. He appeared to Moses, Aaron, Samuel, and others. There are only four *major* "throne-visions." Isaiah saw the throne of God; Ezekiel saw it; Daniel saw it; and John saw it (Isa. 6:1ff; Ezek. 1–3; Dan. 7:1ff; Rev. 4–5). John's vision of the throne was recorded for the seven churches of Asia Minor. If they were to be spiritually armed for their battle against the "beast, false prophet and harlot," it was imperative that they see all their circumstances through the throne-perspective. Only as these churches saw their coming tribulation as under the control of God's throne and as God's purpose for their sanctification and edification would they be able to answer the call to faith and endurance.

At these very crucial eschatological points in God's redemptive work it was necessary that his redemptive people be given a throne-perspective of history as they were experiencing it. Isaiah was called into the temple and saw the Lord on his throne when the respected king Uzziah had died and the Assyrians threatened to destroy the covenant nation. When the faithful remnant was about to lose hope during the Babylonian assault on Jerusalem and their forced exile in Babylon, Ezekiel received a vision of the sovereignty of God's throne over their circumstances. Down in Babylon, when God wanted to prepare the messianic remnant to remain faithful during the 490 years of indignation yet to come upon them, he gave Daniel a throne-vision.

In Isaiah's time, the king of Assyria boasted that he was sovereign of all the world. In the days of Ezekiel and Daniel, the emperor of Babylon arrogated to himself divinity and sovereignty. To each of these prophets a clear revelation was given that Jehovah was Sovereign over all creation. They in turn delivered this revelation to a remnant of believers facing a crisis in their faithfulness to God. They needed to know and believe that, contrary to appearances, no human being had the power to thwart God's redemptive program. God's covenant would be fulfilled in spite of the worst that could be done by man and the devil to stop it.

Now, in the critical centuries of the church of Christ John is given an even clearer revelation of the sovereignty of both God and Jesus Christ. First we have the eschatological notation when a "voice like a trumpet" said, "Come up here and I will show you *what must take place after this*." Then a "door in heaven is opened" for him to peer through! John saw a *person* ("he") sitting on a *throne*. Human language is so inadequate to describe this *Person* in anthropomorphic terms, John described *Him* in symbols; *He* was like "jasper" (diamond) symbolizing eternalness and like "carnelian" (a precious red stone) symbolizing justness and mercifulness. The throne was wrapped around with a rainbow symbolizing covenant-faithfulness of the One on the throne (Gen. 9:8-17; Ezek. 1:26-28; Rev. 10:1). He saw twenty-four "elders" on twenty-four "thrones." This symbolizes the *specially appointed* human beings (i.e., patriarchs and apostles) whom God called and commissioned at specific eschatological points in the divine scheme of redemption. They were given "keys to the kingdom" and "sat in judgment" upon the twelve tribes of Israel" (Matt. 10:40-41; 16:17-19; 18:18-20; 19:28-30; Luke 24:44-49; John 20:21-23; Acts 2:1-47). But their "thrones" are so inferior to the *One* seated in their midst, they fell down before him and worshiped him and cast their crowns before him.

The throne exudes all the symbols of activity, power and majesty — voices, flashing lightning, and peals of thunder (Exod. 19:16; Job 37:1-5; 38:35; Isa. 6:1-6; Ezek. 1:1-28; Dan. 7:9-13; Matt. 17:1-8; 1 Tim. 6:15-16; Heb. 12:18-21; 2 Pet. 1:16-18). The Holy Spirit of God ("seven spirits") was there. Spreading out before the throne was a "crystal sea" of glass symbolizing God's "crystal-clear" revelation of himself from heaven.

> The 'crystal sea' probably symbolizes that the sovereignty of the throne of God in the affairs of history is translucent. Paul wrote in Romans 1:18ff that "the wrath of God *is* revealed from heaven against all ungodliness . . ." and that what could be known about God was *plain* to them — namely God's eternal power and deity — because God had shown it to them in creation. The Old Testament prophets repeated this same principle. . . . In addition to the revelation in creation, God has revealed his sovereignty in history in an even clearer communication, the Bible. . . . God intended this Revelation to be "crystal clear" and expected those who read it to understand it. It does not require theological experts or mystical diviners to interpret what Revelation is saying. It requires only a fundamental knowledge of history, a common sense grasp of human language and its symbols, and an honest heart. *Why* God acts as he does in history may be beyond our understanding . . . but *that he does* is crystal clear! It is plain to all men that there is a Divine Throne occupied by a Divine Being presiding over time and space and history. All who deny it, do so from a moral prejudice (cf. 2 Pet. 3:3-7; 2 Thess. 2:10-12; Rom. 2:14-16, et al.), not from lack of evidential clarity. . . . Those who see from the crystal-surrounded Throne view know that God's grace is sufficient for them even if they must bear a 'thorn in the flesh' all their lives here on earth (cf. 2 Cor. 12:7ff); they see that they need endurance (Heb. 10:35-

39); they see clearly that the chastening of the Lord is for the moment painful, but in the long-haul yields the peaceful fruit of righteousness (Heb. 12:1-11). That is precisely what God wants the seven churches of Asia Minor to do in their historical crisis — see the "beast" from the throne-view. When they do, it will be "crystal-clear" to them that God is sovereign, not the Roman emperor; the tribulation coming upon the church is in the control of God; He will use it to His glory and purpose; believers who remain faithful will come out of the tribulation to rest and blessedness; the church will not only survive but will be victorious.[15]

All living creation (wild beasts, domesticated beasts, human beings, and birds of the air) is symbolically represented as worshiping the *One* on the throne along with the 24 elders. They acclaim the throne *Person's* worthiness to be worshiped and testify that everything which exists does so by *His* willing it and creating it to exist. Members of these seven churches, many of whom were formerly Gentile idolaters, were reminded vividly that the throne of the universe was *not* in Caesar's palace in Rome, but in heaven! The essence of Christian prayer is, "Our Father, which art in heaven; Hallowed be thy name; thy kingdom come, thy will be done, on earth as it is in heaven."

The next thing John saw was a "scroll" in the right hand of the *One* upon the throne. It was "sealed" with seven seals, and no one in heaven or on earth or under the earth was found worthy to open the scroll. Suddenly, one of the 24 elders informed John that the Lion of the tribe of Judah had "conquered" *so that* he could open the scroll and its seven seals. He was worthy *because* he *eschatologically* entered the human frame of reference and *conquered* or *redeemed* human history. He *earned* the right, therefore, to *reveal* and *interpret* history — past, present, and future!

The "scroll" (*biblion*) has a *central part* in the throne-vision. It says, "God reveals — man is to listen!" God knows history from beginning to end. History will accomplish God's ultimate purpose. Human beings cannot discover history's purpose or God's will for them within history unless they let God reveal it to them (Deut. 29:29).

John saw a "Lamb" *having been slain* (*esphagmenon,* perfect tense participle, "having been slain in the past with a continuing result") standing between the throne and the four living creatures. His death interceded for and redeemed all creation. He has divine omnipotence and omniscience and is also the Holy Spirit sent back into the world on God's mission to "convict the world of sin, and righteousness, and judgment" (John 16:8). The "Lamb" is Jesus Christ. By his incarnate redemptive work he *earned the right* to take the scroll from the *One* on the throne and to open it. He is praised by all of heaven as "worthy" to do so. Thus it is being signified that God made "The Lamb" sovereign on the throne of the universe and over all of history — not Domitian! The "Lamb," innocence incarnated, vicarious sacrifice incarnated, he, who was servant of all, is made Greatest of all (Eph. 1:19-23; Phil. 1:5-11; Col. 1:15-20; 1 Tim. 3:16; Heb. 1:5-9; 7:26-28). It is not beastly human power that rules the universe and controls history; rather, it is Lamb-likeness and servanthood. Eschatology, the end of all things, is under the rule of Christ, not men.

The throne vision means: (a) there is an Absolutely Sovereign Being enthroned over all creation and history, and all "crowns" should be cast down before him; (b) this throne is the ultimate source of all truth; every person and event is to be evaluated through this perspective, and without revelation from this throne man is left to weep; (c) what sinful mankind enthrones is opposite from what God enthrones; (d) Jesus, conqueror of death and sin in the flesh is the only Being, ever, with authority to reveal "the scroll" of God's will — **hear ye him!**

Revelation 6:1-17
"... the Lamb opened ... the seven seals ..."

The Lamb, formerly the incarnate Son of God, was exalted to divine sovereignty. It was time now to portray him governing history. He began to open the seven seals, one at a time, to reveal "what was soon to come to pass" in the world of Rome and the seven churches of Asia Minor. The confrontation of the churches with their world was to be a great spiritual struggle with Imperial Rome to become the devil's tool. John's vision of what was to come "hereafter" stretches out over a span of more than three hundred years after he saw it.

A *seal* in both OT and NT represented, either symbolically or literally, that a document was *closed* and to be opened only by someone with authority to do so, or, that the document had been authenticated as authoritative and belonged to the person whose image appeared on the seal, or both. It appears that the *seven seals* symbolize both concepts here. When the seals are opened they will reveal, in a *generic* scope, what will be experienced by the Roman world from approximately A. D. 100 to 450. As a consequence of Rome's ravenous hunger to extend the borders of its territorial and economic rule, a "great tribulation" would come upon all the civilized world. The churches of Asia Minor were to understand that their commitment to Christ did not make them immune to the afflictions of history brought on by the sinfulness of the majority of mankind. Until the Lamb decides to call history to a halt, Christians would remain in the world. They were not to be *of the world* but to endure the distress that came upon the world as a *chastening* from the Lord (John 15:18-21; 16:33; 17:15; 1 Cor. 5:9-10; Heb. 10:32-39; 12:1-17; Rev. 12:10; 14:12). God has ordered his creation so that when human beings disobey the laws he decreed for sustaining social and physical harmony, reprimanding consequences occur (Psa. 119:65-72; Isa. 26:9-10; 59:1-3; Hos. 4:1-3; Joel 1:1–2:27; Amos 4:1-13; Rom. 1:24-32). The Christians of Asia Minor were not to be *surprised* at the fiery trial to come upon *them* as though it were something strange (1 Pet. 4:12). That is the way history is because human beings have allowed themselves to be deceived by Satan to renounce God's sovereignty and attempt to usurp God's rule of creation. "Power corrupts, and absolute power corrupts absolutely," said Lord Acton. Ancient Rome was the epitome and incorporation of all that rebellion in one, crushingly powerful, and decadently sensual empire.

John's vision *after* the Throne-vision, from 6:1–20:6, is *one vision,* seen from different perspectives, running **parallel** to one another. The *one* vision is a prophetic portrayal of Rome's attempt to usurp the Lamb's sovereignty over the world by destroying his redemptive kingdom, the church. As Rome attempts this, the Lamb is seen using the chaos caused, and adding his own providential control of events, to warn Rome to repent. Christ used these events to chasten and save his church, and ultimately, to bring Rome's downfall. **All these predicted (seals, trumpets, bowls, and the fall of the great city) events run parallel to one another until they reach a climax at the destruction of Rome.** The *fall* of Rome severely restricted ("bind") the powers of Satan — a victorious era of the church ensued symbolized by "a thousand years." The fall of Rome and the destruction of the "beasts" typifies and presages the end of all history, the final judgment and the glorification of the church as described by the Lamb in Revelation 20:7–22:5. The time of the end is unknown and unknowable until it takes place.[16] See the chart on Parallelism at the end of notes on the seals.

The **first seal** portrays a rider on a white horse. He symbolized Rome's insatiable lust to conquer the world. The *general idea* of human governments engaged in warfare by the permissive will of God is in both the Old Testament and the New Testament (See Isa. 10:5-23; 13:17-22; 45:1-7; Jer. 27:1-11; Dan. 2,7,9,10,11; Rom. 13:1-7; 1 Pet. 2:13-17). The spirit of greed and conquest was in the heart of the Roman emperors. In their arrogance and ambition they brought war and destruction on the earth. And the righteous suffered along with the wicked. But the absolutely sovereign God turned the tribulation into judgment upon the wicked and spiritual growth for his covenant people.

We do not agree with expositors who insist the rider on the white horse of the first seal must be the same person as the rider on the white horse in Revelation 19:11-21. Context, not similarity of symbolism, must be of first consideration in interpreting the meaning. Furthermore, the Greek syntax of the last phrase of Revelation 6:2 would best be translated, ". . . and he went forth conquering *in order* that he might conquer." This first rider on the white horse represents conquest *as the end in itself.* That is not true of the Rider in 19:11-21. His purpose was to rescue his Bride.

The **second seal** was opened. A rider on a bright red horse was permitted to take peace from the earth so that men slew one another, and the rider was given a "great" sword. War decimated generations of prime young men who served in the Roman army from all the imperial provinces. The Roman war machine kept on swallowing the world's population and wealth for 350 years. Literally millions of Rome's citizens as well as her enemies lost their lives and properties to her imperialistic greed.

Rome's imperial thrust reached as far as the British Isles in the west and Parthia (Iran) in the east. It was Julius Caesar, Rome's first would-be-emperor, who uttered the oft quoted Latin phrase, *"Veni, vidi, vici"* — "I came, I saw, I conquered!" A white horse was always ridden by conquering emperors and generals in ceremonial processions through the streets of Rome. Gibbon wrote that Trajan (A.D. 98–117) was "ambitious of fame" and tried to emulate Alexander the Great in conquering the world. Trajan wrote daily to the Roman Senate of new races and nations surrendered to his conquests.

John depicted the soon-to-come-to-pass history of the Roman Empire as one of imperialistic expansion. The "beast" was going to gobble up ("devour and break in pieces," Daniel 7:7) nations on an international scale as never before. Rome's annexation of Europe and Parthia required massive military power and unimaginable economic expenditure. It produced consequences symbolized by the following three horsemen of the Apocalypse.

Daniel characterized Rome as the "fourth beast" which would be "exceedingly strong" with great iron teeth as it devoured and stamped into oblivion all it could get in its gluttonous grasp. It was to smash and conquer more destructively than all the "beasts" preceding it (Dan. 2:40-43; 7:7-25). But Daniel predicted the "fourth" would be the last universal human "kingdom." It would be conquered by the *fifth universal kingdom*, the everlasting kingdom of God which was to come into existence "in the days" of the kings of Rome (Dan. 2:44-45; 7:26-27). That is precisely what happened!

From the Early Republic (509–264 B.C.) until the Goths and Vandals destroyed her, Rome was in constant warfare. Even in the one era, called *Pax Romana*, i.e., "Roman Peace" (27 B.C.–A.D. 180), Rome was still making war to expand her borders. It was during the era of *peace* that Claudius annexed Britain and Trajan annexed Dacia and Mesopotamia! From A.D. 180 until Rome's complete disintegration she was involved in wars against invaders, civil wars, and a fatal division of the empire between East and West. The carnage and cruelty that came upon civilization through Rome's destructiveness and depravity is unparalleled in history.

The opening of the **third seal** produced a rider on a black horse. As the context indicates, the black horse symbolized *famine*. Basic food staples were at premium prices. Only the rich could afford the luxuries of life. A basic strategy of ancient warfare was the "scorched earth" policy. Crops and food storage were often destroyed by those under attack from invaders to deprive the enemy of their sustenance. Add to that the natural disasters of droughts, floods, earthquakes, and volcanic eruptions predicted for the empire by John (See Rev. 6:12-17; 8:1-12; 16:1-21) and the necessities of nourishment were extremely meager.

The balance-scales and the exorbitant price for *a measure* of wheat (*choinix*, actually less than a quart) predicts the severity of the famine. A *choinix* of wheat was about enough to feed one person for one day. And it would cost one *denarius* which was one day's pay for a laborer. A family of four would have extreme difficulty surviving.

The empire was structured in a tripartite sociological stratification: (a) an extremely rich aristocracy amassing wealth from taxation and extensive land holdings; (b) a massive slave population forced to do practically all labor except commerce and the arts; (c) and a huge "middle-class" of free Roman citizens, unemployed and depending upon "government dole." When economic inflation caused hunger everywhere but among the indulgent aristocracy, there was civil unrest in the form of riots and rebellions throughout the empire. Increasingly heavy taxation upon their provinces precipitated a number of revolts, including the Jewish rebellion (A.D. 66-70) which ended in the destruction of the Jewish nation. Jesus predicted the worldwide wars and natural disasters which would precede the destruction of Jerusalem by the Romans in Matthew 24, Mark 13, and Luke 21.

The rider of the **fourth seal** is upon a *pale horse*. The Greek word is *chloros* (from which we get the English word, "chlorophyll"), and it means, *pale green*. The rider is named *Thanatos*, or "Death." He was followed by "Hades" which is the abode of the dead or the realm of the unknown. These two "riders" were *given* power over a fourth of the earth to kill with sword, famine, pestilence, and wild beasts of the earth. The insatiable lust to conquer produced worldwide war; this brought bloodshed, famine, pestilence, and death in the Roman arenas from wild beasts. The imagery in the fourth seal is exactly like that in the OT prophets Ezekiel and Jeremiah (Ezek. 14:21; Jer. 21:6-9). Disease swept through the Roman Empire time after time, killing people by the thousands. In the years A.D. 157-160 a terrible plague brought back by Roman soldiers from the Parthian battlefields, decimated the Roman world. A second plague which lasted some 15 years (A.D. 251-265) killed half the people of the Roman Empire. John's predictions about wild beasts also had special meaning to the tens of thousands of people who would have to fight and die in the gladiatorial arenas wrestling ravenous animals — both Christian and non-Christian. Suetonius wrote that emperor Marcus Aurelius in one year had 174 days of "games." The bloodbath from animals and humans slaughtered every other day in one year of "games" would be unimaginable.

So, death and Hades, the unknown life beyond the grave, for a *fourth* of the earth is the result of Rome's quenchless thirst for conquest. "Fourth" should not be understood literally. Neither should it be applied to any particular geographical location. Catastrophic death does not necessarily mean the victims are "worse sinners" than any others who die. Jesus spoke to that issue plainly enough.[17] "A fourth" is simply a figure of speech meaning the effects will not be *total*, but will occur all through the Roman world during its closing centuries. It will, of course, include Asia Minor. The fourth seal was a summation of the first three, with pestilence and wild beasts added as further consequences of Rome's mania for imperialism.

Christ's résumé of the history of the Roman Empire here is prophetically realistic. Jesus did not want the churches of Asia Minor to be naive about the world and the effects of sin. They must not be duped by the Satanic lie that man without God is fundamentally good. Rome in rebellion against God's will was evil. As long as those Christians were in the world of Rome's making, they would suffer the same ravages to come upon all who were under the dominion of the "beast." *But when they came out of the great tribulation, they would be home with Jesus!* (Rev. 7:9-17).

The **fifth seal** revealed the martyred saints under the altar of God. The martyrs cried for vengeance. To some it might seem eschatologically inappropriate. Notice first, they have left the matter of accomplishing vengeance up to the Lord; second, they sought no more than God's "beloved" David sought in his imprecatory Psalms when he cried for justice (e.g., Psa. 5:9-10; 7:6; 10:1,15; 12:2). They sought no more than Habakkuk sought (Hab. 1:1-4). They sought no more for a world filled with wickedness and injustice than the Lord himself desires, for when the Lord's judgments are in the earth, the inhabitants of the world learn righteousness (Isa. 26:9-10; see also Eccl. 8:11). In fact, the Lord instructs his people to rejoice when he vindicates their faithfulness by judging their implacable enemies (e.g., Isa. 63:1-9; Jer. 50:18; 51:10-11; Rev. 18:20). God's answer to the martyred saints was given in Revelation 18:20 and 19:1-3. The present tribulation seemed terribly unjust to the persecuted saints. They were told to put their case to rest in the Lord's hands and trust that it was a part of God's great redemptive purpose in history. Then it would make sense to them. John's revelation always keeps the long view of God's redemptive purpose in history preeminent. Because of man's sin war, famine, pestilence, and persecution of the godly "a great tribulation" came to the world. Even the faithful suffered death. But when they were faithful unto death they received the crown of life. God justified their faith and suffering. God took control and brought down with a great demonstration of his wrath the seemingly invincible enemy of the saints.

The **sixth seal** is opened and John paints with words an eschatological, cataclysmic scenario of end-of-the-world dimensions. But this is apocalyptic imagery. It is not intended to be understood as predicting the total end of the cosmos. The OT prophets used the very same imagery predicting the downfall of ancient Babylon or a locust plague upon Judea (Isa. 13:1-22; Joel 2:1-11). Other uses of such apocalyptic hyperbole describing the *end* of ancient kingdoms should be studied (Isa. 14:21ff; 24:23; 34:1-4; Jer. 4:23-28; 15:9; Amos 4:9; Micah 3:6; Hab. 3:11). Jesus used the same graphic figures of speech to predict the destruction of Jerusalem, the *end* of Judaism, and the abrogation of the Mosaic covenant (Matt. 24; Mark 13; Luke 21).

Rome was to suffer God's apocalyptic wrath as a moral consequence of the havoc it wreaked upon mankind. God would not let depraved and violent Rome go on forever. It came to an *end*.[18] God took action through all the forces of creation to bring Rome to judgment. Cosmic forces were used by God to bring judgment crashing down upon those "kings of the earth" and their accomplices who thought they could wrest the control of the world from God and the Lamb. That is the point of this highly figurative picture of the sixth seal.

Even those who ignored God and opposed the Lamb *recognized* their judgment as the direct action of God's wrath! (Rev. 6:16-17; see also Rom. 1:18-23). Other arrogant heathen kings also acknowledged that they could not "stay the hand of the God of heaven" (Dan. 4:35; 5:22-23). A moment's reflection on the magnitude of the catastrophic consequences for the whole world at the disintegration of the Roman Empire provides an explanation for the cosmic, apocalyptic terms used by John to describe it. When Rome fell, it was the "end of the world" for subordinate "kings" and the merchants of the earth who had become "rich" by participating in Rome's wickedness (Rev. 17:1-6; 18:9-19). When Assyria and Babylon fell, it was the "end of the world" for those imperialists. When the Jewish nation was destroyed in A.D. 70, it was *the end of their world*, at least as far as God was concerned, and thus Jesus spoke of it that way in figurative language. It was reported by the historian Pliny that screams, curses and pronouncements of "the end of the world" were heard by those citizens of Pompeii and Herculaneum who were being buried under the 45 feet of scalding ashes of Mount Vesuvius when it erupted in A.D. 79. Historians have described the former empire of Japan and the Nazi "Third Reich" in the same hyperbolic language. Such hyperbole is not uncommon even today and was used by some to describe the wars in Vietnam and Kuwait.

Revelation 7:1-17
"... a hundred and forty-four thousand sealed ..."

"Four corners of the earth" symbolizes the totality of the world or of the land

(Isa. 11:12; Ezek. 7:2). Wind is used repeatedly in the OT and NT as a symbol of judgment and instability. (See Psa. 135:7; 147:18; Prov. 11:20; Isa. 11:15; 32:2; 41:16; 57:13; Jer. 49:36-38; Ezek. 5:2; 12:14; Dan. 2:35; Hos. 8:67; Matt. 11:7; Eph. 4:14; Jas. 1:6.) An angel was sent by God from where creation began ("the rising of the sun") with divine orders to the four angels "holding back" the impending judgments on Rome. Nothing was to be hurt until they had "sealed" the 144,000 servants of God on their foreheads. God was about to send judgment "trumpets" of warning upon civilization but he wanted to reveal that every last one of his servants on earth had been "numbered" and "sealed." These (144,000) were continually "coming *out* of the great tribulation" and forming that innumerable multitude in heaven which no man could number.

Seals of kings and other authorities in biblical times were used to authenticate, ratify, deputize, mark ownership and protect against fraud. This was not a physical seal or a literal "mark." It was to symbolize the manifestation of the Holy Spirit of God in the life of the Christian (2 Cor. 1:22; 2 Tim. 2:19; Eph. 1:12-14; 4:30). God's Spirit living in the saints, directing their lives, recreating the image of God in them, authenticated his genuine ownership of them. The imagery is from Ezekiel 9:3-11. As Ezekiel was given a vision of God's abandonment of Jerusalem to the Babylonians, he also saw a messenger of God going through the city putting a "mark" upon the foreheads of those who were opposed to all the ungodliness of their countrymen. God allowed no one to touch those "marked" by his angel in Jerusalem. That was the same message John gave the Christians of Asia Minor. God's people were all "marked" with the "seal" of his Holy Spirit, and God knew exactly which people belonged to him. They would have to go through the "great tribulation," but when they "came out" of it, belonging to him, they would join the "great multitude which no man could number" standing before the throne of the Lamb clothed in white robes.

These two groups (the 144,000 and the innumerable multitude) have been the subject of much confusion and controversy. But taking into consideration the pervasiveness of symbolic/apocalyptic style in the entire work of Revelation, and the context of the entire *drama*, and the original language of the text, confusion *or* controversy is eliminated. These two groups are one and the same group. They are *all* of God's saints visualized from *two perspectives* — both perspectives are from the throne of God. On earth they were the people in covenant with God, *numbered, identified, and about to go through a great tribulation*. In heaven they *had gone through* the great tribulation and had every tear wiped from their eyes.

The 144,000 were those saints of Asia Minor, and throughout the Roman Empire of that day, *as they were* still on earth. God knew precisely how many redeemed there were among the millions of the empire. He had them "sealed." They had his Spirit dwelling in them and they belonged to him. Even when they suffered death in the arena or through some other persecution of the "beast" they would not be "lost." They would become the innumerable host from every nation, tribe, people and tongue in the presence of God in heaven. The number 144,000 is a symbolic number. It is $12 \times 12 \times 1000$ — a large, complete, "covenant" number. It is **new** Israel (Rom 2:28-29; 4:11; 9:6-8; Gal. 6:15-16; Heb. 12:22-24, et al.). It could not be literal Israel because two tribes, Dan and Ephraim, were omitted from the list while Levi and Joseph (who received no official inheritance) were inserted. The omission and inclusion was designed! These were cryptic notices to tell readers John did not mean genetic Jews in the 12 tribes of Revelation 7:4-8. John called Jews "synagogues of Satan" in the letters to the churches.

"Israel" was not an unusual symbol for the New Testament church. See the following references: "The Israel of God" (Gal. 6:15-16); "The promise to Abraham was to heirs according to faith, not law" (Rom. 4:13ff); Gentiles are "Israel" by faith (Rom. 11:1-36); the true "circumcision" is Christians (Phil. 3:3); the true Jew is the one who is inwardly a Jew (Rom. 2:28); the church is "Israel," "Zion," "The House of David," "Beulah-land," "Jerusalem," "Abraham's offspring." Compare Amos 9:11-12 with Acts 15:12-21; compare Jeremiah 31:31-34 with Hebrews 8:1-13.

The innumerable multitude of Revelation 7:9-17 is identified by the text! It was a great multitude from all over the Roman Empire, of different races, cultures, and languages having gone "through the great tribulation" *as they had arrived* in heaven. These are those who had been and were being "clothed in white robes" (*peribeblemenous*, perfect tense participle). These are those "continuing to come out of the great tribulation" (*oi erchomenoi ek*, present tense participle). These are those who had already "washed their robes . . . made . . . white" (*eplynan*, "washed," and *eleukanan*, "whitened" — both verbs are aorist or past tense) in the blood of the Lamb. They had already become Christians and were **then and there** "coming through the great tribulation." This multitude is *not future* to 1999. It was a multitude whose departure from this world had already begun. It is of significance that the innumerable multitude in heaven was *not* spoken of as being "sealed." They had no need to be numbered and sealed — they were safe in eternity.

The seals are Christ's *vertically realistic* revelation of history versus man's *horizontally unrealistic* interpretation of history. History, from the perspective of heaven's throne-room is that all the tribulations (aggressive wars and their consequences, martyrdoms, natural calamities) were **God's trumpets of warning for the wicked world of Rome to repent**. Thus, when the **seventh** seal was opened, the seven trumpets were ready for sounding.

Revelation 8:1–9:21
"... the seven angels who had the seven trumpets made ready to blow them ..."

Just before the seven trumpets were blown there was momentary "silence" in heaven. What was to be "trumpeted" was *awesome*! What was to be announced should receive the world's undivided attention! It would be the *answer* of heaven's Throne to the intercessory *prayers* of the saints. The trumpets would "throw down on the earth" calamitous chastisements upon the world of Rome. Even heaven paused in silence anticipating the "great tribulation" that was to come upon the Roman world.

Throughout the Bible, trumpets symbolize *warnings* or other *announcements* of significance from God to which human beings are to give heed (e.g., Exod. 19:13, 16,19; 20:19 Lev. 25:9; Num. 10:1-10; Isa. 18:3; 58:1; Jer. 4:5,21; 6:1,17; 42:14; 51:27; Ezek. 7:14; 33:3-6; Hos. 5:8; 8:1; Joel 2:1,15; Amos 2:2; 3:6; Zeph. 1:16; Zech. 9:14; Matt. 6:2; 24:31; 1 Cor. 14:8; Heb. 12:19, et al.) The trumpets are moderately parallel to the seven seals. But the main purpose of the trumpets is to *intensify* the *consequences* of Rome's prostitution of God's creation. The apostle Paul wrote the Christians in the city of Rome detailing the terrible results of Rome's whoredom with idolatry. [19]

The first four trumpets symbolized the judgments of God as he used the elemental forces of "nature" to warn the Roman world that it should repent. God has been using "nature" from the initial sin in Eden as a warning when he "cursed" the earth. He "subjected the creation to futility" and put it in "bondage to decay" (Gen. 3:17; Rom. 8:18-23). The Lord has been announcing through "nature" the doom of this cosmos ever since Eden. The universal deluge in Noah's day (2 Pet. 3:10) and the plagues upon Egypt and Israel (See Exod. 7–12; Joel 1–2; Amos 3–4; Isa. 45:7; Ezek. 7–11; Hag. 1:1-11; et al.). Jesus plainly taught that natural calamities were *signals* for the whole world to repent, and so did Paul (Luke 13:1-5; Rom. 1:26-27). At each blast of the first four trumpets in Revelation 8 a different part of nature was affected. The trumpets harmed only "a third" of the elements, which indicates they were only *partial judgments — not final judgments*. The final judgments upon Rome were symbolized by the seven "bowls" poured out, when the harlot, great Babylon, falls. They were not final and universal judgments, otherwise none would be called to repent.

The **first** trumpet emphasized natural disasters which would "hurt" portions of earth's vegetation. Grain crops, orchards, vineyards, pastures and forests are essential to man's sustenance. Fires, droughts and hailstorms produced a mixture of devastation and death ("blood"). This could also refer to the falling of small meteorites upon the earth. Modern scientific investigation of the ocean floors and the land masses indicates a widespread occurrence of such phenomena in the earth's history. In A.D. 64 "a fire broke out in the Circus Maximus in Rome, spread rapidly, burned for nine days, and razed two thirds of the city. . . . Thousands of people lost their lives amid falling tenements in the crowded streets; hundreds of thousands wandered shelter-less through the nights, crazed with horror . . . ."[20] Josephus wrote of "perpetual droughts" and pestilence in the days of Augustus, Claudius, and Titus[21] Barbarian hordes of Goths, Vandals, and Visigoths burned Roman cities, crops and vineyards as they descended upon the empire in its death throes (A.D. 410-476).

The imagery in the first trumpet may have been appropriated by John from the highly figurative descriptions of judgments symbolized in Ezekiel by "Gog and Magog."[22] The prophecy in Ezekiel chapters 38 through 48 is an apocalyptic portrait of God's defeat of universal humanism at the death and resurrection of Christ and the establishment of his kingdom, the church.[23] Josephus notes the enormous size of hail upon some Egyptians.[24] The OT prophets speak both literally and figuratively of hail as a means of judgment (Josh. 10:11; Psa. 18:12,13; 78:47,48; 105:32; 148:8; Isa. 28:2,17; 30:30; 32:19; Ezek. 13:11,13; 38:22; Hag. 2:17). The prophets also refer to drought symbolically as a "fire" of judgment from God (Isa. 15:6-9; Jer. 50:38; Ezek. 5:13-17; 32:1-8; Joel 1:15-20; Amos 4:7-8; Hag. 1:11).

The **second** trumpet is sounded and "something like a great mountain, burning with fire, was thrown into the sea." Huge portions of sea life and marine commerce were destroyed. This symbolizes catastrophes of the earth's crust such as volcanoes, earthquakes, and landslides. Many volcanic eruptions and earthquakes occurred then, as now, in the seas as well as in the land masses. These cause massive tidal waves which also destroy life and property. There were many active volcanoes throughout the Roman Empire. More than 80 eruptions have been recorded for Mt. Etna. And Mt. Vesuvius, the most famous one, erupted in A.D. 79, turning day into pitch-black "night." For three nights the earth shook; cyclonic winds blew, whole audiences in theaters were "fossilized;" people wailed, screaming that all the gods were dead and the long predicted end of the world had come. Many ships at sea burned and were sunk by great tidal waves. Three cities were entombed under 45 feet of volanic ash — Pompeii, Stabie, and Herculaneum — and everything not consumed by fire was petrified under the ash.

Earthquakes were a part of everyday life throughout the Roman Empire, especially in Asia Minor where the cities of the "seven churches" were practically all built over a huge "fault" and were destroyed numerous times only to be rebuilt. The NT documents a number of earthquakes and so does Josephus. (See Matt. 27:52-54; 28:2; Acts 16:26; Josephus, *Ant.,* IV.5.2.) Roman hisorians Seneca and Tacitus mention earthquakes in places like Asia, Achaia, Syria, Macedonia, Cyprus, Paphos,

Crete, Italy, et al. Virgil spoke of droughts, insect infestations, and sweeping destructive storms in his poem, *Georgics*. Modern statisticians tell us that over two million human beings have been killed by earthquakes *just since A.D. 1900*. How many must have died in the Roman Empire from A.D. 100-450!

The **third** trumpet envisioned a "great star" as it fell from heaven. The star was named "Wormwood," and it made a third of the waters become "wormwood." The Greek word for "wormwood" is *apsinthos*, which in English is *absinthe*, and in German, is *vermuth*. Absinthe is a green, alcoholic liqueur containing oils of wormwood, anise, and other aromatics. Its continued use causes nervous derangement and death! It is a toxic poison. The Hebrew word translated "wormwood" is *la'an* meaning "to talk indistinctly, murmur, talk obscurely and unintelligently like one intoxicated."[25]

This trumpet symbolized man's pollution of fresh water by using it to make alcohol and causing the death of many people. It could be a figure of the pollution of fresh water by floods and sewage which would produce great plagues of typhoid, malaria and other disease. But it is no secret that the Roman Empire was plagued with drunkenness from its aristocracy down to its slave castes. One has only to read Tacitus or Suetonius to see that drunkenness was a chief factor in the ruination of the empire. Italy produced 50 famous kinds of wine. Rome alone drank 25 million gallons of wine per year; that is two quarts per week for each man, woman and child. Every 30 miles on a consular road was a *mansio*, or inn, which was also a store, a saloon, and a brothel. Antioch of Syria, during the feast of Brumalia in December, resembled one huge saloon and the streets ran all night long with revelry and wickedness. People by the hundreds, celebrating the opening of a new bridge built by Caligula, fell into the Tiber River and drowned because they were too drunk to swim. Wine taverns were so numerous in Rome that Martial, the poet, called it one "vast saloon." Many emperors and senators were unrestrained drunkards, i.e., Mark Antony, Tiberius, Claudius, et al. "Custom allowed the diner to empty his stomach with an emetic after a heavy banquet. Some gluttons performed this operation during the meal and then returned to appease their hunger; *vomunt ut edant, edunt ut vomant*, said Seneca — 'they vomit to eat, and eat to vomit.'"[26] Gauls and Germans brought into the empire by conquest, "drank rivers of beer and wine." Open sewage runoff of ancient cities of the empire were constant sources of contamination and disease. What man often calls "natural calamities" are simply the judgments of God built into the moral order of the world as he permits man to suffer the due penalty of his own sinfulness (Rom 1:27). Durant says that deforestation, erosion, and the neglect of irrigation canals was the cause of widespread pollution in Rome's last days. A large portion of the ancient city of Rome was built on a swamp which had not been properly drained. This produced widespread disease from insects and other causes.

When the **fourth** trumpet was blown, a third of the heavenly bodies were darkened and day and night were kept from giving light. The earth's source of light, heat and energy which sustained all human, animal and plant life was affected. The sun, moon, and stars (the atmosphere) have some effect on water, growing seasons and ocean tides. This trumpet was symbolizing droughts, excessive rainfall, cold, heat and a multitude of other atmospheric conditions. Cyprian, ca. A.D. 250, wrote that the empire's misfortunes were because, "the world has grown old, and does not remain in its former vigor. It bears witness to its own decline. The rainfall and the sun's warmth are both diminishing; the metals are nearly exhausted; the husbandman is failing in the fields."[27]

This trumpet was depicting some depletion of the solar system which in turn affected man's circumstances on earth. The second law of thermodynamics, also known as *entropy*, called by Albert Einstein "the premier law of science," shows that the solar energy of our cosmos is gradually, but inexorably, being depleted into an unusable state. The natural order is going from complexity to disorder. Creation has been subjected to futility and the bondage of decay! The ancient philosophers and scientists had some understanding of this "law."

The apostles, Peter and Paul, wrote that the ancient Roman world refused to heed the warnings of God in nature by exchanging the truth of God for a lie and deliberately ignoring the evidence God had placed in the natural order (2 Pet. 3:5-7; Rom. 1:22,25,28). John's Revelation agreed as he wrote, "The rest of mankind . . . did not repent of the works of their hands . . . ," not even after the wrath of God had spent itself in the bowls of wrath (Rev. 9:20-21; 16:8-11).

The next thing John saw was an "eagle" crying, "Woe, woe, woe . . ." The eagle (or vulture) is a bird of prey. Both the OT and NT use the eagle as a symbol of predators which feed on rotten carcasses (Deut. 28:49; Hos. 8:1; Hab. 1:8; Matt. 24:28; Luke 17:37). A bird of prey flying in mid-heaven was a harbinger of death and woe. It was a solemn warning of the terrible trumpets about to be sounded upon the Roman Empire. The cry according to Greek syntax is "Woe . . . to the ones presently dwelling on the earth." The text has a present tense participle. These trumpets were specifically for the Roman world of John's day, not for some alleged millennial age at the end of the twentieth century. The warning anticipated the three remaining trumpets. Calamities in the natural order were severe, but the next trumpets symbolized even more terrible circumstances; one pictured the hell-on-earth corruption from within the society itself, when people sought release by clamoring for death. Another predicted attacks and invasions by countless terrifying warriors on horses. John wrote that the vulture was circling. Rome was about to die. That was precisely how Jesus pictured the death of Judaism in his "Olivet Discourse."

The **fifth** trumpet featured a personalized "star" fallen from heaven to earth. "He" was given the key of the shaft of the "bottomless pit" (*abyssou*, "abyss"). The word *abyssou* is used again in Jude 6; Revelation 11:7 and 20:1,3. It is physically impossible for a pit to be bottomless so this "pit" must exist in the unseen, nonmaterial world. This *abyss* would be the same place as the "lake of fire and brimstone" where "smoke and torment" upon those with the mark of the beast rise up forever (Rev. 14:9-11; 19:20; 20:10,14; 21:8). He did not have the key until it was *given* him and he was *not* given control *over* the abyss. All he did was unlock it by order of the One who had given him the key. The Greek verb *peptokota* is perfect tense and indicates the "star" *had fallen in the past and was in a continuing state of fallenness*. This "star" was the same person as the "king" over the locusts (9:11) whose name was, in Hebrew, "Abaddon," and in Greek, "Apollyon." Both Abaddon and Apollyon mean "Destroyer." It is correct to understand this "star" was the devil or one of hell's angels who had joined him in the "great rebellion" (See Job 1:6-12; 2:1-8; Luke 10:18; John 12:31; 16:11; 2 Pet. 2:4; Jude 6; Rev. 12:9-12). The "throwing down" of the devil in Revelation 12:9-12 was in direct connection with his wrath (through the instrumentality of Roman paganism) upon the churches of Asia Minor (Rev. 12:13–13:1ff).

This "star" was allowed to let the torments from hell belch forth upon earth through Rome's complicity with Satan (Rev. 13:1-18). The "star" does not have the key by his own authority. The Lamb has the key to *everything* — even to "Death and Hades" (Rev. 1:19). That which belched forth from this *abyss* was the demonic forces of hell which took residence in the mentality of Roman politics, religion and culture.

Locusts were always associated with judgments from God upon the sins of mankind. (See Exod. 10:4-19; Deut. 28:38; 2 Chr. 6:28-31; 7:13; Psa. 105:34; Joel 1 and 2; Amos 4:9; Nahum 3:15, et al.) These could not have been literal locusts, for locusts do not have stinging tails. What John sees in this vision represents something much more terrible than literal locusts. This plague of "locusts" harmed only that part of mankind which was without "the seal of God upon their foreheads." They tortured but did not kill. It was *like* the poisonous sting of a scorpion. The Greek word *scorpiou* means "scatter."[28] The work of this huge cloud of "scorpions" was to shatter, scatter, and root out psychological and mental stability. It tormented mankind "five months" until people "longed to die," but they did not find death. (Compare Deut. 28:65-67; Job 3:21-22; 7:15-16; Jer. 8:1-7; Jonah 4:3.) One of the main contributing factors to Rome's downfall was its internal hellishness. Society was bifurcated between extremely rich and almost total welfare state; emperors and senators were little better than thugs killing and confiscating properties; the government became totally bankrupt in the reign of Marcus Aurelius; the army was a mob of untrustworthy mercenaries; assassination of political leaders was rampant; invasion and plundering by the Barbarians "scattered" the population; huge tracts of the countryside were devastated; the "middle-class" was squeezed out of existence into serfdom; streets of cities and highways of the empire were unsafe to travel; the first plague brought back to Rome by Marcus Aurelius' army caused *one fourth of the empire to perish*; the second plague ca. A.D. 252 lasted 15 years and at its peak in the city of Rome *5000 people per day died* while Alexandria lost *two thirds* of its population; Roman cities and villages either fortified themselves or were looted and destroyed by roaming bands of marauders (the city of Rome built a wall around itself 12 feet thick and 20 feet high for protection); economic inflation and devaluation of currency recurred over and over (laborer's wages were about 15-18 cents per day while meat sold at 20 cents per pound, eggs 9 cents per dozen, wheat $1.27 per bushel) — "mere words can scarcely convey the agony through which the inhabitants of that world passed."[29]

In addition to all this, the populace was tormented in soul and conscience by pandemic proportions of sexual profligacy. Practically every emperor and most of the citizenry who could afford it indulged in pederasty (Commodus had 300 little boys by which to satisfy his perverted sexual appetites). Great epidemics of syphilis and other venereal diseases swept central Italy in A.D. 65, 75 and 166. Virtue, faithfulness, cleanness was lost. Incest, abortion and homosexuality were pervasive (Rom. 1:24-32). Most of the nonruling classes of citizens lived on the constant edge of starvation and fear of murder or slavery, or death in the arena. The decadence of idolatrous religion induced the depression of unbelief followed by injustice, despair, and hopelessness. The sheer cruelty and bloodthirstiness of the society drove some to despondency. Seneca, the great philosopher, statesman, and poet said after attending the "games" in the arena: "I come home more greedy, more cruel, and inhuman, because I have been among human beings." The Cynic school of philosophy begun by Socrates found ready disciples in ancient Rome among whom was the famous Zeno. Lucian, the satirist wrote, "A short survey of life had convinced me of the absurdity and meanness that pervade all worldly purposes." Seneca, the Stoic, said, "The final lesson of the Stoic is contempt and choice of death . . . . wherever you look, there is an end to troubles. Do you see that precipice — it is a descent to liberty. Do you see that river, that cistern, that sea — freedom is at their depths . . . ." Marcus Aurelius said: "All that is prized in life is empty, rotten, and petty — and without a change of conviction what is there save a bondage of men who groan and pretend to obey?" Tacitus began his history of Rome with: "I am entering on the history of a period rich in disasters, frightful in wars, torn by civil strife and even in peace full of horrors." There were philosophical schools of Scepticism and Epicureanism which believed people should "eat and drink for tomorrow we die."[30]

It is evident that the suffering caused by the blackness belching from the abyss is, ultimately, *spiritual* suffering. William Barclay quotes a Roman writer named Cornelius Gallus, who said, "Worse than any wound is to wish to die and yet not to be able to do so." The Old Testament prophets recount over and over the hell-on-earth conditions which kill like a deadly plague any society deceived by Satanic idolatries (Isa. 3:1-26; 24:4-13; 57:1-21; Jer. 5:1-31; Hos. 4:1-19; Amos 8:1-14, et al.). Paul described the Roman society as depraved and bestial and warned the Ephesians that such debauchery emanates from hell.

The later chapters of Revelation agree with this symbolic characterization. In chapter 13 Rome's political power is pictured as an incarnation of the devil in what appears to be an invincible "beast." Rome's idolatrous religion is pictured as a vicious humanism incarnated in the second "beast" which has two horns but speaks like a lamb. Rome's carnal materialism and sexual perversion is symbolized as the "great harlot" who seduced the whole world to participate with her in "fornication" (Rev. 13:1-10,11-17; 17:1–18:24). As a result of Rome's opening up the abyss and allowing the tormenting plague of ungodliness to infect the empire, she was given a "like measure of torment and mourning" as her judgment" (Rev. 16:1-21; 18:6-8).

The vision of the fifth trumpet brings to an end the "first woe." Two more "woes" were to come. The "second" woe was the confrontation between the church and the word of God (the two witnesses) and the Roman "beast" (Rev. 11:1-14). The "third" woe was the fall of the *great city* which had dominion over the kings of the earth. The **sixth** trumpet revealed a summation of what the seven bowls brought on the *empire*. The **seventh** trumpet ushered in the judgments of the **seven bowls.** This was "announced to his servants the prophets" which certainly refers to Daniel's prophecy of the judgment of the "fourth beast" (Rev. 10:7). And the **seventh** bowl ushered in the third "woe" which was the final fall of the "great city" which is elaborated in Revelation chapters 17 and 18 (Rev. 16:17-19).

The **sixth** trumpet is blown and the four angels, bound but held ready at the great river Euphrates, were released. The "spirit of the Euphrates" or "Mesopotamia" was released against the Roman world. This goes all the way back to the Tower of Babel. It is the spirit of aggression and rebellion. The OT prophets saw in the plundering warlords of the Euphrates Valley (Assyria, Babylon, Persia) the agents of God for punishing human pride and arrogance (Isa 10:5-19; 13:17; 21:2; 44:24–45:13; Jer. 27:5-11; 55:11). All these Mesopotamian tyrants thought they were acting by their own sovereignty. Indeed, they were acting by their own choice, but they were all being overruled by God and used by him as agents to bring judgment upon those who deserved judgment. The Revelation teaches that same philosophy throughout and especially in this sixth trumpet.

The sixth trumpet symbolizes invasion from external warring forces which served as an instrument of God to destroy Rome because she was set to destroy his church. God's destruction of succeeding Mesopotamian empires by one another was for the same reason — they tried to eradicate the OT covenant people. The author of Revelation expects his readers to understand enough of the history of the OT to grasp the clear symbolism in this army from the Euphrates.

The point of the hyperbolic number of cavalrymen (200,000,000) is to terrify those against whom they would ride. From about 200 B.C. to A.D. 220 the Euphrates region (Persia) was ruled by a virile dynasty called the Arsacid (Parthian) dynasty. This was a related Iranian group that developed a formidable military power based on a fine cavalry using disconcerting and novel tactics, "the Parthian shot." It was a swift attack from all directions, the riders shooting from their horses, then retreating, and scattering in order to attack from all sides again. Because they were such fierce fighters and great tacticians, Rome never succeeded in establishing its sovereignty over the Euphrates Valley. Trajan, Hadrian, and Marcus Aurelius all suffered disastrous defeat in their wars with the Parthians.

Some of these same Mesopotamian hordes, along with Indian and Russian tribes, migrated to Germany and became the most terrifying enemies of Rome. From A.D. 200 to 430 the Roman Empire suffered successive invasions by these people called Goths, Huns, Visigoths, Ostrogoths, and Vandals.

The Visigoths first entered the Roman Empire from southern Russia to escape persecution from the Huns. But the Romans began to persecute them also and the Visigoths began attacking Roman settlements as they moved south toward Italy. In A.D. 378 they defeated a Roman army in battle, and by 395 they had captured Athens and Corinth. About A.D. 395-400 the empire was divided with one ruler in Rome and another claiming rule from Constantinople. In A.D. 410 the Visigoths were powerful enough to sack and burn the city of Rome. The empire was stunned by the news. The Visigoths conquered and took Spain from the empire. Next the Vandals conquered North Africa ca. 430 and ruled it until 548. From their North African ports they crossed the sea and attacked the mainland of Italy and plundered the city of Rome. The last of these fierce peoples to invade the empire were the Ostrogoths and the Huns. Soon the western part of the Roman Empire had nearly cannibalized itself in anarchy. From that time onward the empire began a rapid demise.

These foreign hordes were ferocious warriors. When they attacked, people were paralyzed with fear. They burned, plundered and raped. Eventually the empire lay devastated by them. John's symbolism in these verses was for effect. He did not intend a literal application for all the details of his text. The picture of millions of warriors armed to the teeth, mounted on monstrous horses, was intended to frighten and terrify even once brave Rome. The carnage wrought by this great horde in fire, smoke, rapine, suffering and death is like that of hell. They were so fierce there was no defense against their attack, and they were so well armored they seemed invincible. The description in this passage is such as to terrorize any opponent. The scourge upon the Roman world brought by these millions of destructive warriors was much worse than any of the preceding trumpets. They not only hurt, they *killed* a third of mankind.

Revelation 10:1-11
"... the mystery of God, as he announced to his servants the prophets, should be fulfilled."

There comes a pause in the graphic predictions of awesome and calamitous things to come upon the Roman world. The **seventh trumpet** is not yet to sound. It will be sounded *after* the church gets a picture of its ultimate victory over the "beast" and his kingdom becomes the kingdom of Christ (Rev. 11:14-19). This is a pause with a purpose. Christ reveals to John some solace for the churches of Asia Minor.

A strong angel comes from heaven. He straddles the Mediterranean world because what he has written on the "little scroll" in his hand is for the Roman Empire. He lets out a *mega-roar* like a lion. Then the seven thunders rumbled and boomed. *A storm is coming!* (Exod. 9:23; 1 Sam. 7:10; 12:17-18; Job 26:14; Psa. 104:7; Isa. 29:6; 2 Sam. 22:14; Psa. 18:13, et al.). John is to "seal" what the seven thunders sounded at that moment for it is not yet appropriate to reveal. It will be revealed later as the "third woe" or the "last" when the "wrath of God is ended." Then the angel "swears" by the name of God to validate that his message is from heaven itself. There shall be no more delay. The "mystery of God, as he announced to his servants the prophets," was about to be revealed and fulfilled. "Prophets" should not be thought of as exclusively those of the Old Testament. Jesus and his apostles gave strong clues about the fall of Rome's wicked civilization.[31] But the angel refers especially to the OT prophets, and most specifically Daniel, chapters 2 and 7. Daniel predicted that when the "fourth" part of the image and the "fourth" beast were defeated, the "kingdom of the world would become the kingdom" of the Lord, Christ!

Written on the "little scroll" were the details of the ferocious hurricane of divine judgment that came when the seven bowls of God's wrath were poured out. John was told to "eat" (assimilate) the scroll. It was bittersweet! John's predicting is not finished. He must again prophesy the *doom* of many peoples and nations and tongues and kings. It is sweet revenge and vindication for God's persecuted saints, but it is bitter to the compassionate part of any believer to know that these terrible things were absolutely certain to take millions of impenitent sinners to a Christless hell. If it was bitter to John, think how bitter it is to God! He is not willing that any should perish!

Revelation 11:1-19

"The kingdom of the world has become the kingdom of our Lord and of his Christ...."

The mighty angel has roared to the Roman Empire. God's eschatological "thunder" has sounded. The storms of judgment coming upon Rome as a consequence of her quenchless lust to conquer, symbolized by the seals and the trumpets, is imminent. The intransigent multitudes of mankind not killed by the warnings of seals and trumpets have not repented! There will be no more delay! The **seventh trumpet** will sound and the seven bowls of wrath will be poured out. It will be a terrible time of judgment.

But the Lamb promised his disciples when he ascended back to the Father that he would be with them always. He also commanded his church that it should "go into all the world" and make disciples of all the nations. If terrible times of divine judgment fall upon the world while the church is evangelizing, what will happen to the church? Will the church be left unprotected? Will God withdraw his presence from the whole world? Will the church have the power to carry on with its commission?

The answer to these questions is provided in chapter **eleven**. The imagery in chapter eleven is somewhat Jewish but the application is to the church and the Roman Empire. It does not fit the context nor the time frame of Revelation to apply it to the church and the Jewish nation. The relation of the gospel to Judaism was settled a quarter of a century *before* Revelation was written when Jerusalem was destroyed in A.D. 70. Furthermore the short period when it appeared the "witnesses" of God had been slain (11:7-10) could not apply to the church and Judaism from A.D. 30 to 70, for that is when the gospel prospered by the conversion of thousands. Finally, what transpires in chapter 11 is apparently the "second woe," a period *before* the seventh trumpet which shall be the final "woe" on Rome — its destruction. Chapter 11 must fit into the entire revelation about the "beast" and the church. It would be of little relevance to the churches of Asia Minor to give an anachronistic résumé of the destruction of Judaism. Chapter 11 **does not** predict that Jerusalem will be restored so that the Jews may return as God's "chosen people." That issue had been settled and was thoroughly and plainly stated in the Epistle to the Hebrews (and all the other epistles of the NT). The Holy Spirit does not contradict himself!

The measuring of the temple with a rod is imagery from Ezekiel. Ezekiel's temple (chs. 40–48) was figurative and symbolic of the NT church. It had to be. It certainly was not a prophecy of the "Second Temple" built by Zeruabbabel. Its dimensions are too exaggerated to be predicting anything literal. It would measure larger than the entire ancient city of Jerusalem. Ezekiel's measurements of the city of Jerusalem would have it extending out into the Mediterranean Sea! That entire section of Ezekiel, chapters 38–48, is figurative of the Messiah's **first advent**, his conquest of sin and Satan, and the establishment of God's "temple" (the church, see Ephesians 2:11-22) on earth. Ezekiel's description of the priesthood, sacrifices and vision of the land would be in violation of the Mosaic law. It cannot, therefore, be predicting a return to a Mosaic nation. Ezekiel's predictions, if carried out literally, would have the "city" built squarely at the geographical center of Palestine and the tribal lands divided equally on each side of it. The temple would be in the middle of the city and its surroundings apportioned out in violation of the Old Testament. The "temple" John is told to measure is also the church of Christ. God does not dwell in temples made with hands — he never did! (Isa. 66:1-2; John 4:21-24; Acts 7:48; 17:24-25; 1 Cor. 3:16; 2 Cor. 6:16; Eph. 2:19-22).

In the OT temple only those who were pure, true sons of Israel, could worship at the altar. Gentiles, outcasts and excommunicated Israelites could come into the Court of the Gentiles ('the outer court'), but not into the courts of Israel. John is told to symbolically measure the temple where the altar was. Only those who have accepted Jesus Christ as the Messiah are now true Israelites (Rom. 2:28-29; 9:6-8; 4:10-25; 9:21-26; Gal. 6:15-16). The "saving of all Israel" in Romans 11:13-36 is clearly the saving of **both** Jew and Gentile in **New Israel** by grace and faith. Those who were "measured" and to be protected when the third woe (the seventh trumpet) came upon the Roman Empire were *Christians* whatever their race, ethnic background, or former religion might have been. Christians *only* came to the "New Zion" and had an altar at which they continually offered up sacrifices of praise (Heb. 12:22-24; 13:10-16).

The "outer court" symbolized impenitent Gentiles and Jews. It is **not** to be measured. "Measuring" something symbolized it **belonged** to the one for whom it was measured and was thus "protected." The "outer court" was to be "given over to the nations" (i.e., the Gentiles) to be "trampled" for forty-two months. Those in the "outer court" had no protection against the judgments about to fall. They are to be *recipients* of the judgments! This is closely related to Daniel's prediction of the judgment of God upon both impenitent Judaism and impenitent Rome — all in the same prophecy (Dan. 9:24-27; see also Dan. 7:23-27; 12:7). Jerusalem has been dominated ever since its destruction in A.D. 70 by "Gentiles" (apostate Islam, apostate Christianity and apostate Judaism). God does not intend geographical Jerusalem to be his residence ever again! He now abides in the Jerusalem that is *preeminent*, the *New Zion*, the *heavenly Jerusalem*. The prediction of "forty-two months" refers to the time heathen, imperial Rome will be given what may have seemed to some, complete power over the church. Daniel predicted that the fourth beast, Rome, would "prevail" over the saints and they would be given into the hand of Rome for three and one-half "times." Now "forty-two months" is precisely equivalent to "three and one-half (years) times." John meant to tell the churches of Asia Minor that the "beast" would seem to prevail for some three hundred fifty years from the end of the first century (i.e., until about A.D. 450).

God has always had *two witnesses* in the world. They are his propositional truth, the Bible, and his community of believers (whether patriarchal, theocratic or universal church in the spiritual sense). The number two is a universal symbol for strength. Two are always stronger than one. Many tasks needing to be done require two people. Jesus usually sent his disciples out "two by two" to preach (Luke 10:1). The witness of God through the Bible and the church in a world which seemed to be overcome by evil would be protected and strong. God would *give* power to these two witnesses to accomplish their work even when it appeared the "fourth beast" had warred and prevailed against the saints (Dan. 7:21-27). God "gives" his *two witnesses* **power** to carry out a "sack-cloth" kind of proclamation. The church and the Bible will "wear" the clothing of tribulation and chastening for "1260 days." That is the same amount of time the nations (Rome and its provinces) were given to trample over the "holy city," New Jerusalem (the church), i.e., a symbolic "42 months," or "three and one-half times."

The "two witnesses" are symbolized by two olive trees and two lampstands. The olive tree symbolizes the church composed of both Jew and Gentile in Christ (Zech 4:1-14; Rom. 11:17-24). In Zechariah the olive tree represents Zerubbabel, the king, who represents both the OT people of God and the future messianic people, the church or kingdom of God. The lampstand symbolizes both the church and the Spirit of God convicting the world of sin, righteousness and the judgment, through the instrumentality of the word of God, the Bible. God's word is a light and a lamp, the light of the world (Rev. 4:5; John 16:7-11; Psa. 19:8; 119:105,130; 2 Cor. 4:4; 2 Tim. 1:10; 1 Pet. 2:9; 2 Pet. 1:19). In Zechariah the lampstand symbolizes Joshua the high priest who in turn represents the Word of God in the OT. The two anointed of God in Zechariah's prophecy were Joshua and Zerubbabel, witnesses of God to rebuild the messainic nation in the OT. The church and the Bible are God's two witnesses in the NT. These are the two "witnesses" to the Roman Empire from Domitian (A.D. 81) to Romulus Augustus (A.D. 476) that the Caesars thought they had exterminated.

The symbolic picture of the history of the two witnesses is a remarkable prediction of the history of gospel proclamation during the apostolic age, through the great tribulation of the Roman persecution, and eventual missionary flood over the earth after the death of the "beast." The *first phase* of the history of the two witnesses pictorializes the apostolic age, i.e, from the Gospels to the book of Revelation (Rev. 11:5-6). During the first century, the gospel was preached with great power. Its proclamation was confirmed by "signs and wonders and various miracles." One only has to read the book of Acts to see that God overruled much of the opposition to the gospel by providential signs and wonders. His "prophets" (i.e., apostles and evangelists) were miraculously delivered from prisons, death, false brethren and many other obstacles (Heb. 2:4; 2 Cor. 11:24-29). These early messengers of the gospel were virtual "Elijahs" with great powers given to aid them and protect them. But when these passed from the scene, the church and the Bible were attacked with a ferocity that seemed as if it would devour them.

In the *second phase* of the church's history in the Roman Empire the two witnesses were set upon by Roman ungodliness and paganism to which the devil had given his authority and power. War was made against the two witnesses and *millions* of Christians were martyred and Bibles were burned. Numerous ancient cities of the Roman Empire contained literally miles of catacombs underneath their streets and houses where victims of plagues, gladiatorial contests, and persecution (Christians) were entombed. Refer to Daniel 7:21-27 for a prediction of the "war" by the "fourth beast" (Rome) against the saints and the ultimate victory of the saints over the fourth beast and the kingdom of the saints becoming universal.

In this second phase, the slain *witnesses* will lie in the street of the "great city" which is called **allegorically** (*pneumatikos*, "spiritualized") Sodom and Egypt. The "great city" is Rome — there can be no doubt about that.[32] Egypt and Sodom are appropriately *spiritualized* ("allegorical") designations by which to distinguish Rome. Rome was arrogant and idolatrous, and enslaved the peoples of the world like Egypt; she was filled with decadence, perversion, and wickedness like Sodom. Our Lord was not literally crucified in Rome; but he was not crucified in Egypt or Sodom, either. He *was* crucified *by the order of Rome*. Pontus Pilate gave the official edict that Jesus be crucified. The Jews were not permitted that power by Rome. The two witnesses were "killed." Jesus was "crucified." Two different words in the Greek text.

For "three days and one-half" (i.e., "time, times, and half-a-time" Dan. 7:25; Rev. 11:2-3; 12:14) the Roman Empire will know of the millions of dead bodies of the persecuted saints along with the many scrolls of the Bible burned and destroyed and conclude ("see") they have eradicated the two witnesses. But Rome will only "see" them as dead when in reality the two witnesses would be brought back to life by the Lord. After A.D. 450 the church would survive and eventually become victorious. The beast's refusal to let the two witnesses be buried symbolizes the humiliation and indignity heaped upon Christians by Rome. The empire is also pictured as rejoicing and congratulating itself over having stamped out Christianity. The pagan world was certain it had rid itself of two godly witnesses which had tormented its conscience with guilt and shame. In A.D. 303 Diocletian decreed that every Bible in the world should be destroyed, every church building leveled to the ground and Christians hunted down and killed as seditionists. So effective was that horrible onslaught that in about a year or two the persecutors supposed they had eradicated the Bible and the church from the face of the earth. Diocletian had been told that Christians were a people of the Book and if the Book were destroyed the faith would cease to exist. He considered his efforts so successful he put a sign over one burned Bible, which read in Latin, *extincto nomene Christianorum* (i.e., "the name of Christian is extinguished"). But the name Christian was *not* extinguished. "The court [of heaven sat] in judgment, and his dominion [was] taken away, to be consumed and destroyed to the end" (Dan. 7:26).

The *third phase* of the two witnesses begins at Revelation 11:11. After the great tribulation of Rome's war upon the saints God raised the two witnesses up to new life. The witnesses stood! They were not dead! They were given power. It was evident even to their enemies that their survival and power is divine in origin. These two witnesses went throughout the fallen Roman Empire bringing the fear of God to thousands of those who were former enemies. God "shook" the "great city" and it fell into ruin; some enemies were slain, some were converted.

This last *phase* symbolizes the great missionary success of Christianity in the thousand years following the fall of Rome's imperial power. After Rome fell, the gospel was carried to Ireland and Scotland, Switzerland, and Iceland; to all of Germany; to Scandinavia, and Greenland; to Russia and the Balkans; to Bohemia and Poland; Nestorian Christainity swept over India and Coptic Christianity over Egypt and Ethiopia. History records that this evangelism "explosion" began ca. A.D. 500 *without any discoverable organized mission effort!* The symbolism of John's description predicts the time when the "kingdom of God" (the church) "conquered" Rome by the faithfulness and endurance of the saints.

The *first woe* was Rome's internal decadence (9:1-11); the *second woe* was when Rome suffered the assaults of the "barbarians" (Vandals, Goths, Huns, et al.); the *third woe* was Rome's complicity with the devil to devour the saints of God — the great persecution of the church. God then gave those with the mark of the beast upon them his unadulterated cup of wrath to drink (Rev. 14:9-11; 15:1-8; 16:1-21).

The *third woe* was symbolized by John in the final destroying "plagues" called "bowls of wrath." John dramatized the *third woe* beginning in 12:1 and continued through 20:6.

The **seventh trumpet** sounded and there were loud voices in heaven announcing, "The kingdom of the world has become the kingdom of our Lord and of his Christ [Anointed], and he shall reign for ever and ever." This is a predictive announcement. It had its fulfillment when the "great city fell" and the beast-false prophet-harlot corporation was "cast into the lake of fire and brimstone." It is *significant* that the word "kingdom" in the phrase "kingdom of the world" is singular (*he basileia tou kosmou*). This clearly indicates the Roman Empire is meant. John does not speak here of the end of the world when the "kingdoms" (plural) will all be destroyed. Further emphasis for this is in the fact that the second "kingdom" in the English versions is supplied — it is not in the Greek text. Literally the phrase from the Greek text would read, "The kingdom of the world became our Lord's and his Anointed's." The Greek verb *egeneto* ("has become") is third person, singular, aorist, indicative which means the kingdom of the world *became* the Lord's at some point in the predictive past. It certainly is not speaking of some event *future* to A.D. 1999. The fall of the Roman Empire and the missionary success of the church proved conclusively that the world belonged to God and the Lamb. This is what the vision of the Throne revealed. It was not Roman emperors who were sovereign over this creation, but God and the Lamb.

Those who have had some sort of exalted honor from heaven confirm that there is only one Sovereign. The 24 elders on their "thrones" fall on their faces as this prediction of the Lamb's sovereignty is made, and worship God, with words of agreement about the imminent defeat of the pretended "kingdom of the world." The RSV follows the best Greek manuscripts translating, "We give thanks to thee, Lord God Almighty, who art and who wast." It omits the words, "and art to come" included in the KJV. But John is not predicting the Second Coming of Christ here. He is predicting Jesus' "coming" in judgment upon the Roman Empire. Further substantiation that these verses have to do exclusively with Christ's judgment of Rome, not his Second Coming, is in the Greek verb *eilephas*, ("has taken") which is a perfect tense verb, meaning what was done was in the past time with a continuing result. God "had taken his great power" in the past and had begun to reign. It was not future to John's Revelation. It took place at the cross and the empty tomb and was climaxed in the fall of Rome when God's kingdom went throughout the world. When the Lamb judged the "fourth beast" he proved that his kingdom (the church) was the only kingdom henceforth to reign universally on earth. Even the word "begun" is translated from a Greek aorist verb which means it was not future.

This text (Rev. 11:17-19) is saturated with Greek aorist tense verbs; e.g. "the nations *raged*, but thy wrath came, and the time for the dead to be *judged*, . . . and for *destroying* the destroyers," are all aorist verbs. The Greek verb, *diaphtheirontas*, however, is present tense. In other words, John wrote, "the time when the ones destroying were destroyed came to be." There is nothing future in this text at all!

The "dead" are the *spiritually dead* (Eph. 2:1-10; Col. 2:13-15; John 4:25; Rev. 20:4-6). This cannot be the time for *all* the dead to be judged, for at the end of the trumpets and the end of the bowls there were still people on earth who did not repent. Further, the Greek word *krithenai*, translated "judged," is aorist tense, meaning it happened in the past.

The Greek word *diaphtheirai*, translated "destroyed" is also aorist, but, significantly, the participle *diaphtheirontas*, is present tense which means "the ones presently destroying" would be destroyed. Those who were destroying in John's time would be destroyed. It is also important to remember that in a very similar phrase God predicts through Daniel that the one who is coming "upon the wing of abominations shall [be] one who makes desolate, until the decreed end is poured out on the desolator" (Dan. 9:27). Jesus said the Romans who destroyed Jerusalem in A.D. 70 were those "coming upon the wing of abominations" (Matt. 24:15; Mark 13:14; Luke 21:20). This text, then, is not a prediction of the end of the whole world. It is just the end of the Roman world. It may be *a type* of the final judgment, just as all other judgments in this present world are (Luke 13:1-10), but this is Rome, not Russia!

The temple in heaven was opened. The Greek word *naos* is translated *temple* in this text. It most often means *sanctuary* and does not usually refer to the entire building of the Jewish temple. The Greek word for the entire temple is *hieron*. The word *naos* is used in Paul's letter to the Ephesians to refer to the church; it is used of the inner part of the temple in Jerusalem where only priests were allowed to go (Eph. 2:21; Matt 23:35). This clearly has no reference to the Jewish temple. This temple "in heaven" symbolized the heavenly, unseen, spiritual residence of God. John saw God's heavenly abode opened and in it was the ark of the covenant! The original ark of the covenant built by Moses was never recovered from the Babylonian exile. Jeremiah had predicted just prior to that exile that the ark of the covenant would "not come to mind, or be remembered, or missed; . . . [or] made again" (Jer. 3:15-16; see also Jer. 31:31-34). Jeremiah predicted the annulment of the Old dispensation because when it served its purpose, it was fulfilled in the New dispensation. In the OT God's presence was always associated with the "mercy seat" above the ark of the covenant between the cherubim (Exod. 25:21-22; 30:6; Ezek. 9:3; 10:4; 11:22-23).

The conflict between the church and the "beast" was to grow more ominous. This was to be dramatized in the second major division of the Revelation (chapters 12–20). But the outcome of *victory* for God's *covenant people* (Christians) was announced in chapter 11 before the dark, devilish picture of chapter 12 was revealed. Christians were shown the ark of the covenant to assure them that God *never* forgets his covenant promises. When God makes a covenant, it is before him, on his mind and heart constantly. The ark John saw was symbolic of God's faithfulness to keep his New covenant with his New chosen people — Christians. God would not contradict or revert from his New covenant back to his Old covenant. The New covenant is final, complete, eternal (Heb. 9:9,12,26,28; 10:1-39).

The "nations raged" but they did not embrace the Son (Psa. 2:1-12). Thus the judgment of God fell upon them. God warned the world which opposed his redemptive kingdom. It did not repent. Judgment could not be delayed. Thunder sounded — the storm of divine judgment was on the horizon. God's dwelling place, the church, had been staked out, measured, and set apart for protection. The beastly world thought it had slain the two witnesses to God's sovereignty and reveled in its assumption. These two witnesses had been a "torment" to those with the "mark of the beast." But God gave new life to his two witnesses. The "great city" fell, the spiritually dead were judged, and the saints were vindicated and rewarded. God is always faithful! He keeps his covenant promises.

Notes

[1] Compare Daniel 7:12 with Revelation 13:1-2 where Daniel indicates the first three beasts have their dominion taken away but have their lives prolonged for a season in the fourth. Then John, in the Revelation, indicates the "beast" is a composite of the three (leopard, bear and lion) revealed to Daniel in his dream (Dan. 7:1ff).

[2] Durant, *Caesar and Christ*, p. 289.

[3] Merrill C. Tenney, *Interpreting Revelation* (Grand Rapids: Eerdmans, 1957), p. 19.

[4] See Suetonius, *The Twelve Caesars*, and Durant, *Caesar and Christ..*

[5] Durant, *Caesar and Christ*, pp. 291-292.

[6] Paul T. Butler, *Twenty-Six Lessons on Revelation,* Vol. I (Joplin, MO: College Press, 1982), pp. 1-7.

[7] Durant, *Caesar and Christ*, p. 292.

[8] See Paul T. Butler, *Twenty-Six Lessons on Revelation* in two volumes.

[9] See usage in Matthew 5:25; 28:7,8; Mark 9:39; Luke 15:22; 18:8; John 11:29; Acts 12:7; 22:18; 25:4; 1 Timothy 3:14; Revelation 2:16; 3:11; 11:14, where the word is unquestionably used to mean imminently.

[10] See usage in Matthew 24:32,33; Luke 21:30,31; Hebrews 6:8; 8:13; see the adverb *engyteron* translated in Romans 13:11.

[11] See our comments in this work on Matthew 24:30; Luke 21:27; see also Matthew 26:64; Luke 22:69.

[12] See Revelation 14:6-7, the very "hour" of "his judgment" *has come* (aorist tense verb in Greek, past tense, not future tense).

[13] Daniel 7:9,10; 10:5,6; Ezek. 1:26-28; "son of man" is used 90 times in the book of Ezekiel.

[14] See John 4:47 for the usage of *mellei*.

[15] Paul T. Butler, *Twenty-Six Lessons,* Vol. 1, p. 62.

[16] See notes on the "Olivet Discourse," chapter eight of this work.

[17] See Luke 13:1-9. All calamities in the world merely show that the world has been subjected to futility and decay, Romans 8:18-23, and signify that while creation awaits its redemption, human beings are being summoned to repent by these disasters.

[18] Revelation 15:1–16:21. The *end* of the Roman Empire was "Armageddon."

[19] See Romans 1:18-32; this passage in Romans is an inspired résumé of the book of Revelation!

[20] Durant, *Caesar and Christ,* pp. 280,281,289.

[21] Josephus, *Antiquities,* XV.IX.1; XX.II.5, et al.

[22] See Ezekiel 38:1–39:29; see our comments in this work, Chapter Four; see also Psalms 18:12,13; Joel 2:30.

[23] Connect the following NT references to Ezekiel 38–40; 1 Corinthians 1:18-25; Colossians 2:13-15; Hebrews 2:14-18.

[24] Jospehus, *Antiquities,* II.14.4

[25] See the connection of "wormwood" with "drunkenness" in Deuteronomy 29:18-19.

[26] Durant, *Caesar and Christ,* p. 377.

[27] Ibid., p. 665.

[28] See Matt. 12:30; Luke 10:19; 11:12; in Hebrew the word is *aqrabim* and means "to root out and destroy."

[29] W.G. Hardy, *The Greek and Roman World* (Cambridge, MA: Schenkman, 1960), p. 106.

[30] It is interesting that the apostle Paul quoted that philosophy in 1 Corinthians 15:32-34.

[31] See Matthew 16:28; John 12:31; Romans 1:18-32; 2 Thessalonians 2:7 — in order that the "lawless one" might be revealed, "one had to be taken out of the way" and that one was the Roman emperor, i.e., our notes on "Antichrist."

[32] See Revelation 16:19; 17:18; 18:10,16,17,19,21; the only "city built on seven hills" and that had "dominion over the kings of the earth" was Rome.

chapter 10

THE REVELATION
OF JESUS CHRIST
PART II

Revelation 12:1-17
"But woe to you, O earth and sea, for the devil has come down to you in great wrath, because he knows that his time is short!"

With chapter 12 John began the second main division of the Revelation. The first primary division, chapters 1 through 11, revealed the Lamb sovereign in the historical frame of reference. This second part revealed the Lamb sovereign in the heavenly, spiritual, provinces.

This second division of Revelation explained, in dramatic symbolism, that the earthly struggle of the church against its enemies was inseparably united to the unseen confrontation Satan, the invisible rebel of heaven, made against God to destroy the work of redemption. God carried out his redemptive program through human agents, i.e., Christians (the church). Satan carried out his war against redemption through human agents, i.e., heathen, imperial Rome. More than once Christians of the first century were told that their warfare was not "against flesh and blood, but against . . . the spiritual hosts of wickedness in the heavenly places" (Eph. 6:12; 2:2; 2 Cor. 10:3-5). Jesus referred to his great life and death struggle as "the crisis of the cosmos" (a transliteration of two Greek words, John 12:31; 16:11). An angel of God revealed the same idea — that there was a physically unseen spiritual confrontation which was coincident with the visible, earthly struggle between righteousness and wickedness (Dan. 10:1-21). History's *direct tie* to heaven's battle for man's soul was dramatically portrayed by Zechariah as well (Zech. 1–12; esp. 3:1-10).

In Revelation 12 John summarized and condensed the concept of the unseen spiritual warfare between God and Satan. From chapter 13 through 19 the picture moves to the struggle between the secondary "agents" of God and Satan which are the church versus the beast-false prophet-harlot conglomerate. These latter are the ones in whom the forces of Satan were organized and motivated to "make war upon the saints." The essential concept is: *the involvement of earthly history in heavenly, spiritual matters.* This section of the Revelation is a window opened to heaven for the mental and spiritual eye to behold. It gives reality to the promise, "If God is for us, who can be against us?" (Rom. 8:31, NIV). It is as real as the vision of horses and chariots of fire given the prophet's servant and the promise, "Fear not, for those who are with us are more than those who are with them" (2 Kgs. 6:15-19). Revelation 12:1–20:6 was not written to be fulfilled at some time future to A.D. 1999. It was a message for the seven churches of Asia Minor. *Their* struggle was tied to heaven's plans. *They* were wrestling with cosmic powers who were using Rome as their agent. *Those* Christians needed to know the Lamb would win the struggle and he had invited all who would to prepare for his "marriage supper." Of course, the message is as relevant for the church today as it was then, just as Romans 8, Ephesians 6, 1 Corinthians 15, and 1 Thessalonians 4 & 5 are.

The "woman" symbolized God's *wife*, his church, in both OT and NT (See Isa. 54:1ff; 62:4-5; Jer. 3:14-20; Ezek. 16:1-14; Hos. 1:1–3:5; Eph. 5:21-33; Rev. 19:6-10; 21:2-4). As John saw God's *wife*, she had been clothed and was continuing to be *clothed (peribeblemene*, Greek perfect tense, "clothed in the past with a continuing result") with the glory of the sun and with the moon under her feet. The investiture of God's people with glory and light, symbolized by the sun and moon, is prophetic imagery from the OT (Isa. 9:1ff; 24:21-23; 30:26; 31:35-36; 42:6; 49:5; 60:1-22; Dan. 12:3; Zech. 14:6; Mal. 4:2). The crown of twelve stars symbolized the fact that all the glory of human religious leadership (12 patriarchs, 12 tribes and 12 apostles) in the earth was meant by God to *adorn, protect and equip* God's bride. This bride (mother), gloriously clothed, was a great *portent.* Her glory portended her invincibility. She was glorified and exalted to join with God in redeeming the world (Eph. 1:3; 2:6; Rev. 20:4). Of her it was written: "For all things are yours, whether Paul or Apollos or Cephas or the world or life or death or the present or the future, all are yours . . . ." (1 Cor. 3:21-23). That is the *signal* John was to relay to the seven churches. God's Bride, the church, was exalted and glorified so that she might give birth to the "man-child" (the Messiah).

The cry of travail for the birth of this "man-child" fills all the OT (Isa. 7:14; 9:6-7; 26:17ff; 66:7-11; Micah 4:10; 5:2). Abraham looked for it (John 8:56); Isaiah looked for it (John 12:41); all the prophets looked for it (1 Pet. 1:10-12). The distress and trouble the OT woman would have awaiting the birth is predicted by Daniel as "490 years of *trouble*" (Dan. 9:24-27). Daniel, chapters 7 through 12, is a detailed prediction of those *490 years of trouble* preceding the birth of the Messiah, who would be born and "cut off" in the midst of the last seven years of that "time of trouble." This "time of trouble" would include the rise of the Roman Empire, i.e., Daniel's "fourth beast." See our comments earlier on the book of Daniel.

Another *portent* was revealed to John. It was a *signal* that Satan was the main villain in the "great tribulation." Enemies of God's people were symbolized in the OT as dragons, serpents, and beasts (Isa. 27:1; 51:9; Jer. 53:34; Ezek. 29:3). John borrows from that imagery to symbolize the devil as a "great red dragon" (Rev. 12:9; 20:2). The heads, horns, and crowns symbolized the emperors of Rome pictured in Revelation 17:1-18 as the "scarlet beast" upon whom the "harlot" rode. The "red dragon" invested the "scarlet beast" with some hellish power and authority (Rev. 13:2). John revealed the dragon's "power and authority" was only *pseudo, pretended, and restricted* by God. That is the *point* of the entire book of Revelation. Although some considered the beast to be invincible, John assured the churches that the "beast" was *human*, not divine, and would be *bound* by God (Rev. 13:4,17-18; 20:2-3). Some of the "stars" of heaven (angels) allowed themselves to be caught in Satan's rebellion and were cast out of heaven (2 Pet. 2:4; Jude 6). They were "swept" away by the devil's tail and "cast down" to the earth as they assisted him in his attempt to destroy God's redemptive work. This "rebellion" *began* after creation. Satan and his "angels" were all created by God. The rebellion *focused on man*, first, in the Garden of Eden. It reached its ultimate capacity at Calvary and the Roman Empire. The OT "church" brought forth the "man-child." Satan attempted to "devour" the man-child but God "caught up" the man-child to heaven (resurrection of Jesus Christ and his ascension). The "woman" became the NT church and "fled into the wilderness" to a place *prepared by God* where she was *to be nourished* for 1260 "days." This was apocalyptic phraseology to symbolize that the NT church was dispersed into the *hostile environment* ("wilderness") of the heathen Roman Empire in order that she might be *nourished*. God had *prepared* that heathen, hostile environment to nourish the church by dispersing the Jews, by Pax Romana, the *Koine* Greek dialect, and a hundred other providential details. It was no accident that the gospel began to be nourished among the Gentiles when it was evident that the majority of the Jews had rejected it (Acts 13:44-49). It is extremely significant that the church was to be *nourished* in hostile surroundings. ". . . suffering produces endurance, and endurance produces character" (Rom. 5:3-5; Heb. 10:35-39; 12:1-17).

Now war arose in heaven. The *time sequence* of this "war" must fit *this* context. Contextually it has to do with the devil having been thwarted in his attempt to devour the "man-child" and the flight of the church into the wilderness. The *place* of this war cannot be where the Father and the Son dwell in eternal omnipotence and holiness. It cannot be the throne room of God for no wickedness is able to abide in his immediate presence. The battleground for this war cannot be where God reigns as absolute Sovereign for there his will is done perfectly. The throne-visions of the Revelation show complete subservience and peace in heaven. *But*, the church is a "heavenly place;" the church is called "the kingdom of *heaven*" in numerous places; we, as Christians *now* are blessed with every spiritual blessing in the *heavenly places*; The church *is* "Mount Zion," "the city of the living God," "the *heavenly* Jerusalem;" "innumerable angels in festal gathering," "the assembly of the first born, enrolled in *heaven*;" we, as Christians, are exhorted *now* to "enter the sanctuary by the blood of Jesus;" the OT was a copy and shadow of the "*heavenly sanctuary*" which is the church; Christians are called now to a "heavenly calling" and have a "heavenly rest" (Eph. 1:3; 2:6; Heb. 3:1; 4:1-12; 8:1-13; 10:19-22; 12:22-24; Matt. 13:11; 16:19; 18:1,4; 23:13). Jesus warned that "men of violence sought to take the kingdom for violent purposes" (Matt. 11:12). This war was the attempt of the devil to subvert the church through *Judaizers* and the *Jewish persecution* (see the entire book of Acts; Gal. 1:6-9; 2:1-2; 3:1; 5:1; Phil. 3:2-3; Col. 2:8-23; 1 Tim. 4:1-5; the entire book of Hebrews, esp. Heb. 10:32ff). The Revelation refers to those who said they were Jews but were actually of the *synagogue of Satan* (Rev. 2:9; 3:9). Jesus predicted a "warlike" struggle from the Jews against his new kingdom of heaven involving the forces of hell (Matt. 10:16-33; 24:4-14; Luke 10:17ff). Satan attempted to get Christians to fight one another over the matter of Jewishness, and even tried to get the apostles to fight one another and made every kind of war he could against the apostle Paul (Gal. 2:11ff; 2 Cor. 2:11; 4:4; 11:3,12-15; 12:7). There was "no more any place" for the devil in the church through Judaism after A.D. 70. God won that war! The great dragon was thrown (out). The verb in 12:9 is aorist and there is no preposition indicating which direction Satan was "thrown." Satan's defeat in this "war" had already taken place when John wrote the Revelation. This "war" was not a reference to Satan's original fall, nor to some future "war." It was apocalyptic imagery to describe that great cosmic struggle which took place *after* the ascension of the Messiah and before the church fled into the "wilderness."

When the devil was "thrown" out (there is no preposition for "down" in the Greek text here) John heard a loud voice in heaven announce that the salvation, power and kingdom of God and the authority of Christ *had come*.[1] And the word, "Now," in Greek signifies coincidence, or "just now," i.e., coincidentally with the end of the war in the church by the Judaizers. **At that point** it was clearly manifested that Jesus Christ's church was the repository of salvation, and the power and authority of Christ was shown to be that of God. The Greek word *enikesan*, translated "conquered," is aorist tense and means the Christians *had conquered*. There is nothing future about this text. Once Judaism was completely defeated in A.D. 70, it became evident that the church of Christ *was indeed* the "kingdom" of God predicted in the OT. Satan could indict many through the Law, but once the authority and salvation of Christ was *established,* it was evident the accuser could not accuse those who had conquered by the blood of Jesus.

Heaven and the saints could rejoice over the end of the war with Judaism, but woe to the "world" because the devil came away from this defeat with great wrath. Satan was about to intensify his attack upon God's church by using the "world" (Rome) as his tool. Nearly every verb in Revelation 12:12 is present tense in the Greek text. Literally translated it would read: *"Be rejoicing*, then, O heaven and you that *are dwelling there.* But woe *to you who are inhabiting the earth*, because the devil came ("came" is aorist) to you *having great wrath* because the devil *is knowing* that he has only a little time." Again, the preposition for "down" is not in the Greek text here at all!

The devil was not really the ally of Rome. He seduced that world, used it, exploited it, turned it upon itself, and devastated it (Rev. 17:15-18). The devil infected that world with every despicable and depraved evil possible to the unbelieving human mind (Rom. 1:18-32).

Again the present tense should translate, "the devil *was knowing* that he had just a little time" to use Rome! **No one, not the angels of heaven, nor the Son, knows when the end of *all time* is to be.** [2] But the devil could know times and seasons which God had revealed in the Bible, just as any human may know what God has revealed. The devil's short time with Rome is revealed in Daniel 2:1-45; 7:1-27; 9:24-27! The devil's time allotted to use the "fourth beast" (i.e., Roman pagan power) to halt and eradicate the spread of Christianity was "short" (approximately 350 years). Whatever God chooses to keep secretly to himself, no one can know; but what God has revealed, all higher created beings (i.e., angels and humans) can know, whether they believe it or not (Deut. 29:29). The devil knows the Scriptures and quotes them! (Psa. 91:11-12; Matt. 4:6).

Defeated in his attempt to stamp out the church with a persecuting Judaism, the devil "pursued the woman who had borne the male child" (the NT church). The RSV translates the Greek text "pursued," but the KJV and ASV translate "persecuted." The Greek word for *pursued* and *persecuted* is the same word and is aorist tense (*edioxen*). This action of the devil was transpiring when John wrote Revelation. John did not intend to predict a "tribulation" that was to be at A.D. 2000.

The devil used those who "worshiped" him (Rome) as his tools to persecute the ancient church (Rev. 13:1-4). The church fled into the "wilderness" (*eremon*, "desert, uninhabited place, wilderness, wasteland, barren place."). God deliberately led the OT church (Israel) through a "wilderness" for forty years to "nourish" them (Deut. 8:1-20). God allowed Jesus to be led into the "wilderness" of Judea to be tested by the devil (Matt. 4:4; Mark 1:12; Luke 4:1). The NT church was "tested" and "nourished" in the very inhospitable "wasteland" of Roman paganism. The Greek word for "nourished" is often translated "fed" (*trephetai*, "to rear, to feed, to nourish"). It was *spiritual nourishing* the church was to receive from its testing by the "great tribulation" of Rome. The seven churches of Asia Minor clearly needed spiritual nourishment. Spiritual growth does not preclude the possibility of persecution, suffering, and pain (Acts 14:22; Rom. 5:3-5; 8:18-39; Heb. 10:36-39; 12:1-17; 1 Pet. 4:1-19, et al.).

The Lord gave the church the "wings of an eagle"[3] that she might "fly to the place *prepared* for her to be nourished.[4] Christ *intended* the pagan, inhospitable world of Rome as *her place* for nourishing and survival! The church's "time" in the Roman "wasteland" was to be "a time, and times, and half a time" (i.e., three and one half times). This is a symbolically "rounded" number to indicate approximately 350 years. It is the same time allotted to the two witnesses in chapter eleven. It is the same time allotted to the fourth beast (Rome) in Daniel 7:25. This represented the time from approximately A.D. 100 to A.D. 450. It is, approximately, the time from John's delivery of the Revelation to the end of the Roman Empire. The number "three and one half" is symbolic of incompleteness. Seven is the number symbolic of completeness. The church was not to be persecuted in the Roman wasteland *forever*. Her "wilderness" journey *would* come to an end. But while she was in the "wilderness," the devil loosed a "river" from his *mouth*. It became a "flood." This "flood" symbolized the worldwide *inundation* of false teaching, persecution, and degeneracy associated with ancient Rome's culture.[5] The "earth" came to the help of the woman and *swallowed* the flooding river of the devil. Symbolized here is the fact that there were periods of comparative peace and easing of the persecution of the church "in the wilderness" of Rome. From Domitian through Septimius Servus (A.D. 81 to 211) there was a "flood" of satanic persecution of the church; from Caracalla to Phillipus (A.D. 211 to 244) there was a period of toleration of Christianity; from Phillipus through Diocletian (A.D. 245 to 305) another flood of tribulation; in A.D. 313 Constantine ushered in another period of toleration for the church. Finally, the "fourth beast" (Rome) was "swallowed" up completely, and the church began its missionary endeavors to the ends of the earth.

The devil devised an orgiastic[6] scheme of anger and hate and went off (again the Greek verb for "went" is aorist — past tense) to make war on "the rest" of the woman's "offspring." Satan's war against the *collective* church ("the woman") was thwarted from time to time. But he did not relent. He went off to do battle with those who were keeping and were having (when John was writing) the command-ments of God and the testimony of Jesus.[7] These are *individual* Christians on "every seashore" of the ancient Roman Empire.

> In the Christian faith we need to be careful *not* to think of the relationship between God and Satan in dualistic terms. Satan is an enemy of God, but he is *not* an eternal, independent entity which has forever co-existed with God. He himself is a creature who depends upon God for his very existence. His opposi-tion to God is an ethical choice, not a metaphysical necessity. The "struggle" between God and Satan is not a fight between equals or even near-equals.
>
> This "struggle" exists in the first place not because Satan is so strong in rela-tion to God, but in relation to man. It is man that they are fighting for, and the battle must be waged on the level of man. Thus God's conquest of Satan is not an exercise of sheer divine omnipotence, but is the result of redemptive power wielded by *God Incarnate* as the man Jesus Christ. Nevertheless, because God is the Sovereign Creator, we know concerning the creature Satan that "his doom is sure" and that he will not be an eternal threat. This is the assurance which dual-ism does not permit.[8]

Revelation 13:1-18
"I saw a beast rising out of the sea....
Then I saw another beast which rose out of the earth...."

Why did Christ picture a "beast" to John? Because "beastliness" is an apocalyp-tic symbol of brute force; sensual, lawless and God-opposing human governments are beastly. Isaiah, Jeremiah, Ezekiel, Daniel, Obadiah, and Habakkuk symbolize human governments as "beasts" (Isa. 27:1; 51:9; Jer. 45:15; 46:22; 50:11; Ezek. 32:2; 29:3; Dan. 7:1-8; Obad. 4; Hab. 1:8). Human governments see *themselves* as fierce, powerful animals (e.g., the American eagle, the Russian bear, the English lion or bulldog, etc.). A better way to symbolize human government in its cruelty, fleshly instincts, predatory nature, and cunning could not be found. All human gov-ernments are predatory, more or less. All human governments exist at the expense of their citizens, are absorbed with that which is physical, and all sustain themselves by force. Daniel represents the Roman Empire (the "fourth beast") as "terrible and dreadful and exceedingly strong; and it had great iron teeth; it devoured and broke in pieces, and stamped the residue with its feet. It was different from all the beasts that were before it" (Dan. 7:7).

The first "beast" John saw (Rev. 13:1) arose "from the sea." "Sea" symbolizes a mass of pagan humanity in constant commotion, casting up wreckage (Dan. 7:3; Isa.

8:7ff; 17:2ff; 47:20-21; Jer. 46:7-9; 47:2; Rev. 17:1,15). The "ten horns" represent the collective beastly power of ten successive Roman emperors; Tiberius (Caesar when Christ preached, died and rose again), Caligula, Claudius, Nero, Galba, Otho, Vitellius, Vespasian, Titus, and Domitian (Domitian was Caesar when John wrote the Revelation). The "seven heads" represent the ten emperors in unanimity of mind and action in relation to Christianity. The emperors listed were pleased to be deified as gods. Domitian eventually made an imperial edict that he should be addressed as "Lord God and Savior" and that all persons under the dominion of Rome (except Jews) must burn incense at least once a year as worship to his deity.

The "beast" that arose from the sea was a composite (Rev. 13:2) of a leopard, bear and lion. That was exactly the reverse order from the vision of the four empires related by Daniel of his dream (Dan. 7:1-12). In Daniel 7:12 the fourth beast was destined to be slain and burned. But Daniel revealed that before being slain the first three beasts "had their lives prolonged for a season in the fourth beast." The Roman Empire *did* incorporate, both consciously and unconsciously, numerous aspects of Babylonian, Persian and Greek, refinements into its culture. **This is the point at which Revelation chapter 13 "plugged" right into Daniel chapter 7, and thus Revelation continued and concluded the destiny of all the "beasts" in the "fourth" one.** The connection is unmistakable! The book of Revelation is a prediction of the history of the Roman Empire from the first century A.D., as it relates to the church of Jesus Christ during that time period, until Rome's demise (ca. A.D. 450-500).

The "dragon" *gave* its power and authority to the "beast."[9] The "beast" became the tool of Satan. Satan's "throne" is only pretended. He creates nothing, owns nothing, and any deception he accomplishes is within the sovereign limitations imposed upon him by God (Job 1:6-22; 2:1-13; Zech. 3:1-10; Matt. 4:1-11; 12:22-31; John 12:31; 16:11; 2 Cor. 2:11; Heb. 2:14-15; 1 John 3:8; Rev. 20:1-3). Whatever promises of "power" the devil may make are empty and vain. God alone reigns over all kingdoms (Isa. 10:5-19; 45:1-7; Jer. 27:5-11; Dan. 2:20-23; 3:26-30; 4:34-37; 5:24-28). The devil rules by deception and seduction. His basis of power is all falsehood and can never endure against the truth. *Rome allowed itself to be seduced* (Rom. 1:18-32).

John notes that one of the heads of the "beast" seemed to have a mortal wound, but its mortal wound was healed. At some point within the time frame of this "beastly" Roman Empire it appeared that it received a "wound" that might make it die. This is an apparent reference to the *Nero redivivus* legend. Nero (A.D. 54-68) was a monster of lasciviousness and cruelty. When he killed himself in A.D. 68, many people actually danced in the streets of Rome. A few mourned his death because their positions and fortunes depended on his patronage. And these "friends" of Nero perpetrated a legend that Nero had not really died but had gone to Parthia in the far east and he would return, incarnate in another ruler, leading the dreaded hordes of Parthia, and take up the Roman throne again. Suetonius mentions this legend.[10] Some believed Domitian (A.D. 81-96) was the reincarnated Nero. See our comments on Revelation 17:3-14 for more symbolic use of the *Nero redivivus* legend. John the apostle did not believe in reincarnation, but he used this myth about Nero to identify in cryptic and esoteric language who the "beast" was. John suggested that in Domitian Christians were faced with a "clone" of Nero. Nero's friends propagated the idea that Nero had the powers of the devil and was somehow immortal in his wickedness. Suetonius notes that the Romans could not rid themselves of this idea, and even as late as A.D. 88 a pretender had arisen in Parthia claiming that he was Nero.[11]

Satan worship or demon worship was widespread in all the provinces of the Roman Empire (1 Cor. 10:20ff). The gods of the underworld were believed by the Romans to have powers to make those who worshiped them immortal. Men worshiped the "beast" for it *appeared* to men that the ruler of demons had given his power and authority for immortality to the beast. It was even rumored that Nero had come back to Rome in the person of Domitian and his successors. The "beast" seemed *invincible* (Rev. 13:4). The power of Rome seemed unassailable, unconquerable and more powerful than the gods of mythology. That kind of power clamors to be worshiped. So men began to press for deification of their emperors. Most of the Roman emperors gloried in such flattery. Popular adoration for and self-acclamation of the deification of political tyrants was nothing new to the world. It had been practiced as far back as ancient Egypt, Assyria, Babylon, Persia, and Greece.

Both John and Daniel characterized the "beast" (Rome) as a haughty blasphemer (Rev. 13:5-6; Dan. 7:8,11,20,25). John's reference was to Domitian's *edictum domini deique nostri*, i.e., "Our Lord and God decrees." Domitian commanded that he be addressed as deity; he decreed that anyone who approached him should bow and embrace his feet. Caligula (A.D. 37-41) had earlier ordered that an image of himself be set up in the Holy of Holies in the Jewish temple in Jerusalem. Caligula believed he was the god, Jupiter, and once struck the English Channel with a rod believing he could whip it into submission to his deity. Diocletian declared himself to be a god in the flesh and required all visitors to kneel and kiss the hem of his royal robe. Roman emperors made blasphemous utterances against Christians and their Christ. They accused Christians of sexual depravity, cannibalism, sedition, and cowardice, and scoffed at their God and Christ as powerless.

The beast was "allowed" to exercise its blasphemous power and authority over all who dwell on earth and to make war on the saints for forty-two months (Rev.

13:5-8). Again in Revelation we have exactly the same apocalyptic language Daniel used of Rome ("the fourth beast" Dan. 7:21,25). The time limit of 42 months is the same as 3½ years or 1260 days (see comments on Rev. 12:6). Rome would not have had the power to "make war on the saints" if God had not "allowed" it. Permission from God for severe testing of his people is not strange to biblical history. Israel was put into the "furnace of affliction" from its founding in Egypt, through its exile in Babylonia, and its "time of trouble" in the days of Antiochus IV. Christ could not abide an untested, unpurged, uncommitted church! He allowed his saints to be attacked, to struggle, and to fight because they needed endurance so they could do the will of God and receive what he promised them (Heb. 10:32-39; 12:1-11; 1 Pet. 4:12-19; 2 Cor. 12:7-10). Authority over the whole civilized world was given to this beast, Rome. It was apocalyptic hyperbole and symbolism. John did not mean that Rome had authority over every single individual alive on the face of the earth in the first five centuries A.D. Nor did John intend to predict some time near A.D. 2000 that one "beast" would be given authority over every single human being on the face of the earth. John was describing the power and authority of the ancient Roman Empire over what people then understood to be the "civilized" world of Rome's dominion (Rev. 17:1-18).

All who dwelled in the civilized world under Rome's authority did obeisance to Rome and worshiped the emperor by compulsion. Only those who took their redemption in Christ seriously did not do so. These were distinguished as those who had their names "written before the foundation of the world in the book of life of the Lamb that was slain." When the imperial edict forced Christians to decide about emperor worship, it was not enough to have merely embraced Christianity. Some who failed to count the cost when they became Christians capitulated to idolatry rather than suffer persecution.

When this great "war" and tribulation came, the saints had to trust Christ enough to remain and not seek to avoid the tribulation, renouncing Christ by burning incense to the emperor. *If they must go to prison or death,* they must go (Rev. 13:9-10). John issued a "call for the endurance and faith of the saints." This is imagery taken from the OT prophets as they called the saints of their day to "endurance and faith" (Jer. 14:12; 15:2; 24:10; 43:11; Ezek. 5:2,12). Jeremiah told his people to surrender to God's chastening at the hands of the Babylonians and make the most of it, so that God could deliver them after 70 years of exile (Jer. 29:1-9; 27:1-15; 29:10ff). Jeremiah expected those who trusted God to believe his prediction and obey it no matter what they had to suffer. That is exactly what John told the Christians of Asia Minor.

John saw a "second beast." It arose out of the earth, i.e., out of the empire itself.

200

The first beast was warlike and arose out of the mass of humanity. It represented Roman military and political power in opposition to God's saints. The *second* beast was lamb-like, but it spoke like the dragon. This *second* beast represented the powers delegated to the Roman *concilia* to propagate and enforce emperor worship throughout the empire. *Concilia* (councils), sometimes called *communes*, were organized from politicians and heathen priests nominated from the provinces of the empire. They were charged with administering Roman law, judging in local civil disputes, and enforcing loyalty to the emperor by requiring an annual burning of incense to the emperor as god. Many of the members of these *concilia* were priests of the pagan religions and temples. The president of the *concilia* was usually called *archiereus* (chief priest) or *asiarches*, in Asia Minor. *Asiarch* meant, "Chief officer of Asia," and referred to the high priests of the temples of the imperial worship in the various cities of Asia Minor. Pliny the Younger (A.D. 62-113), governor of Bithynia in Asia Minor, wrote a letter to the Roman emperor Trajan (A.D. 98-117) concerning the prosecution of people for the crime of following Christ:

> . . . the method I have observed toward those who have been denounced to me as Christians is this: I interrogated them whether they were Christians; if they confessed it, I repeated the question twice again, adding the threat of capital punishment; if they still persevered, I ordered them to be executed . . . .[12]

The second beast exercised all the authority of the first beast in the presence of the image of the emperor. The second beast, *the concilia*, got its power to enforce idolatry from the emperor himself. It was after the death of Octavian (i.e., Caesar Augustus) that the Senate decreed his *genius*, or soul, was to be worshiped as one of the official divinities of Rome. But it was not until Domitian that an *official* edict was issued for *all* the subjects of the empire to *annually* worship the image of the emperor. Each *concilia* appointed *inquisitores* (secret investigators) throughout the empire to ferret out the identity of all persons refusing to burn incense to the emperor and bring them to trial. Many Christians were tortured and slain because they would not burn incense to the emperor. Many declared publicly their allegiance to Christ and became "martyrs" for their faith. Others denied their faith and saved their lives by worshiping the image of the emperor and cursing Christ.

Great "signs and wonders" were allegedly "worked" by the second beast. Notice in the first place, that it is *allowed* to work these signs and *by* them it "**deceives** those who dwell on earth into making an image of the first beast" (the one that was wounded but survived). These "priests" were *magicians* who worked amazing feats of sleight of hand and ventriloquism or deception through hypnosis or drugs. Their magic was in no way supernatural or miraculous. What they did was similar to what the "priests" of Pharaoh did.[13] It is clear from Acts 8:5-13 that the "signs" done by "priests" and sorcerers were *pseudo-signs*, for even the sorcerer Simon recognized the true miracles when he saw them.[14] These were not actual miraclesνthey were *pseudo-signs*.[15] These false miracles deceived those who *wanted to be deceived because they had no love for the truth*. The Roman world of the first four centuries was a polyglot of pagan cultism and occultism. Every religion of the world found its way to Rome and her provinces. Priests and priestesses, prophets and prophetesses of every cult imaginable were allowed to practice their "religion" so long as they did obeisance to the emperor. Sorcery, magic, witchcraft, augury, mystery-cultism, occultism of every kind was popular. Rome had long believed in and proclaimed a "sacred flame" which had fallen from heaven and had instituted an order of "Vestal Virgins" who were keepers of this flame. Priests were magicians skilled in sleight-of-hand which amazed and deceived worshipers into believing their tricks were supernatural. Pagan priests often claimed natural phenomena such as falling meteorites as their own magic (Acts. 19:35). This alleged ability of the second beast to make fire come down from heaven to earth in the sight of men is in no way genuinely miraculous. If God allowed Satan and his cohorts to deceive by genuine miracles, he would thereby nullify his own witness to truth. The Bible denominates signs done by sorcerers and cult-priests as pseudo-miracles. If modern "magicians" work illusions on television which mystify the modern mind, how much more might sorcerers do so with those thoroughly superstitious and those who feared for their lives if they did not acknowledge the "beast" as a miracle-worker.

Ancient pagan priests had, for centuries, practiced deceiving superstitious worshipers into believing images made of stone, metal and wood could talk. Many of them used drugs or self-hypnosis to induce in themselves a trance in which they claimed to be speaking oracles from the gods or from idols. One such was the "oracle," a prophetess who inhabited a temple at Delphi in ancient Greece. Alexander demanded from her a revelation. She predicted (of course) he would conquer the world! *Ventriloquism* was a highly skilled and widely practiced art in heathen idolatry. Eurycles of Athens was the most celebrated Greek ventriloquist. They were called *engastrimanteis*, or "belly prophets" because the ancients believed the voices of these "gods" came from the bellies of these "oracles." Priests of ancient pagan religions were masters of this art and to ventriloquism may be ascribed the miracles of the "speaking statues" of the Egyptians, Greeks and Romans. Alexander of Abonoteichus trained a serpent to hide its head under his arm and allow a half-human mask to be affixed to its tail; he announced that the serpent was the god Asclepius come to earth to serve as an oracle; and he amassed a fortune by interpreting the sounds made by reeds inserted in the false "head" attached to this serpent.[16]

Modern archaeologists have found devices in ancient Roman ruins used for secretly piping the human voice beneath the altars bearing the statues of pagan gods. Caligula had a contrivance made by which he could produce a fiery reply to Jove's thunder and lightning stroke for stroke. He claimed that the moon-goddess had come down and embraced him.[17] Vespasian was alleged to have healed blind men with his spittle and lame people with the touch of his foot.[18] The Greek word translated "sorcerer/sorceries" in the NT is *pharmakeion*, and we get the English words, "pharmacology, pharmacist, pharmaceutical" from it (Acts 8:9,11; 13:6,8; Gal. 5:20; Rev. 9:21; 18:23; 21:8; 22:15).[19] The ancient sorcerers practiced the use of drugs, chemicals, minerals, and other elements to produce effects that appeared to be "magical or supernatural" (i.e., powders that could be cast down on a floor which would produce a flash of fire and puff of smoke, etc.).[20] A recent program on television, *Ancient Mysteries*, revealed an ancient battery by which magicians produced an electric charge, as well as an analog computer, both 2000 years old!

The empire's *concilia* (the second beast) had the skill to deceive millions of gullible and superstitious people into believing the statues of Rome's emperor could speak. Worshipers were amazed and awed by the pomp, power and magic displayed. Thus they worshiped the emperor as a god. Whatever the *concilia* of Rome wished to be carried out by its subjects would be obeyed with fear. The *concilia* also had delegated power to execute all who would not worship the emperor (the beast).

Pagan priests and priestesses (the second beast) "caused" all segments of Roman society to be "marked" so that no one could buy or sell unless they had the mark — the *number* of the beast's name. The Greek word translated "mark" is the word from which we get the English word *character* (*charagma*). Some think this was a literal, physical mark placed on the hand (or forehead) of those who had, at the designated time of the year, burned incense to the emperor as a god. Emperor Gaius Messius Quintus Trajanus Decius (A.D. 249-251) issued his edict in A.D. 250 that demanded an annual offering of sacrifice at the Roman altars to the gods and the *genius* of the emperor. Those who offered such sacrifices were given a certificate called a *libellus*. A copy of such a document from that era is extant today. Cyprian (A.D. 200- 258), a Christian, writes that the imperial edict to worship the emperor or be arrested as an *atheotes* ("atheist") struck terror to the hearts of all whose faith was weak. Many weak Christians went to great lengths to show that their sacrifice to idols was done *willingly* so anxious were they to escape arrest. Cyprian pictures many half-hearted Christians running to the marketplace to burn incense to the emperor. Many were so impatient to deny their faith that they could hardly wait their turn. Many others who would neither flee nor sacrifice suffered the most terrible tortures and died in prison, or were sent to labor in Roman mines until they died, or were cruelly executed without delay. Some, by bribing the officials, procured *certificates* of having sacrificed without committing the overt act. Some allowed others to say that they had sacrificed or to procure certificates for them by proxy. Holders of these fraudulent certificates were called *libellatici* and were despised as much as those who openly denied their faith. Some weak Christians who possessed precious copies of the Scriptures gave, under threat, these scrolls to be burned and destroyed. They were called *traditores* ("traitors").

Whatever the "mark" was that distinguished one as loyal to the "beast," it was apparently considered necessary to survive in the economic life of the empire. Anyone not loyal to the emperor and Rome would be banned from the business world and might even be deprived of the fundamental necessities of livelihood such as food, clothing and shelter. This form of persecution may explain in part the scarcity of food symbolized in the third "seal" in 6:5-6. We know some Christians were persecuted this way by Jewish authorities (Heb. 10:32ff).

We believe John's "mark of the beast" is symbolic, not literal. It is probably the figurative counterpart of the "seal" of God on Christians (Rev. 3:12; 7:1-3; 14:1; 22:4). God stamped his image (mark) on Christians through the character of the Holy Spirit living in them as he was lived out in their lives. The devil and the beast "marked" those who belonged to them in the same manner. Those who had the mark of the beast were those who thought and lived like the beast. The mark of the beast was the stamp of paganism impressed upon the character and conduct of idolaters. Men became like that which they worshiped (see Hos. 9:10; Psa. 115:8). Christians were "conformed to the image of God's Son" and idolaters were conformed to the image of their father, the devil (See Rom. 8:29; 2 Cor. 3:18; John 8:42-47; Acts 13:10; 1 John 3:8-10; 3:15).

The "mark" of the beast was a *human number*. John intended *his readers* of *his* book to **understand** what this number meant. He did *not* intend it to be incomprehensible to *them*. Had John written out the literal name of the beast it would have meant a death sentence for John and anyone else who had a copy of the scroll. So John identified the beast in apocalyptic numerology — 666. All this number signified was the humanness of the beast. It was a contradiction of the popular view of the nature of the beast expressed in 13:4 — that the beast was *invincible*, that he was a god. There was no mathematical code contained in the number from which readers were to decipher such individuals as Nero, the Roman Catholic pope, Napoleon, the Czar of Russia or Rasputin, Hitler, Stalin, the CIA, the European Common Market, Saddam Hussein, or some obscure, yet to be revealed, Arab. The following is a sample of egregious errors which have been made in the past by those attempting to make 666 mean a specific person of history:

Hebrew consonants have numerical value as follows: N=50; R=200; O=6; N=50; K-100; S=60; R=200; total — 666; thus NRON KSR, or *Nero Caesar*. But John did not write Revelation in the Hebrew language. He wrote it in Greek, for Christians.

Greek letters have numerical value as follows: L=30; A=1; T=300; E=5; I=10; N=50; O=70; S=200; total — 666; thus *Lateinos*, or pagan Rome (others interpret this formula as predicting the Roman Catholic Church). In the Alexander Campbell–Bishop Purcell Debate in Cincinnati, Ohio, in 1837, Campbell was forced into the unenviable position of affirming a series of negative propositions. In the course of the debate as he was showing the Roman Catholic Church to be the "Babylon" of Revelation, Mr. Campbell totaled the letters of "the Latin kingdom" to be "666." Bishop Purcell cleverly showed that even his opponent's name could be made to total 666![21]

Someone in 1941 applied an English numerology to 666 as follows: A=100; B=101; C=102, etc., through Z=126. H would then =107; I=108; T=119; L=111; E=104; R=117 — total 666. Thus, Adolph *Hitler!*

Roman letters have numerical value (with 0 the value of any letter that has no value in the Roman system): V=5; I=1; C=100; A=0; R=0; I=1; V(U)=5; S=0; F=0; I=1; L=50; I=1; I=1; D=500; E=0; I=1; total — 666; thus the Latin expression, *vicarius filii dei*, or, "in the place of the Son of God." Thus, the Roman emperor, or the Roman pope.

Another suggestion uses the Greek alphabet : T=300; E=5; I=10; T=300; A=1; N=50; — total 666; thus *Teitan*. Teitan could refer in Greek mythology to the Titans who were great rebels against God; or it could refer to *Titus*, the family name of three emperors, Vespasian, Titus, and Domitian.

Students in the author's Bible college course in *Revelation*, deciphered 666 ("lovingly" they said) as follows: A=52; B=53; C=54, etc., then *Butler* would add up to 384; and if the days they had left at that time until Christmas (which was 227) were added, one would get 611; and if I drove 55 mph on my way to church Sunday and added that to 611, one would get 666, a prophetic sign!

All kinds of modern hypotheses have applied the number 666 to a multitude of persons, nations, things, or ideologies. One suggestion was that by using three six-digital units the entire world could be assigned a working credit card number programmed through a universally-centralized computer by which all mankind could be *controlled*. Others have appealed to license plates on cars in the Arab countries bearing the number 666 as an indication that the "beast" (or as they name him, "The Antichrist) is arising there. Some have shown clothing labels from Red China bearing the number 666 as an indication that Red China is the "beast."

While there may be some credence to the idea that 666 may have symbolized Domitian as the reincarnation of Nero, we believe the idea that was symbolized was more general than specific. Seven is the number of sacred perfection or infinitude. Six is short of seven and denoted incompleteness, imperfection and finitude. A trinity of sixes (666) means *fully and absolutely human, evil, and conquerable.* It means the beast is *not* invincible. By pomp, power and sorcery, the beast claimed, and appeared to be, divine and all-powerful. But John had his number! He was not god; he was not divine; he was human! John was not identifying a specific person so much as he was identifying the Roman *emperorship* from Domitian (A.D. 81-96) to Romulus Augustulus (A.D. 476) *in all of its beastliness* until the fall of the western empire.

There can be *no* credence given to the interpretation that this number (666) refers to "The Antichrist" who is alleged to be some very wicked ruler to appear during the "seven years of tribulation," after the "rapture," just prior to the establishment of the "millennial kingdom" in Jerusalem with a reincarnated Christ sitting on his throne there. In the first place, the term *The Antichrist* does not appear in Revelation and is not even, by itself, a biblical term. There had been *many antichrists* already gone out into the world **before** John wrote Revelation (1 John 2:18,22; 2 John 7). Second, none of the ideas concerning a tribulation, a rapture, or a literal millennium are to be found in Revelation. Third, the idea of a very wicked ruler 2000 years subsequent to the time of John would have no relevance or meaning to the churches of Asia Minor.

John could not have more clearly identified the Roman *emperorship* nor exposed its facetious claims to supernaturalness than by using the number 666. In the cryptic symbol 666, hidden to unbelievers but known to Christians, was his message: "Do not fear any Roman emperor and his subordinates to declare himself god — he is not; he is human."

Revelation 14:1-20
"Then I looked, and lo, on Mount Zion stood the Lamb . . ."

While all the Roman Empire trembled at the apparent invincibility of the beast and prostituted itself to a lifestyle like that of the beast, Christians could rejoice and sing the song of redemption for they were secure in the Zion of God (Zion means "citadel"). The scenario which John drew in chapter 13 did not give much hope, from an earthly perspective, for those who refused to worship the beast. Refusal to worship the beast was going to bring war, captivity, starvation and death. Would refusal be worth it? Would faithfulness to death be vindicated? The answer is in chapter 14.

The theme of this chapter is the same as that of chapters 4 and 5 — **Throne perspective.** The great tribulation of the Roman Empire would have to be seen by

Christians through the perspective of heaven. Heaven is in control! The Lamb would be the victor, not Domitian! Persecuted saints on earth were in direct contact with heaven. They were just a breath away from final, complete victory. If they died "in the Lord" they would be ushered immediately into rest and reward. Many were terrified by the first beast; many were seduced by the second beast; Christians, however, were "redeemed" from all this.

The 144,000 with the Lamb on Mount Zion are the same 144,000 as those in 7:1-8. They are the redeemed *still on the earth*, numbered and sealed by God, with Christ in their midst as he was portrayed walking among the seven lampstands. John pictured earthly "Zion" (the church) surrounded by the world of Rome, so indisputably joined to heaven it was, as it were, one and the same in time.

First, Mt. Zion is without question symbolic of the church on earth. It is plainly taught in the OT prophets that Zion is the church of Christ to be established at the first advent of the Messiah (Psa. 2:6; 110:2,6; Isa. 2:2ff; 35:10; 61:3; 66:7-9; Joel 2:32; Micah 4:7–5:2. Jesus and the apostles confirmed that the church was the fulfillment of the prophecies concerning Zion. (Compare Isaiah 62:11 and Zechariah 9:9 with Matthew 21:5 and John 12:15; compare Isaiah 28:16 with Romans 9:33; compare Isaiah 59:20 with Romans 11:26.) Secondly, the *most significant* confirmation of this is found in Hebrews 12:22-28. There, Christians were instructed that they should not have been tempted to return to Judaism which the writer symbolized by Mt. Sinai (Hebrews 12:18-21) **because** they had, by becoming Christians, **arrived** at the **Zion** predicted by the OT prophets. The author of Hebrews used the perfect tense verb which should be literally interpreted, "But you have come in the past and are continuing to come to Mt. Zion . . . ." He declared that "Mount Zion" was not future to A.D. 2000, but was the church of Christ in the first century A.D.

The Father's name "written on their foreheads" was the same name written on those of the church of Philadelphia who kept the faith; it was the seal of God upon the foreheads of the "new Israel" which was the church on earth; it was the mark of God's Holy Spirit contrasted to the mark of the beast (Rev. 3:12; 7:3; 13:16-18; 14:9-11; 19:20-21; 20:4). It was not a literal mark. It had to do with character and spiritual ownership. Jesus called some of the Jews "sons of the devil" and they had no *literal* mark on their foreheads but their spiritual ownership was recognizable in their character and their deeds (John 8:4-47). Those "sons of the devil" did not have 666 literally tattooed on their flesh to be recognized. Christians of the first century did not have to wear "Jesus" tattooed on their foreheads to be recognized as belonging to him (John 13:35; Acts 4:13; Col. 1:4; 1 Thess. 1:6-10; 1 Pet. 1:7; 4:14).

John's attention was directed away from the church on earth (Zion) to heaven. From heaven he heard a sound like "many waters and loud thunder." It was *like* harpers playing on their harps — *like* a roaring, crashing crescendo of musical instruments. He also heard singing — and it was a *new* song. Whoever was singing, it was not the 144,000 of "new Israel" on earth; nor was it the four living creatures; nor was it the 24 elders. Whoever was singing the "new" song was singing it to an audience of the creatures and elders; it was not angels because angels could not learn this song (1 Pet. 1:12; Heb. 2:16). *Only* the redeemed could sing this song!

The 144,000 were on earth. They learned this song while on earth because they were redeemed "from the earth." Just because John "heard" the song being sung from heaven does not necessarily mean the 144,000 had to be in heaven. **No one on earth could learn that song except the 144,000**. They *were being purchased (redeemed)*. The Greek grammar does not indicate they had already been completely purchased from the earth.[22] This 144,000 was not to be redeemed after the year A.D. 2000. John calls them "first fruits" for God and the Lamb. He used the Greek word *aparche*, which means "the beginning ones." These Christians, the 144,000 safe in the citadel of Zion, had not defiled themselves with the filthy woman symbolized as "the harlot" (Rome).[23] The 144,000 were spiritually pure and *chaste* (*parthenoi*, virginal). The 144,000 had not committed spiritual adultery by bowing to emperor worship and idolatry.[24]

The 144,000 learned the new song, also called "the song of Moses and the Lamb" (Rev. 15:3) as they went through the great tribulation. If they had been in heaven, they would not have been "learning" the song; they would have known it completely. Moses learned the "new" song of redemption by going through a "great tribulation" leading the Israelites out of bondage and through the wilderness. The church on earth followed the Lamb wherever he went. Jesus warned his disciples that they would have to follow him through tribulation (John 15:18-27; Mark 10:21-34; Acts 14:22). The 144,000 were abiding in the truth. In their mouth no deceit or falsehood was found. They had not said the Roman emperor was a god because that would have been to acknowledge his deception and depravity as true. They had not renounced Christ as the Son of God, even at the sacrifice of their lives and fortunes.

John saw an angel flying in midheaven who had an *eternal gospel* with which he evangelized those who were dwelling on the earth at the time John was writing the Revelation. John used the present tense Greek verb *kathemenous* ("those now dwelling") to describe the recipients of this proclamation from the angel because he was not seeing a vision of something to happen 2000 years after he wrote. Some commentators have speculated that this was different than the gospel of salvation by grace through faith proclaimed by Jesus and his apostles. They think it is a special announcement of judgment for the "end times" (yet future to today). But what the angel was preaching *must* have been the very same gospel preached by Jesus and

THE REVELATION OF JESUS CHRIST – PART II

the apostles, for the New Testament declares plainly that there is only *one gospel* to be preached for all time (Matt. 28:19; Mark 16:15ff; Gal. 1:8; Jude 3). It is doubtful that God would literally send heavenly beings to preach the gospel to human beings because the gospel was a treasure deposited in "earthen vessels" and something into which angels "long to look" (2 Cor. 4:7; Heb. 2:16; 1 Pet. 1:10-12). This angel symbolized human messengers much the same way the angels of the seven churches symbolized preachers or elders who were "messengers."

It is interesting that reverence for God, obeying God, worshiping God, and preparing for judgment by trusting in Christ's atonement is the very essence of the good news! The "gospel" cannot be preached without a proclamation of judgment to come upon those who disbelieve (Acts 17:30-31; 24:24-27, et al.). This gospel of God was to be proclaimed to every nation and tribe and tongue and people, i.e., to the whole civilized Roman world as it interfaced with the church of the first four centuries. All who followed the Lamb as he dwelt in "Mt. Zion" (the church) would be numbered among the "144,000" and learn the new song of Moses and the Lamb which those already finished with their redemption were singing around the throne (Rev. 15:2-4).

The Greek words *epesen epesen*, "Fallen, fallen," are aorist tense signifying something that has happened. It seems strange that John would not use the future tense and say, "Shall fall, shall fall, Babylon the great" had he meant the fall of some future "Babylon." But when God declares something shall be, it is as good as done already.[25] There is no question in heaven that the "Babylon" (Rome) of John's day would fall. That was part of the "good news" to be proclaimed. The "judgment" announced in 17:7 is *not* the final judgment — it is "Babylon's" judgment. The question is: Who is "Babylon?" That is settled in chapters 17 and 18. It can be none other than ancient Rome. Rome is symbolized by the first beast (political opposition), the second beast (idolatrous emperor-worship), and "Babylon," the harlot, (carnal materialism and sensualism). These were the three main pressures (tribulations) brought to bear on Christians and others during the age of the Roman Empire.

The destiny of those who worshiped "the beast" and received his mark was, in this particular context, to drink the "wine of God's wrath, poured unmixed into the cup of his anger" (Rev. 14:9-11). Whether that was to be on earth or in hell is problematic. The context of the whole chapter is concerned with "Zion" on earth. However, that the torment of Zion's enemies went up "forever and ever" seems to indicate the worshipers of the beast had already been cast into hell. Again, it is possible that John was writing from a "predictive-present" perspective, predicting what worshipers of the beast would be subjected to during the "great tribulation" upon the Roman Empire as well as their *ultimate destiny*. The statement, "Here is a call for the endurance of the saints . . . ." would support the latter view. If this is correct, the "predictive-present" should be applied to John's vision of the circumstances for those who would "die in the Lord." Those Christians who would die in the "great tribulation" were to be counted as "Blessed, indeed!" They would rest from their "labors" (trials, tribulations) and their *ultimate destiny* would be that of the "innumerable multitude" around the throne, serving God, sheltered in his presence, hungering and thirsting no more, shepherded by the Lamb to springs of living water, every tear wiped from their eyes (Rev. 7:9-17).

John's next vision is a prediction, in symbolic form, of the imminent judgment by the Lamb upon the Roman Empire. The imagery of the Son of man coming on a cloud does not necessarily have to be restricted to Christ's Second (final) Coming.[26] In fact, what John saw here may not be Christ on a cloud at all. The one on the cloud was *like* a son of man. That phrase is used of angels (See Gen. 18:1-2; Ezek. 9:1-2; Dan. 3:25; 10:5; 12:6, et al.). Furthermore, an *angel* shouted with a loud voice to the "one on the cloud" giving him orders. Christ would not take orders from an angel. Finally, the one having "the sickle" is said to be an *angel*. This angel had a crown, but that is not unusual since the 24 elders also had crowns.

The imagery of a "sickle" associated with God's judgment is from the OT prophets, and from Jesus' parables about reapers (Joel 3:13; Matt. 13:24-30, 36-43; Mark 4:29). The angel with the sickle was told to gather the *clusters of the vine* (*botruas tes ampelou tes ges*, "clusters of the vine of the earth"). The "grapes of wrath" were ripe! The Greek word used for "vine" here was to be understood as *vintage* (a season's produce of grapes) and not as the whole vine. The *earth* was the whole vine, but *only the clusters* of the vine (earth) were to be gathered. In other words, God was not going to reap the whole earth in this judgment — only vintage pagan Rome. The angel gathered pagan Rome and threw it into the great wine press of the wrath of God. Wine presses were usually sunk into a hole in the ground or excavated in a rock. Clusters of grapes were poured into these round or square excavations and men and women climbed into them barefooted and squeezed the juice from the grapes by *treading* back and forth upon the ripened grapes.

This is apocalyptic hyperbole. It is figurative and exaggerated. Julia Ward Howe adapted this apocalyptic language to write her poem about America's cataclysmic Civil War, *Battle Hymn of The Republic*. The wine press was trodden *outside the city*. The "city" was undoubtedly the capital city, Rome itself (Rev. 16:19; 17:18; 18:10). Thus, John ensured his readers that, not only shall the "great city" itself suffer the judgments of God, but the rest of the Roman Empire had "stored up for itself the grapes of wrath." That which was to flow from this winepress was blood, not grape juice. This was a figurative scene. It was not intended to be literally fulfilled — certainly not in Palestine, especially not in the valley of Meggido ("Armageddon"), for there is no place for a river 200 miles long (1600 stadia) there. If the river of blood was intended by John to be understood literally, so must the sickle and the winepress! Similar apocalyptic imagery was used by the OT prophets (Isa. 34:5-7; Ezek. 38:19-23; 39:17-24, et al.). John was describing the awful carnage that would attend the destruction of the Roman Empire. Jesus used the same kind of apocalyptic language to describe the fall of Judaism. The essence of chapter 14 is its contrast to chapter 13. The forces of evil were strong. They seemed invincible to some. But the forces of righteousness were stronger. The persecuted saints were reassured of their relationship to the Lamb and their *ultimate destiny* of blessedness. It was time for the Lamb to unleash his wrath upon "Babylon," the "harlot," "the two beasts." And that is what John wrote about next.

Revelation 15:1-8
". . . seven angels with seven plagues, which are the last . . . ."

John saw the Lamb as he stood in "Zion" receiving the worship of the saints who followed him wherever he went. Let a petty emperor of the earth assert his deity for a decade or two. Let an entire dynasty of tyrants pretend to rule the world. That would be infinitesimal compared with the Christ of eternity! Enforced worship of a depraved emperor was a cheap sacrilege viewed against the worship of God; a dictator's required praise was nothing compared with the new song of the redeemed. Men and nations were warned against worshiping an impotent earthly potentate. They were urged to pay obeisance to Almighty God. Those who did not would suffer judgment — *ultimately forever*. The "Babylon" (Rome) of John's day had caused the nations to follow after lies and depravity. Rome, the seat of Satan's rebellion, was therefore to be judged by the gospel it had rejected. Jesus Christ brought the gospel to the world to save it. However, that "good news" became "bad news" (judgment) upon those who, because their deeds were evil, refused to love the truth (John 3:19-21; 5:22ff; 9:39-41; Rom. 1:18-32; 2 Thess. 2:10-12). Rome's judgment built to a crescendo of the seven plagues which were *the last*.[27] This judgment of Rome had been in execution since the beginning activity pictured in the *seven seals* and the *seven trumpets*. Rome's insatiable lust to conquer, rule and prostitute God's "good" creation, inexorably brought God's judgment upon her (Rom. 1:18-32). This judgment intensified as time passed and Rome did not repent. The time came for God to pour out bowls full of wrath and bring an *end* to the beastliness.

These seven plagues were the *last*. The Greek word *eschatas* does not necessarily always mean "the end of all time" in Scripture.[28] It is used frequently in the NT to signify that God has reached some goal, *in time*, on earth, during his redemptive program (cf. 1 Cor. 15:45; Acts 2:17; Heb. 1:2; 1 John 2:18; 1 Pet. 1:20, et al.). The phrase "last days" in the OT and NT usually means the end of the Mosaic dispensation and the beginning of the Christian dispensation. These *last* plagues signified God had reached the *goal* of judgment he had put into operation with the *seals and trumpets*. This is clearly evident from the use of the Greek word *etelesthe*, and translated, "ended." This Greek word would have been better translated, "completed, finished."

John saw through the same crystal-clear sea he had seen through earlier in the "throne-vision." The crystal sea now reveals the *fire* of God's judgment ready to fall in the form of seven plagues upon Rome. It was necessary to see God's judgment upon Rome through the "throne-perspective." Standing *beside* this fiery crystal sea were those who "were conquering" the beast and its image. The Greek participles *nikontas* and *estotas* are present and perfect tense participles, respectively. This indicates the vision is of saints presently *in the tribulation on earth* as if they had already conquered the beast and were standing *with a view toward* the throne of God. The Greek preposition *epi*, translated *beside*, does not necessarily mean "upon" but can mean "toward, near, with a view toward." In other words, "those conquering the beast" in John's day, were standing "with a beside-the-throne perspective" on the judgments that were coming upon Rome. These saints who were seeing their tribulations through the perspective of God's clear revelation were *singing* (present tense Greek verb) the song of Moses and the Lamb.[29] The "Song of Moses and the Lamb" in Revelation (and in the OT) was totally about God. It was not about man's religious emotions. Those who see history and man through the "throne-perspective" see, at last, all of self and self-importance lost in the presence of the greatness and the glory of God. A most interesting phenomenon about music or singing from the viewpoint of the Revelation, or the throne of God, is how much singing is done *about* God's judgments and justice and wrath upon the world! The judgments and justice of God as the subject for singing and praise permeates the OT prophets (e.g., Exod. 15:1ff; Isa. 5:1ff; 26:10). The world will never learn righteousness unless the judgments of God are in the world (present tense). Yet most people, and some Christians, consider any and all judgment or tribulation to be unfair and unjust. God's *way* (judgment upon sin; redemption upon repentance) is always just and true.

One of the four living creatures gave the seven angels (messengers) their bowls of wrath. God executes his wrath on Rome through secondary agents. The sanctuary of the tent of witness was opened and the order to pour out wrath comes from the sanctuary. Smoke filled the sanctuary and no one could enter until the plagues "reached their goal (*telesthosin*, "completed"). The sanctuary is inaccessible! God is unapproachable for any intercessory request on behalf of the beast until judgment is completed. Rome refuses to repent — God refuses to hear any intercession (see Jeremiah 7:16; 11:14; 14:11; 15:1; 16:5; 17:1).[30] When the Jews refused to "know the day of their visitation," there was nothing Jesus could do but weep and pronounce their inexorable doom! (Luke 19:41-44; Matt. 23:29-39; 24:1-35; 1 Thess. 2:15-16).

Revelation 16:1-21
"Go and pour out on the earth the seven bowls of the wrath of God."

The seven seals *reveal*, the seven trumpets *announce* and *warn*, and the seven bowls *execute* God's judgments. Bowls symbolize *fulness* of God's wrath (Isa. 51:17; Jer. 1:13; Zech 9:15; et al.). Seven is the numerical symbol of sacred completeness. The order to pour them out came from the "temple." It was God's edict that judgment upon Rome be executed. We know this referred to Rome because people are left alive, refusing to repent, *after* the bowls are poured out (Rev. 16:6,9,11). At the end of all time, at the Second Coming of Christ, there will be **no** opportunity to repent! (Matt. 24:36-51; 25:1-46; Luke 17:26-37; 1 Thess. 4:13-18; 5:1-11; Heb. 9:25-28; 2 Pet. 3:8-13, et al.). The context which precedes chapter 16 and the context which succeeds it clearly indicate the "bowls-judgment" is to fall upon Rome, "the great city" and its subordinate "kingdoms." The "nations" who had listened to Rome, had "drunk the wine of her impure passion," and had profited by imbibing of her exploitative commerce would first, hate her, then cannibalize her, and then mourn over her destruction (Rev. 14:8; 17:12,15; 18:9,11,16,19, et al.). The bowls were symbols that God used natural or secondary agencies as instruments of judgment upon the Roman world rather than the *direct, divine, miraculous interposition* he will use at the Second Coming of Christ.[31]

If there be any doubt that the wrath of God could be executed through the agencies of mankind and nature, let the terrible destruction and carnage visited upon Nazi Germany through the Russian winter and the allied armies suffice. This is not to place upon Germany, nor all Germans, the blame for World War II. Nor is it to solve all the mysteries connected with the suffering of the innocent as a result of that conflict. The same principle is true of the terrible judgments which came upon the ancient Roman Empire as predicted by John in the Revelation.

The first bowl represented painful and mortal diseases of the plagues brought back to Rome from its military sorties among the barbarians. The second bowl symbolized God's judgments by the use of the sea as an instrument of destruction of life. It is parallel to the second trumpet. Rome shed the blood of the saints and prophets in terrible persecutions, and God poured out her blood in retribution. The assassinations by paranoid emperors and subordinate rulers contributed to the bloodbath of the empire; the wars of aggression, the invasions of barbarian hordes, crime, disease, famine, and natural disasters made humanity a "sea" of blood. The second and third bowls are definitely connected to the statement in 16:5-7 which places the results of the bowls in a situation contemporary to the time of Revelation's writing. The Greek verbs (16:6) translated "have shed" and "hast given" are aorist and perfect, respectively. This clearly indicates that the bowls were poured out long before the twentieth or twenty-first century! John was picturing God's literal use of fresh water sources as instruments of judgment in the third bowl. It is parallel to the third trumpet.

The sun "allowed" to scorch men with fire, in the fourth bowl, symbolized a physical use of the elements of the heavens (i.e., droughts, entropy, changes of seasons, etc.). It parallels the fourth trumpet.

The fifth bowl poured out darkness until men gnawed their tongues in anguish and cursed God because of their pain, but they did not repent of their deeds. This symbolized the same kind of "torment" of the human psyche as is pictured in the *fifth trumpet*. The "darkness" was the depraved mindset of that society (Rom. 1:18-32). It was poured out upon the imperial city, Rome, "the throne of the beast" and it "darkened" the whole empire.

The sixth bowl is parallel to the sixth trumpet. Both symbolized the invasion of the Roman Empire by the barbarian Parthians, Goths, Ostrogoths, Visogoths and Huns. In the sixth trumpet only a third of mankind was hurt, but in the sixth bowl the whole world is assembled to do battle with *the kings from the east* (i.e., from the direction of the Euphrates River). Out of the mouths of the "dragon" (the devil), the beast, and the false prophet, came three *unclean spirits*. These had the symbolic appearance of frogs, but they were demonical. Frogs were "unclean" in Jewish mentality (Lev. 11:9). In Egyptian mythology a frog-god Khnum allegedly created human beings out of the dust of death and his wife, Hekt, a frog-goddess breathed life into them. These were fitting symbols for Roman emperors and their idolatrous priests who claimed to be gods in whose hands men's lives rested.

These "frogs" were said to be performing lying signs and wonders throughout the Roman world to bring together all the kings of that world for battle with God on his great day of judgment on Rome. This unclean, demonic, breathing represented the "river" of lies issuing from the three "tools" of the dragon (i.e., the beast, the false prophet and the harlot).[32] Rome assimilated false religions from all over the world, including Egypt. The false prophets of Rome kept deceiving their world with their "signs" of Rome's invincibility and immortality so that all the subordinate "kings" of Rome aligned themselves with Rome. Then God judged them *with Rome*.

The battle on the great day of God the Almighty is the battle the Lamb had with the Roman Empire for sovereignty. It is the same battle described in Daniel 2:44-45 and 7:7-27 between the saints of the Most High and the fourth beast (Rome). It is not predicting or referring to the end of time. Armageddon is not a real, geographical, place! The Greek word in Revelation 16:16 is Ἁρμαγεδών (*Harmagedon*), and is a **transliteration** of the Hebrew word מְגִדּוֹן (*Megiddon*). The meaning of the Hebrew word is "place of troops, throngs, or multitudes; or sometimes, Hill of Slaughter." A city and a plain are given the name Megiddo in the Old Testament. The prefix "Har" in Hebrew means "hill or mountain." There were some famous battles at, or near, Megiddo (Josh. 12:21; 17:11; Judg. 1:27; 5:19; 1 Kgs. 4:12; 9:15,19; 2 Kgs. 9:27; 23:29-30, et al.). But Megiddo is infinitesimally too small to crowd into it "all the nations of the earth" in the twenty-first century! The armies of just the two most populous nations of the world could not fit on the "Hill of Megiddo." Most modern eschatological theories that "Armageddon" is a *literal* battle at a *literal* place in the future try to make Armageddon the same as the battle of Gog and Magog (Ezekiel 38-39) and the Valley of Jehoshaphat (2 Chronicles 20; Joel 2–3) and Bozrah (Isaiah 34). If "Armageddon" is all of these, *it cannot be literal* since they are all located in different places!

The contexts immediately preceding and following deal unquestionably with the Roman Empire. "Armageddon" is the final downfall of the Roman Empire. The main activity of unclean spirits is to involve all the world of unbelief in a battle of *deception*, not a fleshly war. If this is a literal place and a physical war, then consistency would demand that the frogs, the dragon, the beast, and the false prophet be literal and physical. "Armageddon" is symbolic. It symbolized the decisive conflict between the worship of Caesar and the worship of Christ. Victory at "Armageddon" cleared the way for the kingdom of the saints to break out of the constraints of pagan Rome and go to the farthest corners of the globe. "Armageddon" symbolized the same great battle as was symbolized by the Valley of Jehoshaphat, Gog and Magog, and Bozrah.

Bowl seven — **it is done!** The Greek verb translated "it is done" is perfect, active, indicative, singular.[33] That means that what was done had been done, and was *not* to be done in the future. It is another example of "predictive present." The "great city" (Rome) was split up. The great division of the Roman Empire into Western and Eastern sections precipitated its fall. The "cities of the nations" fell. "Babylon" drained the cup of the fury of God's wrath. **This is none other than Rome and her empire**. It was John's use of apocalyptic, hyperbolic language just as Isaiah 13:10ff, Jeremiah 4:23ff; and Ezekiel 32:1ff used it. It was **not** a prediction of the end of time and the Second Coming of Christ. Men were still on earth cursing God!

Revelation 17:1-18
"Babylon the great, mother of harlots and of earth's abominations."

In the Old Testament Nineveh, Tyre, Jerusalem, and Babylon are all symbolized by the word "harlot" (Nahum 3:1-4; Isa. 1:21; 23:15-17; 45:5-15; Jer. 2:20). God's judgment on ancient, Mideast, Babylon is effusively pronounced in the Old Testament (See Isa. 13 & 14; Jer. 50 & 51; Dan. 1-5; Hab. 1 & 2; Zech. 2:7; 5:5-11). Ancient Rome is portrayed as a "harlot" because of the seductive attractiveness of her appeal to that civilization to consort with her in prostituting God's creation. Rome *prostituted and perverted* all the natural order, social, religious, intellectual, physical, moral, and material. Such great importance was attached to the city of Rome as the center of forces opposing God and profaning all of that civilization, three chapters were devoted to portray her doom. The seventeenth chapter focuses on identifying the great harlot (or "Babylon"). A number of symbols were given in detail for the benefit of the church of the first four centuries. They were *expected* to understand the "mystery of the woman" (Rev. 17:7).

It is appropriate that one of the seven angels who had the *seven bowls* should explain the judgment on "Babylon." That tied the seven "last" plagues, or bowls, directly to the "city" identified in chapters 17 and 18. The awful judgment predicted and portrayed to fall upon the "beast" was the same judgment to fall upon the "harlot" because they were one and the same entity. The beast, the false prophet, and the harlot were all the ancient Roman Empire, seen from the perspective of Rome's three-sided attack upon Christ's church then.

Notice the following symbolisms which were attributed to the harlot (Rome): (a) she was *sitting* (present tense) upon many waters, i.e., enthroned over many nations; (b) kings and nations of the earth had committed fornication with her, i.e., joined with Rome in prostituting God's creation; (c) she was sitting on the back of a scarlet beast, i.e., she was a cohort with the beast whom the devil had selected as one of his tools, i.e., carnality supported by political power; (d) she wore gaudy clothing, i.e., enticing and seductive; (e) she became drunk (intoxicated, inebriated) with the feeling of rebellion and power to kill; (f) she has a name written on her forehead, i.e., she advertises; (g) she is a "mother," i.e., she reproduces children of her character; (h) her drunkenness comes through the shedding of the blood of martyrs for Jesus.

Rome inebriated herself on pride, arrogance and opposition to the kingdom of God. She sated herself on the blood of the saints and martyrs of Jesus until she was "drunk." Intoxicated with what she thought was absolute power and eternal perpetuity, she lost all ability to function realistically and became, as the apostle Paul described her: (1) suppressing the truth; (2) ungrateful; (3) senseless and futile in her thinking; (4) filled with idolatry; (5) impure and lustful; (6) dishonorable to the human body; (7) exchanging the truth of God for a lie; (8) exchanging natural sexuality for unnatural; (9) obsessed with homosexual lust; (10) receiving in her own person the due penalty of her errors; (11) base in mind and improper in conduct; (12) filled with all manner of wickedness; (13) evil; (14) covetous; (15) malicious; (16) envious; (17) murderous; (18) contentious; (19) deceitful; (20) malignant; (21) gossip-filled; (22) slanderous; (23) hating God; (24) insolent; (25) haughty; (26) boastful; (27) inventing of evil; (28) disobedient to parents; (29) foolish; (30) faithless; (31) heartless; (32) ruthless; (33) and encouraging of others to evil (Rom. 1:18-32). It is no wonder that ancient Rome would be called the "harlot" and the "mother of harlots." In fact, John was told "not to marvel" because God would tell him the mystery of the woman. He is told the woman (harlot) resided (sat) upon "seven hills," and she was "the great city that had dominion over the kings of the earth" (Rev. 17:18). That was Rome! Identification of Rome as "*the great* city" is even more apparent in chapters 18 and 19.

The "beast" that carried the woman was the same "beast" introduced in Revelation 13:1 — Imperial Rome. Seven specific emperors are symbolized. The symbolic picture began with *Tiberius* (A.D. 14-37), the emperor when Christ died, rose from the dead, and established the church. The six following "kings" were: *Caligula* (A.D. 37-41), *Claudius* (A.D. 41-54), *Nero* (A.D. 54-68), *Vespasian* (A.D. 69-79), *Titus* (A.D. 79-81) and *Domitian* (A.D. 81-96) who was ruling when John wrote the Revelation. Five of these had fallen: Tiberius, Caligula, Claudius, espasian and Titus. Nero, although one of the seven, is *not* one of the five *because* he is regarded as "coming alive" in the adaptation of the *redivivus* (reincarnation) *myth*. Thus, to speak *mythologically*, Nero had not "fallen." *One is*, refers to Domitian who was the only one of the seven then living. *The other who has not yet come* was the symbolic personality of Nero revived in Domitian. According to Suetonious, Domitian certainly displayed a "Nero" personality in his later years. The "Nero personality" that had been revived in Domitian lasted only a "little while." The "ten horns" symbolically represent the *complete* coalition of *subordinate* rulers of Roman provinces who had been given the title "king" by the Roman emperors (e.g., the Herods, et al.).

Millions of heathen people throughout the Roman Empire (i.e., those whose names had not been written in the book of life) "marveled to behold the beast." They marveled *because* the beast existed in the past, was not presently existing, yet did exist. The Revelation John received here about the beast was enigmatic and esoteric. John was attempting, in cryptic language, to identify Domitian as the "beast" who had existed in the past, was not presently existing, yet was existing! In other words, John was describing Domitian as a *reincarnation of Nero*. John continued his abstruse identification and described the "beast" as "seven kings, five of whom have fallen, one is, the other has not yet come and when he comes he must remain only a little while." And again, "the beast that was and is not, it is an *eighth* but it belongs to the *seven*, and it goes to perdition." It works out chart-wise as follows:

1. Tiberius — fallen
2. Caligula — fallen
3. Claudius — fallen
4. Nero — one who was, is not, and is to come for a little, who also was an eighth, but was of the seven, making Nero both a *seventh* and an *eighth*.
5. Vespasian — fallen
6. Titus — fallen
7-8. DOMITIAN — the one who *is*, *Nero reincarnated*, therefore, an *eighth* — belonging to the *seven*, yet symbolically having Nero reincarnated in him, making Domitian both a *seventh* and an *eighth*.

In other words, Domitian was the "beast" then existing, but he was Nero who had come back in the person of Domitian. There was no question that Domitian behaved much like Nero in beastliness nor was there any question that he was going to perdition. The *Nero redivivus* ("resurrection") *myth*, already mentioned in our comments on chapter 13, was **widely** and **continually** (for more than twenty years) perpetuated.[34] It is used satirically by John here to identify and characterize Domitian. We see no other possibility by which to explain this enigma. Remember, the seven churches of Asia Minor *were* to *understand* what was written in this Revelation. Further, John was told by the angel of God, "I will tell you the mystery of the woman, and of the beast.

The "ten kings" of 17:12 were the same subordinate rulers called "ten horns" in 17:3. The number "ten" represented a totality of puppet "kings" throughout the empire who were of "one mind" with the imperial policies, but later cannibalized the empire (17:6ff). These "kings" were united in purpose with the beast (Rome) and surrendered their sovereignty to Rome. Their appointment as "kings" was conditioned upon their complete subservience to Rome's imperial authority in politics and religion. That, from Rome's viewpoint, included the church of Christ. Puppet "kings" joined the beast in making war on the Lamb and his followers. Rome allowed absolutely no competition to her sovereignty or glory. She demanded her emperors be worshiped as gods by all peoples. She demanded all her subjects to be ready to die in battle against any self-perceived form of sedition or revolution. The worship of Jesus Christ was considered sedition. Christianity and Rome were at *war!*

The Lamb and those with him would win that war. The conquest of the fourth "beast" was predicted by Daniel some 600 years before John wrote the Revelation (Dan. 7:26-27), and it was the fundamental theme of Christ's revelation to John.

In the Old Testament "waters" was used as a symbol for people (Isa. 8:7; Jer. 47:2). John symbolized the entire Roman Empire, comprising many ethnic groups, cultures and languages with "waters." The "harlot" sat upon that world, seduced it, prostituted it and exploited it for her own profit and pleasure. She paid for it with her life at the hands of her puppet-kings. Rome was devoured by her former "lovers." Her wickedness inevitably led to her self-destruction (See Micah 3:2-3; 7:2; Ezek. 22:27; 34:1-6 for examples of self-cannibalizing).

> The armies of Rome were no longer Roman armies; they were composed chiefly of provincials, largely of barbarians; they fought not for their altars and their homes, but for their wages, their donatives, and their loot. They attacked and plundered the cities of the Empire with more relish than they showed in facing the enemy; most of them were sons of peasants who hated the rich and the cities as exploiters of the poor and the countryside; and as civil strife provided opportunity, they sacked such towns with a thoroughness that left little for alien barbarism to destroy. . . . In this awful drama of a great state breaking into pieces, the internal causes were the unseen protagonists; the invading barbarians merely entered where weakness had opened the door, and where the failure of biological, moral, economic, and political statesmanship had left the stage to chaos, despondency, and decay."[35]

This picture of self-cannibalization, incredible as it may have seemed in the glory days of Rome, was predicted some 350 years *before it took place* when John wrote the Revelation.

Precisely how God "put it into their hearts to carry out his purpose" (Rome's self-destruction) we are at a loss to know. The Greek text says God gave[36] it into their hearts. It is the same Greek word used by Paul to describe how God "gave them up" to the lusts of their hearts, dishonorable passions, a base mind and improper conduct (Rom. 1:24-32). Rome's destruction by self-cannibalization brought to *fulfillment the words of God*. The process took 350 years or more beyond the time John predicted it but it came, inexorably and irrevocably. God built this moral judgment of self-destruction into his moral creation. It is an undeniable doctrine of the Bible and an unimpeachable fact of history.

The angel identified the "beast." It was Rome. Now, in one terse sentence, the angel identified the "woman." She was Rome. Babylon, the harlot, the woman, was (as the RSV describes her) that "great city which has dominion over the kings of the earth." Babylon cannot, therefore, be Jerusalem or the Roman Catholic Church.

In the 35 years between Alexander Severus and Aurelian (A.D. 235-270) 37 men were proclaimed emperor. Decius gave orders (249-251) for Christianity to be destroyed, but later he watched his own sons slain in battle and was himself struck down in one of the worst defeats of the entire history of Rome. Assassination of emperors by their troops became a regular occurrence. Revolts broke out everywhere. The Western Roman Empire ended its days with a *boy of 6-7 years of age on the throne* (Romulus Augustulus, A.D. 475-476).

Cheap imports, high taxes, pestilence among human workers, caused large scale migration of farmers to cities and reduced production in the empire. The army often joined in attacking the wealthy. Barbarian raids and piracy made trade routes unsafe. People were too poor to buy the goods that could be produced. Precious metals ran low. War was almost continuous. Rome repeatedly devalued its currency. The government issued cheap coinage. Prices rose rapidly. In Palestine they increased 100 percent between A.D. 70 and 299. In Egypt inflation ran out of control. A measure of wheat costing eight drachmas in the first century cost 120,000 drachmas at the end of the 3rd century. Trust funds were nullified, business failed, capital funds for trading and loaning disappeared. "The empire had begun with urbanization and civilization; it was ending in reruralization and barbarism."[37]

Although the devil was severely bound when Rome fell, and his accomplices (the beast, the false prophet, and the harlot) were destroyed, today he continues to deceive those who refuse to come to the glorious light of the gospel. And he still uses, though with less power, those three tools. The beastliness of ungodly political power still persecutes; the masquerading of the devil in false religions still leads astray; the attractiveness of worldliness and carnality still seduces millions into spiritual prostitution. Thanks be to God life and immortality have been brought to light through the gospel. Christ destroyed the power of the devil, the fear of death, and the devil's power to deceive has been forever truncated (Heb. 2:14-18).

Revelation 18:1-24
"Alas! alas! thou great city . . . . In one hour has thy judgment come."

This chapter portrays, in symbolic terms, the devastating prostration of the city of Rome. It was to be many years future to the time John wrote, but it was so certain John spoke of it as an accomplished fact! The glory of ancient Rome did disappear from the earth in exactly the manner John predicted.

Chapter eighteen presents a vivid picture of the contrast between heaven's attitude and the world's attitude when the judgments of God fall on wicked worldliness. Heaven and the saints rejoice; the worldly-minded mourn. To some people it may seem out of character for heaven to call for rejoicing over the devastation of

Rome, but heaven knows that the life of the godly on earth is one of persecution, deprivation and injustice (John 15:18-21; 16:33; Acts 14:22; Rom. 8:18-25; 2 Tim. 3:12; 2 Cor. 1:8-11; 4:16-18, et al.). Christians are not permitted to carry out any personal vengeance and must trust God to punish wickedness as he sees fit. God has ordained human government to punish the wrong doer and reward the right doer and thus maintain justice and order (see Rom. 13:1-7; 1 Tim. 2:1-4; 1 Pet. 2:13-17).[38] But human governments do not always acknowledge that God-ordained mandate and become corrupt and unjust — as Rome did. In such cases it is altogether biblical for Christians to rejoice at every clear judgment of wickedness in history.

It is clearly a distinguishing mark of Christian character to hate evil and love good. Christian character insists on a demand for justice and an uncompromising call for an end to evil. Righteous people will rejoice when wickedness is brought to an end, either by conversion or judgment. But they will let God accomplish this through the faithfulness of his word. Moses and the Israelites sang for joy at the fall of Pharaoh's army. The OT prophets repeatedly exhort the believing "remnant" to rejoice at the promised destruction of their enemies. The Christian is not to love the world or anything in it. He may use it and whatever is good in it as a steward of God, but he must be ready and willing to rejoice at its destruction. Because that is how it is in heaven, forever!

"After this" does not mean chronologically. It is a phrase used in the Revelation to distinguish one vision from another, but not necessarily in time. Chapter 18 is merely a continuation or an amplification of the subject matter of chapters 15, 16, and 17. The angel coming down from heaven apparently was not one of the seven who had the bowls. This angel was one of great power and authority, directly from the presence of the glory of God; the earth was made *bright* with his glory. He cried with a *mighty* voice. What he said *thundered; it roared; it was ear-splitting.*

"*Fell, fell,* Babylon the great," would be a literal translation of the Greek aorist verbs, *epesen, epesen.* Rome's fall, though not for 350 years after John, is so *certain* it may be said from heaven's perspective to have already taken place! Rome and her consorts did not see themselves as ever to fall (Rev. 18:7), but from heaven's vantage point their doom was sealed.

Rome *became* (aorist tense verb) a dwelling place of demons. Rome had become a "haunt" (*phylakē*). The once proud, rich and splendid buildings of Rome became haunts of "demons, unclean spirits and unclean, hateful birds." Tertullian wrote concerning the Colosseum, "There are as many unclean spirits as there are men there."[39] It is doubtful that John meant the ruins of Rome would become haunts of actual demons. There is no evidence that evil spirits were then, or are today, living in the ruins of the ancient Colosseum. John was symbolizing the devastation of ancient Rome and the contempt with which history would hold it for its arrogance, its injustices done to Christians, and its insane depravity which brought self-destruction. In a figurative way the ruins of ancient Rome *speak* of the demonic, depraved, foulness of the human spirit in league with Satan. *No civilization or culture has ever been able to outdo Rome in depravity.* Many have imitated her but none have exceeded her. And why should Rome escape total devastation when the wicked cities which had preceded her suffered it? (Isa. 13:19-22; 34:8-15; Jer. 50:39; 51:37; Zeph. 2:13-15, et al.).

All the world known to civilized man was seduced by ancient Rome to participate in her ungodliness. She built her empire by military conquest and economic extravagance. Practically all the cultures and races of the world of that time willingly joined in political and military alliance with Rome, and followed her depraved ways to gain powers and favors from her. Puppet kings and influential men, like the Herods, grew rich through political and business advantages granted them by Rome. By fawning to the indulgent whim of the Caesars, even when it meant exploitation and treason against their own people, the politicians and merchants of that world grew rich. By imposing exorbitant taxes upon their subjects, by selling many of their own peoples into slavery, and by exporting to the lascivious and insatiable imperial Rome all their best national products, these provincial kings and traders engaged in intercourse with the "harlot" and became as guilty as she. *Wantonness* is "insolent, insatiable, luxuriating."[40] Kings and merchants sacrificed truth, justice and kindness in their *wantonness* to grow rich with Rome.

Christians were exhorted by God, through John, to "Come out of her [Roman carnality], my people, lest you take part in her sins . . . ." The Greek verb *exelthate*, is aorist imperative. God did not merely suggest Christians should "come out" of that worldliness, he *commanded* it. John was not, of course, ordering Christians to make a *geographical exodus* from the Roman Empire. Neither did John mean that Christians then should withdraw from the world into monastic societies. *Geographical* separation from ungodliness cannot be done (see 1 Cor. 5:9-13), but *spiritual* separation certainly may!

Many of the Christians to whom John wrote had to make great sacrifices to live their lives separated from Rome's idolatry and depravity. Some had pagan family members turn against them. Others were accused of treason against the emperor and were slain. Some were deprived of employment, food and property. But whatever the cost, the separated life would eventually deliver them to glory. God was for them — who could be against them? Nothing Rome could do to them could separate them from the love of God. But those who shared in Rome's sins would also share in her plagues and eventually be cast into the lake of fire and brimstone.

Sin after sin had been "glued"[41] together in ancient Rome until a huge mountain of wickedness reached even up to heaven. No nation or people on the face of the earth can long postpone the wrath of God if it continues to pile up sins against him (see 2 Chr. 28:9; Jer. 51:9; Ezra 9:6, et al.). Men may forget some of their sins, but God will not forget any sins not covered by the vicarious death of Jesus Christ. So after calling his people "out" of "Babylon," God called those angels who would execute his wrath upon her. They gave her what she had given. The Greek phrase, *diplosate ta dipla*, is translated "double for her deeds," but literally it would be "double for her double." God was evenhanded in his justice. Rome did not suffer any more than she had handed out. Rome magnanimously gave out double portions of wickedness to the world, so she was to receive a double portion of God's wrath. The same phrasing is used in "Mix for her what she has mixed-double." When Rome's crimes against the world had reached a point beyond God's tolerance, he executed his justice, double for double.

Rome did not see herself as a profligate or derelict. She told herself that she was enthroned as the "queen" of the world. Isaiah portrayed ancient Semitic Babylon saying the same thing of herself (Isa. 47:7-15). Ancient Nineveh, and Tyre said the same of themselves (Zeph. 2:15; Ezek. 28:2). Many emperors and nations have boasted they would last forever; Cyrus the Great's Persia; Alexander the Great's Greek empire; the British empire; Hitler's Third Reich. None of these were as powerful and rich as the Roman Empire of the first century, but they are all gone, including Rome! The Roman Forum which was the seat of her power is today only ruins visited by tourists. Rome's power and grandeur is only a cadaver of the past upon which historians pronounce *post mortems*.

Rome said she would *never* mourn. God said, "in one day" her plagues and destruction would come! One, twenty-four-hour day is not meant to be understood literally. It is figurative language, poetic in style, to symbolize the suddenness and unexpectedness of Rome's fall. In A.D. 410 the entire world was *stunned* when the once proud city of powerful emperors was sacked, looted and burned by the Visigoths. That was just the beginning of the plundering of Rome, but it was sudden and unexpected, and signaled her demise. God showed the world he was equal to the challenge of Rome for eternal sovereignty of the world. She boasted she would never relinquish her hold on the world. But God was mightier than Rome!

What a strange paradox! The kings of the earth turned in hate upon the harlot and joined in making her desolate; *now they weep* and wail at her destruction. But that is the way of the worldly-minded. These kings did not weep out of compassion for the harlot. They mourned their *own loss*. When the harlot passed away, what they had enjoyed by her power was gone. There is no "rhyme or reason" for the actions of most unbelievers. The unbelieving mind does not think logically, for it is a mind in rebellion against the very Source of logic and reason — God. It is a mind in anarchy, a mind gone mad. That is why Paul wrote to the Corinthians, "Come to your right mind, and sin no more" (1 Cor. 15:34). Lenski commented here, "The lover of a whore strangles her and then weeps like a fool." But that does not mean the "lover" is not guilty. These "allies" of Rome stood afar off as she burned. They could not help her and were careful to stay at a distance to avoid sharing in her doom.

The city of Rome was like a voracious and insatiable wild animal. Roman aristocrats and the *nouveau riche* spent money in unbelievable quantities. Modern man's most extravagant luxury is poverty compared with the riotous extravagance of ancient Rome. One of Nero's "freemen" was so rich he regarded a man with a fortune of $12 million a pauper. Apicius squandered a fortune of $2 million in refined debauchery, and then committed suicide when he had only $250,000 left because he could not live on such a pittance. In one day Caligula the emperor squandered the taxes of three provinces amounting to $250,000, and in a single year boasted of spending $40 million. There was an insanity of wanton extravagance in first century Rome without parallel in history. Rome raped and plundered the civilized world of its resources and treasures, material and human, to an extent unmatched even by the Nazis of the 20th century.[42]

John's list of goods no longer being sold in Rome is an amazingly detailed inventory of first century merchandise. It shows the indulgent luxury of Rome and how widespread Rome's commercial empire was. Gold and silver came from Spain. Pliny the Elder writes of hydraulic mining for gold in that age which would put recent operations to shame. Roman aristocrats and emperors used gold and silver in building and crafts like we would use steel and marble today. Jewels and pearls and the various spices all suggest the Orient. Silk and cinnamon apparently came from China. Silk was usually purchased to make clothing for the rich. One pound of silk was sold for one pound of gold, or approximately $10,000 today. Extremely costly wood from a special citrus tree which grew in North Africa, prized for its coloring which was like a peacock's tail or the stripes of a tiger, was imported to make furniture. One table made from this wood would cost anywhere from $8,000 to $30,000. Ivory was shipped from India and Africa and was very costly. It was used to make furniture and decorative pieces. Fine linen, made of flax, came mainly from Egypt and only the very rich could afford it. Purple and scarlet cloth was dyed in Asia Minor and transported to Rome for making clothing for Roman emperors, senators, and their wives. Wine was a universal table drink in that age. Water was usually unfit to drink. Italy could not supply enough wine for her own people, so Rome paid high prices to have wine from other countries imported. Oil, used for lamps, medicine, cooking and a number of other things, was also in short supply and therefore very expensive. Metals and lumber, mined and harvested all over the world, were voraciously consumed by Rome in her worldwide public works programs and in extravagant beautification of the city of Rome. Agricultural products and animals were imported by the ton to be consumed daily by the hundreds in the games, and sacrificed to the "gods." Horses and chariots were imported by the rich to become part of the stables of the aristocrats as well as resupply for the massive Roman military complex.

The Greek words *somaton kai psychas* are translated, "human souls" (18:13) in the RSV. Literally it would be "bodies and souls" of men. The slave markets of that ancient world were called *somatemporos*, or "body emporiums." Slaves were sold and owned, body and soul. The slave was no more than the livestock on the farm. There were over 60 million slaves in the Roman Empire. In the city of Rome alone there were 400,000 slaves, half the population of the city. It was not unusual for an aristocrat to own 500 slaves. One Roman left 4116 slaves in his last will and testament. Emperors often had households of at least 20,000 slaves. People from every nation and culture were sold into slavery — even Hebrews. Those who owned slaves held over them the power of life and death. Slaves might be legally killed by their owners or set free on the slightest whim. Slavery was a worldwide industry and many became rich by trading and selling human beings.

The Roman Empire of John's day had an astoundingly well-organized passenger, freight, and express system. For the transport of goods, there were *mansiones*, which in English means, "waiting places." These *mansiones* maintained riders, drivers, conductors, doctors, blacksmiths, wheelwrights, and about forty horses and the appropriate amount of rolling stock. In this way the trade of the empire was kept moving. Where in our world there are scores of obstacles to free trade, in that Roman world there were no such obstacles. From the Great Wall in Britain to the Sudan in Africa, and to Mesopotamia and China there was one huge trading unit. There was such an immense volume of trade and prosperity that credit, capitalism and banking were well advanced. Checks were used, letters of credit were common, and Roman currency was valid exchange anywhere. The Roman Empire was a *paradise for businessmen*. Commerce was frenzied. Only a very few ever warned of the dangers of inflation and fiscal irresponsibility. But the crash came! And it was one of the contributing factors to the death of the empire.

The merchants (*emporoi*) all over the Roman Empire and those in countries not under Roman rule, i.e., China, Africa and the Orient, mourned and wailed because the luxurious "fruits" of their commercial traffic with Rome were gone when she fell. The sumptuous and luxurious life merchants of the empire were making for themselves by selling to Rome was all over with when Rome fell. Like the subordinate "kings," the merchants did not try to come to Rome's rescue but stood "afar off" afraid for themselves. They did not care for Rome — only for their own loss. The merchants did not think of Rome as "mighty" like the "kings," but they thought of her as "wealth," clothed in fineness and bedecked with precious jewels. Their market collapsed! Suddenly, completely, and disastrously they lost everything.

All international, seafaring traders "stood far off and cried out as they saw the smoke of her burning." Throwing dust on the head was a sign of great grief in that civilization. But again, the grief was selfish. There was no pity for Rome. Trade and commerce of themselves are not wicked; they are good when used for the welfare of humanity. However, when used for selfish luxury and the gratifying of fleshly lusts, they become unrighteous, profane and wicked.

The martyred saints in heaven, under the altar, had cried out for God's justice to be done on their murderers (Rev. 6:9-11). Heaven, saints and apostles and prophets, were *commanded*[43] to be glad about Rome's devastating death. Throwing a millstone into the sea symbolized a punishment of severity for extreme wickedness or perversion (Jer. 51:63-64; Matt. 18:6). It depicted that the one thus punished would never rise again! Rome's death was characterized as passionate, impulsive, violent. John used the double negative, "no, no," six times in chapter 18 to emphasize *total obliteration.*[44] Never again would the empire of Rome be found. This is exactly what Daniel predicted when he interpreted Nebuchadnezzar's dream of the "great image" (Dan. 2:36-45; see also Dan. 7:26-27). Daniel predicted the "fourth" empire would be the last universal secular empire. The fifth "universal empire" was to be God's kingdom, the church. Ancient Rome will never rise again!

John's prophecy of Rome's fall parallels the historical reality: first the beast, i.e., political structure of the empire; second, Rome's allies, i.e., the provinces and their merchants; and last, the harlot, i.e., the capital city itself. All the wild orgies, the bloody contests in the arenas, the gluttonous feasts, the indecent and blasphemous theater productions and the pomp and extravagance of the royal processions — all attended with music and trumpets, would *not ever* be experienced in Rome again. Industry would cease. No more would there be found craftsmen plying their trades. Rome's great commercial capital was to die. Third, all vestiges of family and home life were to disappear. No more lighted homes, no more marriages, no more Rome! Some interpreters excising certain verses and words from their contexts and using them to construct a millennial melange envision a resurrected and restored Roman Empire prior to what they call "the end of the age." Some are declaring the European Common Market is the "new Rome." During World War II a number of books on prophecy were written announcing that Benito Mussolini was about to resurrect the Roman Empire as prophesied in Revelation. Adolph Hitler was supposed to be "The Antichrist" and, together with Mussolini, he would usher in the seven years of tribulation before which Jesus Christ would "rapture" the church and after which Jesus would come to earth and set up his millennial kingdom. Jesus would then rule over all the nations with "a rod of iron" from the city of Jerusalem. Needless to say, those books are now obsolete and out of print! Rome, a universal power of wickedness, is *never* to be again! Because ancient Rome was destroyed, and Satan was "bound," the church has become a universal kingdom. It is composed of citizens from "all nations, races, tongues and cultures." The next time Christ comes to this world, this existing cosmos will melt with a fervent heat and he will create a new heaven and earth (2 Pet. 3:8-13).

In the last two verses we are reminded of the three *reasons* God judged Rome and obliterated her. First she made dominion, wealth, and worldliness her chief ambition. Second, Rome deceived and exploited the whole world with her "sorceries." Third, Rome is accused of the murder of God's prophets and saints. But Rome's guilt does not stop there. She is also accused of the blood of all who have ever been slain on earth! Rome was in complicity with the Jews by giving the ultimate order to crucify the Son of God. Jesus pronounced the Jewish leaders to be guilty of all the blood shed from creation to their own time (Matt. 23:29-39).

The apostle Paul delineates the horrible crimes of that Roman civilization (Rom. 1:18-32). The universal pagan sovereignty Rome enjoyed is gone, never to be revived. But the triad of forces opposing the church of Christ which were so powerful in Rome live on with less concentration and in subdued influence in the present world, i.e., political persecution, humanistic idolatry, and carnal indulgence of the flesh. The subduing of these powers resulted in the missionary thrust of the gospel into the far reaches of civilization. Truth sets people and nations free from ignorance and falsehood and Satan's powers are bound to a greater degree than they were when Rome controlled the world.

Revelation 19:1-21
"And the beast was captured, and with it the false prophet. . . . These two were thrown alive into the lake of fire that burns with brimstone."

John brought to its grand climax the apocalyptic drama of the sovereignty of God in Christ versus the pretended sovereignty of the devil and his allies (the beast, the false prophet, and the harlot — Rome). The opposing characters had all been clearly defined. From the birth of the Man Child, it was apparent that the old dragon (the devil) was in a rage to devour the Child. But he could not do it. God caught the Child up from death and back to heaven. So the dragon gave his power to deceive to the beast, the false prophet and the harlot. They set upon the Woman (the church) in the wilderness of pagan depravity. But God pronounced his final judgment upon Rome — especially the prostitute-city itself. Rome's doom was sealed. Her death was imminent. She would even cannibalize herself. There would be none to help her.

God through the Lamb was going to defeat Rome and throw her into the lake of fire and brimstone. The Lamb would take on the character of the Warrior-King (Messiah) and completely defeat his enemies. The Lamb would prove his sovereignty by dramatically saving his church (his Bride) on earth and by destroying that fourth world empire (greatest of all according to Daniel) which the world believed to be invincible.

So, John would give an apocalyptic, highly symbolic vision of victory for the ancient church. The vision would be in the form of a glorious contrast between the defeat of "the city of the world" (Rome) and the revelation of the Perfect City of God coming down out of heaven from God. But first, the climactic battle between the King of kings and the allies of the devil — the beast, false prophet and the harlot.

John heard a loud cry of a multitude of angels, living creatures, and martyred saints together in heaven. All heaven had been commanded to rejoice at the revealed fall of the harlot (18:20) and so heaven's corridors were ringing with shouts of hallelujah and praise to the name of God for that victory. The rejoicing of heaven was in sharp contrast to the weeping and wailing on earth over Rome's fall! The world saw Rome's fall as a detriment to its indulgence and greed. Heaven saw it as beneficial for all creation. The power of Satan would be bound. The good news of salvation would be able to go to the farthest reaches of human habitation on earth.

God proved himself just and fair and true to his word. He kept his promises to avenge wickedness done to those who trusted him. The Greek text, by placing the article before each noun, makes it emphatic that *the* salvation and *the* glory and *the* power belonged to God. When Rome fell, it was apparent to all the world there was a power greater than that of Rome.

God *judged* the great harlot who *had corrupted* the whole world with her "fornication."[45] The word translated "corrupted" means literally "to destroy by bringing to a state of moral rottenness." The decadence of Roman aristocracy permeated the whole of Roman society and killed it.

The blood of the saints shed by Rome was *avenged*.[46] There was no capriciousness or vindictiveness in God's vengeance — it was simply the fair, deserved, right and proper result of Rome's wickedness. God gave them up to eat the fruit of their deeds. Rome tried to stamp out the church, to stamp out all that stood for goodness, righteousness and truth. The church was a "torment" to Rome's conscience. So God simply gave Rome what she wanted — profligacy, depravity, falsehood. God made all his creation to function on the principles of right, justice, faith and love. He also built into his creation a constant revelation of these principles, and consequences for obeying and disobeying them. All God had to do to Rome was simply give her the consequences of the choices she made. So, God gave Rome up to the lusts of her heart, to dishonorable passions, to base minds and improper conduct (see Rom. 1:18-32).

Access to the throne had been halted (Rev. 15:8), and no intercession for the world could be made. Once the judgment of Rome was sealed with prophetic certainty, the throne was seen again. All of God's obedient creation was seen paying homage and praise to his righteousness and justice. "So be it!" or "Amen," they said, in perfect agreement with God's final world on Rome. At that point it was announced that the "marriage of the Lamb has come." The announcement came with a *roaring* that drowned out all other voices or announcements. God was about to reveal something extremely significant. The harlot had brought ultimate pressure upon the church (Christ's Bride) to seduce her, but the Bride remained faithful to her husband. It may have seemed to the church that the *whole world* had committed fornication with the harlot, but Christ's Bride had not done so. She married him and adorned herself in the righteousness Christ had provided for her. She did not dirty her garments with compromise or strip them off by unfaithfulness. Once again, the Greek verbs are aorist tense to indicate the "marriage" pictured here has *already happened in the past.*[47] The betrothal (engagement) was considered as binding as marriage in the customs of John's day (See Matt. 2:20,24). People were considered married *before* there were any ceremonies or celebrations and before the sexual consummation. The time lapse between betrothal and other ceremonies (including the marriage supper) was pictured in Jesus' parable of the ten virgins (Matt. 25:1-13). Marriage was considered to have taken place long before any feast might be given.

It is evident from many Scripture passages that the church on earth has been married to Christ. In the OT the relation of Jehovah to his covenant people is portrayed as a marriage (Hos. 2:1ff; Isa. 50:1; 62:4ff; Jer. 2:32; Ezek. 1:16ff, et al.). Isaiah 62:4-5 is a prophecy that when the Messiah came in his *first* advent, those who believed and followed him would be "married" to God. In the NT the church *on the earth* is the Bride of Christ (John 3:29-30; Eph. 5:22ff; Rom. 7:4; 2 Cor. 11:2). So the "marriage of the Lamb" as John portrayed it was not picturing some future event. It was past. It took place at the *first advent of Christ* when the church was established on the Day of Pentecost, Acts 2. The *consummation* of the marriage (not the "supper") is yet to take place at Christ's *second advent*.

Those "invited to the marriage supper of the Lamb" were those who were becoming Christians in John's day. First, the Greek word translated "invited" is a perfect tense verb, meaning, "having been invited and continuing to be invited."[48] The marriage supper had already come when John wrote Revelation and people were continually being invited to it and participating in it. John clearly would not have used a perfect tense verb to predict some *future* event to take place more than 2000 years afterward. Remember, the consummation comes *after* the marriage supper.

The whole Christian age is depicted in the NT as a festival. Jesus likened the kingdom of God unto a "feast" many times (e.g., Matt. 22:2ff; Luke 14:15ff; 15:1-32; Rev. 3:20). The OT prophets pictured the Christian age as a "feast" (Isa. 55:1-2; 65:13, et al.). The NT indicates the feasts of the Mosaic dispensation were types of the NT experience (i.e., 1 Cor. 5:8; Heb. 13:10, et al.). Both the "marriage" and the "marriage supper" of the Lamb have already begun and are continuing to take place as men and women are becoming Christians on earth. The Spirit and the Bride are *still* saying, "Come," and inviting whosoever will to come (Rev. 22:17). To say that the marriage and the supper have already come does not imply the marriage has already been *consummated*. The ultimate union of the Bride and her husband will take place at Christ's Second Coming.

For some reason John thought the one speaking to him should be worshiped. John was quickly corrected. The testimony of *Jesus* is the *spirit* of prophecy. What has been testified by Jesus, and about Jesus, is the *pneuma* ("spirit") or focus of all the prophecies of the Bible, both OT and NT (including Revelation). That awesome fact should make all men focus their worship on the *Lamb* instead of the servants who delivered the *testimony of Jesus*. The testimony that Jesus is the Sovereign Lamb, is the very point of the book of Revelation. No secular ruler or empire is sovereign — Jesus, the Lamb is!

The Groom appeared on a "white horse," not to consummate the marriage, but to *rescue* his Bride by destroying the beast and false prophet (and the harlot). Heaven was opened and Christ, the Warrior-King, rode forth on a white horse. This Warrior-King was called "Faithful and True!" Jesus Christ was called "the faithful witness" (Rev. 1:4-5). What he revealed to John about the conflict between the Roman Empire and the early church was absolutely true and faithful. To millions of *unbelievers* Rome was no "beast." To them she was man's beneficent god! To millions of *unbelievers* Rome was eternal. She was invincible. But the true and faithful Revelation of Christ declared Rome was a beast and she would be destroyed. The Warrior-King had a name which only he knew. If he alone knew it, we can only speculate. It probably had to do with the nature of the "Trinity." Who understands that? In him dwelt all the fulness of the Godhead bodily (Col. 1:9; 2:9). He wore a robe "dipped" in blood. The imagery is unquestionably following that of Isaiah where the Lord Jehovah is seen in a vision coming from the destruction of those who were enemies of his redemptive program (Isa. 63:1-6; see also 34:1-17). The Lamb revealed that he was going to tread the awful winepress of God's wrath upon Rome and that he was going to assemble all the world of Rome for the battle at Har-Mageddon. Awesome defeat and judgment upon the world of Rome was predicted numerous times in Revelation. Now the Lamb, as the Warrior-King, needed to be visualized in his robe spattered by the blood of his enemies. The context and a similar vision in Isaiah would preclude this blood being that of the Lamb or his saints. It was the life-blood of his enemies!

The Warrior-King was called "The Word of God." The use of *Logos*[49] or "Word," was a favorite title of John for Jesus Christ (John 1:1,14; 1 John 1:1, et al.). Jesus was the Word of God, the personality of God, in human flesh. Jesus was God's word to mankind — God's final word to mankind. He appeared to John in the Revelation clad in a robe dipped in the blood of a fallen Roman Empire. The Logos is God's judge of the world. The Logos is God!

The "armies of heaven" which followed him did not have to come from heaven. This "army" was undoubtedly the church on earth "riding" to victory over the Roman Empire. It most certainly did not refer to some battle at the end of time and Christ's Second Coming. There will be no "battle" at his second advent — only judgment and salvation (Heb. 9:27-28). John did not intend to portray a literal battle of swords, spears, chariots and horses. John is using symbolism. The Christians of the first century were told their war was a *spiritual* war — not one of flesh and blood, and the weapons they were to take up were *spiritual* weapons, not carnal ones (Eph. 6:10-20; 2 Cor. 10:3-5).

The "sword" that issued from the mouth of the Warrior-King was symbolism and so was the "rod of iron." The sovereign, faithful, Word of God was going to rule, not Caesar. What *God's* Word says about the world, not what human rulers say, will come to pass. This parallels the clear teaching of the OT. (Psa. 2:9; Isa. 10:5-10; 11:4; Jer. 27:5-7; Dan. 2:20-23; 2:46; 3:28-30; 4:34-37; 6:25-28, et al.). God's rule (or kingdom) is in the minds and hearts of believers. His rule is established by persuasion, not by force. The word John used in this text and translated "rule" is *poimanei*, which literally means "shepherd." People out of every nation were to be "smitten" and persuaded and shepherded with the indestructible and sovereign Word of God. The Warrior-King was to do the work of fulfilling God's wrath. The Messiah, whom Rome thought they had crucified, would squash Rome and all her influence like grapes in a winepress. The One whom Pontius Pilate scorned and crucified for claiming to be "king of the Jews" was seen by John as having the title "King of kings and Lord of lords."

Another feast is portrayed! A "feast" for "vultures!" The fall of Rome was symbolized as a great, gory feast for carrion-eating birds. The imagery is, again, from the OT prophets and especially Ezekiel (Isa. 34:6; Jer. 46:10; Ezek. 39:17-20). The fallen are from across the entire spectrum of humankind. Mighty people, kings, princes, men and women of all categories of life, emperor and empress, slave and free, rich and poor, opposing God's kingdom. Satan did not discriminate when he deceived people into joining him in rebellion against God. He took his wicked helpers wherever he could seduce them.

The imagery of this great devastation and death is borrowed from Ezekiel's symbolic battle between the Lord and the forces of Gog and Magog. Just as Ezekiel's vision was described symbolically, so John's details in the vision of the fall of Rome were not intended to be literal but symbolic. Every living individual was not slain when Rome fell. Many of those individuals who had worshiped the Caesars and opposed the church went right on living when Rome fell. But God had John describe it *symbolically* as an enormous slaughter for the sake of *impression*. God does not have to literally slay people and leave billions of rotting cadavers strewn on a battlefield in order to defeat his enemies and rescue his saints — neither in OT times or NT times! God delivered the OT saints from Persia, "not by might, nor by power, but by [his] Spirit" (See Zech. 4:6; 2 Chr. 36:22-23; Ezra 1:1-4). God merely "stirred up the spirit of Cyrus" and the faithful remnant was delivered.

Earlier, John described this battle of the Warrior-King versus the beast and false prophet as the "battle on the great day of God the Almighty" at the place which is called in Hebrew, Armageddon. It pictured the "great city" as split into three parts, the cities of the nations falling, and Babylon draining the cup of the fury of God's wrath (Rev. 16:12-21).

Now, for the third time, the great spiritual struggle for the allegiance of mankind and sovereignty over the ancient world of Rome are predicted. The battle itself is never described in its details — only its consequences are predicted. It would be defeat for humanistic depravity and victory for the holy followers of Christ. The Warrior-King "seized"[50] the beast and the false prophet who had "deceived"[51] those who had received[52] the "mark of the beast." The Greek word translated "mark" is *charagma*, from which the English word *character* derives. The false prophet had worked pseudo-signs by which he misled those willing to receive the "character" of the beast and who were worshiping[53] its image.

The beast and the false prophet were thrown into the lake of fire that burns with brimstone. They were forever overcome. They were banished from earth to the eternal prison. They would never rise again to the extent they were in the ancient Roman Empire. This, of course, does not mean that the devil did not continue to oppose God and his kingdom. The devil was not banished forever (Rev. 20:10). But with Rome's fall, the *devil was bound* — his sphere or power was to be limited for a *long time* (symbolically, "a 1000 years," Rev. 20:1-3). He no longer had a *universal* secular and carnal power by which to dominate the civilized world as he had with Rome.

The beast and the false prophet were cast *alive* into the lake of fire. This symbolized that the "life" of Rome's power to oppose the church of Christ was no more! The "wrath of God [was] revealed from heaven against all ungodliness and wickedness of [those people] who by their wickedness suppressed the truth. . . . and [they suffered] in their own persons the due penalty for their error" (Rom. 1:18-32). Universal paganism with all the accumulated wealth and power of the ancient Roman Empire could not thwart God's redemptive program in the world. Will Durant made a succinct comment to this effect:

> There is no greater drama in human record than the sight of a few christians, scorned or oppressed by a succession of emperors, bearing all trials with a fierce tenacity, multiplying quietly, building order while their enemies generated chaos, *fighting the sword with the word* (our emphasis), brutality with hope, and at last defeating the strongest state that history has known. Caesar and Christ had met in the arena, and Christ had won.[54]

The life of universal paganism which had total domination of the civilized world was banished. The "rest of them" symbolized *all* those who had the "mark" of the beast and false prophet upon them. Those were slain by the sword (the Word of God) which issued from the mouth of the Warrior-King. That it was the word of God and the church which defeated pagan Rome is extensively documented in Durant's *Caesar And Christ*. He devotes the last two chapters and the epilogue (52 pages) of this work to describing the collapse of Rome and the triumph of Christianity.[55] His analysis of the causes and results of the fall of Rome correlates *exactly* with the Revelation given to John!

> The two great problems in history, says a brilliant scholar of our time, are 'how to account for the rise of Rome, and how to account for her fall.' We may come nearer to understanding them if we remember that the fall of Rome, like her rise, had not one cause but many, and was not an event but a process spread over 300 years. Some nations have not lasted as long as Rome fell.
>
> A great civilization is not conquered from without until it has destroyed itself within. The essential causes of Rome's decline lay in her people, her morals, her class struggle, her failing trade, her bureaucratic despotism, her stifling taxes, her

consuming wars. Christian writers were keenly appreciative of this decay. Tertullian, about 200, heralded with pleasure the *ipsa clausula saeculi* — literally, the *fin de siecle* or end of an era — as probably a prelude to the destruction of the pagan world. Cyprian, towards 250, answering the charge that Christians were the source of the Empire's misfortunes, attributed these to natural causes. . . . The cause, however, was no inherent exhaustion of the soil, no change in climate, but the negligence and sterility of harassed and discouraged men.[56]

Durant specifies the reasons for the fall of Rome as he analyzed her history in his "Epilogue." He attributes her demise to a serious decline of the native population and a rise in an alien population produced by infanticide (abortion), sexual emasculation (castration and homosexuality); pestilence; revolutions and wars; epidemics of major proportions; the welfare dole; moral decay of social structures; despotism in the political ruling classes; taxation; excessive expenditures in public works. "Powerless to express his political will except by violence, the Roman (citizen) lost interest in government and became absorbed in his business, his amusements, his legion, or his individual security."[57]

Look again at Durant's description of the mood of the soldiers as the empire crumbled:

The armies of Rome were no longer Roman armies; they were composed chiefly of provincials, largely of barbarians, they fought not for their altars and their homes, but for their wages, their donatives, and their loot. They attacked and plundered the cities of the Empire with more relish than they showed in facing the enemy; most of them were the sons of peasants who hated the rich and the cities as exploiters of the poor and the countryside; and as civil strife provided opportunity, they sacked such towns with a thoroughness that left little for alien barbarism to destroy.[58]

Rome cannibalized itself! (Rev. 17:15-18).

Homer Hailey's excellent summarization of Revelation, chapters 16-19, bears repeating here:

The victory is won, and the defeat of the beast and his ally, the false prophet, is complete. The Roman power and the paganism which it supported are now destroyed forever. The vision of Daniel is fulfilled (Dan. 7:11), and in this defeat and destruction is revealed the destiny of all such powers that should ever arise to fight against God and his kingdom. This is God's guarantee of victory to the saints who lived then and to all who would come after them, even until the end of time. . . . Not a vestige of the anti-Christian forces was left; the destruction was complete. The sword of truth and judgment prevailed over the sword of political force and human wisdom in false worship.[59]

Revelation 20:1-10
**"Blessed and holy is he who shares in the first resurrection!
Over such the second death has no power . . .
they shall reign with him [Christ] a thousand years."**

We have chosen the sixth verse as the key verse to chapter 20. This is the focus of chapter 20's message! The focus of the chapter is *not* on the binding of the devil. It is *not* on the "thousand years." The focus is to *contrast the destiny* of those who had taken part in the "first resurrection" and those who had worshiped the beast and its image.

Chapter and verse numbers in the Bible are not inspired! The earliest Greek manuscripts of the NT have no numbers for chapters or verses; in fact, they have no paragraph indentations or punctuation marks. Although the English versions begin a new chapter here, we believe this chapter is merely a summarization of, and perhaps an extension of, what has been pictured from chapters 12 through 19 dealing with the defeat of the beast and false prophet and the victory of the saints. In the last half of the Revelation the two beasts and the harlot are intimately allied with Satan to suppress the truth and make war on the saints. Their defeat would unquestionably produce a devastating *limitation* on Satan's sphere of influence.

Chapter 20 is the most talked about chapter of the Revelation. Many people know *about* the chapter but have never analyzed the chapter in its context. Many articles and books have been written taking Revelation 20 out of its context and, mixing it with numerous texts from the OT, have cooked it into a "mulligan stew" of eschatology. This chapter has been pressure-cooked into a basis for various theories of a literal, physical, thousand-year reign of Christ on earth. The *general* theory, with variations among different eschatological schools, is:

a. Within a generation (35-40 years) from the time the Jews reoccupy the land of Palestine, Christ will begin his 1000-year reign. (The modern state of Israel was established in 1948).

b. Just prior to the millennial reign of Christ, the saints, both living and dead, will be "raptured" (caught up into the heavens to meet with the coming Christ).

c. There will be seven years of tribulation on earth, while the "raptured" will be enjoying the "marriage supper" of the Lamb.

d. After the Antichrist ("beast") manifests himself and initiates seven years of tribulation, Christ and his saints will come to earth and, in a literal, carnal, battle, defeat the Antichrist.

e. At this point, God will set up his kingdom, which he tried to set up when Christ came the first time but had to put the church parenthetically in its place because Christ was crucified before he could set up his kingdom on earth. At this time a visible Christ will visibly sit on a literal throne of David in the literal city of Jerusalem.

f. This will begin Christ's millennial reign, and he will force "with a rod of iron" the nations to be at peace. A new Jewish temple will be built in Jerusalem; OT worship (with modifications) will be reinstated; Jews will be converted by the millions ("all Israel will be saved"); Satan will be bound for a literal 1000 years.

g. At the end of 1000 years, exactly, Satan will be loosed for "a little while" and make furious war upon the saints on earth. But Christ and his army of saints, engaging once again in a literal battle with carnal weapons, will defeat Satan and his hosts at the literal place called Armageddon.

h. Following this, the wicked dead will be raised and, with the wicked remaining alive, will be judged and sent to hell, forever, while all the righteous will dwell on a renovated ("new") earth.

A careful analysis of Revelation 20:1-10 will note the following:

1. There is no unequivocal mention whatever of the *Second Coming* of Christ.
2. There is no unequivocal mention of a *bodily* resurrection. The NT, in other places, provides for a resurrection *other than* and *prior to* a bodily resurrection.
3. There is no mention of a literal reign of Christ *on earth.*
4. There is no mention of a literal *throne of David.*
5. There is no mention of a literal *Jerusalem or Palestine.*
6. There is no mention of a *rebuilt Jewish temple* or the *salvation of all Israel.*
7. There is no mention of the church being *raptured.*

This vision began as John saw an angel coming down from heaven. It was not Christ coming down, but an angel *sent* down. Whatever was to happen in this vision, was to connect immediately to what had happened in 19:1-21. The angel held in his hand the key of the *bottomless pit* and *a great chain*. Most of the Greek verbs in this text, i.e., "seized, bound, threw, shut, sealed," even "loosed," are aorist (past) tense. None of them are future tense. Clearly, this is symbolic language. There is literally no such thing as a "bottomless pit" or a "chain" capable of binding spiritual beings. The "key" symbolized *authority,* the pit symbolized *safe-keeping*, and the chain symbolized *limitation*. The Greek aorist verb for "bound"[60] is used to report that Herod had bound John the Baptist in prison (Mark 6:17), to describe people bound in marriage vows (Rom. 7:2), of physical incapacity (Luke 13:6), of that supernatural power to "bind" with which Jesus anointed the apostles (Matt. 16:19; 18:18), and in rabbinical literature used of that which "is forbidden." Evidently the *bottomless pit* is not the final destiny of Satan (Rev. 20:10). It is *Hades*, the *abyss*, or *nether darkness*, to which Jesus had sent demons (Luke 8:31; 16:23; 2 Pet. 2:4; Jude 6).

The Greek word used for "bound" in this text is a derivative of the same root word from which the word used in Jude 6 is derived and translated "reserved" in the KJV, and "kept" in both the RSV and NIV. *Satan was bound, or restrained for 1000 years by the angel with the keys to the abyss to be forbidden, or kept from the power he had exercised through the Roman Empire.* This text refers to a *binding* of Satan *as a result of the fall of the Western Roman Empire* which took place ca. A.D. 450-500. This interpretation best fits the context because:

1. The terms "bound" and "loosed" in the text are Greek aorist tense.
2. The terms "bound" and "loosed" in connection with Satan are always *relative* in the Bible to God's determinations, i.e.,
   a. God is almighty. He is the *only* almighty being in existence!
   b. Satan, therefore, is *always bound* to some degree or other.
   c. Any "binding" or "loosing" Satan has is by God's sovereign permission, and according to God's purposed limitations.
   d. The record of Job's experiences shows God kept Satan in check (bound) to some degree even in OT times. God allowed certain freedoms with Job that Satan could not have otherwise taken (Job 1:6–2:8).
3. Revelation chapter 20 is *only one* of a number of passages in the Bible that deal with the "binding" of Satan and his hosts. Thus the passage must be interpreted in the light of the consistent teaching of these other Scriptures. Revelation 20 must *not* be used to *outweigh or contradict* the cumulative statements on this subject from all other passages, e.g.,
   a. Mark 3:27; Matthew 12:25-29; Luke 11:17-22 all make it plain that Jesus claimed to be "binding" or restricting Satan's sphere of influence at his *first coming* to the world. He proved his claim by casting out demons.
   b. Jesus claimed that his death and resurrection "threw" (Greek aorist tense verb) out the pretended ruler of this world (John 12:31). In other words, Jesus' redemptive accomplishment at his first advent placed severe limitations on Satan's sphere of influence.
   c. Discussing the work to be accomplished by his death, resurrection and return as the Holy Spirit (John 16:11), Jesus said the pretended ruler of this world (Satan) had been judged and would continue to be judged (perfect tense verb in the Greek text). When Satan was "judged" he was handcuffed and restrained, but not then consigned to eternal incarceration.
   d. The author of the Epistle to the Hebrews wrote (Heb. 2:14-15) that Jesus shared the flesh and blood experience of humankind, died and rose again, so he might "cause to cease to operate the one having the power of death, that is the devil." The Greek verb in this Hebrews text is *katargese*, which means "to deprive of force, influence or power."[61]

     e. Jesus said he "was seeing" (Greek imperfect tense verb, *etheoroun*) Satan fallen as lightning falling out of heaven. Jesus spoke of Satan's fall in his own time, not in the future (Luke 10:18). This was said when Jesus gave miraculous power to the seventy disciples over demons.

     f. John wrote that the Son of God was revealed at his *first coming* to *undo* the works of the devil (1 John 3:8).

     g. Paul wrote that Jesus' death and resurrection *disarmed* the rulers and authorities (spiritual hosts of wickedness) and *triumphed over them publicly* (i.e., historically, Col. 2:13-15).

     h. When Jesus ascended, *captivity* was taken *captive* (Eph. 4:8-9).

     i. Peter preached that the devil *could not hold* Jesus in the bonds of death (Acts 2:24).

     j. Christians *overcame* the devil in the blood of Christ (Rev. 12:11).

3. From these passages it is clear that the "binding" of Satan was initiated at the onset of Jesus' earthly ministry and *finished at the downfall of Rome*. Rome was the last of the four great empires which Daniel predicted would exert *all possible* human and Satanic power to erase God's work of redemption from the face of the earth (Dan. 7:19-27). But Daniel also predicted that "during the days" of the fourth kingdom (Rome) God would establish a *fifth* universal kingdom (the church) which would overcome the last universal humanistic empire and continue forever (Dan. 2:44-45). Rome's military-politico, religio-idolatrous, and sensually depraved stranglehold (as the tool of Satan) on the civilized world was a classic example of what it was like *all over the earth* before Satan was "bound" or limited by the ascendency of the gospel and the spread of Christianity to the ends of the earth. The fact that God could rescue his covenant people from the worst that men could do and from the worst that demonic powers could do is proof even in the OT that *God keeps Satan bound all the time* to the extent he wishes to have it, so that his redemptive work might be carried on. The binding of Satan in Revelation 20 *is relative to the needs of God's redemptive work in the NT age* which is the last of the ages (1 Cor. 10:11). Satan's final incarceration will take place at the end of the world and the final judgment.

    To understand the relative binding of Satan, someone has suggested we think of Satan as a vicious animal on a chain tied to a tree. In OT times, the chain binding Satan was extended to greater length and his sphere of influence to deceive and destroy was wide. In NT times, because sin has been atoned for historically and been brought to light historically, because forgiveness has been wrought, because life and immortality have been brought to light historically, God, through the

Gospel of Christ, has *shortened* the chain binding the devil and has severely restricted the power the devil has to deceive the world. The devil is still active, like a roaring lion, seeking whom he may devour. And though his chain (sphere of influence) is shorter than it was, anyone who steps within that sphere of influence will be deceived and devoured.

Another way to understand the relative nature of Satan's present binding is to contemplate what widespread area of influence the devil had when the *only verbal* revelation of God before Christ was to a small nation of Jews surrounded by many nations of paganism. The whole world (except for isolated and exclusivistic Judaism) was held hostage by Satan in ignorance, superstition and fear. Most of the ancient civilizations were controlled, life and death, by one-world government. We introduce the following charts as aids to understanding this concept.

Limitations ("binding") imposed upon Satan by the force of God's truth and mercy through the historically-accomplished redemptive work of Christ, written in the New Testament and established all over the world after the fall of the Roman Empire.

1. Incomplete revelation of God, given in only one language to one nation, the Jews.

2. Man a hostage of guilt through Law which brought only a fearful expectation of judgment.

5. Demons were allowed to inhabit men's bodies and hurt mankind.

Complete revelation
Forgiveness by grace
Worldwide gospel and church
Satan bound by Christ's incarnation and fall of Rome
Demonic activity greatly curtailed
No pagan one-world government

Satan's sphere of influence before

Christ was very wide and powerful.

3. Only one locale where God's spiritual sovereignty ruled with all the physical, social benefits thereof.

4. Pagan imperialism dominated all the civilized world (except Judaism) with idolatry and wickedness.

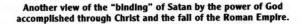

Another view of the "binding" of Satan by the power of God accomplished through Christ and the fall of the Roman Empire.

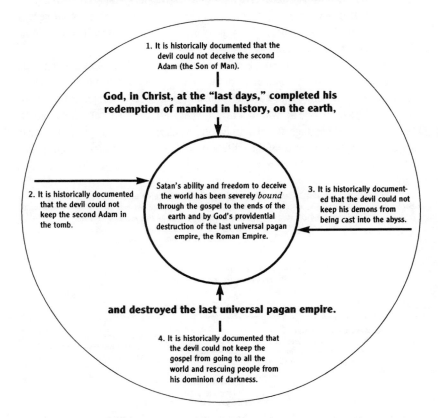

The "thousand years" started *after* the "time, times and half a time" when the *two witnesses* were victorious (Rev. 11:11-19) and *after* the "time, times and half a time" of the woman's nourishing in the wilderness (Rev. 12:13-17). The beast, false prophet and harlot, prompted by the devil, brought *great tribulation* upon the woman and her offspring for "three and one half times." That came to an end when those wicked forces were defeated and the devil was "bound." That was when the 1000 year reign of the saints began.

It is clear that the Bible often uses the number "thousand" (as well as many other numbers) in a figurative, symbolic sense. Surely, more than all the cattle on a thousand hills belong to the Lord (See Psa. 50:10). Did the Lord multiply Israel exactly, or figuratively, a thousand times more than they were at the time of the exodus?[62] John's use of numbers throughout the Revelation is altogether figurative and symbolic — why should he suddenly select such a "round number" to predict something literal?

The "little while" Satan was to be "loosed" is the same time Satan is "loosed" in Revelation 20:7. It is *not* the same as the "short time" of Revelation 12:12. The "short time" of 12:12 is the same as the three and one half times (350 years) of 11:3-13 and 12:13-17, the limited time Satan knew he had left to use Rome as his tool to make war upon the woman and her offspring.

How does one account for the fact that ancient Rome has been dead for *more* than one thousand years and yet Revelation 20 seems to indicate the final judgment follows immediately after the thousand-year binding of Satan and the death of Rome? The 1000 years is simply symbolic of a *vast, indeterminate, yet incomplete* time known literally only to God! Why doesn't John tell us in detail what will transpire during this "thousand-year" binding of Satan if it is predicting the time-span between the death of ancient Rome and the end of time? *Because it is not necessary for the faithfulness of any saint to have that information!* (Acts 1:7; Matt. 24:36; Mark 13:32; Acts 17:26,31). The OT prophets left centuries of blanks in their eschatology, just as John does here. Many of them jumped, eschatologically, from their own times (800 B.C.) to the beginning of the messianic age (the first advent of Christ and the establishment of the church) *with hardly any details of the intervening centuries being revealed at all!*

For God to leave a huge hiatus in biblical revelation between what a prophet wrote about his immediate time and what he might predict about some future time is not unusual. This is a unique vehicle of prophetic, apocalyptic literature and we have discussed it under "Shortened Perspective" in Appendix A. It is the same perspective one gets as he approaches head-on a mountain range on the horizon. The mountains appear to be jammed up against one another without any space or valleys between them. Once the traveler arrives alongside the mountain range, he sees that there are valleys in between. The prophet Joel furnishes us a classic illustration of shortened perspective. In Joel 2:27 the prophet is speaking of the blessings God gave the land after the locust plague of Joel's day. In Joel 2:28, the prophet leaps some 800 years into the future, from one verse to the next, and predicts the messianic age and the establishment of the church. *We have that interpretation on divine authority!* Peter interpreted Joel 2:28 for the world in Acts 2:16ff. Joel sums up what will happen in the messianic age from the establishment of the church until the "great and terrible day of the LORD" comes by saying there will be "signs in the heavens and on the earth" and whoever calls upon the name of the Lord during that time will be saved. Joel goes on in chapter 3 to explain that what he has prophesied about the messianic age will be God's defeat of all the forces of worldliness and wickedness. All of Joel's prophecy from 2:28 through 3:21 is figurative and symbolic of the messianic age. But the important point is to see clearly how the prophet *shortened the eschatological perspective* by jumping over 800 years from one verse to the next.[63] This is precisely what John has done in Revelation. He jumped over centuries and centuries of time (now more than 1500 centuries) from 20:6 to 20:7. The two charts on pages 247 and 254 will aid in understanding the "Shortened Perspective" concept.

The devil was caged — thrown into the abyss (pit) with the opening shut and sealed so that he could no longer *deceive the nations*, i.e., the whole civilization of ancient Rome (except a minority of believing Christians) *until* the thousand years are ended. The devil's only power is that of falsehood. He has no real authority. Jesus said the devil "has nothing to do with the truth because there is no truth in him. . . . he is a liar and the father of lies" (John 8:44). The devil's primary goal with ancient Rome was to deceive it into believing that he was the ruler of this earth. The recurring theme of this book of Revelation centers in Satan's *false claim to sovereignty in the universe*. Deception is really the only power Satan has. The book of Revelation is a refutation of that deception. That claim was totally and empirically refuted in the historical work of Christ's redemption. Essentially, Satan was bound when Christ was raised from the dead and proved that "*all authority was given to him in heaven and on earth*" (Matt. 28:18).

After the fall of the ancient Roman Empire with her military and economic powers broken, whole nations could no longer be deceived and led into idolatry because the gospel freed many people in every nation, tribe, tongue, and race. Satan no longer had the awesome, and to some, invincible, power of Rome to use to deceive the whole world into believing that demons and idols and emperors should be worshiped. Once the eyewitnessed testimony that Jesus Christ had conquered death permeated the world, people from every nation turned away from allegiance to satanic falsehood and toward the truth of God.

It should be noted that this text never says that the church of Christ was deceived. Before Christ came and instituted his kingdom of truth, practically the whole world had joined Rome in idolatry. The church remained for a while confined, with a few exceptions, to the land of Palestine. The "nations," therefore, were being deceived by Satan. Then the great apostle to the Gentiles began invading the "nations" with the truth of God. Thousands of Paul's converts also took the Gospel to the ends of civilization. Eventually, the veil of Satanic deception began to fall away from the eyes of those in the "nations" and the empire of darkness began to crumble. When Rome fell, Satan's power to deceive the whole world was *severely restricted — Satan was bound!*

E. A. McDowell says it most succinctly:

> Let it be repeated that this is not the termination of Satan's power; he has not been cast into the lake of fire; he is confined for a 'thousand years' to the abyss, the home of the demons. In the vision John teaches that with the failure of the Caesars to make Christianity subordinate to the imperial rule, the reign of Christ as King of kings and Lord of lords in history was confirmed. . . . So far as the span of history which stretches from the triumph of Christianity in the first and second centuries to our time is concerned, we may say that no instance is on record of a general challenge to the rule of Christ *paralleling the challenge made to that rule by the empire of Rome which ruled almost all the civilized world.*[64]

Immediately after having seen the devil seized and bound, John saw the souls of those who had been "axed"[65] or, beheaded, for their testimony to Jesus and for the word of God. The Greek participle is perfect tense indicating a continual slaughter of Christians. Christians *had been* and *were continuing to be* martyred during Rome's attempt to stamp out Christianity. These were the "two witnesses" Satan and Rome believed they had eradicated, but God raised them up. Rome died but these saints came to life! The Greek verb *edothe*, translated "was given," is aorist, indicative, passive. The action was taking place upon the subjects. *The martyred saints were **given** thrones of judgment to sit upon!* Now they were the judges — not the beast and false prophet! This is the "court" of Daniel 7:26.

These "axed" saints "came to life," and reigned with Christ a thousand years. The Greek verb translated "came to life" is actually aorist tense and would literally read, "they lived."[66] Satan and Rome had tried to deceive the world into believing that martyred Christians and Christianity were dead forever, while the empire would live and be enthroned forever. Christ revealed through John that those martyred Christians, faithful unto death, had not died but really lived and the kingdom to which they belonged reigned and judged the world. This was a visionary, figurative, resurrection — *not a bodily one.* It symbolized the resurrection of the kingdom of Christ on earth and its sovereignty over Rome. John did not see Christians in bodies living and reigning; he saw souls. It is symbolic. It represents a principle. At Rome's defeat, the sovereignty of Christ as King of kings and Lord of lords was *proven!* Those martyrs John saw in his vision as "coming to life and judging and reigning" symbolized that Christ's kingdom would "come to life," defeat and judge Rome. This revelation of the martyred saints alive and reigning was not intended to single them out as a group holier than other Christians, or as a group appointed to positions higher than others. It was designed to make a sharp distinction or contrast to "the rest of the dead." The "rest of the dead" — the pagan contemporaries of the Christian martyrs — were those *unbelievers* who had died from the same tribulations of the empire which claimed Christian lives. The unbelieving dead did not live during the thousand years — they remained forever dead. *The second death had claimed them.*

The "rest of the [spiritually] dead" did not come to life *during* the *completion* of the thousand years. That is the way the sentence should be translated in 20:5. The Greek word *achri* (translated "until" RSV) is a conjunction, expressing time expiring up to a point. It may be accurately translated, "during." The Greek word *telesthe*, translated "ended," may also be accurately translated, "completion" or "consummation." The context should determine the translation of these words. Proper translation would emphasize the absolute difference between the martyred Christians and dead pagans who had worshiped the beast and the false prophet. That is the point of this context. The Greek word translated "rest" is *loipoi* and means "the *other* things." The "rest" were *different* than those martyred saints. Contrary to the devil's lie, those *faithful* to Christ who had been slain came to life and reigned. The "rest of the dead" never did. They came to the "second death."

The martyrs had, earlier, experienced symbolically, "the first resurrection." It was *not* a bodily resurrection from the grave. There will be only one resurrection from the grave. These martyred saints still await the uniting of their souls with a new "body" in a resurrection along with all Christians who have departed this life and those of us who still remain! The NT speaks of the act of becoming a Christian as a "resurrection" from being dead in sin (Rom. 6:12-13; Eph. 2:4-7; Col. 2:13; 1 John 3:14). But even more explicitly, Jesus denominated the *two resurrections* in his great sermon recorded in John's Gospel, chapter five. There Jesus talked about a "first" resurrection in present tense verbs, when he said, "Truly, truly, I say to you, the hour is coming, *and now is,* when the dead will hear the voice of the Son of God, and those who hear will live" (John 5:25). Every verb in that sentence except one is present tense. Jesus was talking about the "resurrection" that takes place at belief and baptism into Christ — the new birth. Later, in the same sermon, Jesus said, "Do not marvel at this; for the hour is coming when all who are in the tombs will hear his voice and come forth, those who have done good, to the resurrection of life, and those who have done evil, to the resurrection of judgment" (John 5:28-29). This last, is the *only* bodily resurrection of mankind. There, in Jesus' sermon we have *two resurrections* and *two deaths.*

In the phrase, "This is the first resurrection," the word "is" is a *supplied* word. It is not in the Greek text. The Greek text reads, *haute he anastasis he prote,* literally, "this the resurrection, the first." The word "This" is an adjectival demonstrative pronoun, meaning, "Namely this, or, This is what I mean." In other words, John wrote, "The other kind of dead ones did not come to life during the 1000 years, and this is what I mean, they did not take part in the 'first resurrection' so as to become Christians." John specified that was his meaning when he continued by saying, "Blessed and holy is he who shares in the first resurrection! Over such the second death has no power . . . ."

Nowhere in the NT are we led to believe there will be more than **one** *bodily resurrection*. The vision was graphic symbolism. It was not declaring some complex, detailed eschatological schedule for *multiple bodily resurrections* and *multiple judgments*. Symbolic "resurrections" are not uncommon to Scripture. The OT prophets symbolized Israel's return from the captivities as a "resurrection" (Isa. 26:19; Hos. 13:14; Ezek. 37:1-14). Daniel was told that during the troubled times of Antiochus IV there would be a "resurrection" of many Jews to faith and loyalty to God's word (Dan. 12:1-4). The seemingly dead "witnesses" were "raised up" by God (Rev. 11:11-13). Mothers, because of their faith in God, during the Syrian persecutions under Antiochus IV "received" their dead sons in a symbolic resurrection (Heb. 11:35).

The saints martyred by Rome not only symbolized the perpetual life of God's kingdom, they also symbolized its perpetual reign. Daniel had predicted that at the death of the "fourth beast," the warred-upon saints would reign and judge (Dan. 7:19-27). John's vision was a fulfillment of Daniel's prophecy. Christians as they remain faithful to Christ in this life are said to be reigning with him and judging with him (See Eph. 2:6; 2 Tim. 2:12; Rom. 5:17; Rev. 5:10; Matt. 7:1-20; 1 Cor. 5:9-13; 6:1-6; Heb. 11:7).

The phrase "first resurrection" is being used here symbolically and metaphorically to describe the status of the "souls" (not bodies) of the saints who "came alive" to judge the Roman Empire and reign with Christ from their martyrdom to the Second Coming of Christ (the 1000 years). This interpretation would be especially possible if the phrase "came alive" is simply a contrast of *perspectives*, i.e., if the point is to reveal that those saints the Roman pagans had killed were not "dead" after all, but "alive." The contrast apparently was that the "rest of the *other* kind of *dead*," i.e., the pagans who had died during the great tribulation, were the ones who were really dead for they had been claimed by the *second death!*[67]

These Christians who "came to life" when they were baptized into Christ also came through the great tribulation to reign with Christ and to judge the Roman Empire and also "came to life" to minister before God as priests. And that correlates to the teaching of the NT, for believers are said to become "a royal priesthood" from the moment they become Christians (1 Pet. 2:9; Rev. 1:6).

Contextual analysis of this highly symbolic and apocalyptic passage, and studied comparison with what the rest of the NT teaches on resurrection, judgment, and priesthood, should bring the reader to a sensible and harmonious interpretation. It goes without saying that the Holy Spirit would not contradict himself. He would not reveal a doctrine of *multiple* bodily resurrections in Revelation 20:1-6 and then contradict that by declaring in the rest of the NT that there is *only one bodily resurrection of the saints.*

> No basis is found in the symbolism (of this passage) for a literal reign of a thousand-year reign of the saints with Christ on earth either before or after his second coming. No basis is found in the symbolism for multiple resurrections and judgments. Theological systems which have majored on a literal interpretation of these verses and have interpreted the clear teachings of the New Testament in the light of the obscure have found several resurrections and several judgments taught. They find a resurrection of believers at what they call the "rapture"' when Christ comes to call his people out of the earth before the great tribulation which is also interpreted as future. Seven years later, at the "revelation" (the second stage of the program of the Lord's second coming), they find a resurrection for those who have become believers and died during the period between the "rapture" and the "revelation." According to their system, people are converted and die during the millennium which is set up at the "revelation." So there must be a resurrection of this group at the close of the earthly millennium when the heavenly order is set up. If the wicked dead are raised at a separate judgment, the system has at least four (perhaps more) resurrections. In similar fashion they find multiple judgments ranging from two (one before and one after the millennium) to seven, according to the particular interpreter.
>
> This is pure fantasy read into a literal interpretation of these highly symbolical verses. By the "proof-text" approach one can prove practically any proposition by perverted use of Scripture passages. When the entire New Testament is studied, it teaches *one* general resurrection (of both good and evil) and *one* general judgment (of both good and evil), both of which are directly related to the second coming of Christ which brings to an end this world order and ushers in the eternal heavenly order.[68]

The Bridegroom (Messiah-Warrior) rode forth into the arena of history to defend his Bride against the beast, false prophet, and harlot. John saw these enemies of the Bride captured and thrown in the lake of fire, along with the "rest" of the pagan dead. With the most powerful allies he ever had destroyed, Satan was "bound" for a thousand years; his power to deceive was severely restricted. The martyred church had "come to life" when it confessed Christ and was baptized into his name. It was to reign with Christ, judge the Roman Empire, and minister before God for the thousand years. Death could not prevail against the church. However, the others (pagans), those who had the mark of the beast upon them, had not come

The Binding of Satan and the "Thousand Years" in Perspective

by Paul T. Butler

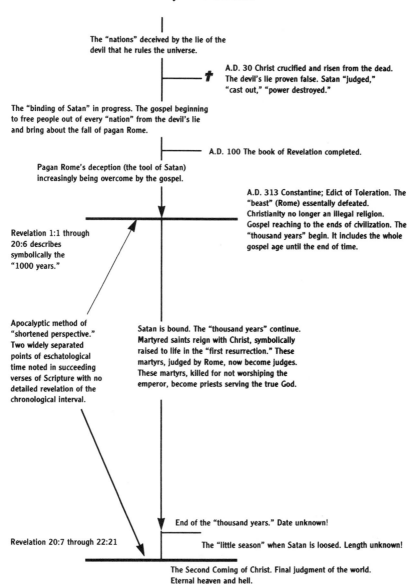

The "nations" deceived by the lie of the devil that he rules the universe.

A.D. 30 Christ crucified and risen from the dead. The devil's lie proven false. Satan "judged," "cast out," "power destroyed."

The "binding of Satan" in progress. The gospel beginning to free people out of every "nation" from the devil's lie and bring about the fall of pagan Rome.

A.D. 100 The book of Revelation completed.

Pagan Rome's deception (the tool of Satan) increasingly being overcome by the gospel.

A.D. 313 Constantine; Edict of Toleration. The "beast" (Rome) essentially defeated. Christianity no longer an illegal religion. Gospel reaching to the ends of civilization. The "thousand years" begin. It includes the whole gospel age until the end of time.

Revelation 1:1 through 20:6 describes symbolically the "1000 years."

Apocalyptic method of "shortened perspective." Two widely separated points of eschatological time noted in succeeding verses of Scripture with no detailed revelation of the chronological interval.

Satan is bound. The "thousand years" continue. Martyred saints reign with Christ, symbolically raised to life in the "first resurrection." These martyrs, judged by Rome, now become judges. These martyrs, killed for not worshiping the emperor, become priests serving the true God.

End of the "thousand years." Date unknown!

Revelation 20:7 through 22:21

The "little season" when Satan is loosed. Length unknown!

The Second Coming of Christ. Final judgment of the world. Eternal heaven and hell.

to life and were claimed by the "second death." This is Christ's answer, through John, to the challenge of the Caesars about sovereignty. The Lamb was sovereign — not the Roman Empire. Rome fell! The church lived on and spread throughout a larger world than the Caesars ever dreamed existed. God won — as he always has and always shall!

John was told twice that after the 1000 years were ended, the devil would be "loosed." Only *once* does it say "for a little while" (Rev. 20:3,7). Naturally any reader would want to know *why* the devil *must* be loosed. We are not told the reason. Some speculate that it is to allow the social climate of the whole world to get as chaotic as it was *prior* to the evangelistic victories of the gospel over ancient Rome. This is supposed to be God's final attempt to *drive* more of mankind to repentance and discipleship. A parallel is cited from the history of Israel. Israel showed no desire to leave Egypt and return to Canaan after the famine was over which drove Jacob and his family to Egypt for refuge. So God permitted the Egyptians to heap tribulations upon them until they cried out for deliverance. Israel's experience in the wilderness and its exile into Babylon might also be cited as illustrations. The apostolic church in Jerusalem (and even the apostles themselves) showed no inclination to preach the gospel outside Judea until persecution scattered them! (Acts 8:1).

But the question that most piques the human imagination about Satan's being loosed for a little while is, When? Again, John does not say — he gives no time table. What John has done is leap over *more* than one thousand years from Revelation 20:6 to 20:7. The "1000 years" began with the fall of Rome, ca. A.D. 475. It has been almost 1500 years since that momentous event and the devil has *not* been loosed from the restraints which the universal preaching of the gospel placed upon his power to deceive.

The main concern of this passage (20:7-10) was *not time*. It was the revelation of Satan's ultimate defeat, the victory of the saints of God. The Lamb revealed victory; the saints did not need a time schedule. It was as good as done! The Lamb is the Faithful and True Word of God! When the purpose of God no longer needs severe restrictions upon Satan, he will loose Satan to some extent. There are numerous important matters to note in connection with Satan being loosed here:

a. Satan is *always bound* to some extent. He is never completely free from the sovereignty of God, nor is he ever able to stand as an equal to God.

b. John did not reveal *when* the "little time" would begin, nor did he reveal how *long* the "little time" would be. The Greek text *micron chronon* means literally, "little, small in quantity of time."

c. Satan's work does not *most efficiently* consist in persecution and tribulation. His major work is *deception*. Deception "catches more flies with honey (false teachings and carnality) than with vinegar."

d. It is the *nations* (unbelievers) who are deceived — *not the church of Christ.*

e. Satan's deception reaches to the "four corners of the earth," that is, "Gog and Magog." John used the same symbolism Ezekiel used. It is not just Russia and China, but the majority of mankind. Jesus warned that while many are "called," few are "chosen." He also said that only a few find the "narrow and difficult way" which leads to life but many will go to hell on the "broad and easy" way.

f. Sometime before Christ comes a second, and final, time to earth, Satan, and those he has deceived, will make a worldwide push to deceive as many people as possible. He will successfully deceive the vast majority of mankind. The church will be surrounded with a siege of falsehood in all manners of expression (perhaps even physical persecution).

g. But we note the church is *not harmed!*

h. The devil has not made a successful prison break, for he is released *only by God's permission and for God's purpose.*

i. There is *no battle,* and *no great tribulation.* There is only a "gathering" for battle!

j. It is *not* stated in 20:7 that the devil is loosed *for a little while.*

k. At the moment the church is surrounded by deception and worldliness, God delivers her by destroying Satan. *The micro-time could be instantaneous!*

l. The church is rescued by heavenly power. This is the *same kind of action* Ezekiel symbolized of God's victory over his enemies, Gog and Magog.

m. The devil and his forces are consumed by fire from heaven and thrown in the lake of fire and brimstone where the beast and false prophet had already gone. Contrary to popular opinion, Satan does not rule over hell! He will be tormented right along with all others who have been deceived by him. He controls nothing, he rules nothing. He never has — he only deceived the majority of the world into believing he did.

Notes

[1] The Greek verb, *egeneto,* is aorist tense, meaning the "kingdom had come in the past."

[2] See Matthew 24:36 and Jesus' parables following (see our discussion of the Olivet Discourse in this work).

[3] See the OT "church" borne by God on "eagles wings" in its wilderness trek, Exod. 19:4; Deuteronomy 32:11.

[4] The Greek phrase in Revelation 12:14 is *hina petetai eis ten eremon eis ton topon autes,* literally, "in order that she might fly to the desert, to the place of her."

[5] See these OT passages for symbolism: Psalms 18:4; 32:6; 42:7; Isaiah 43:2; Jeremiah 46:7-8; 47:2; Daniel 9:26; 11:22; Nahum 1:8, etc.

[6] The Greek word translated "angry" in Revelation 12:17 is *orgisthe,* from which we get the English words "orgy" and "orgasm." In Greek it means "cold, calculated, vengeful, long-lasting anger."

[7]Both Greek participles, *terounton* and *echonton*, are present tense. These were Christians present when John was writing the Revelation.

[8]Jack Cottrell, *What the Bible Says about God the Creator* (Joplin, MO: College Press, 1983), pp. 65-66.

[9]*edoken*, aorist tense, "gave." John is writing about something that had happened when he wrote, not about something 2000 years future to Rome.

[10]Suetonius, *The Twelve Caesars*, pp. 238-241.

[11]Ibid., p. 241.

[12]Durant, *Caesar and Christ*, p. 648.

[13]In Exodus 7:11 the Hebrew word *keshaphim* is translated "sorcerers" who "performed their secret arts" to try to discredit the real miracles God worked through Moses.

[14]Acts 8:9 depicts the work of Simon the Sorcerer with the Greek words *mageuon* and *mageiais*, which are translated "magic" in the RSV and "sorcery" in the KJV. These words may also be translated, "conjure." These Greek words are the words from which we get the English word "magic." The KJV translates the Greek word *existon* as "betwitch" to describe the results of Simon's "magic."

[15]See 2 Thessalonians 2:9-10 where Greek words *pseudous* and *apate* ("false" and "cheating") are used to describe the alleged "signs" and "wonders" of the "lawless one."

[16]Durant, *Caesar and Christ*, pp. 522-527.

[17]Ibid., pp. 265-268, 388-389.

[18]Ibid., pp. 311-313, 467.

[19]The Hebrew word *kesheph* is translated "sorcery" in Exodus 7:11; Isaiah 47:9,12; Jeremiah 27:9; Daniel 2:2; Malachi 3:5.

[20]Durant, *Caesar and Christ*, pp. 58-67.

[21]Tom Friskney, *Strength For Victory, Verse by Verse Study of the Book of Revelation* (Cincinnati: Friskney, 1986), p. 127.

[22]The Greek word *egorasmenoi*, translated "redeemed," is a perfect participle meaning the 144,000 "had been and were continuing to be" redeemed from worldliness.

[23]The Greek verb *emolynthēsan* is aorist, indicative, passive, and translated "defiled."

[24]Idolatry is symbolized in the Bible as "spiritual adultery." See Hosea 1:2; 2:1; Ezekiel 16:1-63, and in Revelation 17:1,2,4,5; 18:3,9; 18:4,20; 19:2,6,7,8; see also 1 Corinthians 10:14-22; 2 Corinthians 11:2-3; 1 John 5:21.

[25]Isaiah 13:1–14:21; Isaiah 46:10; 48:3; Jeremiah 51:8, etc. The "predictive-present" (speaking of something in the future as if it has already happened) is an often used vehicle of communication in prophetic literature. This is due to the fact that God is revealing it within his frame of reference. God sees all time and eternity as "Today."

[26]See our comments, chapter eight, in this work, Matthew 24:30, "coming on the clouds . . . ."

[27]*tas eschatas*, the word from which the English "eschatological" comes.

[28]See Appendix B in this work, "Word Studies in Prophetic Literature."

[29]The "Song of Moses" is found in Exodus 15:1ff; and Deuteronomy 32:1–33:29

[30]The mind that is **set** on the flesh (Rome) is hostile to God and cannot please God, Romans 8:6-8.

[31]See Matthew 24:36–25:46; 1 Thessalonians 4:16; 5:3; 2 Thessalonians 1:7-10; 2 Peter 3:8-13, et al., for the *direct invasion* of creation by God at the end of time.

[32] See also Revelation 12:15 for the "flood" and 13:13-17 for the "signs and wonders" to *deceive* those who dwell on earth.

[33] *gegonen*, perfect active indicative, 3rd person singular of *ginomai*, "it became."

[34] Suetonius, *The Twelve Caesars*, p. 240-241.

[35] Durant, *Caesar and Christ*, p. 669.

[36] The Greek word is *edoken*, aorist tense, meaning "gave."

[37] Durant, *Caesar and Christ*, pp. 620-633

[38] See also Paul T. Butler, *What the Bible Says about Civil Government* (Joplin, MO: College Press, 1990).

[39] "The Roman Arena," on television's History Channel, March 4, 1997.

[40] The Greek word *strenous* is translated "wanton" in 18:3,9, and means "to run riot, to indulge voraciously."

[41] *ekollethesan*, is translated "heaped," but literally means "glued, fastened together."

[42] Hardy, *The Greek and Roman World*, pp. 90-111.

[43] *euphrainou*, "Rejoice . . . ." is an imperative mood verb which is a command.

[44] *ou mē*, translated "no more" (RSV), Revelation 18:21,22,23, i.e., "not at all."

[45] The Greek verbs *ekrinen* and *ephtheiren*, or "corrupted, defiled," are both aorist tense, emphasizing John speaks of an action that was in the immediate present or future — not distant from his own day.

[46] *exedikesen* is translated "avenged" and means "a vindication proceeding from justice."

[47] *ēlthen*, "has come," and *etoimasen*, "has made herself ready."

[48] *keklēmenoi*, is perfect tense, "having been called in the past and continuing to be called."

[49] *ho logos tou theou*, "The word of the God."

[50] Greek aorist tense verb *epiasthē*, translated in RSV "captured."

[51] Also aorist tense in Greek, *eplanēsen*, "led astray."

[52] Also aorist tense in Greek, *labontas*, "having received."

[53] This is the only Greek present tense verb in this context —*tous proskynountas*, "those worshiping."

[54] Durant, *Caesar And Christ*, p. 652.

[55] Ibid., pp. 620-672.

[56] Ibid., p. 665.

[57] Ibid., p. 668.

[58] Ibid., p. 669.

[59] Homer Hailey, *Revelation: An Introduction and Commentary* (Grand Rapids: Baker, 1979), p. 388.

[60] *edēsen*, aorist active indicative verb "bound"

[61] Compare the same usage in 1 Corinthians 2:6; 15:24; and 2 Timothy 1:10.

[62] See Deuteronomy 1:10-11; for other figurative uses of the number "thousand" see Job 9:3; Psalm 90:4; Ecclesiastes 6:6; 7:28; 2 Peter 3:8

[63] See chapter three of this work.

[64] E. A. McDowell, *The Meaning and Message of Revelation* (Nashville: Broadman, 1951), p. 190.

[65] The Greek word *pepelekismenōn* is literally the word for "axe" but is translated "beheaded." It is a perfect tense verb participle.

⁶⁶*ezēsan,* "they lived," and *ebasileusan,* "they reigned," are both aorist tense verbs.

⁶⁷See also Norman Shepherd, "The Resurrections of Revelation 20," *Westminster Theological Journal* (Fall 1974): 34-43.

⁶⁸Ray Summers, *Worthy Is the Lamb* (Nashville: Broadman, 1951), pp. 205-206.

chapter 11

THE REVELATION
OF JESUS CHRIST
PART III

Revelation 20:11–22:21
"Then I saw a new heaven and a new earth; for the first heaven and the first earth had passed away, and the sea was no more."

Remember, in the original Greek autograph of Revelation there were no chapter, verse, or paragraph numbers or divisions. John could very well have begun a totally new phase of the Revelation at 20:11. We believe he did!

The last act in this fascinating pageant of redemption pictures God's judgment and final destiny of the righteous and the wicked. All earlier judgments in the drama dealt with the fall of the Roman Empire. All through history God has judged and destroyed nations and forces which have opposed his redemptive program. At the *consummation of time* and history God will judge each human who has ever lived.

Just how this revelation of the *consummation of all time* relates to the fall of the Roman Empire we are not told. But, we repeat, "shortened perspective" is not an unusual phenomenon in prophetic literature in the apocalyptic *genre*. In fact, leaps from contemporary circumstances to distant future events (usually fulfillments) without any revelation of history between is widely used from Isaiah to Malachi. Jesus employed this vehicle for his "Olivet Discourse" (Matt. 24:1–25:46; Mark 13:1-33; Luke 21:5-36). The apostles often "shortened their perspective" in their epistles as they exhorted churches concerning contemporary problems and then, immediately, predicted the Second Coming of Christ.

We do know from the epistles of the NT that the apostles and their first century brethren *believed* Jesus' warnings that they should *expect his Second Coming at any moment in time*! Jesus taught believers to *watch constantly for his return*. No one would know when it was to occur. His Second Coming will slip up on those who do

Apocalyptic Method of "Shortened Perspective" as Applied to Revelation 1:1–20:10 and 20:11–22:21

by Paul T. Butler

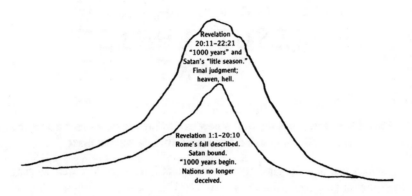

Revelation 20:11–22:21 "1000 years" and Satan's "litle season." Final judgment; heaven, hell.

Revelation 1:1–20:10 Rome's fall described. Satan bound. "1000 years begin. Nations no longer deceived.

Shortened perspective: Jesus reveals to John two "mountain peaks" — *Rome's fall* and the *consummation* of all things, final judgment and eternal heaven and hell . . .

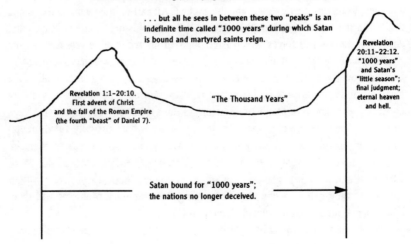

. . . but all he sees in between these two "peaks" is an indefinite time called "1000 years" during which Satan is bound and martyred saints reign.

Revelation 1:1–20:10. First advent of Christ and the fall of the Roman Empire (the fourth "beast" of Daniel 7).

"The Thousand Years"

Revelation 20:11–22:12. "1000 years" and Satan's "little season"; final judgment; eternal heaven and hell.

Satan bound for "1000 years"; the nations no longer deceived.

believe in him and those who do not believe in him. It was to occur at a time the whole world would not expect it. Only Christians will be prepared for it because they expect it at any moment.

The proper attitude in every age is to expect him momentarily! That he has not yet appeared to consummate all time does no violence to the integrity of the Scriptures. The *time* of the end is a matter for God's knowledge alone and was hidden even from the incarnated Son and all other inspired writers of the NT. Modern "end-times" prognosticators should exercise extreme caution about setting a schedule for God when he has made it plain he will not give any signs or reveal the time of Jesus' Second Coming.

When God acts to consummate time everyone will know it. There will not be any "secret raptures." When he appears earth and sky will flee away from his presence and no place will be found for our physical cosmos as it is now. Peter's description of "the end" is more vivid (2 Pet. 3:7-13). This present cosmos will disappear when the Lord appears to "dissolve it with fire." All physical matter is transitory and temporary. When its Creator decides it is no longer useful to him, it will disappear. This corrupted creation will not stand in the awful presence of perfect holiness. This present creation was subjected to futility and decay by its Creator (Rom. 8:18-25). It is God's determination to destroy it immediately at the time of judgment and to create a new place for those who have taken part in the "first resurrection" (the spiritual one).

John's vision now includes all the dead from Adam to the end of the world standing before the "great white throne." We know this is the final judgment because "Death and Hades" were thrown into the lake of fire (Rev. 20:11-15; see also John 5:28; Acts. 24:15; Rom. 2:6,16; 2 Cor. 5:10). The apostle Paul's revelation of the final judgment also predicts that death, man's last enemy, will be destroyed (1 Cor. 15:24-26). God does not need "books" to keep a record of men's deeds. He is omniscient and infallible. "Books" is a word of human language to symbolize that every deed, every thought, every secret of every human being is known and remembered by God. The Bible tells us, however, that God, if he wishes to do so, may "blot out" and forget or "remember no more" the sins of people who have trusted in the atoning death of Jesus Christ on their behalf (Psa. 51:1-9; Micah 7:19; Isa. 43:25; 44:22; Acts 3:19; Heb. 8:12, et al.). Those human beings whose names are written in "the book of life," also known as the "Lamb's book of life," will not be judged by what is in the "book of deeds." The impenitent, those who have not taken part in the first (spiritual) resurrection, will be judged according to what they have done — and what they have *not done* (Acts 10:42; 17:31; 24:25; Rom. 2:12-16; 14:10; 2 Cor. 5:10-11; 2 Thess. 1:5-10; Heb. 10:26-31; James 4:17, et al.).

Those who have accepted the atonement and justification provided by Christ, through an obedient exercise of their faith will be found written in God's "book of life." This book of life is mentioned a number of times in the Bible (Exod. 32:32ff; Psa. 69:28; Isa. 4:3; Mal. 3:16; Luke 10:20; Phil. 4:3; Rev. 3:5; 13:8; 17:8; 21:27). Those who have washed their sins away by accepting God's gracious offer of the atoning death of his Son will be rewarded for the good they have done. Christians may forget some good things they have done, or they may consider even what good they have done unworthy to be acknowledged by Almighty God (Luke 17:7-10). But God does not forget! (Matt. 25:37-40; Heb. 6:10). The saint appears before God's throne of judgment to hear God vindicate his faith in Christ and to hear God say, "Well done, you good and faithful servant, enter into the joys of your rest." The saint will receive that inheritance prepared for him which is beyond all comparison.

As there is a second higher life, so there is also a second and deeper death. And as after that life there is no more death, so after that death there is no more life! At the final judgment there will be only two classes of humanity — the saved and the lost. Human beings will be either cast into the lake of fire or they will be found written in the book of life and live forever in Paradise. There will be no "in between" categories. It is no wonder that Jesus told seventy disciples that they should simply rejoice that their names were written in heaven and *not* rejoice over their miraculous deeds (Luke 10:20). One does not have his name written in heaven merely because he is religious, or even because he may have done some miracles (Matt. 7:21-23). One's name is written in heaven by "having the Son of God." The same apostle who wrote this Revelation also wrote, "And this is the testimony, that God gave us eternal life, and this life is in his Son. He who has the Son has life; he who has not the Son of God has not life" (1 John 5:11-12; see also 1 John 2:3,5,6,24; 3:19-24; 4:6-15).

The Revelation has, in the scene of the "great white throne," pictured the defeat of all forces opposed to God. Final judgment will consummate the victory of God. Satan and his hosts will be incarcerated in the lake of fire. God will reign on his throne in undisputed sovereignty. But what is the status of the redeemed? This question was of imminent interest to the persecuted saints in Asia Minor. It is a question of utmost relevance to saints through all the ages. The "Babylon" which was described in chapter 18 was Rome. It was the epitome of earthly, humanistic rebellion against the rule of God. It was a self-appointed substitute for the eternal God and the kingdom of God on earth.

The symbolic unity of Revelation would be incomplete without a picture of the ideal kingdom of God which in some way unites heaven and earth. As a means of portraying the ideal kingdom of God, John is given a vision of the *new Jerusalem* "coming down out of heaven from God." No carnal kingdom can accomplish God's purposes for man. God has instituted a heavenly kingdom, even on this present earth, to serve his ultimate purposes for humankind. This heavenly kingdom, even while on this present earth, is the ideal and should be functioning, as nearly as circumstances will allow, in all respects as God has revealed his ideal (refer to Matt. 6:10). One day, in the sovereign time schedule of God, the ideal kingdom will be taken out of this world order, which is to be completely dissolved, and placed in a new world order, with all new blessed circumstances. This is what the last vision of Revelation is all about. The two world orders are only the "twinkling of an eye" apart!

The central dynamic of heaven will be the glorious presence of the eternal Father and Son and Holy Spirit. No more separation for human beings from their Creator. God will put up his "tent" in the midst of our "tents." It will be like living in the presence of Jesus when he was on earth — only infinitely better! There will be no sadness, no weeping, no death or pain in heaven. Those not allowed into this blessed Paradise are the cowardly (those afraid to confess their belief in Christ, afraid to suffer persecution for his name); the faithless (those disobedient to God and those to whom God cannot trust good and holy matters); the polluted (those who have succumbed to the corruption of carnality); murderers (those who have killed others outside the sanctions of God's revealed will — includes abortion, euthanasia, aggression in war, genocide, and all degrees of homicide); fornicators (those guilty of illicit sexual intercourse — includes adultery, homosexuality, incest, and bestiality); sorcerers (those devoted to sorcery, witchcraft, occultism); idolaters (those who worship — devote their being to — any person or thing other than Almighty God and his Son — includes the love of money, covetousness, humanism); and all liars — those who speak and live contrary to the truth. Heaven is the inheritance of those who are lovers of truth, those who are honest, and those who speak and live the reality of what God's word says as opposed to living what is false. God's eternal kingdom cannot tolerate liars. A kingdom of liars would be a kingdom in rebellion against the King of Truth. It is of utmost significance that spiritual character is emphasized prior to the description of the New Jerusalem. Life upon earth is preparatory to life in heaven. Here character is formed; there character is savored!

New Jerusalem, heaven, is described in human words. We must constantly remember that human language is composed of words which may only describe that which falls within human experience and is therefore inadequate to describe anything beyond human experience. This forces us to admit that God has merely *symbolized* the indescribable glories of heaven. Heaven is actually far beyond any human experience. There are no human words that would be capable of describing it

(2 Cor. 9:15; 12:1-4). The main idea symbolized by the details of this highly figurative vision of the heavenly city is *perfection*. While the harlot (Rome) has her rotten decadence exposed and hell as her destiny, the Bride of the Lamb, the church of Christ, has her faithfulness testified to and perfect Paradise as her destiny.

Suggested Symbolism of the New Jerusalem

1. A great high wall
1. Perfect inclusion showing a clear separation between those within and those without, Rev. 22:14-15

2. Twelve gates
2. Perfect and abundant access, Heb. 10:19-21

3. Twelve foundations
3. Perfect security; it will never be shaken from where it is, Heb. 12:25-29

4. The city foursquare (a perfect 1500 mile cube)
4. Perfect spaciousness, room for all the redeemed, 2 Pet. 3:9

5. Walls and foundations built out of every precious jewel and pure gold
5. Perfect or infinite purity, infinite costliness, infinite beauty, no flaws or imperfections, Rev. 22:3

6. No temple but the Lord
6. Perfect, completely satisfying, worship and service in the actual presence of the Lord, Heb. 9:11ff

7. No sun or moon
7. Timelessness, perfect knowledge or insight; nothing hidden; perfect guidance; perfect reality — no shadows or images

8. Into it comes the glory and
8. Perfect universality of redeemed mankind; no more racial or cultural or social hostilities, John 17:20; Eph. 2:11-22

9. Nothing unclean entering
9. Perfect holiness, righteousness and goodness. Nothing bad or false.

10. The water and tree of life
10. Perfect fulfillment, satisfaction, enjoyment, sustenance, health, harmony

Those who had overcome by the grace of Christ and their faithfulness to his word now have their reign extended from the "thousand years" with Christ in this age to a reign forever and ever, ages without end. The dominion man lost in Eden by rebelling against God's will for his life is restored in New Jerusalem by man's repentance and surrender to the will of God for his life as accomplished by Jesus Christ.

It is important that the reader of Christ's Revelation to John return to the letters to the seven churches at this point and reread the promises to those struggling Christians who overcame their world by faith. They were promised: (a) to eat of the tree of life which was in the paradise of God; (b) not to be hurt by the second death; (c) to be given some of the hidden manna, a white stone, with a new name written on it; (d) to be given power over the nations to rule them with a rod of iron, and given the morning star; (e) to be clad in white garments, not have their name blotted out of the book of life, and confessed before God by Jesus Christ; (f) to become a pillar in the temple of God, never go out of the temple, and have the name of God and the city of God and Christ's own new name written on them; (g) to sit with Christ upon his throne.

What Christ promised the faithful saints of Asia Minor, God allowed John to look down the corridors of time and see fulfilled when time is transferred to eternity, when the mortal takes on immortality. What glory! What blessedness! What fulfillment! Let those who belong to Christ and are overcoming by the power of their faith in him say, "even so, come Lord Jesus!" Let those who do not belong to him yet, but wish to, say, "What must I do to inherit eternal life?" and turn to his Word to find their answer and obey it!

Most people who study the book of Revelation give chapter 22 only cursory treatment. Most are intrigued with the fast moving, highly symbolic drama of the middle portion of the book.

However, the very idea that chapter 22 probably contains the last words, the last revelation, to be spoken by God to man before the Second Coming of Christ, make these words take on tremendous importance. These last words were declared by God, to be soon fulfilled and would, therefore, be important to every believer of every age as an aid to understanding the early church's confrontation with the Roman Empire. This closing chapter of the last Word of God to man is a beautiful *recapitulation* of the purpose of the whole Bible.

These words are, first, a message of *divine authority*. The Lamb affirmed that what John had seen and recorded was from the same God whose Spirit was in all the prophets of the Bible. The message of Revelation is part of the fulfillment of the plans and purposes that God revealed in the whole Bible, namely that nothing in this world or in any other world can thwart the program of God to redeem his creation. The timing of the *greatest tribulation* to face the kingdom of God on earth was important. *It is to come speedily!*[1] It was the judgment of Christ upon the Roman Empire — not his Second Coming. The immediate promise of a "speedy" coming in judgment was to the saints in Asia Minor. The Lamb promised *quick* relief to the beleaguered saints of Asia Minor. One year after John received the Revelation, Domitian died. From that point, Rome began to crumble. The "beast" began to lose power. It took another three and one-half centuries for Rome to fall, but God works within his own time schedule. Suffering saints of every age have felt that Christ's intervention on their behalf has been slow in coming. But the Lord promises that those who cry out for vindication should always pray and not lose heart for he will vindicate them "speedily" (Luke 18:1-8). Therefore, blessing comes from the Lord to those who keep the words of the prophecy of Revelation. In the Revelation the words "to keep" are *endurance, repentance, separation from the world, conquer temptation, overcome, open the door for Jesus' entrance.*

Second, the closing chapter is a message of *immediate importance.* John was forbidden to "seal up the words" of the Revelation. The Greek word for seal (*sphragises*) is aorist subjunctive. This means the action has not taken place as a fact yet, but it is desirable because of some contingency. That "contingency" was the fact that the message of the book was needed *immediately* for the ancient church! The churches of Asia Minor needed it *then and there.* It was *not* a message to be fulfilled two thousand years or more *after* John wrote it. It was to strengthen the church for *that* great tribulation. The Lamb warns about his *speedy coming* again, using the same Greek word (*tachi* and *tachu*) he used in Revelation 1:1 and verses 6 and 7 of chapter 22. The Greek verbs translated, "Let the evildoer still do evil, and the filthy still be filthy, and the righteous still do right" are aorist imperfect and represent a linear action in past and present time. The Revelation was written to exhort people contemporary with its writing.

Chapter 22 is a message of *divine invitation.* The Spirit and the Bride say, "Come." The invitation is present active indicative and means the Spirit and the Bride *are continuing to say, Come.* Everyone hearing and believing the message of the Spirit through God's written word, and the pleading of Christ's church should come to Christ and partake of the water of life freely. Since it is the invitation of the Spirit (through the written Word) and the Church, those who wish to come must do so according to the singular message authorized by God to be proclaimed by the Spirit and the Church.

Chapter 22 is a message of *divine warning.* Everyone who hears the words of the prophecy of this book is warned against tampering with it. This warning is made a number of times in God's Word (Deut. 4:2; 12:32; Prov. 30:5ff; Matt. 15:6; 2 Cor. 4:2; Gal. 1:6-9). And yet, many bizarre and impossible eschatological systems have been imposed upon this book in disgraceful and underhanded ways until there is widespread confusion among believers as to the fundamental message and meaning of Revelation. Sincere mistakes about the book will be forgiven, but indifference toward it and exploitation of it for human profit will result in eternal condemnation! People who would never literally omit an English or Greek word from the printed text of Revelation will *neglect to read* the book and especially *refuse the book to be studied in church assemblies.* In our opinion, this comes dangerously close to "taking away from the words of this book." *Christian people must not neglect this book!* That is a divine warning! Because of the confusion generated through "end times" mania, the church of Christ has neglected the *real* message of the book of Revelation. The real message of the book is the *imperative* need of the church in any era to *repent*, to *endure*, and to have *faith*, because the Lamb is sovereign *in* and *over* all heaven and earth. "Even so, come, Lord Jesus!"

Notes

[1] *en tachei* literally means "with speed."

chapter 12

THE "CATCHING AWAY" AND THE MAN OF SIN

"But we would not have you ignorant, brethren, concerning those who are asleep . . . ."

A final chapter is needful to discuss briefly two passages in the NT: first, 1 Thessalonians 4:13–5:11 which is alleged to teach a "secret rapture" of God's saints *before* the "tribulation, millennial reign of Christ, and the final judgment"; and second, 2 Thessalonians 2:1-12, which is alleged to teach the identity of *The* Antichrist.

"The Rapture"

First, no specific term such as "*the rapture*" appears in the entire Bible! Etymologically, the root for "rapture" is from the Latin, *raptus*, which means, "violent snatching, or dragging away; robbery, carrying off, abduction." The Greek word used by Paul in 1 Thessalonians 4:17 is *harpagesometha*, a future passive verb. English versions translate the Greek word, "caught up" in KJV, RSV, and NIV. The Greek word was translated *simul rapiemur* in the Latin Vulgate.

Second, most dispensationalists use the passage in 1 Thessalonians to make their case for "the rapture" by pointing to an alleged distinction between Jesus coming "*with* his saints" and Jesus coming "*for* his saints." But the Bible does not make such a distinction anywhere. The Bible does not use the expression, "coming *for* his saints."

Third, 1 Thessalonians 3:13 would preclude the possibility that Christ is coming back *with* his saints *after* having taken them earlier out of the earth. Resurrected saints transformed and taken to be with Jesus would need no further "establishing, unblamable in holiness." Furthermore, the verse could be accurately translated, "so that he may establish your hearts unblamable in holiness before our God and Father in the presence of our Lord Jesus Christ in the midst of his saints." The verse *does not necessarily need to refer to Jesus' Second Coming!*

Fourth, the word "saints" (*hagiois*) is frequently applied to *angels* as well as people! (Deut. 33:2: Dan. 4:13; 8:13; Psa. 88:5-7; Luke 9:26). And many verses in the NT plainly teach that when Christ comes in his second advent he will be accompanied by his *hagiois* or "holy" angels (Matt. 16:27; 25:31; Mark 8:38; Luke 9:26; 1 Thess. 4:16; 2 Thess. 1:7). Thus, the "holy ones" coming with Jesus at his second advent are angels, not human beings. This correlates to the statement in Jude that the Lord came with *myriads* of his "*holy ones*" (*hagiais myriasin*)(see also Zech. 14:5). The only way it can be "proven" that *people* will be with Christ at his second advent is to insist that the word *hagiois* must always be interpreted to mean *people*. Clearly, it does not necessarily always mean *people* — it can refer to *angels*.

Fifth, there is no indication that Christ's second advent will be *unseen* and *unheard* by the whole world. Scripture plainly states that at his Second Coming he will be heard and seen by all mankind. There will be a "shout of command, the archangel's call, and the sound of the trumpet of God." and *all* are to be "changed" (given immortal bodies) together to be taken home with the Lord (John 5:28; 1 Thess. 4:16; 1 Cor. 15:51-52). The veritable elements of this cosmos will pass away with a "loud rushing noise" and be dissolved by burning (2 Pet. 3:10).

Sixth, *contextually*, 1 Thessalonians 5:1-4 belongs to what has immediately gone before in 4:13-19. That being the case, it is clear that Paul was writing about the last judgment and makes it clear he was not denoting a "seven-year rapture" intervening between Christ's second advent and the judgment.

Seventh, there would be *no surprise* about the Second Coming of Christ at all *if the "rapture-tribulation" theory is correct*, for once the "rapture" came, the seven-year period of the alleged "Antichrist" and the alleged "tribulation" would follow. Once the seven-year period began, all that would need to be done by those left on earth to anticipate his coming for judgment is count exactly seven years and they would know precisely when Jesus was to return. **"But of that day and hour no one knows, not even the angels of heaven, nor the Son, but the Father only."**

Eighth, Jesus made it unequivocally plain in his great sermon recorded in chapter five of John's Gospel that there is going to be only *one* bodily resurrection of the dead (John 5:28-29). As we have pointed out elsewhere the Greek word in that text translated, "the hour" is *singular* and the Greek word translated "resurrection" is *singular*. John always used the Greek singular when recording Jesus' statement about "raising" people from the dead on *the* "last day" (See John 6:39,40,44,54).

Ninth, the "first" resurrection in Revelation 20:4-5 is either a resurrection of souls only, for nothing is said of a bodily resurrection, or the "resurrection" to the new birth at baptism. As we have pointed out in our comments on Revelation 20:4-5, the second option is most likely the correct interpretation.

Tenth, *actually, 1 Thessalonians 4:13-17 was written to caution against any ideas of separate resurrections!* Paul emphasized that the *believers* living when the Lord returns at his second advent, **will not precede** those who have died. The obverse is clearly true also — those who have *died* **will not precede** those who are alive!

Eleventh, in Jesus' parables concerning the final judgment (Matt. 13:24-30, 36-43, 47-50) the entire "harvest" is reaped "at the consummation of the age." Jesus does not teach two, separate, resurrections and judgments — only *one!* When Jesus comes back it will be on *one day* just as it was when Sodom was destroyed and when the flood came in Noah's day (Luke 17:26-36). *All the saints* will meet Jesus at the same time, at a specific "hour" or "moment" (John 5:28; 1 Cor. 15:51-52). He has appointed "a day" (singular) when he will judge *all* men (Acts 17:31).

Yes! The Bible does predict that when Jesus comes again (his Second Coming) *all the saints* (both alive and dead) will meet *together* with him in the "air." It will be the "moment . . . in the twinkling of an eye" when *all* the saints will be given an immortal body in which they will *all* be "at home with the Lord." So, the Bible does teach that at the Second Coming of Christ those who are alive will "by no means, in no way"[1] **precede** those who are "dead in Christ." Those who are dead will by no means **precede** those who are alive. Those who are alive will be "seized or snatched"[2] **together** in the clouds to meet the Lord in the air and so **always** they shall be with the Lord. That is the only "rapture" there is in the Bible!

Russell Boatman quotes a significant statement by the venerable Bible scholar and preacher, G. Campbell Morgan:

> . . . a question . . . was put to the renowned Bible scholar, G. Campbell Morgan, by Paul G. Jackson, reported in *Christianity Today*, Aug. 31, 1959, p. 16,17:
>
> *Jackson*: After your long and full study and extensive exposition of the Bible, do you find any Scriptural warrant for the distinction which Bible teachers draw between the 2nd coming of the Lord *for* his own (the rapture) and the coming of the Lord *with* his own (the revelation) with a time period of 3½ to 7 years between?
>
> *Morgan*: Emphatically not! I know this view very well. In the earlier years of my ministry I taught it and incorporated it in one of my books (*God's Method with Man*). But further study so convinced me of the error of this teaching that I actually went to the expense of buying the plates from the publisher and destroying them. The idea of a separate and secret coming of Christ is a vagary of prophetic interpretation without any Biblical basis whatsoever.[3]

"The Antichrist"

A plague of theological confusion has infected the church of Christ because of a plethora of eschatologists who have misinterpreted what the NT says about "antichrist." The primary cause of the confusion lies in the faulty equation of *ho antichristos* ("the antichrist") in the apostle John's writings (1 John 2:18,22; 4:3; 2 John 7) with *ho anthropos tes anomias* ("the man of lawlessness") in the apostle Paul's letter to the Thessalonians (2 Thess. 2:3,8). *They are not the same person(s)!* John makes it clear that *antichrist is more than one person.* He says emphatically, "there are **many** antichrists (plural *antichristoi polloi.* 2:18). John uses *plural* pronouns and verbs to denote "us" and "they" referring to the fact that the "antichrists" went out from among the saints. Even in 2 John 7, the apostle equates "the" antichrist with "many" deceivers" who have gone out into the world. *There is more than one antichrist.* In fact, anyone then or now, or in between, who does not confess that the Anointed One of God (the Christ) has come in the flesh in the historical person, Jesus Christ, is "antichrist."

The second chapter of 2 Thessalonians was written to remove some misapprehensions about the Lord's Second Coming, apparently bothering the Thessalonian brethren from their misreading of Paul's *first* epistle to them. Second Thessalonians chapter 2 reveals to these brethren that the Lord would not come in his second advent *until* two incidents had taken place. First, *the apostasy* would have to occur (2 Thess. 2:2). Second, *that* specific apostasy could not occur until *the one restraining* the "man of lawlessness" was *himself* out of the way. Paul revealed that the "mystery of lawlessness was already "operating"[4] as he was writing 2 Thessalonians. But *someone* was holding back the coming of **the man** (singular) **of lawlessness** who would usher in **the** great apostasy. The one "restraining" would have to be "taken away" *before* the lawless one could commit the great apostasy. All of Paul's nouns in this text are *singular.*

This revelation of Paul should silence all the theories that the "man of lawlessness" is the same as the "spirit of antichrist." It should also stop all the misinterpretations of 2 Thessalonians that the "man of lawlessness" is to appear *after* an alleged "secret rapture." The "man of lawlessness" in this text was to "be revealed" immediately[5] *after* the "one restraining him" was out of the way.

Note the following: (a) Paul spoke of "the" apostasy, not "an" apostasy; it is a *particular apostasy*; (b) it is "the" man of lawlessness, not "a" man of lawlessness; it is a particular personage — it is *not* "the" antichrist for the Bible speaks of *many antichrists,* some even in the days of the apostle John; (c) "the apostasy" clearly refers to the incorporation into the true apostolic doctrines taught in the NT of that paganism which *began* as early as the first century A.D. (even as it was occurring in

Paul's day). By the time of the fall of the Western Roman Empire the Roman bishop, Simplicius (468–483), was free from civil authority. Thus began the evolution of true NT Christianity into what is known today as Roman Catholicism;[6] (d) "the one restraining" the lawless one was undoubtedly the Roman emperor, for the paganization of Christendom was accomplished only when the Roman bishop obtained "universal lordship" of the church.

This being so, Paul certainly was not predicting the "revealing" of the "man of lawlessness" in the twentieth or twenty-first centuries. Other NT Scriptures document that false doctrines and power-grabs were already occurring in the first century A.D. (e.g., Acts 20:29-30; 2 Pet. 2:1; 3 John 9; Jude 4, et al.). Paul wrote to Timothy about this pagan "falling away" and used the same Greek word.[7] "The" apostasy which occurred, and is still in existence in Roman Catholicism, is the greatest "falling away" of the centuries. Paul predicted the "man of lawlessness" would be perpetuated until the Lord comes to "slay him." *No one knows when the Lord is to come.* He cannot be the "beast" of Revelation chapter 20, for the "beast" was slain and cast into the abyss *before the judgment.*

We have attempted to survey only the texts of the Bible most often used (or abused) by some who have made, and are still continuing to make, what we think are improper eschatological interpretations. *Any* appeal to "signs of the times" and *any* specification of the time (whether it be century, year, hour or day) of the Second Coming of Christ and the "consummation of the ages" is sheer foolishness in the light of Jesus' *clear* and *repeated* statements that he is coming back when no one expects him to do so, and *no one*, not even the angels in heaven, knows when that will be!

We do not claim to have dealt with every minute detail of the numerous eschatological theories proclaimed through the centuries. Surely, the *fact* that thousands of calculations thus far have been wrong should counsel extreme caution on the part of any Christian voice predicting the coming of Christ, or alleging that "the rapture, the antichrist, the tribulation, and the millennium" will transpire at Anno Domini 2000!

For more discussion of subjects related to eschatology we urge the reading of the epilogue and the appendixes which follow.

Notes

[1] *ou mē*, Greek phrase is emphatic!

[2] *harpagēsometha*, Greek "seized."

[3] Russell Boatman, *What the Bible Says about the End Time*, p. 190.

[4] Paul used the Greek word, *energeitai*, from which we get, "energized, at work."

[5] *tote*, is the Greek adverb used here, meaning, "at that point in time, thereupon."

[6] See *Halley's Bible Handbook*, 24th ed., 1965, p. 770ff.

[7] Paul used the Greek word *apostesontai* in 1 Timothy 4:1-3.

epilogue

In late 1990 and early 1991 Saddam Hussein, dictator of Iraq, invaded Kuwait. American President George W. Bush, threatened retaliation and was successful in forming a "United Nations" coalition armed force to drive the Iraqi army out of Kuwait. Saddam Hussein declared that should U.N. forces attack his army it would be "the mother of all wars." Any person who watched television, read newspapers, or listened to "talk radio" in those months remembers the eschatological frenzy that swept through America (and perhaps other western countries also). There were predictions that "Armageddon" was imminent. Prophecy preachers were calling Saddam Hussein "the antiChrist." It was prognosticated with much certainty that Russia (declared to be "Gog and Magog") would soon invade Israel and the United States would be at war with Russia.

As we have documented in chapter two, this kind of impetuous, doomsday forecasting has been going on for centuries. There were those in the *first century* Thessalonian church saying that the "day of the Lord" had already come (sometime before Paul wrote 1 & 2 Thessalonians ca. A.D. 52). Apparently the doomsday date-setters have not learned from history and are therefore doomed to obsessive repetition of the errors of their predecessors.

A better epilogue for this brief work could hardly be made than a recent article in the bimonthly Christian periodical, *Does God Exist?* John N. Clayton, editor and publisher of the magazine wrote an article which, with his gracious permission, we quote in part herewith:

"The New Millenial Madness"

"'The second coming of Christ will occur in 1997.' — Mary Steward Relfe

"'I predict the absolute fulness of man's operation on planet arth by the year 2000 A.D. Then Jesus Christ shall reign from Jerusalem for 1000 years.' — Lester Sumrall

"'The confrontation with Iraq — points to fulfillment of Bible prophecies that 'the nations of the world are going to come against Israel" in the latter days and the Middle East is "going to explode." It's exactly what the Bible said.' — Pat Robertson

"'Four major prophecies in the Bible pinpoint Iraq and the Persian Gulf as the prelude to the Battle of Armageddon, a conflict that will begin at the Euphrates River in Iraq.' — Jack Van Impe

"'The Persian Gulf crisis and the West's need for oil may very well be . . . what unites the West under one man that the Bible calls the Antichrist.' — R. L. Hymers

"'There are spiritual forces at work in the Persian Gulf confrontation. History has gone full circle, and we are coming back to these [Bible] lands. This is not another Korea, it is not another Vietnam — it is something far more sinister and far more difficult.' — Billy Graham

"'The Iraqi crisis may spark the terrible war that will herald the Messiah's arrival.' — Rabbi Menachem Schneerson

"In the ten years prior to A.D. 1000, the world was exposed to a period of religious panic. Frederick Marten in his book, *The Story of Human Life and Doomsday*, described prisoners being released, debts forgiven, food given away, possessions sold, and people going to mountain tops to observe the second coming of Christ. On December 31, 999, Pope Sylvester II held a midnight mass so the Pope's followers could witness the end of the world in the presence of the man they considered to be God's leader on earth. Needless to say, the new century entered without the return of Christ. Now as we approach 1999, the same mentality is approaching. The New Age writers, Ken Carey and David Spangler, attach special significance to the year 2000. Elizabeth Clare Prophet, of the Church Universal and Triumphant, claims a Russian invasion is imminent. Hal Lindsay's 1970's book, *The Late Great Planet Earth* has jumped 83% in sales and Zondervan Publishing is releasing a re-write of John Walvoord's 1974 book *Armageddon, Oil, and the Middle East Crisis.* Even the sales of books by Nostradamus (a sixteenth century French astrologer) have jumped dramatically.

"Ron Rhodes recently wrote an article titled 'Millennial Madness' in *Christian Research Journal* (Fall 1990, page 39). Rhodes does not get into the major problems theologically of all this activity. What he does do is list eight logical, solid reasons why we need to stay out of the new millennial madness. We think these reasons are important to consider.

"First, over the past 2,000 years, the track record of those who have predicted and/or expected 'the end' has been 100 percent wrong. The history of doomsday predictions is little more than a history of dashed expectations. Though it is *possible* we are living in the last days, it is also possible that Christ's Second Coming is a long way off.

"Second, those who succumb to millennial madness may end up making harmful decisions for their lives. Selling one's possessions and heading for the mountains, purchasing bomb shelters, stopping education, leaving family and friends — these are destructive actions that can *ruin* one's life.

"Third, Christians who succumb to millennial madness (for example, by expecting the rapture to occur by a specific date) may end up damaging their faith in the Bible (especially prophecy) when their expectations fail.

"Fourth, if one loses confidence in the prophetic portions of Scripture, biblical prophecy ceases to be a motivation to purity and holiness in daily life (see, e.g., Titus 2:12-14).

"Fifth, Christians who succumb to millennial madness may damage the faith of *new* and/or *immature* believers when predicted events fail to materialize.

"Sixth, millennial soothsayers tend to be sensationalistic, and sensationalism is unbefitting to a Christian. Christ calls his followers to live, *soberly* and *alertly* as they await his coming (Mark 13:32-37).

"Seventh, Christians who get caught up in millennial madness can do damage to the cause of Christ. Humanists enjoy scorning Christians who have put stock in end-time predictions (especially when specific dates have been attached to specific events). Why give 'ammo' to the enemies of Christianity?

"Eighth, the timing of end-time events is in God's hands, and we haven't been given the details (Acts 1:7). As far as the Second Coming is concerned, I close with the sound advice of David Lewis: 'It is better to live as if Jesus were coming today and yet prepare for the future as if He were not coming for a long time. Then you are ready for time and eternity.'"[1]

Let all who love Christ say, Amen!

Notes

[1] John N. Clayton, *Does God Exist?* (March/April, 1991), pp. 2-4.

appendix a

INTERPRETATION OF BIBLICAL PROPHECY

The Biblical Requirements of a True Prophet from God

1. His predictions of the future, far and near, must come to pass in every detail, e.g., Deut. 18:20-22; Isa. 41:21-24; 42:8-9; 43:9-13; 44:6-8; 45:20-21; 46:9-11; 48:3-7; Ezek. 13:1-16; Jer. 28:8-9.
2. He must be able to reveal the unknown past, e.g, Isa. 42:22; 43:9.
3. He must not teach anything that is contrary or contradictory to the Word of God already revealed in the Scriptures, e.g., Jer. 23:21-32; Ezek. 13:10-23; 2 Pet. 2:1-22; 1 John 4:1-6.
4. He must not predict or prophesy in order to exploit others for personal gain, e.g., 2 Pet. 2:1-22; Ezek. 13:17-19; Micah 3:5.
5. He must not live an ungodly life or teach others to do so, e.g., Jer. 23:1-40; Ezek. 13:1-23; Micah 2:6-11; 2 Pet. 2:1-22; Jude 4,23.
6. He must be able to tell both dreams and interpretations of dreams, e.g., Dan. 2:1ff; 4:1ff.
7. He must preach a message that brings people to repentance, e.g., Jer. 23:21-22; Ezek. 13:2-23; 2 Pet. 2:1-22.
8. He must prophesy to edify and instruct so that people will learn God's will as God alone has revealed it, e.g., 1 Cor. 14:26-33.
9. He must have his own spirit under his own control, e.g., 1 Cor. 14:24-25.
10. He must prophesy the secret thoughts of men, e.g., 1 Cor. 14:24-25.
11. He must not cause division in the body of Christ, e.g., 1 Cor. 12:1–14:40; Jude 19; Jas. 3:13-18.
12. He must be called by God himself, e.g., Ezek. 13:1-19.
13. It must be realized that in the New Testament dispensation, after the coming of

273

the completed canon of Scripture, the prophetic call and office would cease. This was predicted in Zech. 13:1-6, and confirmed in the NT in 1 Cor. 13:8f.

The Vocation of a True Prophet

1. Primarily and foremost, a prophet was a preacher of God's revelation to sinful people. His primary message was the law of Moses in the OT dispensation; in the Messianic Age he proclaimed the New Testament Scriptures and the Old Testament Scriptures as they were fulfilled in the New.
2. Secondarily, a prophet was a predictor of history and a proclaimer of any message God saw fit to reveal to him apart from the written Word.
3. Prophets were also often counselors to the leaders of their societies.
4. Prophets were authors and orators. Many of them committed parts of their proclamations to written form to be preserved until the end of time.
5. Prophets were human beings with feelings, fears, doubts, and failures, but with faith and courage and conviction that ultimately God's Word and God's glory would be vindicated.
6. As a preacher, the prophet viewed his *present* in the light of the *future*, i.e., he interpreted contemporary events and persons as they were supposed to fit into and affect the future — mainly the messianic future.
7. As a predictor, the prophet viewed the *future* in light of his *present*, i.e., he indicates that the unexperiencible future of which he gloriously speaks should be affecting his audience's present actions.

Seven Axioms or Principles for Interpreting Prophetic Literature of the Bible[1]

1. **Times Coloring** (or Historical Contemporaniety). The OT prophets *colored* all their messages with terminology, symbols, figures of speech which were *contemporaneous* to their own day. They communicated God's message, both present and predictive, in their own *vernacular*. That is normal. Every generation and every culture does the same. The OT prophets spoke and wrote colloquially. This should be obvious. It should also be obvious that if we are to understand them, we must learn their vernacular, as nearly as possible, from adjunct studies of history, literature, and archaeological artifacts contemporaneous to their age.
2. **Covenant Background** (or Theological Accentuation). Every judgment, every redemptive promise made by God to the "Chosen people" was made on the *background* of God's moving of history toward the fulfillment of his covenant

with Abraham (cf. Gen. 22:18 with Rom. 9:6-13 and Gal. 3:15-29). *Everything* that was happening, or going to happen, was, from God's perspective, ultimately to fulfill that covenant of messianic redemption. The Old covenant was not the best God was going to do. He had a glorious, spiritually speaking, covenant future for his people. The coming Messianic Age, i.e., the "latter days," (Acts 2:14f) and "the end of the ages" (1 Cor. 10:11) would be "the time of the end" for the Old covenant and the *filling-up-full* of the covenant made with Abraham. The law, which came 430 years after God's promise to Abraham did not annul the promise (Gal. 3:17-18).

3. **Eschatological Significance** (or A Philosophy of History). God spoke through the prophets and revealed to the world a divine philosophy of history. The prophets predict where history is going and why it is going in that direction. Along the way, they predicted a number of different *terminals* in history. The OT prophets spoke of the **Messianic Age** (the first advent of the Lord's "Anointed One") as, "the last days," or, "the end of the times," or, "the time of the end," or "the day of the Lord." The prophets were emphatic and unequivocal that God was working in their times toward an END. Prophetic literature is *goal-oriented.* **In the literature of the OT prophets that goal is the Messianic Kingdom (i.e., the church of Jesus Christ).** Their philosophy of history teaches that:

   (a) history is controlled by the Omnipotent Creator, eventually and ultimately serving his divine goal of the redemption of his creation;

   (b) history is *forward* or *climactic* in orientation — not cyclical, and is purposeful;

   (c) history's goal is the redemption of creation through a restored rule of the Lord over a regenerated people ("God is going to take back what belongs to him");

   (d) history will experience an incarnation of deity, and the institution of a universal, undefeatable, spiritual society, i.e., the Messianic Kingdom of the church ("Zion" will be glorious — cf. Isa. 60:1–66:24 with Heb. 12:22-29);

   (e) historically, this will be accomplished in the "last days" (i.e., the end of the Mosaic dispensation [cf. Jer. 3:15-16 with Heb. 1:2 and 8:1-13]), and will involve a **new covenant**.

4. **Shortened Perspective** (or Chronological Discontinuity). The prophet stands at one point in time (his own), and looks by divine revelation across a span of years and centuries and reveals a future point in time (near future or distant future). The prophet usually does not have revealed to him any of the history **between** those two points of time. Often the prophet will skip a chasm of hundreds,

perhaps a thousand, years of time **at the end of one sentence and the beginning of the very next sentence!** Thus, God has "shortened" the prophet's and our perspective from his present day to centuries or millennia later by going from one sentence to the next sentence, leaving the hundreds of years of history between the two points unrevealed. A classic example of this axiom is found in Joel 2:27 (a time contemporaneous with the prophet himself) and Joel 2:28 (approximately 800 years in the future of the prophet, see Acts 2:14-21). Jesus used the same principle in Matthew 24:35 — 24:36. In 24:35 Jesus ends his prediction of the destruction of Jerusalem and the Jewish nation which took place A.D. 66-70. He then makes a verbal leap to begin in 24:36 speaking of the time which no one knows, his Second Advent and the end of the world. *Chronological discontinuity is a common vehicle of prophetic literature.*

5. **Fulfillment Is Greater Than the Prediction** (or The Bloom Is Greater Than the Bud). It is axiomatic that the fulfillment of a prophecy is **greater**, more desirable, than the prediction. Therefore the New Testament church (i.e., the Messianic Age or "the latter days") is **greater** than the OT prophecies foretelling its institution. The NT is more to be desired and more advanced toward God's ultimate goal of the **end of time and inauguration of eternity** than the OT which only symbolized and predicted the church. The reality of the spiritual kingdom of God and her spiritual blessings (Eph. 1:3) are **greater** than the physical symbols and metaphors contained in the OT promises. Thus, God would **not** be saying in the OT prophets that his *ultimate* plan was to give the Jews back their land, rebuild their temple, and reinstate their religion! God would not contradict in the OT prophets what he has declared in the NT (e.g., Romans, Galatians, Hebrews). The reinstatement of OT religion after the First Advent of the Messiah is NOT the message of the OT prophets — not anywhere, in any of them! The OT prophets have nothing to say about a restored Judaism in the time of the Messiah. In fact, they clearly indicate that when the Messiah was to come, Judaism would be done away — **forever** (e.g., Isa. 56:3-8; 66:1-24; Jer. 3:15-18; 31:32-34; Dan. 9:24-27; 12:6-7); Jesus is unequivocal about the end of Judaism (John 4:19-26; Matt. 5:17; 21:43: 23:37-39; 24:1-35; Mark 13:1-32; Luke 21:5-33; 24:25-27; 24:44-49). The entire Epistle to the Hebrews is devoted to the "**once-for-all**" abrogation of the OT system.

6. **Double Emphasis** (or The Dualistic *Modus Operandi* in Divine Redemption). The OT prophets preach that God is carrying out his program to redeem creation in a process that seems from a strictly human perspective to be antithetical. That is precisely why God had to reveal his process through the prophets. Man must see the history of redemption from the divine perspective. When he

does so, he sees a theme that runs throughout the OT prophets — in fact through the whole Bible from Genesis through Revelation — that God is "managing" the history of the world by a "double-emphasis" schematic, e.g.:

J Judgments	b. Redemptions
The Noahic Flood	The Ark & Noah's Family
The Egyptian Bondage	The Exodus
The Mesopotamian Captivities	The Restoration of Israel
The Crucifixion of Christ	The Resurrection of Christ
The Roman Persecution of the Church	The Victory of the Church
The Consummation (the above are types)= Final Judgment & Redemption	
Hell	**Heaven**

All the judgments and redemptions within the continuum of time are prefiguring and providentially using people and events toward the *final* judgment/ redemption event which will be eternal (see Luke 13:1-5). Any judgment-redemption may be called by the OT prophets, "the day of the Lord" because all such events are not only prophetic of, but are also components of, the *final events*.

7. **Unifying Focal Point** (or "The Fullness of Time"). This principle proposes that all the Bible, including *all* prophecy of both OT and NT, has Jesus Christ as its "unifying focal point." "For the testimony of Jesus is the spirit of prophecy" (e.g., Rev. 19:10; see also Luke 24:25-27; 24:44-49; Col. 1:15-20; 2:3; Heb. 1:1-4). The redemptive work of God's Anointed Son is the point upon which *all human history converges*. And this includes the rising and falling of all human empires and emperors (Dan. 2:20-22; 4:44-45, et al.). Nearly every word in the Bible, from Genesis to Revelation looks forward or backward primarily, to Christ's work of vicarious, substitutionary atonement, his resurrection from death, the establishment of the church, and the continued intercessory ministry of the Spirit of Christ both in this time-space continuum and in the presence of the Father. Thus, we must keep **Christ and the church** constantly in mind as being the **essential message of the OT and NT prophets**. The Bible holds out no hope for salvation of anything or anyone in eternity except the church! The OT prophets were concerned with nothing beyond the Messiah's first advent, the establishment of his kingdom (the church) and its redemptive work in the world. And NT prophecy is not extravagant concerning the eschatological future of Christians and the church beyond the promises of its eternal certainty (e.g., Luke 16:19-31; Rom. 8:18-39; 1 Cor. 15:35-58; Phil. 3:20-21; 1 Thess. 4:13–5:11; 2 Thess. 2:1-12; 1 Pet. 5:4; 2 Pet. 3:8-13; 1 John 3:2; Rev. 7:9-17; 21:1-27; 22:1-5).

The language of prophecy is (a) vernacular; (b) vivid; (c) poetic; and (d) cryptic. That invests it with majesty, power, and enchantment; but because it is a revelation from God (undiscoverable by human wisdom alone), it demands a childlike spirit to understand it. Prophetic preaching and writing has to be all of this because of the incorrigible sinfulness of its audience (e.g. Isa. 1:1-31; 6:9-13; 30:1-18; Jer. 2:1-37; 5:1-31; 6:16-19; ⌐ ek. 2:1–3:15; Hos. 4:1-6; Amos 7:12-13; Micah 2:11; Rom. 1:18-32; 2 Thess. 2:10-12; 2 Pet. 2:1-22, et al.). Preaching prophets were sent to a people who did not want to hear them, people who had no interest in spiritual matters. The prophets had to get their attention by "hitting them between the eyes" of their minds with verbal clubs! The language of prophecy is of the calibre of genius (which is to be expected of God, of course!). It is versatile, optimistic, spiritual, eloquent, imaginative and emotional. The prophetic literature of the OT and NT was written by scores of different authors, from vastly different social and economic backgrounds, in all kinds of social circumstances and in different generations. Yet it has an unassailable unity and a goal, a remarkable magnetism, and produces a salutary spiritual effect upon all honest and careful readers.

An Hermeneutical Approach to Prophetic Literature

Fact #1: God expects all human beings to understand the Bible! All of it! Yes, even prophecy (e.g., Rev. 1:1-3; it must be understood to be "kept"). "The secret things belong to God, but the *things that are revealed* [*golah*, literally, "uncover the ears"] belong to us . . . forever, that we may do all the words of this law" (Deut. 29:29; see also John 20:30-31; Rom. 15:4; 16:25-27; 1 Cor. 10:11).

Fact #2: Jesus rebuked some of his disciples (Luke 24:25) for failing to comprehend the OT prophecies concerning the Messiah! He rebuked Jewish religious leaders and scholars for not knowing the Scriptures and what they said of the Messiah (Matt. 21:42; 22:20; Mark 12:24; Luke 11:52; John 5:39). What will the Lord say at the judgment to the dull comprehension and/or misinterpretation by people twenty centuries later with all the advantages they have to assist them to understand biblical prophecy? God expects Christians to "grow up" spiritually, *through understanding* his Word (1 Cor. 3:1-2; Eph. 4:14). God *deplores* scriptural illiteracy and ignorance for he has created human beings with minds capable of logic and has given them a clear revelation of his existence in "nature" (Rom. 1:18-21; Acts 14:16-17; 17:26-31); a clear revelation of his mind and his will in human language in the Bible (e.g., Rom. 11:25; 1 Cor. 2:1-16; 10:6ff; 12:1; 2 Cor. 1:8; 10:3-5; 1 Thess. 4:13; 2 Pet. 3:5,8).

Five Basic Principles of Hermeneutics[2]

A. *The true interpretation of **any** biblical passage is what the **author intended** to say.* This applies not just to the Bible but in every area of life where there are spoken or written words to hear or read! It is clearly asinine for a person to read a book or listen to a discourse deliberately intending to understand it by some personally preconceived, self-centered agenda (e.g., 1 Cor. 5:9-13). Applying this principle of "author's intent" requires a serious effort by the reader to project himself as much as humanly possible into the writer's historical, cultural, mental, emotional, and linguistic frame of reference. One must take the author's *stated* purpose, time, addressee(s), language, context, personal background, claims and proofs of sources into account. **Author's intent — first, last, and always!**

B. *God's word has **one** intended meaning, not many conflicting ones!* This does *not* mean that every word in the Bible is to be understood in a literal sense. We do not apply total literalness in everyday attempts to communicate or understand any and all nonbiblical literature or discourse. Neither does it mean that every prophecy has *only one point* of fulfillment (cf. Hos. 11:1; Isa. 7:1-25; 28:5-13, et al.). But *it does mean* that symbols and other figures of speech, and just plain prose, are all intended to **mean one thing or idea or principle** as they are read in their own contexts and that **one** meaning is to be **understood alike by all who read it**. We must adhere to the **rules** by which all language is to be commonly understood; otherwise we shall have a subjectivism that can only produce literary chaos and a total lack of communication.

C. *God is able to say what **he** wants to say, and he knows to whom he is speaking!* After all, he created us and he created thought and language. **God spoke in order to be understood!** God did not set out to speak to man so he might be *misunderstood*! The Bible then, will be the absolute best instrument of communication known to man. It will be the clearest, most available, most moral, most appealing, most artistic, most profound work of literature ever produced (cf. Psa. 19:7-10; 119:98-100; 1 Cor. 2:1-16, et al.). If men do not understand God's word, they would not understand any other communication (Luke 16:16-31). When people do not understand God's revelation in human language, the hindrance is evidently moral, not intellectual (cf. John 5:39-47; 8:43-47; Rom. 1:18-32; 2 Cor. 4:1-6; Gal. 4:16; 2 Thess. 2:10-12; 2 Tim. 4:3-5; Titus 1:15-16; Heb. 5:11-14; 2 Pet. 3:3-7).

D. *The language of the Bible is the **language of man** and is to be interpreted by rules for understanding all human language.* The language of the New Testament is expressly the language of "common" (*koine* Greek) verbalization of the time in which it was originally written. While the Hebrew language was not as "commonly" used in the world of its day, still it was "common" to most of its surrounding Semitic neighbors and was translated into other languages upon the dispersion of the Israelites through the captivities of 722–586 B.C. The language of the Bible is *not* the language of sophists and technicians (1 Cor. 1:28–2:16). It may be understood by any literate, honest minded (Luke 8:15) human being when translated into his language. In some matters God felt it necessary to communicate the unknowable or unexperiencible. If he was to communicate it to human beings he would have to express it in humanly-known or experienced terms. That is why we have a plethora of symbols, parables, metaphors, similes, hyperbole, and other figures of speech in the Bible — and especially in prophetic literature. God does *not* communicate to mankind in an unknown tongue! Nor does man communicate to God in an unknown tongue. Perhaps people may occasionally be unable to find human words adequate to express their thoughts and feelings to God (Rom. 8:26; 2 Cor. 12:4), yet God is never at a loss to find exactly the right human words to communicate to human beings precisely what he wants them to believe, understand, and do.

E. *God expects **straight thinking** from human beings as they read and teach his Word.* Paul exhorted Timothy to handle aright the word of truth (2 Tim. 2:15). The Greek words there are *orthotomounta ton logon tes aletheias.* Literally, Paul has said, "correctly slicing the word of truth." It does make a difference how you "slice" the Bible! You had better do so "straightly" or "correctly." The Greek word, *ortho,* is prefixed to many English medical words and means, "correction of a deformity, or straightening a crookedness." In theology, *orthodox* means "straight, or correct thinking." The Greek word, *tomounta,* means to "plow a furrow, cut a line." Paul rebuked false teachers who "huckstered" (*kapeleuontes,* "peddled, hawked, exploited for gain") the word of God (2 Cor. 2:17) and those who "adulterated" (*dolountes,* "use bait, use to deceive, snare, beguile") the word of God (2 Cor. 4:2). Paul was always careful in his use of the word of God as he communicated it to others (1 Thess. 2:3-13). Every searcher of the Scriptures should be like the Bereans (Acts 17:11). It is hard work to make oneself biblically *orthodox.* It takes intensive study. But Christians are not permitted the luxury of *lazy-mindedness*! They must **exercise** (*gegymnasmena,* the word from which we get the English word, "gymnasium") or **train** their mental faculties to be able to **distingush** (*diakrisin,* from which the word "diacritical" comes) the good from the bad, the true from the false. Peter exhorts Christians to **gird up** the loins of their minds (1 Pet. 1:13) and be **serious** about knowing God's word. Increasing in the knowledge of God's word is a Christian **imperative** (1 Pet. 3:15; 2 Pet. 3:18).

The Symbolic and Apocalyptic Style of Prophetic Literature

Perhaps the **most disctinctive style of prophetic literature** may be called **apocalyptic-symbolic.** The purpose of **symbolic** language is to try to make the invisible, visible! **Symbols** communicate characteristics of persons and events that are not otherwise discernable through human observation. *A symbol is essentially:*

(a) an emblem, a token, a type — A flag is a symbol; a logo is a symbol; even some events may contain a symbolic communication;

(b) a vivid, sometimes bizarre, representative likeness — e.g., all civil governments are essentially predatory; they exist only by taking, through taxation, the citizen's hard-earned productivity; thus, all human governments are **symbolized** in the Bible by a variety of rapacious beasts; while the harmless innocence of Christ and his kingdom are **symbolized** by lambs and sheep;

(c) not the meaning itself, but a suggestion that some reality resembling the person or event being symbolized is there in the object used as the **symbol**;

(d) an attempt, by hyperbole or bizarreness, to stimulate the mind and the emotions of the reader;

(e) something that arises out of, and is related to the cultural, traditional, racial, religious and historical backgrounds of those using it;

(f) an invention of necessity; or arbitrarily fixed; some **symbols** soon become obsolete, while others are universal and enduring.

Apocalyptic language is essentially:

(a) a message-style for times of crisis — usually oppression or disaster; it tries to give a look beyond the wicked, cruel and seemingly hopeless human circumstances through the perspective of God who knows and sees the ultimate spiritual victory and glory; thus, it is highly symbolic in its terminology (classic examples are found in Daniel, Ezekiel, Zechariah, Matthew 24, Mark 13, Luke 21, and Revelation);

(b) a message-style suited to depict divine control and divine intervention in catastrophic and cataclysmic proportions (whether to be literally fulfilled or understood figuratively depends on the basic rules of hermeneutics already cited);

(c) a message-style dealing with the whole cosmic struggle of good and evil, truth and falsehood, right and wrong, judgment and redemption — symbols are strange and fantastic; time periods are varied and esoteric and not usually to be understood literally;

(d) a message-style which alone is suited to reveal the divine frame of reference — literal language is totally inadequate to communicate the unseen realities, **because**:

   (1) of the brevity of the human attention span;

   (2) of the need for making the human mind curious;

   (3) of the need for exciting human beings to action;

   (4) of the need for the human mind to expand its conceptual horizons to understand ultimate realities which are apart from this world.

(e) a message-style portraying essentially the same message, only in different time-slots, whether in Daniel or Revelation — thus, through the apocalyptic style history is made to transcend time; through the apocalyptic style we are shown that human history is not separated from heaven's awareness and is thus linked directly to and functions within the purposes under the control of the Sovereign of all existence; human history is shown, through apocalyptic language, to be the stage upon which the cosmic controversy between Almighty God and the rebellious prince of demons (who pretends to be the "god" of this world) is acted out; the one certain fact of history, as God knows it and reveals it (apocalyptically), is that his church will survive all the devil and his assistants ("beasts and harlots") can possibly do to stamp her out!

(f) a message-stye that is esoteric, cryptic, and "coded" — it is intended to be that way; it is a "secretly-coded" message from God so that only those who are really interested in what God has to say will "dig" it out by "decoding" it; but the God who encodes the message graciously gives the tools, and even supplies the motive, for decoding it!

Any interpretation of prophetic literature which places a meaning on its figures and symbols that is contrary to the rest of the teaching of the Bible (both OT and NT) must be erroneous — either deliberately so, or innocently so — but still erroneous. **God does not contradict himself!**

Actually, the writings of the prophets are **epistolary** just as the writings of Paul in the NT. The only difference is in style, not in content or intent. God meant all people to understand prophetic literature. And he meant all people to strive, under common hermeneutical rules, **to understand it alike!**

Notes

[1] A brief summary of John P. Milton, *Prophecy Interpreted*, Augsburg, adding this author's observations of interpretative principles from 35 years of teaching the OT Prophets in the Bible college classroom.

[2] An adaptation of this author's class notes from Seth Wilson's Bible college course on *Hermeneutics*, 1958.

appendix b

WORD STUDIES
IN PROPHETIC
LITERATURE

We offer here a study of some of the pertinent words (e.g., "last days, last day, end of the age(s), latter days, and end times") bearing on biblical eschatologly. The Greek words τέλειος, τελειότης, τελειόω, τελείως, τελείωσις, τέλον, τελεσ–φορέω, τελευτάω, and τελέω, are all from the same root word τέλος, used in the *Koine* Greek of the NT and the papyri, as well as classical Greek, and all mean, generically, "having attained the end or purpose intended," i.e., **completed**. These words are used to refer to "ends or purposes attained" that may have already occurred at varying points along the line we call "time." They may also refer to **points yet to occur** in the line of time, or to the end of all time. Context, usage, and fulfillments determine their meaning.

The Greek words, συντέλεια and συντελέω, are compounded from the preposition prefix, *syn*, which means, "altogether, fully," and the root word τέλος as defined above. Thus, in συντέλεια/συντελέω we have words that mean *"emphatically* having attained the end or purpose intended," i.e., **consummated**. These words are also used to "ends or purposes attained" in the past, in the future, or at the end of all time according to context and complementary passages.

The following are related to the New Testament phrase, "end or consummation of the age(s)"

The phrase "the consummation of the age(s)," or "the end of the age(s)" in the Greek New Testament and the Septuagint (the Greek Old Testament) is συντελει–΄ας τοῦ αἰῶνος, or transliterated, *synteleias tou aiōnos*. The word συντελείας is most accurately translated "consummation."

Matthew 24:3 in the Greek text is Εἰπὲ ἡυῖν πότε ταῦτα ἔσται καὶ τί τὸ σημεῖον τῆς σῆς παρουσίας καὶ τῆς συντελείας τοῦ αἰῶνος (gen. sing.), or transliterated, *eipe hēuin pote tauta estai kai ti to sēmeion tēs sēs parousias kai tēs synteleias tou aiōnos.* Translation — "Tell us when this will be, and what is the sign of your coming and of the end ("consummation") of the age?" *Contextually* this concerns the destruction of Jerusalem A.D. 70 and the close of the Mosaic Age.

Mark 13:4 in the Greek text is καὶ τι τὸ σημεῖον ὅταν μέλλη ταῦτα συντελεῖσθαι πάντα, *kai ti to sēmeion hotan mellē tauta synteleisthai panta.* Translation — ". . . and what will be the sign when these things are all to be finished" ("consummated"). This is a parallel to Matt. 24:3 and refers to the destruction of Jerusalem and the end of Judaism. The parallel account of the Olivet Discourse in the Gospel of Luke does *not* include the use of the Greek word συντελείας, or any of its cognates.

1 Corinthians 10:11 in the Greek text is πρὸς νουθεσίαν ἡνῶν εἰς οὓς τὰ τέλη τῶν αἰώνων (gen. pl.) κατήντηκεν (*katēnteken* is 2p. perf. ind.), *pros nouthesian heñon eis hous ta telē tōn aiōnōn katēnteken.* Translation — ". . . for our instruction upon whom the end (or "**consummation**") of the ages has come and continues to come." *Gramatically* and *contextually*, this **undeniably** refers to the Christian Age, the First Advent of Christ.

Matthew 28:20 in the Greek text is ἐγὼ μεθ᾽ ὑμῶν εἰμι πάσας τὰς ἡμέρας ἕως τῆς συντελείας τοῦ αἰῶνος (gen. sing.), *egō meth᾽ hymon eimi pasas tas hēmeras heōs tēs synteleias tou aiōnos.* Translation — ". . . I am with you always, to the end ("**consummation**") of the age." *Contextually* Jesus is promising to be with the apostles and all who become Christians through their ministries until the end of time and his Second Advent.

Hebrews 6:5 is γευσαμένους (acc. pl. mas. part. aor. 1) . . . τε μέλλοντος (gen. sing. mas. and neut. part. pres.) αἰῶνος (gen. sing.), *geusamenous . . . te mellontos aiōnos.* Translation — ". . . has tasted at some point in the past . . . the coming age (or the age coming)." *Contextually* and *gramatically* this refers to the Messianic Age, the First Advent of Christ.

Hebrews 8:8 is καὶ συντελέσω (1 pers. sing. fut. ind. act.) ἐπὶ τὸν οἶκον Ἰσραὴλ καὶ ἐπὶ τὸν οἶκον Ἰούδα διαθήκη καινήν, *kai synteleso epi ton oikon Israel kai epi ton oikon Iouda diathēkē kainēn.* Translation — ". . . and I will **consummate** upon the house of Israel and upon the house of Judah a covenant, a new one. . . ." *Contextually* this refers to the ushering in of the New Testament through the redemptive work of Christ which will, as predicted by Jeremiah 31:31-34, abrogate the Old Covenant. Why did the Hebrews author use συντελέσω here? Did he mean to say that the New Covenant was the **consummate covenant — the final covenant**? That is clearly the emphatic teaching of the book of Hebrews. This adds to the cumulative evidence that the phrase "**consummation** of the ages" *usually* refers to the Messainic Age (the NT church).

Matthew 13:39,40,49 is ὁ δὲ θερισμὸς συντέλεια αἰῶνός ἐστιν (gen. sing.), *ho de therismos synteleia aiōnos estin.* Translation — "and the harvest is the end ("**consummation**") of the age." οὕτως ἔσται ἐν τῇ συντελείᾳ τοῦ αἰῶνος (gen. sing.), *houtōs estai en tē synteleia tou aiōnos.* Translation — "thus it shall be at the end ("**consummation**") of the age." οὕτως ἔσται ἐν τῇ συντελείᾳ τοῦ αἰῶνος, *houtōs estai en tē synteleia tou aiōnos.* Translation — "So it will be at the end ("**consummation**") of the age." *Grammatically* and *contextually* these refer to the Second Advent of Christ and the final judgment.

Hebrews 9:26 is νυνὶ δὲ ἅπαξ ἐπὶ συντελείᾳ τῶν αἰώνων (gen. pl.), *nyni de hapax epi synteleia tōn aiōnōn.* Translation — ". . . but now once for all at the end ("**consummation**") of the ages . . . ." *Contextually*, this **unequivocally** refers to the Christian dispensation, the First Advent of Christ.

The following are related to the New Testament phrases, "last days," and "last day"

The word ἔσχατος, *eschatos,* and cognates, is the only word in the Greek NT to be translated, "last." The same is true of the word ἡμέρα, *hēmera* translated "day."

Acts 2:17; 2 Timothy 3:1: ἐν ταῖς ἐσχάταις ἡμέραις, *en tais eschatais hēmerais*; also **Hebrews 1:2; 2 Peter 3:3**: ἐπ' ἐσχάτου [or ἐσχάτων] τῶν ἡμερῶν, *ep' eschatou* [or *eschatōn*] *hēmerōn.* Translation — "in the last days." Acts 2:17 and Heb. 1:2 are categorically interpreting OT usage of "last days/latter days" as referring to the First Advent of the Messiah (the Messianic Age and the church). This would infer that 2 Tim. 3:1 and 2 Pet. 3:3 were also to be applied to the Messianic Age.

Ephesians 2:7: ἐν τοῖς αἰῶσιν τοῖς ἐπερχομένοις (pres. pl. dat. m. part.), *en tois aiōsin tois eperchomenois.* Translation — ". . . in the ages now coming upon . . . ." *Contextually* and *grammatically* it clearly refers to Christ's First Advent.

1 Peter 1:20; Jude 18: ἐπ' ἐσχάτου τῶν χρόνων (pl. — Jude has sing. τοῦ χρόνου), *ep' eschatou tōn chronōn.* Translation — "in last of the times." *Contextually*, it must refer to the First Advent of Christ. The definite article *ton* is absent in Jude 18. *Contextually*, Jude too, is writing of something *contemporary* with the gospel/apostolic age.

1 Timothy 4:1: ἐν ὑστέροις καιροῖς, *en hysterois kairois.* Translation — "in latter times." Timothy was to instruct people of his own time about circumstances which were to **begin in his own time** (see 4:6,11,13) and **continue** until the **end** of time.

1 John 2:18: ἐσχάτη ὥρα ἐστίν (pres. tense), *eschate hōra estin*. Translation — "a last hour **it is**." The definite article is absent, thus it would be *indefinite* and literally translated, "this hour in which I am writing is the last hour." (John does **not** write, "**the**" last hour).

John 6:39,40,44,54; John 11:24; 12:48: ἐν τῇ ἐσχάτῃ ἡμέρᾳ (sing), *en tē eschatē hēmera*. Translation — "In the last day." Jesus used the definite article *te* to speak of **the** end of time and the end of the world.

1 Corinthians 15:52: ἐν τῇ ἐσχατη σάλπιγγι (sing.), *en tē eschatē salpingi*. Translation — "at the last trumpet." *Contextually*, Paul is writing of the Second Advent of Christ and the resurrection of the dead.

1 Peter 1:5: ἐν καιρῷ ἐσχάτῳ (sing.), *en kairō eschatō*. Translation — "in time last." *Contextually* it appears to be referring to the end of time, the Second Advent of Christ.

Thus it is apparent that more is said in the terminology of "last days, consummation of the age(s)," etc., even in the NT, of Christ's First Advent.

Some words in the Old Testament of significance in this study. (There are no predictions of the Second Advent of the Messiah in the OT, thus all the following terminology concerns his First Advent and the Christian dispensation.)

בְּאַחֲרִית הַיָּמִים (Hebrew language is read from right to left) transliterated would be *bᵉ'achᵉrith hayamim*. Translation — "in the end of the days" — or, "in the latter time." This is probably the most **significant** of all the words and phrases in the Old Testament relating to eschatology. It is a prophet phrase specifically denoting the final period of the history of Israel *as far as the speaker's perspective reaches* (which is no farther than the Messianic Age). Almost without exception, it is an OT expression denoting the ideal or messianic future (Gen. 49:1; Num. 24:14; Deut. 4:30; 31:29; Isa. 2:2; Jer. 23:20; 30:24; 48:47; 49:39; Ezek. 38:8,16; Dan. 8:23,26; 10:14; Hos. 3:5). *Bacherith* stands alone in Dan. 8:23 (not followed by *hayamim*).

לְעֶת-קֵץ (*lᵉ'eth-qēts*). Translation — "the time of the end" or "for the time of the end." Dan. 8:17; 9:18,26; 11:35,40; 12:4-9. Literally it is "season of cutting off." This Hebrew phrase is often used to speak of summer, or of gathering summer fruit (see Amos 8:1). Daniel's context clearly indicates he is speaking of "the time of the end, or cutting off" of the OT dispensation which was going to occur at the end of the era of "the contemptible one" (none other than Antiochus IV, the Syrian tyrant whose army occupied Palestine ca. 178-165 B.C., see Dan. 8:1-27; 11:1-45). Daniel predicts the coming of the messianic kingdom (the church) along with the end of any monolithic, universal secular rule, when he interprets Nebuchadnezzar's dream-image (Dan. 2:44-45) and his own dream of the four beasts (Dan. 7:1-28). In addition to Daniel's eschatological predictions in 9:24-27 of the coming of the Messianic Age and the end of the OT dispensation, he includes a prophecy in Dan. 12:5-13 of "the shattering of the power of the holy people" (i.e., the destruction of Jerusalem and Judaism).

קֵץ (*qēts*). Translation — "end." It is the word used in Dan. 9:26 for "end" in both places, and in every other place in Daniel (8:17,19; 11:27,35,40,45). In all these instances the word is translated in the Septuagint either *telous* or *horasis*. The word *telous* is the word from which we get the English prefix on words like "telemeter, telephone, telegraph, television" and means "at a distance." The word *horasis* is the word from which we get the English word "horizon" and means "boundary, limit, end." The Hebrew word *qēts* is the generic word for "end." Daniel 9:26 reads, *v''ad qēts* and is translated in the Septuagint *kai heos telous polemou*, "to the end of the war." The word *ketz* is also used in Dan. 12:4,13, but is translated in the LXX by the Greek words, *kairou synteleias* and *synteleian*, or "consummation."

לְמוֹעֵד (*lamo'ed*). Translation — "at the time set." It is in Dan. 11:29. Also in Daniel 11:29 is the word, וּכְאָחֲרוֹנָה, *v'ka'ach'rōnah*, Translation — "but it shall not be this time as the latter."

וְעַד־כָּלָה (*v''ad-kalah*). Translation — "the decreed end," Dan. 9:27. The LXX translates this *kai heos tes synteleias kairou synteleia dothesetai epi ten eremosin.* The Hebrew word *kalah* means, "finish, consummate." A literal English translation of the LXX would be, ". . . and at the finish of this time (when the Anointed One shall be cut off) a finish will be put to the desolation."

אַחֲרִית (*'ach'rith*). Translation — "after part, latter part, actual final lot" (Deut. 32:20,29; Jer. 12:4; 31:17). Sometimes refers to "the close of a man's life" (Num. 23:10); "the end or ultimate issue of a course of action" (Jer. 5:31; Prov. 14:12; 23:32; Isa. 46:10; 47:7; Dan. 12:8, etc.). The Hebrew root of this word, *achar*, means "that which comes after; that which follows, which is next." Thus, the days *immediately after* the Mosaic days were the "*last days.*"

Hebrew words from Jewish rabbinic and apocryphal literature

עוֹלָם הַבָּא (*'ōlam habbah*). Translation — "the eternal world." In Jewish rabbinic and apocryphal literature, especially in the apocalyptic style, this phrase almost always refers to the Messianic Age. Rabbinic interpretation of the Messianic Age has always been one that would *end* the world-order as they knew it (but not end the existence of the planet earth). An eternal physical order would be instituted in which a beneficent Jewish state would rule and Gentiles would be given opportunities to serve this Jewish state.

עָתִיד לָבָא (*'atid labbah*). Translation — "the future to come." In Jewish rabbinic and apocryphal literature, this phrase also refers to the Messianic Age.

עוֹלָם (*'ōlam*). Translation — "ever, forever, eternity." This is a biblical word and may (and often does, in context, mean something other than "eternal." It may mean "a long duration, during a lifetime" (Gen. 9:12, where it means, "a future generation"). In 2 Chronicles 33:7 it speaks of God's name in Solomon's temple "forever," but Solomon's temple has not lasted "forever," thus it means "for a long time." In Deuteronomy 15:17; Exodus 21:6; Leviticus 25:46, certain persons are said to be bondservants "forever" but that is another literal impossibility. Jeremiah 20:17 talks of his mother's womb as, *olam*, "forever" great; Job 41:4 speaks of Leviathan being made a servant of man *olam*, "forever." Both of these are literal impossibilities. However, the Messiah, the "Ruler of Israel" (Micah 5:2) is to come from *olam* and in this case it literally means, "from eternity." It is apostolically authenticated as referring to God incarnated in Jesus Christ (Matt. 2:1-6).

Thus from this brief study of Hebrew words it is clear that "end time, time of the end, and latter days" are phrases which, for the most part, apply to the Messianic Age (the church). Further, it is observed that "forever" (*olam*) in the OT, does not often mean "eternally."

Important Note about the Following Appendixes

Appendixes C and D of this book are included at the author's insistence and he accepts full responsibility for their contents. While some might argue about the relevance of the physical descent of the Ashkenazi Jews, the claim of modern Israelis to the land of Palestine is based in the minds of many on descent from Abraham, and a continuation of God's promises to him. Arthur Koestler, himself a Jew, pointed out that there is no such physical right of succession for what he called, in the title of his book, *The Thirteenth Tribe*. The sources employed for these appendixes are Jewish sources. Koestler wished to place Zionism on a separate footing from the Abrahamic promises. The discerning reader may judge for himself/herself how much or how little physical descent has to do with claims to the land of Israel. That these claims are very relevant to the study of prophecy, however, is readily evident from the shelves of Christian bookstores, and from this recent statement in *U.S. News and World Report*:

> No single modern event has stirred more apocalyptic excitement, however, than the founding of the State of Israel. Since much of the end-times drama revolves around Israel, its nearly 2,000-year absence from the world scene had posed something of a problem for generations of prophecy believers. So when the United Nations chartered Israel in 1948, premillennialists exulted that the final countdown had begun. For many Orthodox Jews, Israel's founding also stirred Messianic expectations linked to biblical prophecies that the Temple in Jerusalem, destroyed by invading Romans in A.D. 70, would be rebuilt and herald the coming of the Messiah. [1]

---

[1] Jeffery L. Sheler, "Dark Prophecies," *U.S. News & World Report*, December 15, 1997, 62-71.

ZIONISM

"... and you shall be plucked off the land .... And the LORD will scatter you among all peoples, from one end of the earth to the other ..."
(Deuteronomy 28:63-64)

The land of Palestine, so named from the ancient land called Philistia in the Bible, was essentially depopulated of Jews by the Romans at the Jewish revolt in A.D. 66-70 when, as Josephus writes, 1,100,000 Jews died and another 100,000 were taken as prisoners of war and dispersed throughout the Roman Empire as slaves. A second revolt of the few Jewish nationalists left in Palestine led by Bar Kochba, the pseudo-Messiah (A.D. 132-135) was utterly crushed by the Romans, who then established the Roman city of Aelia Capitolina on the ruins of Jerusalem and banned all Jews from the city. Most of the Jews that happened to be left after this ban fled Palestine for more accommodating places, while some doggedly remained in the hills and villages.

Palestine became noted as an outstanding center of religious scholarship in the 2nd and 3rd centuries. The Mishnah was compiled there in A.D. 200; Origen, the great Greek Christian scholar, lived at Caesarea ca. A.D. 280; Jerome, the greatest Latin Christian scholar of his day, lived at Bethlehem in the late 4th and early 5th century.

The Muslim Arabs conquered Jerusalem in A.D. 637 and Palestine came under the rule of the Ottoman Turks. Between 1096 and 1099 the Crusaders from Europe began coming, captured Jerusalem, and set up a Christian kingdom which lasted about one hundred years. The land was retaken by Muslims under Saladin of Egypt and was ruled by his successors for some 300-400 years. In 1517 Palestine was once again conquered by the Ottoman Turks and remained under their rule for the next 400 years.

During all these centuries the *Palestinian people* were never a "nation" with their own centralized government and infrastructure. They were Semitic and Arab genetically, and Muslim theologically, but socially and culturally they were an amalgamation of nomadic sheikdoms much like their Arabic brothers east and south of them (the Arabic emirates).

At the beginning of the 20th century a fervent nationalism, initiated in Turkey by the "Young Turks," also took root among the Palestinian Arabs and other Arab emirates which portended revolt against Turkish rule. Questions of language, particularly in education, as well as issues of autonomy for the Arab provinces, became matters of contention. The Ottoman establishment dealt with the "revolt" quickly and harshly. In 1915 eleven Arab nationalist leaders were hanged in Beirut. In May 1916 another 20 Arab leaders, including two from Palestine, were hanged for their participation in an attempted Arab revolt which had been encouraged by Britain.

When World War I began, the Ottoman Turks took the side of Germany and Austria-Hungary. Many Arabs felt that by aiding Britain they could bolster their claim to independence. The British promised the Palestinian Arabs independence for their help, but secretly they had agreed with France that they would occupy and rule Transjordan and Iraq while France would occupy and rule Lebanon and Syria and that an international coalition of the victorious nations of WW I would administer Palestine until a peace conference could decide its fate.

On April 25, 1920, the conference of European powers at San Remo allotted the mandate for Palestine (including Transjordan) to Britain, and on July 1 the British military government was replaced by a British civil administration headed by Sir Herbert Samuel, *a Zionist sympathizer.* The Palestine mandate, which now contained provisions for a Jewish national home in Palestine, was ratified by the League of Nations on July 24, 1922.

The Arabs adamantly rejected this mandate as a violation of the Covenant of the League of Nations and the principle of self-determination that it enshrined, especially Article 22, which provisionally, but specifically, recognized Palestine and other Arab regions as "independent nations." In 1919 Arabs were still an overwhelming majority of the population, more than 90 percent. The British government in Palestine determined the number of immigrants allowed in Palestine but they allowed the Jewish Agency to issue the visas. Under this arrangement, the number of Jewish immigrants to Palestine rose from 5,000 in 1920 to nearly 34,000 in 1925, and soared again in 1933-1940 so that in 1944 it was estimated there were 565,000 Jews in Palestine.[1]

Zionism is the movement that gave impetus to the establishment of the modern secular State of Israel in the land of Palestine. According to some opinions, Jews have been returning to "their land" ever since the ancient exiles at the hands of the Assyrians, Babylonians and Romans. Evidently individual Jews and small increments of them migrated to Palestine during the "Spanish" Jewish period. Notable among those was Judah Halevi (A.D. 10 5-1141). Halevi, famous as a Jewish poet and philosopher, was born in Toledo, Spain, and traveled extensively in Spain and Egypt. We mention him here because of his later polemic entitled, *Kuzari*, which was named after the king of the **Khazars**. The Khazars play an extremely significant role in the later history of Zionism (see Appendix D following).

Judah Halevi, disillusioned with any possibility of the Jews ever being secure as expatriates in foreign lands, with an intense longing for some redemption of his people, and influenced by strong messianic fervor until he dreamt that the redemption would come in the year A.D. 1130, decided to emigrate to *Erez Israel*. In September 1140 he arrived in Alexandria, Egypt. Friends tried to convince him to stay in Alexandria, and some believe the evidence indicates he died and was buried in Alexandria. Others believe a legend that he boarded a ship bound for Israel, arriving there in 1141. According to the legend he finally reached the city of Jerusalem, but, as he kissed its stones, a passing Arab horseman trampled him to death just as he was reciting his elegy, *"Ziyyon ha-lo tishali."* Judah Halevi's apology, *Kuzari*, was to explain why the **Khazars** chose Judaism as their national religion rather than Christianity or Islam. The *Kuzari* exercised a great influence on Judaism throughout its subsequent history, particularly in Kabbalistic (mystical) circles. His contention was that Christianity and Islam, while recognizing Jewish elements in both, could not base their doctrines on an unequivocal historical revelation such as the one granted to Israel at Sinai, when 600,000 people were granted the experience of prophecy where God spoke to man and commanded him to observe the laws of the Torah. According to Halevi, wherever Christianity and Islam diverge from the Torah or supplant it, they are falsehoods which cannot claim historical validity.[2]

The article on "Zionism" consumes 149 pages in the *Encyclopedia Judaica*.[3] The article includes subjects on "Zionist Organization of America," "Zionist Socialist Workers Party" (in Russia), and "Christian Zionism."

From about A.D. 1500 until 1800 there were sporadic attempts by self-appointed Jewish prophets urging Jews to emigrate to the land of Palestine. But even these incidents faded as the Enlightenment with its stress on religious tolerance swept Europe. Some Jewish leaders (e.g., Moses Mendelssohn, 1729-1786) attempted to win over Jews to modern Western civilization. In the early nineteenth century interest in Zionism and a Jewish state in Palestine was kept alive mainly by Christian chiliasts (premillennialists and dispensationalists) whose eschatology viewed the restoration of Jews to the "Holy Land" as a "sign" of the coming millennial kingdom of Christ.

The impetus toward creating a Jewish state enjoyed a revival among Jews in the late nineteenth century because of the severe persecution they met in Russia, Poland and other East European countries. In Austria there lived a journalist by the name of Theodor Herzl. The origin of modern Zionism is attributed to Theodor Herzl. He spent vast sums of money bribing Turkish officials in order to gain the Sultan's approval of a Jewish settlement in Palestine.[4]

Antisemitism was, at this time in history, strongest in Austria. In 1897 Herzl convened the first "Zionist Congress" at Basel, Switzerland. Soon the movement was centered at Vienna, Austria, where Herzl published a weekly called *Die Welt* (The World). In his novel, *Altneuland* ("Old-New World"), Herzl depicted future life in an ideal Palestine in terms of a modern secular state, *neutral in religion* and in cooperation and cohabitation with Arab Palestinians. The headquarters of Zionism was transferred to Germany in 1904 when Herzl died at age 44. Its great membership came from Russia (Khazarian Jews who were Gentile proselytes), and at that time only a small minority of Judaism favored Zionism. Some wanted a strictly orthodox religious homeland. Herzl's followers wanted a modern political state. There was much conflict and disagreement within the movement at this point.

After the start of World War II, the leadership of Zionism moved to the United States. In 1942 a conference in New York City demanded the founding of a Jewish state in all of Palestine with unlimited immigration. The United Nations, on November 29, 1947, proposed "partition" of Palestine between Arabs and Jews. The issue was settled in armed conflict between Arabs and Zionists called by some Jews their "War of Independence." The state of Israel was proclaimed on May 14, 1948, and, with some reservations, recognized by the United States. The "partitioning" gave the modern state of Israel the land of Palestine, essentially that which was occupied by their ancient ancestors under Joshua *except* an area approximately 30 miles wide and 75 miles long known as the "West Bank." This region is in the very center of modern Israel and borders on the west at Jerusalem and on the east at the Jordan River. It was allotted to the Palestinians.

The secular state of Israel has attempted to mold Jews from all over the world, who have grown up as citizens of differing cultures, into one nation. At the same time it has tried, at times by diplomacy but at other times by militarily defending Jewish citizens who became "squatters" on Palestinian properties, to assimilate a large Arab population into its political and economic structure. Israelis have aimed to accomplish this without sacrificing what they claim to be their values and religious and cultural traditions which initiated the Zionist rebirth.

The total population of Palestine in 1982 was slightly more than 4 million people; 84 percent were Jewish and the remaining 16 percent were mainly Arab

(Palestinian). The population density is 603.2 persons per square mile; 80 percent are urban and 20 percent rural. Modern Israel is a modified parliamentary state. The Knesset (parliament) is the only legislative body. It has 120 members elected every four years through proportional representation. The Knesset elects the Prime Minister, who heads the cabinet. All local authorities are elected by their respective communities. Their Supreme Court heads the civil and criminal judicial system. Judaism and Islam have independent courts with jurisdiction over religious matters, including marriage and divorce.

Israel has no written constitution. They consider their laws, as they enact them, to be an "evolving constitution." Political life is organized around two main political parties, "Labor" and "Likud." Until 1977 the Labor (liberal) and its ally, the Worker's party, dominated Israeli governments. In 1977 the Likud (conservative) party with religious and small right-wing allies, took control of the government. The core of the Likud party is a coalition of Zionist Revisionists, founded in 1948 by former Prime Minister Menachem Begin. The Labor party generally seeks accommodation with the Palestinian Arabs through territorial compromise and linking the West Bank with Jordan. Likud stands for an unpartitioned land of Palestine based on their imagined "biblical mandate" for possession of *all* the land.

Israel's economic structure is basically socialistic. The Histadrut, or General Federation of Labor, which includes most Israeli workers, is more than a trade union. Its health system insures 83 percent of the population, and, along with the Israeli government, runs most of the hospitals. It also owns factories, banks, and construction companies as well as wholesale and retail cooperatives. The Kibbutz communities were actually "communes" and ideological and physical experiments in radical socialism. They are not as popular now as they were in the 1950s and 1960s because they were found to be impractical and unworkable.

The immigration of Zionists from 1920 to 1948 led to waves of Arab rioting in 1920, 1921, 1929, 1936 to 1939, and to a larger scale warfare in 1947. While the Jews grudgingly accepted the partitioning of Palestine into Jewish and Arab states, the Palestinian Arabs and neighboring Arab countries unequivocally rejected the United Nations resolution.

The new Zionist state prevailed against the objections and military resistance of the Arab states with extensive financial aid and political pressure in her favor from the United States, Great Britain and other western powers in the United Nations. War broke out along the Gaza strip in April 1956; the 6-day war in the 1960s followed; next, war with Egypt in 1973; and war with Lebanon in the 1980s. With the establishment of modern "Zionist" Israel and the partitioning of the land of Palestine, the Middle East has been a firestorm of unabated political intrigue, racial

hatred, war, and terrorism. The Zionism of those who succeeded Herzl has no tolerance for Palestinians living alongside Jews in the land of Palestine as the following
quotations cited by Pike in *Israel: Our Duty . . . Our Dilemma*, reveals:

> "The Jews energetically reject the idea of fusion with the other nationalities
> and cling firmly to their historical hope of world empire." [Max Mandelstam,
> World Zionist Comgress, 1898]
>
> "Jerusalem is not the capital of Israel and world Jewry, it aspires to become the
> spiritual center of the world." [David Ben-Gurion, *The Jewish Chronicle*, 1949]
>
> "In Jerusalem, the United Nations (a truly United Nations) will build a Shrine
> of the Prophets to serve the federated union of all continents, this will be the seat
> of the Supreme Court of Mankind, to settle all controversies among the federated
> continents, as prophesied by Isaiah." [David Ben-Gurion, *Look Magazine*, 1962]
>
> "The Jewish people cannot ever be destroyed, but rather they and their God of
> History will emerge in days to come triumphant over the evils and the foolishness
> of all other nations. Zion will and must emerge as the mount to which all other
> peoples turn." [Rabbi Meir Kahane, *The Jewish Press*, 1973]
>
> "You shall have no pity on them until we shall have destroyed their so-called
> Arab culture, on the ruins of which we shall build our own civilization."
> [Menachem Begin, quoted at a Tel Aviv Conference by *The South African
> Observer*, 1997]
>
> "Some years ago, the prominent journalist Russell Warren Howe asked Begin
> whether he considered himself 'the father' of terrorism in the Middle East. Begin
> answered expansively, 'No, in the entire world.'" [Georgie Anne Geyer, *The
> Washington Star*, 1981][5]

Christian Zionism is rooted in the beginnings of chiliastic theology after the
Reformation (A.D. 1515). Insisting on a literal interpretation of the prophecies of
both the OT and the NT, some of the pietistic Protestant groups and certain English
Puritans held that the Second Coming of Christ was imminent in their day and that
he would rule from Jerusalem for 1000 years. The early Christian chiliasts not only
anticipated the return of the Jews to their land but also their conversion to
Christianity as conditions and "signs of the time" prior to the Second Coming of
Christ. A few Christian groups made this belief the center of their theology. In 1830
the Plymouth Brethren were founded in England by John N. Darby (1800-1882)
whose doctrine of dispensationalist premillennialism asserted that *all* the biblical
prophecies relate to the return of the Jewish people to their homeland prior to the
Second Coming of Christ. Before that, however, according to Darby, the Jews and
all the other nations will be judged during a period of tribulation, after which Jesus
and the Jewish remnant will rule over all the nations from Jerusalem.

Numerous Protestant fundamentalist churches and pseudo-Christian sects adopted this outlook and continue to promote it today. From their founding in 1844, the Christadelphians supported the return of the Jews to the land of Israel. Founded in 1830, by Joseph Smith, the Mormons held that Jews would return to their land as "a sign of the time" of Christ's Second Coming. The Adventist movement, founded in 1830, also views the return of the Jews to the land of Israel as a fulfillment of their eschatological beliefs, and some Adventists have moved their base of operations to Israel. In 1851 Clarinda Minor and her followers moved from America to Israel (near Jaffa) and formed an agricultural settlement to await the imminent coming of Christ. In 1866, Rev. G. Adams and a group of Americans from the Church of the Messiah moved near Jaffa (ancient Joppa) also believing the second advent of Jesus was impending. Both groups failed and disbanded.

The most famous American Zionist was William Blackstone (1841-1933) of Chicago, who wrote *Jesus Is Coming Soon*. In his book he insisted that the land of Israel belonged to the Jews and that they would reclaim it as a sign of the Second Coming of Christ. He attempted a political realization of his ideas through memoranda to presidents of the United States, Benjamin Harrison in 1891, and Woodrow Wilson in 1916. He demanded American intervention for the return of the Jews to the land of Israel as a solution to the czarist anti-Jewish persecutions. Hundreds of eminent Americans signed these petitions.

In 1932 the American Palestine Committee was founded to promote Zionist aims. Its members included prominent public figures, statesmen, and officials. The Christian Council of Palestine was founded in 1942 and had a membership of 3000 clergymen in 1946, mostly from liberal churches. The latter two organizations merged in 1946 as the American Christian Palestine Committee, which had at that time a very influential membership of 15,000. [6]

Countless so-called "statesmen," historians, theologians, idealogues, military experts, geo-politicians, moralists, celebrities, and economists from the Western bloc have lined up on the side of Zionist Israel's "right" to move into the land of Palestine and dispossess hundreds of thousands of Palestinian Arabs of territories in which they had lived for almost two millennia! But such opinion has not been unanimous throughout the world. Granted, a Zionist-Israel state in immediate proximity to the world's largest oil deposits is pragmatically strategic (politically and economically), but is it "mandated" or sanctioned by the Bible? Perhaps, more importantly, is it *right*?

By the precepts of the Old Testament prophets concerning international imperialism, Zionist dispossession of Palestinians from their lands stands under the judgment of God (See Amos 1:13-15; Obad. 1-16; Nahum 3:1-7; Hab. 2:1-11, et al.). Evaluated by the consequences — relentless bloodshed and destruction of property by both Palestinians and Israelis, it is a disastrous and tragic mistake.

Zionism has been no "balm for Gilead." It has been no boon to world peace. It is not God's revealed plan for the redemption of the world — not even a part of his plan. God's program for peace and redemption is in the Person of Jesus Christ. Only when men and women are united to Christ by faith and obedience does love and reconciliation reign. Faith in Christ is produced through the hearing of the gospel (Rom. 10:14-17).

Zionist invasion and occupation of the land of Palestine has *no biblical mandate*. This is apparent in a few Scriptures:

a. Jews have not been "careful to do all the words" of God's law, particularly the admonitions to accept their Messiah when he came. Their divine "mandate" to the land was always conditioned upon this (e.g., Lev. 18:28; 20:22; Deut. 28:15-68; Jer. 27:10; 44:22; Hos. 9:3; Amos 9:9; Zeph. 3:1-7, et al.).

b. Jewish rejection of the Messiah was *the ultimate* sin and resulted in the pronouncement of Christ's judgment that their "house" was to be forsaken and their "land" desolate (Dan. 9:24; Matt. 23:29-39; Luke 19:41-44).

c. Jesus predicted the dispossession of the Jews by God in his parables (Matt. 21:33-46 and parallels; Matt. 22:1-10).

d. Jesus predicted the Jews would be led captive into all the nations and be trodden down until the times of the Gentiles were fulfilled (Luke 21:24).

e. The apostle Paul, writing of the Jews nationally, said that God's wrath came upon them *to the end* (i.e., completely). From the divine perspective Judaism cannot be revived, although individual Jews may be reconciled to God by accepting the gospel of Christ (1 Thess. 2:16).

f. Since the Messiah has completed redemption, God has dispensed forever with a special *place* of worship and any *other system of worship* (John 4:21-24; Acts 17:24-25; Heb. 9:26; 10:12-14).

g. Paul's Epistle to the Galatians is unequivocal that "in Christ" there are no more racial, social, or theological distinctions ever again. Those who are in Christ are "Abraham's offspring" (Gal. 3:26-29; 6:15-16; see also Rom. 4:9-15; 9:6-13).

h. True "Zion" is the church of Christ, and true "Israel" is composed of those who are "new creations" (Heb. 12:22; Gal. 6:15-16).

i. Christianity is the *only* kingdom that *cannot be shaken*. Judaism is no lasting city, and to go to Christ one must go outside the "camp" of Judaism (Heb. 12:28; 13:13-14).

j. The twelve tribes of Israel in Revelation 7:1-8 cannot refer to a literal return of OT Israel to Palestine because that list leaves out the tribes of Dan and Ephraim, and inserts the tribes of Levi and Joseph not originally given an inheritance.

k. It is *remarkably significant* that no NT writer mentions a future return of the Jews to the land of Palestine. Obviously the return of the Jews to the land as it was promised in the Old Testament had already occurred literally in the restoration of the Jews from Babylonian captivity, and occurred figuratively in the establishment of the church of Christ on the Day of Pentecost, Acts 2.

l. Daniel clearly teaches that God would *finish his work with the Jews* in the redemption of mankind 490 years after the "going forth of the word to rebuild" Jerusalem. From 457 B.C. to A.D. 34 is 491 years; the discrepancy of one additional year added to the "490" is accounted for due to the fact that there is no year zero ("0"). The stoning of Stephen and the initial taking of the gospel to Gentiles occurred approximately A.D. 34 (Acts 7:54–8:40).

m. Isaiah predicted that God would establish a "new" nation before the "old" one passed away and that the new would be established with one stroke. A land and a nation was brought forth with one stroke before the old passed away on the Day of Pentecost, A.D. 30 (Isa. 66:7ff; Acts 2:14-47).

This does *not* mean, of course, that some who call themselves Jews today *will not* and *have not* returned to the land of Palestine. They may even build a new temple there some day. But it *does* mean that as any of them go back, they do so entirely apart from any covenanted purpose or "biblical mandate." Their repossession of the land is entirely outside of Scripture prophecy. No Scripture blessing is promised for a project of that kind. It may be that in years to come the Israelis will possess a larger part, or even all, of Palestine. But if they do, they will secure it as other nations secure property, through negotiation, purchase, or conquest — *not by virtue of any as yet unfulfilled prophecies in the Bible.*

Arthur Koestler, himself an Eastern-European Jew, writes that it is a *fact*

> that the large majority of surviving Jews in the world is of Eastern European . . . mainly of Khazar . . . origin . . . their ancestors came not from the Jordan but from the Volga, not from Canaan but from the Caucasus, once believed to be the cradle of the Aryan race; genetically they are more closely related to the Hun, Uigur and Magyar tribes than to the seed of Abraham, Isaac and Jacob . . . . then the term "anti-Semitism" would become void of meaning, based on a misapprehension shared by both the killers and their victims. The story of the Khazar Empire, as it slowly emerges from the past, begins to look like the most cruel hoax which history has ever perpetrated.[7]

Zionism travels under false colors, whether wittingly or unwittingly, and shares in the responsibility for nearly three centuries of terrorism and bloodshed in the Middle East and throughout the world. Because it failed to recognize and identify its origins in Caucasian-Gentile (Khazarian) ancestry it ought to bear some responsibility for allowing the victimization of six million "Jews" in the Nazi holocaust. That is apparently what Koestler means by "the most cruel hoax which history has ever perpetrated."

Notes

[1]Rashid Khalidi and Phyllis Bennis, "Palestine, Ancient," *Colliers Encyclopedia*, Vol. 18 (1995), pp. 364B-365.

[2]*Encyclopedia Judaica*, Vol. 10, pp. 356-366.

[3]Ibid., pp. 1031-1180.

[4]H.D. Leuner, "The Tragedy of the Herzl Family," *The Hebrew Christian*, Vol. L, No. 4, Winter 1977, 152-155.

[5]Theodore W. Pike, *Israel: Our Duty... Our Dilemma* (Oregon City, OR: Pike, 1984), pp. 198-199.

[6]*Encyclopedia Judaica*, Vol. 16, pp. 1152-1155.

[7]Arthur Koestler, *The Thriteenth Tribe* (New York: Random House, 1976), p. 17. Mr. Koestler's book received a very favorable review for its historical documentation in the *Wall Street Journal* of Aug. 11, 1976.

THE KHAZARS AND MODERN JUDAISM

Not all who claim to be Israeli are descended from Abraham (See Rom. 9:6-7).

By the time you finish reading Appendix D we hope to have given you pause for more than a perfunctory attitude toward a fascinating and consequential body of research into the issue of "Who is *really* a Jew?"

Jacob Gartenhaus, born a "Jew" in Austria, educated there in rabbinical schools, wrote in a national periodical that no Jew today can trace his ancestry back beyond two or three hundred years. It is therefore impossible to document pure Jewish lineage. [1]

Fifty thousand black people from East Central Africa, called "Falashas," sought citizenship in Zionist Israel. They said they had practiced Judaism since 600 B.C., and they claimed to be descendants of King Solomon and the Queen of Sheba. They said they observed *all* the Jewish rites, sacrifices, and festivals except Hanukkah. [2] Are these people Jews with all the rights and privileges to the alleged heirs of the OT promises and prophecies?

But the most astonishing data concerning Judaism to be made public in recent years is that most East-European Jews, or Ashkenazim Jews (i.e., Polish, Hungarian, Czechoslovakian, Yugoslavian, and Austrian Jews) are *not really* descendants of Abraham, but descendants of the Caucasian **Khazars** who became converts or proselytes to Judaism about A.D. 740. The Khazars were Gentiles from south Russia! They were not even as closely related to the Jews as the Semitic Arabs!

Numerous modern encyclopedias, including the prestigious *Encyclopedia Britannica*, have articles concerning the Khazars. But the most thorough and best documented information on these ancient Caucasians is to be found in *The Thirteenth Tribe*, by Arthur Koestler. *The Wall Street Journal*, reviewing the thesis of Mr. Koestler's book concerning the Caucasian ancestry of today's Western Jews, said:

> Though familiar to few other than scholars, it is not a new question but arises from a large body of scholary inquiry, Jewish, and non-Jewish, for over 100 years, having its roots in many ancient chronicles and histories. It was asserted in 1944 by A. N. Poliak, Professor of Medieval Jewish History at Tel Aviv University.[3]

Mr. Koestler was born in 1905 in Budapest. He was a foreign correspondent for various European newspapers in the Middle East, Paris, Berlin, Russia and Spain. He has been honored with many awards for his contributions to European culture. His works are republished in a collected edition of twenty volumes. Mr. Koestler begins:

> The country of the Khazars, a people of Turkish stock, occupied a strategic key position at the vital gateway between the Black Sea and the Caspian, where the great eastern powers of the period confronted each other. It acted as a buffer protecting Byzantium against invasions by the lusty barbarian tribesmen of the northen steppes — Bulgars, Magyars, Pechenegs, etc. — and, later, the Vikings and the Russians. But equally, of even more importance both from the point of view of Byzantine diplomacy and of European history, is the fact that the Khazar armies effectively blocked the Arab avalanche in its most devastating early stages, and thus prevented the Muslim conquest of Eastern Europe.[4]

Some scholars believe their origins are from the nomadic tribes associated with Attila the Hun (A.D. 400-550).[5] Arthur Koestler cites numerous other Jewish scholars who have concluded that the preponderance of Eastern European "Jews" are descended from the proselyted Caucasian Khazars. He cites, particularly, the work of A. N. Poliak, Professor of Mediaeval Jewish History at Tel Aviv University, entitled, *Khazaria*, as one of the most "radical" propositions concerning the Khazar origins of Jewry.[6] Nesta Webster in the 1920s, and a few other scholars such as H. von Kutschera, had expounded the concept of the Khazarian origin of Ashkenazim Jewry. Their conclusions were dismissed as "antisemitic" until Koestler, a liberal Jew with impeccable academic credentials, made the same claim.

The Jewish encyclopedias, as well as the *Encyclopedia Britannica*, recount the Khazarians' history and their conversion to Judaism, but they do not, like Koestler, on the basis of new information, follow through concerning the forced migration of the Khazarian "Jews" into Eastern Europe. Koestler cites the article in *Encyclopedia Judaica* on the Khazars as "written with the obvious intent to avoid upsetting believers in the dogma of the Chosen Race."[7]

These Khazarians, after the Hun empire faded from history, apparently built an empire in southern Russia that lasted for nearly four centuries. Soviet archaeologists unearthed evidence for a relatively advanced civilization in that area, but the Soviets, in order to minimize the contributions of Khazarian "Jews" to Russian culture, submerged Sarkel, famous fortress and priceless archaeological site of Khazarian history, under the waters of the Tsimlyansk reservoir.[8]

The conversion of the Khazars to an unadulterated Judaism is unique in history. What was their motivation?

> At the beginning of the eighth century the world was polarized between the two super-powers representing Christianity and Islam. Their ideological doctrines were welded to power-politics . . . . The Khazar Empire represented a Third Force, which had proved equal to either of them . . . . But it could only maintain its independence by accepting neither Christianity nor Islam — for either choice would have automatically subordinated it to the authority of the Roman Emperor or the Caliph of Baghdad.[9]

The contact the Khazars had with Christianity and Islam revealed to them that their pagan shamanism was barbaric and incapable of producing the more civilized benefits that seemed to accrue from the two religions vying to assimilate them into their folds. The Khazars were well acquainted with Jews and their religion. For at least a hundred years prior to their adoption of Judaism (in A.D. 740) there had been Jews taking refuge among them from the persecutions of Jews in the Byzantine Empire to the far west.

In A.D. 740 the Khan (ruler) of the Khazars summoned representatives of Christianity, Islam and Judaism to his presence and instructed each of them to declare the evidence for, and the tenets of, their religion. According to the Khazarian literature, the Jewish representative poisoned the Muslim spokesman prior to the debate. The Khazarian Khan reasoned that the religion to select would be the one that embraced doctrines from all three presentations. Ultimately the Khan chose Judaism.

For over 400 years, well into the thirteenth century, a proselyted Judaism was rigidly practiced by several million Khazars in that vast region north of the Caucasus Mountains between the Caspian and Black Seas which included an area as far north as where the modern Ukrainian cities of Kiev and Kharkov are located. They became fluent in the Hebrew language they studied the Talmud and Torah, anticipated the coming of Messiah, and advocated the retaking of Jerusalem from the Moslems in order to return to "the land of their forefathers." Koestler writes, "Thus the Judaization of the Khazars was a gradual process which, triggered by political expediency, slowly penetrated into the deeper strata of their minds and eventually produced the Messianism of their period of decline. Their religious commitment survived the collapse of their state, and persisted, as we shall see, in the Khazar-Jewish settlements of Russia and Poland."[10]

Much of what we now know about the Khazars is gleaned from "Khazar Correspondence" which is an exchange of letters between Hasdai In Shaprut, the Jewish chief minister of the Caliph of Cordoba, and Joseph, King of the Khazars which took place afer A.D. 954 and before 961. There is an interesting passage in one of the letters concerning the date of the coming of the Messiah:

> We have our eyes on the sages of Jerusalem and Babylon, and although we live far away from Zion, we have nevertheless heard that the calculations are erroneous owing to the great profusion of sins, and we know nothing, only the Eternal knows how to keep the count. We have nothing to hold on to only the prophecies of *Daniel* [our emphasis], and may the Eternal speed up our Deliverance . . . .[11]

About a century after the Khazar Correspondence, Jehuda Halevi wrote his now venerated work called *Kuzari* (referring to the Khazars). It is mainly a book proposing a view that the Jewish nation is the only mediator between God and the rest of mankind. At the end of history, all other nations will be converted to Judaism; and the conversion of the Khazars appears as a symbol or "prophecy" of that ultimate event.[12] This, of course, indicates that Halevi had either read the "Khazar Correspondence," or had other sources of information about the Khazars. Koestler notes, "A warrior-nation of Turkish Jews must have seemed to the rabbis as strange as a circumcized unicorn."

There is even a Christian source on the Khazars that antedates the "Khazar Correspondence." About A.D. 864, a Westphalian monk, Christian Druthmar of Aquitania, wrote a Latin treatise *Exposito in Evangelium Mattei*, in which he reported that "there exist people under the sky in regions where no Christians can be found, whose name is Gog and Magog, and who are Huns; among them is one called the Gazari, who are circumcized and observe Judaism in its entirety."[13] About the time Druthmar wrote what he knew about the Jewish Khazars, the Byzantine Emperor sent no less a figure than St. Cyril, "apostle of the Slavs," and designer of the Cyrillic (Slavic, Russian) alphabet, to convert the Khazars to Christianity. He had no success whatever among the Khazars.

By the ninth century, the Vikings were sending their boats full of Norse warriors down the Volga and Don Rivers to attempt a conquest of Khazarian territories and peoples. The Khazars were as fierce warriors as the Vikings and were successful in repelling all intrusions. The particular tribe of Vikings roaming into this area were called "Rhos" by the Byzantines, and "Varangians" by the Arabs. Toynbee thinks the word "Rhos" (which others have called "Rus") is from a Swedish word "rodher" which means "rowers." They apparently inhabited the far northern reaches of Russia near Novgorod (just south of Saint Petersburg).

The "Rus" Norsemen (forefathers of modern Russians), gradually gained access to the Khazars — what they had not gained by violence — through trading and cultural interchanges. Then the Rus formed an alliance with Byzantine forces and together in A.D. 1016 they invaded the Khazarian Empire and forced its disintegration. This brought to an end one of the most powerful and strategic nations of the ancient world. The *National Geographic*, March, 1985, p. 288, presents a fascinating review of the contribution of the Rus to modern Russia and how "they reached the Volga, where the entrenched *Jewish Khazars* and Muslim Bulgars forced them to pay tribute for a lucrative silver trade."[14]

According to Koestler, about A.D. 950, the Khazars became interracially mingled with the Magyars who lived west of the Khazars and these people conquered and inhabited what is today called Hungary. They took their Jewish religion with them. In the twelfth century there arose in Khazaria a messianic movement, an attempt at a Jewish crusade, aimed at the conquest of Palestine by force of arms. The initiator of the movement was a Khazar Jew, Solomon ben Duji (or, Roy), aided by his son Menahem. They wrote letters to all the Jews in all the lands around them and said that the time had come in which God would gather Israel, his people from all lands, to Jerusalem, the holy city, and that Solomon Ben Duji was Elijah, and his son the Messiah. Menahem assumed the name David al-Roy, and the title of Messiah. Among the Jews of the Middle East, David al-Roy aroused fervent messianic hopes when one of his messengers instructed Baghdad Jewish citizens to assemble on a certain night on their flat roofs, when they would be flown on clouds to the Messiah's camp. Numerous Jews spent that night on their roofs awaiting the miraculous flight. It never came! David al-Roy was assassinated in his sleep by his own father-in-law, but the cult did not disband. According to one theory, the six-pointed "shield of David" which adorns the modern Israeli flag, started to become a national symbol with David al-Roy's crusade. Before that it had been used as an occult amulet along with the pentagram in pagan shamanism.

In spite of declining autonomy and a disintegration of its imperial cohesion, the Khazarian population retained their independence and their Judaic faith well into the thirteenth century. Koestler quotes S.W. Baron's work, *A Social and Religious History of the Jews, Vols. III and IV* concerning the ultimate demise of the Khazarian empire:

Its population was largely absorbed by the Golden Horde (Genghiz Khan and the Mongols) which had established the centre of its empire in Khazar territory. But before and after the Mongol upheaval the Khazars sent many offshoots into the unsubdued Slavonic lands, *helping ultimately to build up the great Jewish centres of eastern Europe.*[15]

While the "offshoots" to which Baron refers helped form the "cradle" of the majority of modern Jewry (the Ashkenazim), that "cradle" had already been forming by Khazarian immigrants into Eastern European territories long before the destruction of the Khazar state by the Mongols. By the time of the Mongolian conquests of Khazarian territory, Khazar communities were well established in Hungary and the Ukraine, in the Balkans, Southern Russia, in Slavic lands, in Lithuania, but most of all, in Poland!

About A.D. 962 numerous Slavonic tribes united under the leadership of the strongest among them which happened to be the *Polans*, from which the Polish state was formed. The Polish state began just as the Khazar empire was disintegrating. And it is significant that Jews play a decisive part in the birth of the Polish kingdom. Legend has it that this alliance elected a king to rule them named Abraham Prokovnik, a Jew, who soon abdicated the crown in favor of a native peasant named Piast, founder of the historic Piast dynasty which ruled Poland for four centuries (A.D. 962-1370).[16]

Whether the legend is accurate or not, the Khazars, because of their work ethic and expertise as artisans, merchants, and builders were welcomed as settlers within Polish territory. The Khazars set about to build Jewish synagogues. In one Polish city there were five synagogues and most towns and villages had at least two synagogues. There were Byzantine Christians in Poland, but Khazarian Jews continued to flee from their former homeland in the east until in the fifteenth and sixteenth centuries Poland had become the "new Khazaria" with over a half-million Khazarian Jews settled there.

The *Jewish Encyclopedia*, in its article on Jewish population "Statistics," indicates a total Jewish population of the world during the Middle Ages of about 1,000,000. Koestler cites Poliak, Kutschera, and Webster who have all documented that during the Middle Ages the majority of those who professed the Judaic faith were Khazars. A large part of the Khazars went to Poland, Lithuania, Hungary and the Balkans, where they founded that Eastern Jewish community which in its turn became the dominant majority of world Jewry known as the Ashkenazim Jews.

In the late seventeenth century the Caucasian-Khazar "Jews" living in Poland came into contact with "true" Israelite descendants of Abraham from Spain, Germany, and France. As a result of the Moslem invasions and the Jewish exodus

from Babylon in the eleventh century, most "true" Jews had settled in the lands surrounding the Mediterranean — Alexandria in Egypt, Greece, and Italy, but mostly
in Spain. These Jews were called Sephardim. The Sephardim were very few in number in the northern parts of Europe, i.e., Germany, Belgium, Holland (even as they
are today). Despite the claims by Jewish historians that mass migrations of
Sephardic Jews moved east into Khazar territories as a result of the Crusades, the
Black Death and the Spanish Inquisition, Koestler documents extensively the
absence of any historic basis for such allegations. This is what Koestler has to say
about any and all alleged Jewish migrations from the German Rhineland eastward
toward Poland before and after the first Crusade:

> The traditional conception of Jewish historians that the Crusade of 1096 swept like
> a broom a mass-migration of German Jews into Poland is simply a legend — or
> rather an *ad hoc* hypothesis invented because, as they knew little of Khazar histo-
> ry, they could see no other way to account for the emergence, out of nowhere, of
> this unprecedented concentration of Jews in Eastern Europe. Yet there is not a sin-
> gle mention in the contemporary sources of any migration, large or small, from the
> Rhineland further east into Germany, not to mention distant Poland.[17]

It is a matter of history that the Sephardic Jews ("true" Jews) were extremely
small in number in northern Europe from A.D. 500-1800. Koestler shows that those
Jews who did live in heavily Roman Catholic northern Europe did not flee their
homes when persecuted but simply suffered and survived the best they could. These
persecutions were so severe as to almost decimate the entire Jewish population of
western Germany, Belgium and Holland. Kutschera asks, "How, then, in these circumstances, should they have been able to lay the foundations in Poland of a mass
population so dense that at present (A.D. 1909) it outnumbers the Jews of Germany
at the rate of ten to one? It is indeed difficult to understand how the idea ever gained
ground that the eastern Jews represent immigrants from the West, and especially
from Germany.[18]

Ultimately, the first widespread contact between Khazars and Jews of the west
occurred as a result of the antisemitic massacres in Poland of 1648-1649 which
caused a huge influx of Khazar migration out of Poland to the west. This mass
movement of Ashkenazim Jews (Khazarian Jews) from Poland and Hungary toward
Germany and Holland in the west continued almost three centuries until the Second
World War. This migration, which began about 1650, is responsible for the Jewish
settlements in western Europe, and later in England, and the United States.

Koestler reveals that a study of the Yiddish language, the language of the Polish
Khazarian Jews, also confirms the absence of Sephardic Jews in Poland. Yiddish is
a "curious amalgam" of Hebrew, medieval German, Slavonic and other elements,

written in Hebrew characters. "No linguistic components derived from the parts of Germany bordering on France are found in the Yiddish language. Not a single word from the entire list of specifically Moselle-Franconian origin . . . has found its way into the Yiddish vocabulary. . . . The history of the German Jews, of Ashkenazi Jewry, must be revised. The errors of history are often rectified by linguistic research. The conventional view of the erstwhile immigration of Ashkenazi Jews from France belongs to the category of historic errors which are awaiting correction."[19]

Theodore Pike sums up Koestler's history of the Khazars and their conversion to Judaism succinctly:

> We have the strongest evidence, then, from historic and linguistic sources, that the Ashkenazi-Khazarian population of Eastern Europe, *the source of most "Jews" today, if not 100 percent Gentile before the mid 17th century, was very near it* [emphasis ours]. With this in mind, the Jewish claim that all Jews of Eastern Europe contain at least some of the blood of Abraham becomes spurious — the crudest attempt to preserve the Ashkenazim from being as Gentile as the verdict of history decrees them to be. Rejecting history, Khazar-Jewish scholarship scrabbles for even the smallest claim to the patrimony of Abraham, since such is essential not only to the self esteem of Eastern European "Jewry," but to legitimize the present Jewish claim to Palestine — a claim which has been most insistently made by those of Khazar origin. But, as Koestler documents so formidably, the most any Eastern European "Jew" can claim with confidence is that his forefathers were *converted to Judaism out of paganism* [emphasis ours]. As Koestler (himself most likely a German Jew of Khazar origin) laconically concludes: *"The story of the Khazar Empire, as it slowly emerges from the past, begins to look like the most cruel hoax which history has ever perpetrated."* [emphasis ours].[20]

Koestler states that he is aware of a danger that his book, *The Thirteenth Tribe*, the history of Khazarian Jewry,

> may be maliciously misinterpreted as a denial of the State of Israel's right to exist. But that right is not based on the *hypothetical* [emphasis ours] origins of the Jewish people, nor on the *mythological* [emphasis ours] covenant of Abraham with God; it is based on international law — i.e., on the United Nations' decision in 1947 to partition Palestine, once a Turkish province, then a British Mandated Territory, into an Arab and a Jewish State. Whatever the Israeli citizen's racial origins, and whatever illusions they entertain about them, their State exists *de jure* and *de facto*, and cannot be undone, except by genocide.[21]

While we think the origin of the Jewish people was, originally, from Abraham and from an historical and factual covenant made by God, what Koestler says about modern Israel's right to the land of Palestine is precisely what we are contending to be the case. *There is no biblical mandate for the "Jews" to return to the land of Palestine.*

It is interesting to read Koestler's evaluation of Jewish orthodoxy and its *kulturkampf.* He maintains that

> Orthodox Jewry is a vanishing minority ... and it is the vast majority of enlightened or agnostic Jews who perpetuate the paradox [that orthodox Jewry is significant] by loyally clinging to their pseudo-national status in the belief that is their duty to preserve the Jewish tradition. ... Talmud, Kabbala, and the bulky tomes of biblical exegesis are practically unknown to the contemporary Jewish public. ... to sum up, the Jews of our day have no cultural tradition in common, merely certain habits and behaviour-patterns, derived by social inheritance from the traumatic experience of the ghetto, and from a religion which the majority does not practice or believe in, but which nevertheless confers on them a pseudo-national status. [22]

Oh, church of Jesus Christ, it is our *duty* to winsomely, firmly, and eagerly proclaim the gospel to every creature under heaven, which includes Jews, both real and Khazarian!

Location of Origin of the Khazar Jews

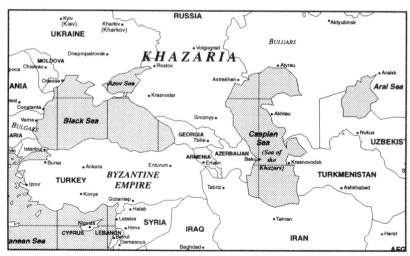

Modern names are in san-serif type; historical names in *Times italic*
More names of surrounding tribes and details of the area rivers and mountains are shown on the original map in Koestler's book.

Notes

[1]Jacob Gartenhaus, "The Jewish Conception of the Messiah," *Christianity Today* (March 13, 1970): 520-522.

[2]Glenn Everett, "Black Jews: A House Divided," *Christianity Today* (December 7, 1973): 52-53.

[3]Edmund Fuller, "A Jewish Nation in the Caucasus," *Wall Street Journal* (Aug. 11, 1976), p. 1.

[4]Koestler, *The Thirteenth Tribe*, p. 13.

[5]*Encyclopedia Judaica, Vol. 10*, p. 944.

[6]Koestler, *The Thirteenth Tribe*, p. 16.

[7]Ibid., p. 16.

[8]Ibid., p. 85.

[9]Ibid., p. 58.

[10]Ibid., p. 74.

[11]Ibid., p. 75.

[12]Ibid., p. 78.

[13]Ibid., p. 81.

[14]Pike, *Israel*, p. 299.

[15]Koestler, *The Thirteenth Tribe*, p. 141.

[16]Ibid., p. 147.

[17]Ibid., p. 164.

[18]Ibid., pp. 162-168.

[19]Ibid., pp. 172-173.

[20]Pike, *Israel*, p. 303.

[21]Koestler, *The Thirteenth Tribe*, p. 223.

[22]Ibid., pp. 224-226.

select bibliography

Allis, Oswald T. *Prophecy and the Church*. Philadelphia: The Presbyterian and Reformed Publishing Company, 1945.

Asheri, Michael. *Living Jewish: The Lore and Law of Being a Jew*. New York: Everest House, 1978.

Aune, David E. *Prophecy in Early Christianity and the Ancient Mediterranean World*. Grand Rapids: Eerdmans, 1983.

Baker, William W. *The Theft of a Nation*. Las Vegas: Defenders Publications, 1982.

Berkhof, L. *The Kingdom of God*. Grand Rapids: Eerdmans, 1951.

Bible Readings for the Home. Mountain View, CA: Pacific Press Publishing Association, 1942.

Boatman, Russell. *What the Bible Says about the End Times*. Joplin, MO: College Press, 1980.

Boettner, Loraine. *The Millennium*. Philadelphia: The Presbyterian and Reformed Publishing Company, 1972.

Brown, David. *Christ's Second Coming: Will It Be Premillennial?* Reprint. Rosemead, CA: Old Paths Book Club, 1953.

Bruce, F.F. *Israel and the Nations: From the Exodus to the Fall of the Second Temple*. Grand Rapids: Eerdmans, 1969.

Butler, Paul T. *Daniel*. Third Edition. Joplin, MO: College Press, 1982.

_____. *Twenty-Six Lessons on Revelation*. 2 Vols. Joplin, MO: College Press, 1982.

_____. *Isaiah*. 3 Vols. Joplin, MO: College Press, 1975-1978.

3

_____. *Minor Prophets: Hosea, Joel, Amos, Obadiah, Jonah*. Joplin, MO: College Press, 1968.

_____. *The Gospel of Luke*. Joplin, MO: College Press, 1981.

Cox, William E. *Amillennialism Today*. Philadelphia: The Presbyterian and Reformed Publishing Company, 1975.

DeCarlo, Louis A. *Israel Today: Fulfillment of Prophecy?* Philadelphia: The Presbyterian and Reformed Publishing Company, 1974.

DeMar, Gary. *Last Days Madness: The Folly of Trying to Predict When Christ Will Return*. Brentwood, TN: Wolgemuth & Hyatt, 1991.

Durant, Will. *Caesar and Christ: A History of Roman Civilization and of Christianity from Their Beginnings to A.D. 325*.The Story of Civilization. Part III. New York: Simon and Schuster, 1944.

Erickson, Millard J. *Contemporary Options in Eschatology*. Grand Rapids: Baker Book House, 1977.

Farfield, Kenny. *The Prophet Motive: Examining the Reliability of the Biblical Prophets*. Nashville: Gospel Advocate, 1995.

Fairbairn, Patrick. *Exposition of Ezekiel*. Grand Rapids: Sovereign Grace, 1971.

_____. *Prophecy: Viewed in Its Respect to Its Distinctive Nature, Special Function, and Proper Interpretation*. New York: Carlton and Porter, 1866.

Feinberg, Charles L., ed. *Focus on Prophecy: Messages Delivered at the Congress on Prophecy, Convened by the American Board of Missions to the Jews at Moody Memorial Church in Chicago*.

Fields, Wilbur. *Thinking Through Thessalonians*. Joplin, MO: College Press, 1963.

Fowler, Harold. *The Gospel of Matthew*. 4 Vols. Joplin, MO: College Press, 1968-1985.

Friskney, Tom. *Strength for Victory, A Drama in Four Acts: A Commentary on the Book of Revelation*. Cincinnati: Friskney, 1986.

Froom, Leroy Edwin. *The Prophetic Faith of Our Fathers*. 4 Vols. Washington, D.C.: Review and Herald, 1950.

A Glimpse into the Future: God's Clock Is on Time. Portland: Apostolic Faith Church, n.d.

Green, Joel B. *How to Read Prophecy*. Downers Grove, IL: InterVarsity, 1984.

Hailey, Homer. *A Commentary on the Minor Prophets*. Grand Rapids: Baker, 1972.

_____. *Revelation: An Introduction and Commentary*. Grand Rapids: Baker, 1979.

Hendriksen, William. *Israel in Prophecy*. Grand Rapids: Baker, 1974.

Jenkins, Ferrell. *The Old Testament in the Book of Revelation*. Grand Rapids: Baker, 1976.

Josephus, Flavius. *The Complete Works of Flavius Josephus*. Translated by William Whiston. Philadelphia: John E. Potter & Company, n.d.

Keil, C.F. *The Prophecies of Daniel*. Biblical Commentary on the Old Testament. Grand Rapids: Eerdmans, 1950.

_____. *The Prophecies of Ezekiel*. Biblical Commentary on the Old Testament. Grand Rapids: Eerdmans, 1950.

Kimball, William R. *What the Bible Says about the Great Tribulation*. Joplin, MO: College Press, 1983.

Kik, J. Marcellus. *Matthew XXIV: An Exposition*. Philadelphia: The Presbyterian and Reformed Publishing Company, 1948.

Kligerman, Aaron. *Old Testament Messianic Prophecy*. Grand Rapids: Zondervan, 1957.

Koestler, Arthur. *The Thirteenth Tribe: The Khazar Empire and Its Heritage*. New York: Random House, 1976.

LaHaye, Tim F. *Revelation: Illustrated and Made Plain*. Grand Rapids: Zondervan, 1974.

Lindsay, Hal. *The Late Great Planet Earth*. Grand Rapids: Zondervan, 1970.

_____. *There's a New World Coming*. Santa Ana, CA: Vision House, 1973.

Mauro, Philip. *The Wonders of Bible Chronology*. Swengel, PA: Bible Truth Depot, 1961.

Newman, A.H. *A Manual of Church History*. 2 Vols. Valley Forge, PA: Judson Press, 1899.

North, Stafford. *Armageddon When?: A Reply to Hal Lindsay*. Oklahoma City: Oklahoma Christian College, 1982.

Pentecost, Dwight. *Things to Come*. Grand Rapids: Eerdmans, 1972.

Peters, George N.H. *The Theocratic Kingdom*. Vol. 1. Grand Rapids: Kregel, 1952.

Pike, Theodore Winston. *Israel: Our Duty. . .Our Dilemma*. Oregon City, OR: Big Sky Press, 1988.

Smith, James E. *What the Bible Says about the Promised Messiah*. Joplin, MO: College Press, 1984.

_____. *Ezekiel*. Joplin, MO: College Press, 1979.

Speck, Willie Wallace. *The Triumph of Faith.* Athens, AL: C.E.I. Publishing, 1961.

Strauss, James D. *The Seer, The Saviour, and The Saved: A Study of the Book of Revelation.* Joplin, MO: College Press, 1963.

Walvoord, John F. *The Millennial Kingdom.* Findlay, OH: Dunham Publishing, 1959.

Reference Works

Arndt, William F. and F. Wilbur Gingrich, eds. *A Greek-English Lexicon of the New Testament and Other Early Christian Literature.* Chicago: University of Chicago Press, 1957.

Brown, Francis, S.R. Driver, and Charles A. Briggs, eds. *A Hebrew and English Lexicon of the Old Testament.* Oxford: Clarendon Press, 1978.

Davidson, Benjamin. *The Analytical Hebrew and Chaldee Lexicon.* London: Samuel Bagster & Sons, 1967.

Green, Jan. *The Interlinear Hebrew/Greek English Bible.* 4 Vols. Wilmington, DE: n.p., 1976.

Harrison, Everett F., Geoffrey W. Bromiley, Carl F. H. Henry, eds. *Baker's Dictionary ofTheology.* Grand Rapids: Baker, 1960.

Hastings, James, ed. *A Dictionary of the Bible, Dealing with Its Language, Literature andContents, Including the Biblical Theology.* New York: Charles Scribner's Sons, 1905.

_____. *A Dictionary of Christ and the Gospels.* New York: Charles Scribner's Sons, 1911.

_____. *Dictionary of the Apostolic Church.* New York: Charles Scribner's Sons, 1951.

Kittel, Gerhard, ed. *Theological Dictionary of the New Testament.* Translated by Geoffrey W. Bromiley. 10 Vols. Grand Rapids: Eerdmans, 1969.

Latin Dictionary. Compiled by S. C. Woodhouse. Berks, England: Cox & Wyman Ltd. Reading, 1991.

Nestle, D. Eberhard, D. Erwin Nestle, and D. Kurt Aland, eds. *Novum Testamentum Graece.* New York: n.p., 1952.

Orr, James, ed. *The International Standard Bible Encyclopedia.* Grand Rapids: Eerdmans, 1957.

The Analytical Greek Lexicon. New York: Harper & Brothers, n.d.

The Septuagint Version of the Old Testament, with English Translation. Grand Rapids: Zondervan, 1976.

Pick, Aaron. *The English and Hebrew Bible Student's Concordance.* Grand Rapids: Kregel, n.d.

Roth, Cecil, ed. *Encyclopaedia Judaica.* 16 Vols. Jerusalem: Keter Publishing House, 1971.

Strong, James L. *The New Strong's Exhaustive Concordance of the Bible.* Nashville: Thomas Nelson, 1984.

Vine, W.E. *An Expository Dictionary of New Testament Words.* Westwood, NJ: Fleming H. Revell, 1957.

Periodicals

Anderson, Bruce W., ed. *Moody Monthly.* Chicago: Moody Bible Institute.

Awake! New York: Watchtower Bible and Tract Society of New York.

Beirnes, William F., ed. *The Midnight Cry.* Shoals, IN: Midnight Cry Publishing.

Clayton, John N., ed. *Does God Exist?* South Bend, IN: Donmoyer Avenue Church of Christ.

DeMar, Gary, ed. *Biblical Worldview.* Smyrna, GA: American Vision.

Fruchtenbaum, Arnold G., ed. *The Chosen People.* Englewood Cliffs, NJ: American Board of Missions to the Jews.

Lewis, Ronald H., ed. *The Hebrew Christian.* Ramsgate, England: Thanet Printing Works.

Myra, Harold L., ed. *Christianity Today.* Carol Stream, IL: CTI.

Olasky, Marvin, ed. *World.* Ashville, NC: American Vision.

Stone, Sam, ed. *Christian Standard.* Cincinnati: Standard Publishing.

Thompson, Bert, ed. *Reason & Revelation.* Montgomery, AL: Apologetics Press.

Zuckerman, Mortimer B., ed. *U.S. News & World Report.* New York.

ABOUT
THE
AUTHOR

Paul T. Butler is also the author of thirteen Bible commentaries in the College Press Bible Study Textbook series, and What the Bible says about Civil Government. Some Bible Study Textbook commentaries have been translated into seven different languages and are used around the world. He has also authored seven family genealogical books.

Butler served in the Navy for 10 years. After graduating from Ozark Christian College, he was appointed Registrar and a full-time professor of Bible. Later he received the Doctor of Theology degree from Theological University of America.

Butler retired in 1998 from Ozark Christian College, but continues to write Sunday School lessons and teach in the Sunday School of his local congregation. He continues to be in wide demand to speak on Bible, history, and genealogical subjects.